191203270

10 —

17½

D1512284

RACE RELATIONS

Race Relations

MICHAEL BANTON

Basic Books, Inc., Publishers   NEW YORK

© 1967 by Michael Banton

Library of Congress Catalog Card Number: 68–13937

Printed in the United States of America

THIRD PRINTING

Rober⸱ ⸱   ⸱ ʼibrary

JAN 30 1978

Tallahassee, Florida

for

Nicholas & Dagmar

Cph. - Jan - 26 - 1978

'The problem of the twentieth century is the problem of the colour line – the relation of the darker to the lighter races of men in Asia and Africa, in America and in the islands of the sea.' W. E. B. DUBOIS, 1903

Contents

Illustrations

FIGURES

TABLES

MAPS

Acknowledgements

Portions of this book are based on the author's Munro lectures for 1966. It was an especial honour to be invited to deliver these lectures at the University of Edinburgh, in view of the great contributions that university has made, both in previous centuries and in more recent years, to the study of race and race relations. It was also a personal pleasure to lecture under the chairmanship of Professor Kenneth Little, since it was from him that, as an undergraduate, the author received his first instruction in the study of race relations.

Other portions of the book derive from some of the author's previous publications, though in many cases they have been extensively revised. Chapters One to Three, and Fifteen, reproduce certain passages from *White and Coloured*, published by Jonathan Cape in 1959. Chapter Nine uses material that first appeared in *Race* (Vol. 5, 1963: 42–55); other chapters quote shorter passages from contributions to the same journal, which is published by Oxford University Press for the Institute of Race Relations. Chapter Ten develops further the line of thought that underlay a review of research published in the *International Social Science Journal* (Vol. 13, 1961: 197–214). Chapter Thirteen draws upon an article that originally appeared in the *Sociological Review* (Vol. 8, 1960: 169–83).

The author is obliged to the publishers concerned for permission to reproduce the material mentioned above, and to the publishers and others listed below for permission to quote from the published works of other authors: George Allen & Unwin Ltd in respect of *Out in the Mid-day Sun* by Boris Gussman; the American Psychological Association and Professor Bruno Bettelheim in respect of 'The Dynamism of Anti-Semitism in Gentile and Jew'; Ernest Benn Ltd in respect of *The Place of Prejudice in Modern Civilization* by Sir Arthur Keith; Cambridge University Press in respect of *Caste in India* by J. H. Hutton, and *Colonial Policy and Practice* by J. S. Furnivall; Dr E. J. Dingwall in respect of *Racial Pride and Prejudice*; Edinburgh University Press and University of Chicago Press in respect of *The Structure of American Life* by W. Lloyd Warner; The Free Press, a division of The Macmillan

Company, in respect of *Race and Culture* by Robert E. Park; Harper & Row, Inc., in respect of *An American Dilemma* by Gunnar Myrdal, and *The Authoritarian Personality* by T. W. Adorno, Else Frenkel-Brunswick, Daniel J. Levinson, and R. Nevitt Sanford; Holt, Rinehart and Winston, Inc., in respect of *The American Class Structure* by Joseph A. Kahl; Alfred A. Knopf in respect of *Slave and Citizen* by Frank Tannenbaum; Lady Listowel and the Editor of *The Listener* in respect of 'Journey's End at Johannesburg'; The Merlin Press in respect of *Politics and Law in South Africa* by Julius Lewin; Oxford University Press in respect of *A Study of History* by Arnold J. Toynbee, and *Granville Sharp and the Freedom of Slaves in England* by E. C. P. Lascelles; Prentice-Hall, Inc., in respect of *Strangers Next Door* by Robin M. Williams, Jr; A. H. Richmond in respect of *The Colour Problem*; Secker & Warburg Ltd and Ernest Benn Ltd in respect of *Portrait of the Anti-Semite* by Jean-Paul Sartre; the Society for Applied Anthropology in respect of 'Intercultural Communication' by Edward T. Hall and William Foote Whyte; University of Chicago Press in respect of *Black Nationalism* by E. U. Essien-Udom.

The writer who ventures outside the confines of conventional academic specialization is more than usually dependent upon the advice and assistance of his university colleagues. The author has been especially fortunate in the help he has received in many ways, most notably from Christopher Fyfe, Kenneth Little, George Shepperson, and T. F. Torrance of Edinburgh University. Several colleagues and friends have commented upon particular chapters or portions of chapters: Ian Whitaker, P. D. Marshall, J. Clyde Mitchell, and Nicholas Deakin. Their support has been a great reassurance.

M. B.

Department of Sociology
The University
Bristol

CHAPTER ONE

The Study of Race Relations

The political importance of racial tension in the modern world is beyond dispute. But the claim that the study of race relations can constitute a coherent field for teaching and research is more contentious. The chapters that follow show why racial conflict has cut so deep into patterns of human relations, identifying the nature of racial friction and analysing its constituent elements. The author has tried to explain racial relations rather than merely to describe them. His contribution is therefore an attempt to demonstrate the utility of the social scientist's academic studies and to state a case for the recognition of this field of work as one possessing a coherence comparable to that of many of the more generally accepted fields of specialized teaching and research. The study of race relations takes in an enormous section of human experience, but this breadth has its advantages. Nearly all the major problems of human co-operation can be detected in the exploration of so extensive a field, though this does not mean that they can all be investigated simultaneously. Teaching in any intellectual discipline must neglect certain applications in order to concentrate upon the most instructive discoveries and lines of reasoning. Disciplined study seeks to give the student an intellectual training rather than a ready-made set of answers.

It is from this standpoint that the author has reviewed what seem to him the most instructive discoveries and lines of reasoning for someone studying race relations after elementary tuition in sociology. That particular attention has been paid to the regions where studies have been most intensive and to the interests of English-speaking students may explain some of the book's limitations: the neglect of much relevant literature concerning intergroup relations in Israel, India, and the Far East, of writings in languages other than English, etc. Nor has it been easy to hold a balance between chapters when the source material differs so greatly. For example, the history of racial thought sketched in the second and third chapters should be regarded as no more than an outline. Until very recently, hardly any worth-while studies had been published on this theme, but historians are now taking greater interest in questions of racial thought and its influence, so that it may soon be possible to delineate the historical perspective more firmly.

For a variety of reasons it is unlikely that the study of race relations will ever occupy a place in the map of learning similar to those held by physics, economics, and French literature. But there are other fields of research and teaching, such as engineering, criminology, commerce, international relations, social administration, and public health, which also bring together knowledge gained within other disciplines. The difference between these two kinds of 'subject' is sometimes expressed as the difference between pure and applied sciences. A pure science, such as physics or economics, concentrates upon distinctive theoretical problems. An applied science, such as engineering, draws upon work in the pure sciences (as, in this case, physics, chemistry, mathematics, etc.) for the elucidation of particular problems which tend to be of a less abstract character. In this light the study of race relations may be viewed as an applied social science. It brings together all that other sciences can contribute to the solution of problems within its own special field. It draws not only on the pure social sciences, such as psychology, economics, political science, and sociology, but upon the perspective and expertise which historians and geographers can furnish for the better understanding of relations in particular regions. As with other applied social sciences, how a particular course is taught in a particular university may be influenced by the discipline in which the teacher has received most of his training, but this is not necessarily a disadvantage, since a certain bias towards a particular discipline may give a teaching course greater coherence.

The student of psychology, economics, political science, or sociology is not interested in race relations as such, but in questions of human behaviour. Studying a complex situation, the pure social scientist will concentrate his attention upon just a few variables in it which he will try to relate to similar phenomena in other situations. His task is one of analysis. At other times, however, both social scientists and general readers need a synoptic interpretation of the position in a particular region. The political problems of race relations in different parts of the world have become so pressing in the last half-century that there is an urgent need for the public to have a better informed understanding of what is involved in these circumstances. The political argument for systematic instruction about race relations is undeniable. The academic argument is also strong. It rests upon two claims. On the one hand, the accumulation of theoretical and descriptive material in this field during the past two generations is now so extensive and interrelated that it can be used as a basis for imparting intellectual discipline and for training students in the marshalling of data and argument. On the other hand, the progressive specialization of the pure social sciences increases the significance of subjects which bring together modes of analysis used by other departments of study. One weakness of specialized training is that students become wedded to particular theories and approaches, regarding them as better than any others, so that they are unable to appreciate the limits within which these ideas are useful. Thus an applied social science provides a measure of synthesis which is an essential balance to the analytical propensities of the pure sciences.

BIOLOGICAL AND SOCIAL ASPECTS

One of the more common objections to the study of race relations as outlined above concerns the conceptions of race as a biological and as a social phenomenon. The objection can take either of two forms. It may be claimed that, since differences between groups of men may be biological in origin, it is necessary first to establish how much variation must be attributed to genetic differences. Patterns of relations between groups may be an outgrowth of different inherited capacities or capabilities. Contrariwise, critics may protest that the theory of races as separate and distinctive groups of mankind has been quite exploded and that it would be foolish to construct a subject upon the idea of relations between bogus units of analysis. The answers advanced here to both of these objections are similar. They stem from the consideration that, when studying any kind of phenomena, the scholar is obliged to restrict his field of operations if he is going to deal adequately with any topic. Patterns of race relations during the last two hundred years have been influenced by what people believed to be the nature of race and it is necessary, therefore, to take account of these ideas. But many theories concerning the nature of race have subsequently been proven wrong, and it would be inconvenient if the study of race relations had to be reoriented every time biologists changed their views. It would, in any case, be exceedingly difficult to keep them completely consonant in that biological opinion is not monolithic: there are always divided views and contrasting approaches. Yet such a procedure is unnecessary in any event. Relations between categories of people have a logic of their own which is very largely and sometimes entirely independent of human biological make-up, and the task of the social scientist is to study these social systematics; he is not called upon to be an amateur biologist. If some socially significant racial inequality were to be discovered, this would not invalidate the arguments for studying the social elements in relations between racial groups; it would probably require us to pay them even more attention. The evidence from the biologists indicates that the socially significant group differences are culturally and not genetically transmitted. Cultural differences therefore occupy a central place in the study of race relations whereas, on present evidence, genetical factors are peripheral to the analysis of the social systematics. Yet it would also be undesirable to banish completely the notion of race from the study of social relations between categories of people who are popularly identified in racial terms. Beliefs about the nature of race – whether true or false – still have considerable social significance, and, when a category is labelled in the popular mind by racial terminology rather than by religious or class criteria, certain predictable consequences ensue. The social significance of the racial label compared with other identifications is a matter that properly forms part of the study of intergroup relations.

The relevance of biological research is frequently brought up in connection with doctrines of racial superiority or equality. A common pitfall in the discussions that result is the failure to make a sharp distinction between statements of fact and judgements of value. There are powerful philosophical reasons for believing that it is impossible to infer judgements of value from statements of fact. Assertions about racial inequality or equality usually refer to moral standards and they can therefore be grounded only in political or philosophical reasoning. If, tomorrow, a biologist were to report experimental results indicating an inherited inequality between particular social groups, let us say a reported superiority of Scotsmen over Englishmen, what would this imply for social policy? Higher tax allowances for Scottish parents to encourage them to have more children? Higher expenditure on education in English schools to make up for the genetic handicap? A little reflection will show that policy decisions are not logically entailed by statements of biological fact; policy decisions cannot be agreed unless some value premiss is accepted. The validity of the declaration that all men are created equal in dignity and rights does not depend upon a permit from the biologists that has to be renewed at regular intervals.

Arguments about racial superiority frequently start from the proposition that among the races of the world only the Negro race has never developed any major civilization. David Hume, in a footnote to his essay *Of National Characters* (published in 1748), stated that on this account he suspected that Negroes might be 'naturally inferior to the Whites'. Arnold Toynbee in *A Study of History* (1934, I: 233) concludes that, since all other races have contributed to a major civilization, there is no reason for supposing that the Black Race has been born without this birthright just because it has not made such a contribution yet. From the proposition that Negroes have not developed a civilization, racists infer that the probability of their doing so is negligible. African nationalists infer from the same proposition the belief that it is their turn next. Historians of Africa question the factual accuracy of this proposition itself, but, in so far as it is accepted, the ideas and beliefs to which it gives rise lie primarily within the philosophy of history. When anthropologists enter this arena today they adduce evidence to show that cultural development is independent of biological inheritance (indeed, Lévi-Strauss refers to the identification of race and culture as 'the original sin of anthropology'). But if they go on to maintain that the distinctive contributions of cultures are to be accounted for by geographical, historical, and sociological circumstances they must beware the philosophical traps concealed in the view that moral judgements are always relative to particular cultures. Lévi-Strauss's own arguments against the idea of cultural superiority have been criticized as mutually inconsistent. They imply that: (i) the question of cultural superiority has no meaning; (ii) in any case, this superiority proves nothing; (iii) besides, where it exists it is because of chance or borrowing. The idea of cultural superiority in this way makes progress at each stage of the argument (Lévi-Strauss, 1952; Caillois, 1954–55). This is no place to pursue this controversy but it may serve as a cautionary tale to those who believe that the factual conclusions of anthropology prove either superiority or relativity in matters of culture. The student of race relations does well to concentrate upon the elucidation of more immediate problems.

An approach to race relations from the standpoint of social science requires that race be viewed not as a biological category but as a sign by which a social category is identified. As Chapter Four explains, the two categories overlap but they do not coincide. In all social systems, physical distinctions are vested with more significance than physiological requirements would dictate. Differences between male and female roles, for example, cannot be completely accounted for by biological differences; the notions of propriety that restrict a woman's conduct stem entirely from the structure of the social order. In any racially divided society people are obliged to play the role conventional to their group in situations where racial background is considered a relevant criterion of behaviour; if they do not do this they are subject to social sanctions just as when they do not fulfil the obligations of any other role. Physiological differences serve as signs or emblems telling others what a person's role is, just as differences of costume or demeanour distinguish roles of sex and class. Hilda Kuper has written of the 'uniform of colour', and if race is viewed in this way it becomes possible to assimilate most of race relations studies to the more general field of intergroup relations studies. Certain similarities can be observed in relations between social groups of any kind, be they racial groups, religious groups, class groups, work groups in industry, or categories such as policemen and the public. The social scientist's goal is to develop a general theory which will comprehend these fields and build up a body of general propositions which, with the necessary specifications, apply in all of them. In this way, lessons learned in the field of industrial relations can be transferred to that of racial relations and vice versa. Similarly, general sociological theory will be of great relevance to the problems in these fields, and research carried out there will repay the debt to general theory by developing it further.

A social science approach to race relations will then be primarily oriented to developing the science, not to immediate practical applications, though in the long run its practical utility will probably be greater if it concentrates upon improving its explanatory power instead of pursuing passing problems. The study of race relations should not be conceived as a course in current affairs. To explore the dynamics of intergroup relations it is best to take the most illuminating studies, irrespective of whether the position they describe is still current. A good case-study of social relations in another era or in another region of the world should reveal more about the nature of man and of society than the morning newspaper does. So while race relations may be seen as an applied science this does not mean that it will always disintegrate into particular applications and lose its elements of synthesis and intellectual discipline. Nor does it mean that scholars in this field will necessarily be successful in separating fact and value. The ideal of complete objectivity remains an aspiration in any science. The physical sciences are able to approximate to it much more closely than the social sciences are ever likely to, though there are important variations in this respect between different fields within social science. The bias of particular scholars is restrained by the scientific tradition of criticism, directed at any work by a man's colleagues and by the man himself. It is therefore desirable that the academic study of race relations should provide a forum in which scholars and students with different biases can engage in the sort of dialogue that can take them nearer the truth.

THE THREE APPROACHES

Many areas of research in the social sciences deal with problems of great contemporary importance. Consequently, discoveries by scholars are quickly absorbed, like many of their concepts, into general discourse so that the work of the academic student seems less distinctive than it really is. What distinguishes the social scientist's chief contribution from the journalistic commentator's is that he seeks new questions which will open up aspects of the problem insufficiently comprehended in common speech. The obstacle to greater understanding is often not that of finding new answers but of discovering new questions, which, by reformulating the old ones, make possible their solution.

In popular discourse one of the tendencies that do most to hinder the understanding of race relations is to seek for explanations in terms of a single factor, for instance the inclination of some people to maintain that racial friction is caused by instinct, custom, exploitation, or the limitations upon human sympathy – as if, say, inflation in an economic system could be explained as caused by human greediness. An analogy may make the contrast clearer. When the ordinary motorist presses the starter knob but fails to start his car, he may ask himself, 'Why won't my car start?'; but this question is too general to help him to locate the fault. He stands more chance of success if he asks specific questions: 'Is the ignition switched on?'; 'Is the electrical system working?'; 'Is the choke out?'; 'Have I flooded the carburettor?' Such questions may enable him to get the engine working. If they do not, he may find that he has run out of constructive questions and has to call in a mechanic who has the skill to ask and answer more technical questions. To ask, 'Why do Columbians dislike Danireans?' is like asking 'Why won't my car start?' It is necessary to identify the important elements in racially divided societies, and the mechanisms that relate them to one another, if the student is to use the mechanic's kind of skill in formulating and answering the sorts of question that permit the discovery of the causes of trouble.

Social scientists have made considerable progress in this direction. Three lines of questioning have proved particularly fruitful and have led to the formulation of three major models of racial friction. A model of social relations is a conception of them as the product of a set of interrelated factors, the various interrelations being specified as closely as possible. The first model utilizes the approach from *ideology*, which has *racism* as its basic concept and has received its theoretical elaborations primarily from the disciples of Karl Marx. By racism is meant the doctrine that a man's behaviour is determined by stable inherited characters deriving from separate racial stocks having distinctive attributes and usually considered to stand to one another in relations of superiority and inferiority. It is to be distinguished from *racialism*, which does not refer so much to the doctrine as to the practice of it, though it is often loosely used to refer to activities that serve the interests of a particular racial group. Second, there is the approach from *attitude*, which utilizes *prejudice* as its basic concept. Prejudice has been defined as 'a generalization existing prior to the situation in which it is invoked, directed toward people, groups, or social institutions, which is accepted and defended as a guide to action in spite of its discrepancies with the objective facts' (Vickery & Opler, 1948). The essential features of prejudice would appear to be its emotional character, in that it serves psychic functions for the individuals who display it, and its rigidity, in that when someone tries to demonstrate that an opinion is false, prejudiced people do not modify their views but, indeed, often twist the new evidence to fit their preconceptions. This emotionality and rigidity are, in practice, characteristic only of hostile dispositions. Third comes the approach from *social relationships*, based upon the concept of *discrimination*. This mode of analysis does not derive from any particular theorist but has been built up by a variety of scholars. Discrimination is the differential treatment of persons ascribed to particular social categories, and it can be generalized to form a measure of *social distance*. Discrimination may be exercised either against a social category or in its favour. Discrimination may be morally reprehensible, but it is not necessarily so: the sociological concept deals only with factual statements about differential treatment.

The nature of these concepts may be illustrated by reference to a hypothetical example. A white employer has advertised a vacancy for a truck driver; he turns away a qualified West Indian applicant and engages a white man. This action is, on the face of things, discriminatory. There is the possibility that the employer rejected the man on other grounds than racial ones, and to be certain about this it would be desirable to have a series of observations about how the employer tended to act. If he has refused to hire qualified coloured workers on previous occasions, the probability is increased that his action is part of a pattern of discrimination and not a response to particular individuals. However, even when discrimination is proven, no certain inference can be made about the motives underlying it. Without additional evidence it would be illegitimate to infer that the employer subscribed to a racist ideology or that he was actuated by prejudice. For one reason or another, true or false, he might believe that it was in his economic interest not to take on coloured workers. Discrimination may be caused by other things than an attitude of prejudice. Prejudiced people do not give vent to their feelings in all situations; sometimes the possibility of punishment for doing so appears too threatening, and prejudice does not produce discrimination. Similarly, discriminators and prejudiced people often do not subscribe to a racist ideology, and people who do are not always prejudiced or likely to discriminate. The three factors are often associated in particular situations but they are in principle independent.

A further possibility has also to be considered. The imaginary employer might reject a West Indian would-be truck driver because he believes he already has too many West Indians on his staff. This is discrimination, because the only grounds for rejecting him are that he belongs to a particular social category. The employer may believe that if the proportion of coloured staff is allowed to rise too high this will occasion resentment and either produce friction at the works or cause the white workers to leave for other employment, so that the firm becomes typed as a 'coloured man's firm'. The employer who fixes a ceiling to the proportion of coloured workers in these circumstances is operating a 'benign quota', which may be morally justified and may, indeed, be in the interests of the West Indian workers themselves if it promotes their dispersal throughout the employment market. Whether it is justified or not is an ethical or political issue on which the sociologist does not, in his scholarly capacity, have to make any judgement. But quotas do entail discrimination.

The three approaches can be seen as attempts to solve rather different problems. The approach from racism is useful in demonstrating the political and economic functions of such doctrines, especially in cases of overseas expansion, and is of particular relevance to the era of imperial annexation starting in the late nineteenth century. Neither of the other two approaches can answer these questions so well. The approach from prejudice, on the other hand, is much more illuminating when it comes to problems of anti-semitism, of individual variation in intergroup behaviour, and of irrational behaviour. A focus on the dynamics of particular social relationships becomes necessary, however, when the problems to be solved are those of the patterns of discrimination in different contexts, and of the way in which such patterns continue as part of a society's customs. Nevertheless, it has not always been appreciated that the three approaches are complementary, and social scientists coming to this field from particular disciplines have been inclined to assert that the factor of interest to their discipline is the fundamental one that, in the end, determines the other features. Psychological writers, in particular, have thought of individual disposition as the dynamic element in behaviour ultimately responsible for intergroup antagonism, and have seen social factors as repressing, permitting, or encouraging the display of this disposition. One way of thinking about this view, which facilitates comparison with a contradictory conception, is to draw an analogy with water flowing along a pipe. For the psychologist, individual disposition constitutes the flow, while social factors are a tap which may turn it down or boost it up. Sociologists see things the other way about. They have tended to argue, for example, that a white man in the American South will act aggressively towards a Negro who claims privileges customarily reserved to Whites. To explain apparently contrary instances they may introduce qualifications about the influence of non-sociological factors, such as: 'provided he does not have economic interests which might be endangered'; or, 'provided he has no strong emotional predisposition in favour of Negroes'. In this case, it is the structure of the situation that is singled out and seen as the flow along the pipe; individual and other factors are regarded as acting like the tap which modifies the flow.

The psychologist and the sociologist examine the same data, the same 'facts', but from different aspects, each singling out the variable that interests him and viewing other influences only as modifying factors. The point that must be emphasized – for it has often been overlooked – is that this is a characteristic of the method of investigation, not a characteristic of the way things are arranged in the real world. The isolation of one factor at a time is the proper way to carry out an investigation, for nothing can be examined from two standpoints simultaneously. The research worker must concentrate upon 'his' variable as if it were all-important; the confusion enters when he writes as if he believed it to be all-important, as if the model were a complete representation of reality. The psychologist thinks of social factors as the 'tap' regulating the expression of individual dispositions, but that does not mean that the task of sociology is no more than to explain why in given situations the tap is open or closed, or why the flow of hostility is directed upon one group rather than another. The sociological approach lies in a different way of looking at the same phenomena and in isolating a different variable. Events present different problems to scholars trained in different disciplines; each attempts to answer the questions of interest to him rather than to seek an exhaustive explanation of the event itself. The chapters that follow are biased towards the concerns of the sociologist but, since there have been few treatises by sociologists to set beside the psychologically oriented texts (e.g. Allport, 1954), this bias may, in the long run, be constructive.

CHAPTER TWO

Racial Thought before Darwin

Racial differences seem to have been recognized from the earliest periods of human history, to judge by prehistoric cave paintings and the decorations in ancient Egyptian tombs (Casson, 1939: 23–26). Discrimination against strangers and particularly against dark-skinned people is probably of equal antiquity. But 'race' as it is known today is a relatively new idea. Only in the last two hundred years or so has an ideology of race claiming scientific validity been added to the rhetoric of national, economic, and social conflict.

THE INFLUENCE OF ARISTOTLE

The views of race espoused by different writers have depended in large measure on their ideas as to man's place in nature and the extent to which it is legitimate to study man's social behaviour by the methods of science. Any account of these views must therefore start with Aristotle. He classified man as an animal, though to be distinguished from other animals by features such as the relative size of brain, two leggedness, mental characters, etc. Aristotle further maintained that slavery was a natural state of affairs: 'Those who are so much inferior to others as is the body to the soul, and beasts to men, are by nature slaves and benefit, like all inferiors, from living under the rule of a master.' This was a racist theory, at least in embryo. It was used for many centuries to justify the *status quo*, for the proof of the natural superiority of the rulers could only be their success in maintaining their position, and if another group defeated them that was proof of the newcomers' right to rule. Aristotle's doctrine was thus of major significance as a justification for patterns of racial relations maintained by force.

But the intellectual systems of the philosophers do not always have an influence in the market place, and the attitude of the Greeks towards other peoples was based upon cultural rather than biological premises.

An Asian appearance signified to a man of classical Greece that the stranger was probably a barbarian and no good company for a cultured Greek. Macedonians were excluded from the games, but so were Greek slaves. From the fifth century onwards, it was participation in the culture of the city-state that developed as the criterion of Hellenism.

It is difficult to generalize about the racial element in the thought of earlier civilizations. Some writers, wishing to stress the iniquities of modern racism, have minimized evidence of a similar outlook in earlier periods lest their readers should conclude that racism was a normal feature of human attitudes towards strangers. Expressions of something rather like racism can be found in many quarters (Gossett, 1963: 3–10), but it is dangerous to infer that in their cultural context they had a meaning similar to that which they would have for a contemporary audience. There may also be a contrast between the way in which a scholar emphasizes ideas of race when elaborating a philosophy of history and the sort of action he recommends in relations with other peoples. Cedric Dover considered that the first racial philosopher of the Middle Ages was Jehuda Halevi of Cordova (c. 1080–1141), whose verse extols the supremacy of Judaism, challenging Christianity and Islam. Halevi's arguments constitute a closely rationalized racial philosophy, the culmination of two thousand years of Jewish racial thinking. But it is a negative racism, responding to persecution, not a justification for aggression (Dover, 1952b: 312, 322). Dover also held (1954: 188) that in the verse of Antar, the sixth-century Arab poet born of a Negro slave woman, can be glimpsed the handicaps and conquests of 'the greatest of the early half-castes of our own era', and that in the work of his co-religionist Ibn Khaldun of Tunis (1332–1406) there is an early Muslim racial philosophy (Dover, 1952a).

Arnold J. Toynbee (1934, I: 223) has maintained that the spirit of mediaeval European Christendom was free from race feeling, regarding the stranger and the heathen as potential converts to Christianity. But there is evidence to the contrary. Martin Luther's writings on the Jews and the Turks belong with the mediaeval tradition and they never imply that Christ died for Turks and infidels or that Jews belong to the one people of God. Modern historians would be more disposed to agree with one of their number who remarks, 'There is plenty of evidence of what looks to me like race prejudice among the European peoples of the Middle Ages' (Deighton, 1959: 20). Generalizations about the spirit of an age cannot permit too many exceptions. It would also seem that mediaeval Christendom was less than tolerant to scientific inquiry in the field of anthropology. A. C. Haddon, in his history of the subject (1934), sketched Aristotle's contribution and then continued, without any comment: 'Vesalius (1513–64) is the next great name in the history of physical anthropology'. Nineteen centuries have passed without a mention. The formidable St Augustine must bear as much responsibility as anyone for the hostility shown towards those who believed that whether or not man was 'a little lower than the angels' his form and his origin could be the objects of rational inquiry. Augustine had emphasized that man, 'whatever colour, gait, voice – whatever strength, proportions, or natural qualities he may have . . . has sprung from one protoplast'. There could be no men in unknown lands on the other side of the world because the idea of some of Adam's descendants having sailed there was 'excessively absurd'.

The discovery of the New World consequently required that Europeans rethink their conception of human life to find a place for the new peoples. Many Spaniards were intensely interested in the American Indians. Kings and the Council of the Indies instituted prolonged and formal inquiries in both Spain and America into the Indians' nature. Haddon states that some Spaniards excused their barbarities to the natives on the grounds that they could not be descendants of Adam and Eve, but there were other views about this. The controversy became so heated and the king's conscience so troubled over the question of how to carry on the conquest of the Indies in a Christian way that Charles V actually suspended all conquests in America while a commission of foremost theologians, jurists, and officials assembled in the royal capital of Valladolid to weigh the arguments. The critics of Spanish policy were represented by the Dominican friar Bartolomé de Las Casas, a former bishop of Chiapa in Southern Mexico. His opponent was the ghost of Aristotle speaking through contemporary interest groups. In 1510 a Scots professor in Paris, John Major, had first applied to the Indians the Aristotelian doctrine of natural slavery, approving the idea that force should be used as a preliminary to the teaching of the faith. Aristotle's theories had not been used to justify slavery in mediaeval Spain, so when Las Casas first encountered this argument he objected that Aristotle was but a 'gentile burning in Hell, whose doctrine we do not need to follow except in so far as it conforms with Christian truth'. Later, he was to be more respectful of the philosopher whose approach dominated Renaissance thought and whose writings were of great importance to the philosophical substratum of Catholicism (Hanke, 1959).

The occasion for the debate at Valladolid was the presentation of a treatise maintaining that wars against Indians were just and constituted a necessary preliminary to their conversion. Its author was Juan Ginés de Sepulvéda, a much respected scholar and theologian. The disputants were to direct themselves to the specific issue: is it lawful for the king of Spain to wage war on the Indians before preaching the faith to them in order to subject them to his rule, so that afterwards they may be more easily instructed in the faith? Sepulvéda answered 'yes', because of 'the gravity of the sins which the Indians had committed', 'on account of the rudeness of their natures, which obliged them to serve persons having a more refined nature, such as the Spaniards' (which argument he declared to accord with the doctrine of natural slavery), and more to the same effect. Las Casas argued for peaceful colonization and persuasion; he believed that 'mankind is one, and all men are alike in that which concerns their creation . . . the savage peoples of the earth may be compared to uncultivated soil that readily brings forth weeds and useless thorns, but has within itself such natural virtue that by labour and cultivation it may be made to yield sound and beneficial fruits'. The proceedings, however, brought a clear victory to neither side, perhaps because Las Casas's views found considerable favour but could not be put into effect in the American colonies where the town councils and governmental bodies insisted on more authoritarian policies. Nevertheless, the confrontation between Las Casas's protests and Sepulvéda's defence echoed round Western Europe and America, for it dramatized a continuing problem of ethics and policy (Hanke, 1959). An ironical feature of the occasion in the eyes of later generations lies in its exclusive concern with the treatment of Indians. Negroes were not considered. Early in his career Las Casas proposed the introduction of Negro slaves to the islands, in order to spare Indians the heavy labour that was destroying them; but he later repented and opposed Negro slavery also 'and for the same reasons'. The Iberian peoples never fought as hard or consistently against Negro slavery as they did on behalf of Indians; perhaps they had become accustomed to dark-skinned Muslims – both as slaves and as masters – in their own country. Despite his later rejection of Negro slavery, Las Casas himself owned several Negro slaves as late as 1544 – a reminder that the dispute of 1550 centred on the nature of the Indians, not, as in later debate, upon the political status of slavery.

The discovery of peoples whose existence Augustine had declared to be impossible came as a severe blow to the authority of the Fathers on matters of science and gave a great stimulus to independent studies of the diversity of mankind. For a long time there was little or no speculation about biological causes of racial differences, all interest being in the problem of origins. Two schools of thought contended: the monogenists, who held that all mankind was derived from a single pair, and the polygenists, who believed in a multiple origin. The first scholar to state the polygenetic theory seems to have been Theophrastus Paracelsus; in 1520 he argued that peoples 'found in out-of-the-way islands' were different kinds of men, not descended from the sons of Adam (Bendyshe, 1865: 353). In 1655 the luckless Isaac de Peyrère published his *System of Theology on the Pre-Adamite Hypothesis*, in which he held that Adam was the first of the Jews and that the Gentiles had been created earlier. He wrote: 'I would that St Augustine and Lactantius were now alive, who scoffed at the Antipodes. Truly they would pity themselves if they should hear and see those things which are discovered in the east and west in this clear-sighted age . . .' But the book was burned and the author forced to recant. Though previously a Protestant, he was obliged to spend his remaining years in a Catholic monastery (Casson, 1939: 114–18).

ANTICIPATIONS

The first appearance of the word race in English occurs in the poem *The Dance of the Sevin Deidly Sins* (1508) by the Scotsman William Dunbar. Among those who followed Envy he listed:

> *And flatteris in to menis facis;*
> *And bakbyttaris of sindry racis,*
> *To ley that had delyte;*

During the next two and a half to three centuries it was used with growing frequency in a literary sense as denoting a class of people. The anatomists wrote mostly in Latin.

The first time the notion of race was used as the basis for a taxonomy of mankind was in an essay by the French traveller and physician, François Bernier, published anonymously in 1684. He writes of 'four or five species or races of men in particular whose difference is so remarkable that it may properly be made use of as the foundation for a new division of the earth'. The criteria for his classification were the outward features of skin colour, hair, and physiognomy. Bernier drew from his distinctions no particular conclusions as to the nature of man or of the various races (Bendyshe, 1865: 360–4). No further work of significance concerning race was published for almost another century.

BELIEF IN THE IMMUTABILITY OF SPECIES

The belief that the Old Testament embodies a historical record of the human species has at times inspired both a biblical anthropology and a biblical chronology. Dr John Lightfoot in 1644 maintained that 'Man was created by the Trinity about the third hour of the day, or nine o'clock in the morning' on 12 September 3928 BC. Six years later, Archbishop James Ussher calculated that 'the beginning of time fell upon the night before the twenty-third day of October in the year of the Julian calendar 710' (4004 BC). The literal acceptance of the Creation story entailed not only a monogenetic theory of human origins but a belief that the number and nature of species were fixed. *Species tot numeramus, quot diversae formae in primitione sunt creatae*, as Linnaeus stated in his *Philosophia Botanica* of 1751. This is the Idealist doctrine that each species is distinct, having its own essential nature and representing a separate idea of the Creator. By the end of the nineteenth century it could seem strange that the question of the mutability or immutability of species should ever have appeared to be a religious question. Who had invented it? Not Augustine nor Aquinas nor Bacon; the true culprits were Milton, Ray, and Linnaeus (Willey, 1961: 7-8). Milton's description in *Paradise Lost* of creatures emerging fully-formed had been especially influential:

> *The Earth obey'd, and straight*
> *Op'ning her fertile womb team'd at a birth*
> *Innumerous living creatures, perfect forms,*
> *Limb'd and full grown . . .*

Thus burst the tawny lion into life, followed by the tiger, stag, river horse, and scaly crocodile in quick succession.

Yet to group Linnaeus with Milton is not altogether accurate. It is in the first edition of the great Swedish naturalist's *Systema Naturae* (1735) that man recovers his Aristotelian place among the animals, this time classed as a quadruped, and, together with apes and sloths, constituting the order *Anthropomorpha*. As early as 1744 in his dissertation on *Peloria* Linnaeus recognized a plant that constituted a new species, intermediate between two others, 'no less extraordinary than if a cow gave birth to a calf having a wolf's head'. But he hesitated to draw the full implications of this discovery and continued to repeat his earlier view, though with more and more qualifications. Towards the end of his days he regarded *species animalium et plantarium* and *genera* as the works of time, but the *ordines naturales* as the works of the Creator (Hagberg, 1952: 200). In the tenth edition of his *Systema* (1758) Linnaeus recognized four varieties of the human species: (a) *Americanus* – reddish, choleric, erect; (b) *Europaeus* – white, ruddy, muscular; (c) *Asiaticus* – yellow, melancholic, inflexible; (d) *Afer* – black, phlegmatic, indulgent; in addition he created a fifth division, *monstrosus*, to accommodate certain supposedly abnormal forms. But in one of his late lectures he insisted: 'Man, my hearers, is distinguished from all other animals principally by *reason*, through which he surpasses them to such a degree and in so many ways, that we must confess that nature here has made its greatest leap.' To this idea of nature's leap reference will be made later.

THE DOCTRINE OF MUTABILITY

Faith in the moral and spiritual equality of mankind generally went with the belief that all races descended from Adam and Eve. Blumenbach himself was very sympathetic to the cause of the Negro: 'God's image he too, although made out of ebony'. But that an acceptance of the Genesis story could be combined with a doctrine of mutability to the discredit of other races is seen in the writing of the Scottish judge, Henry Home (later Lord Kames). In 1774 he offered to explain racial diversity on biblical grounds. God had created only one pair of the human species. What had happened since then? The confusion of Babel had scattered men over the face of the earth, depriving them of society and rendering them savages. From that state of degeneracy they had been gradually emerging. Some nations, stimulated by their own nature, or by their climate, had made rapid progress; others had advanced slowly, and yet others had remained as they were. By thus insisting on a racial distinctness originating at Babel and persisting ever since, Kames placed the nature of racial differences beyond human inquiry. Others before him (such as Boulainvilliers) had appealed to racist doctrines to justify political claims but they had not applied them systematically outside their own sphere of interest.

One of the most important of the monogenists and a writer of major significance for the development of ideas about races was J. F. Blumenbach. He first elaborated (in 1781) the fivefold classification: Caucasian, Mongolian, Ethiopian, American, Malayan. Blumenbach criticized the belief in the 'continuity or gradation of nature'; man was a distinct species, and races were but subdivisions of it: 'no variety exists, whether of colour, countenance, or stature, etc., so singular as not to be connected with others of the same kind by such an imperceptible transition, that it is very clear they are all related, or only differ from each other in degree'. Blumenbach was uncertain about the causes of variation and refrained from speculation, but the philosopher Immanuel Kant showed greater ingenuity. Rejecting either an environmentalist or a variation-and-selection explanation of human variety, Kant in 1785 expounded a monogenist theory holding that the ancestral human stock had been

endowed with a range of latent powers which could be evoked or suppressed as new conditions of life required (Greene, 1954a). Thus the
monogenist theory was freed from any assertion of the immutability
of types.

Some of the most significant developments in eighteenth-century
biological thought were associated with the widespread belief in a 'Great
Chain of Being', according to which any one creature was differentiated
from others only by a series of gradations (Lovejoy, 1936). The doctrine
was summarized in the popular phrase *natura non facit saltum* ('nature
makes no leaps') to which Linnaeus was referring and which Blumenbach criticized. The influence of the Great Chain of Being outlook is
very apparent in the work of the French naturalist Buffon, who for a
time denied the very concept of species. He taught the mutability of
species under the direct influence of environment. Erasmus Darwin
maintained that 'all animals undergo transformations which are in part
produced by their own exertions in response to pleasures and pains,
and many of these acquired forms or propensities are transmitted to
their posterity' – a view that was further developed by Lamarck. Buffon,
Erasmus Darwin, and Lamarck raised serious objections to any view of
species as qualitatively distinct and fixed for all time.

If natural phenomena were to be seen as developing in a long sequence
it was an obvious inference that the different races of men represented
stages of development. The assumption that this was in fact the case
coloured the way in which the evidence was presented and complicated
the scholar's task further. Naturalists searched for creatures who might
constitute the 'missing links' in the chain, and the reports which they
received were often already distorted in the desired direction. The
orang-outang was misleadingly termed *Homo sylvestris*, and in 1774
the Royal Society were so excited about its relation to man that they
proposed to send a special investigator out to Africa. One set of stories
attributed near-human abilities to the orang-outang; another described
the Hottentots as near-brutes and scarcely human. Given, then, the
belief in the continuity of natural varieties, a statement like that of
Edward Long, the Jamaican historian (vehemently anti-Negro though
he was), that 'Ludicrous as the opinion may seem, I do not think that
an orang-outang husband would be any dishonour to an Hottentot
female' (1774, II: 364) appears more easily comprehensible. As late as
1831 it was possible to publish respectably a multi-volume work in
which orang-outangs and chimpanzees were classified as human and
set in a regular hierarchy along with the other races of man (Curtin,
1964: 368).

Consideration of late eighteenth-century racial thought prompts a more general reflection. When writing on this topic it is easy to fall into the trap of judging contributions by what is now known to be scientifically acceptable, instead of evaluating them in the context of their intellectual milieu. This is part of what Joseph Agassi (1963) has castigated as 'inductivist history', in which the historian of a science takes as his standard an up-to-date textbook, distributing credit to all historical figures who have contributed to modern knowledge and passing over any of their work that has been less fruitful – as if mistakes were simply due to a failure to make the logical inductions. Many modern writers have been over-ready to attribute to prejudiced thinking the errors about race made by their predecessors, when closer examination suggests a less simple conclusion. Take the case of the Manchester surgeon, Charles White, who in 1799 published *An Account of the Regular Gradation in Man, and in different Animals and Vegetables; and from the former to the latter*. White measured anatomical features of over fifty Negroes, compared them with figures for Whites, and concluded that in respect of 'bodily structure and economy' the Negro was closer to the ape than was the European. In seeing, hearing, smelling, memory, and the powers of mastication the European was 'least perfect, the African more so, and the brutes most perfect of all'. As the title indicates, White's thought was dominated by the idea of the Great Chain of Being. The author obviously felt uneasy about the implications of his conclusions, for he expressed at the beginning of the book his hope 'that nothing advanced will be construed so as to give the smallest countenance to the pernicious practice of enslaving mankind, which he wishes to see abolished throughout the world'. He held that 'the negroes are, at least, equal to thousands of Europeans, in capacity and responsibility; and ought, therefore, to be equally entitled to freedom and protection'. To those who would consider his book 'peculiarly ill-timed' White answered that his object was 'simply to investigate a proposition in natural history'. What should he have done? Suppressed his results? If he subjected his observations and inferences to criticism but still found them politically objectionable he might feel they were best ignored, but someone in this position cannot be sure that another research worker may not shortly publish the results of a similar investigation with inferences which might be even less welcome to him. Honest conclusions are not overthrown by personal attacks or dogmatic inferences but only by further analysis. As it happened, White's inferences did receive some critical attention, as from the American divine, Samuel Stanhope Smith, who discovered numerous errors without ever being able to controvert the overall effect of White's study (Smith, 1810: 151–76; Greene, 1954b: 393).

THE NOBLE SAVAGE

A notable consequence of the discovery of America and other distant lands was that the more educated people in Europe learned of living societies very different from their own, and from the comparison of their own ways with what they believed to be the customs of others a new criticism was born. In the diaries of Columbus and the accounts of subsequent explorers, the life of coloured inhabitants of distant lands is described in glowing terms. The French essayist Montaigne (1533–92) describes what he has learned about customs of the peoples near the bay of Rio de Janeiro and suggests that there is no more barbarism in their eating men alive than in some of the things he and his readers have lately seen in France. Three men of this foreign nation, he says, visited Rouen in the time of Charles IX, who talked with them a great while. Montaigne also did his best to question them on many points, and reported: 'I find there is nothing in that nation, that is either barbarous or savage, unless men call that barbarism that is not common to them' (cf. Hodgen, 1964: 191–4). The understanding of cultural variability began to make ground and to raise questions in men's minds. Bacon referred to custom as 'the principal magistrate of man's life'. Montesquieu's satirical *Persian Letters* (1721) started a new fashion, in holding up to a European nation a picture of itself as it might appear in the eyes of people from another culture.

The tendency of the early explorers to describe these foreign peoples in genial terms was partly an outcome of the initial lack of tension in their fleeting acquaintance with them. But the building up of these accounts into the myth of the noble savage reflected eighteenth-century romantics' attitudes towards their own society. Thus the visit to England in 1775 of Omai, a native of the Society Islands, provided verse satirists with a stock figure of great use in the attack upon the morals and manners of contemporary society. Such a figure could be made to observe of Europeans:

> Not rul'd like us on Nature's simple plan,
> Here laws on laws perplex the dubious man.

The significance of the romantic attitude went deeper, however. To believe that the savage is noble is to believe that man is naturally good. If evil does not have its origin in human nature, it must spring from the faulty organization of society (Hirn, 1941: 11–12). As Rousseau urged: 'God makes all things good; man meddles with them and makes them evil.' To believe that man is naturally good is to believe that under another régime he could lead a better life, and such an outlook must therefore be a powerful spur to the radical reorganization of existing institutions. Voltaire and the Encyclopaedists in France did not appeal to the 'noble savage' myth in their arguments for reform, and the Tory Samuel Johnson, who did not hold human nature in high esteem, scornfully dismissed 'cant in defence of savages'. Dryden had written:

> I am as free as nature first made man,
> Ere the base laws of servitude began,
> When wild in woods the noble savage ran.

But though the romantic image disappeared from the literary scene as bourgeois opinion recoiled from the French Revolution, it has appeared in new forms in later generations. Bernard Smith has shown how this image caused the progressive distortion of visual representations of savage life; how later – as mission activity in the Pacific increased – it was replaced by 'the evangelistic picture of an ignoble and degraded brute', and later still it gave way to a new conception of the romantic savage 'representative of the childhood of man, interesting because he possessed the unrealized accomplishments of the child' (Smith, 1960: 22–23, 108, 251). During the high noon of imperialism it was not the revolutionary who extolled the nobility of the unacculturated tribesman but the conservative who deplored the mixing of cultures. The notion that savagery is, in Rousseau's words, 'the real youth of the world' and its innocence, too, still has a firm grip on the Western imagination.

THE WILBERFORCEAN AGE

In the seventeenth and eighteenth centuries Negroes were employed as domestic servants in many fashionable British households. Most of them had been brought to Britain as slaves from plantations in the West Indies and while in Britain they not infrequently ran away from their owners. The legal position was confused. England prided herself on the personal liberty which Englishmen enjoyed under the common law. At the same time, she sanctioned and even promoted a rigorous system of slavery in her colonies. It was therefore inevitable that the problem would arise whether a Negro slave who was brought to England forthwith became free under the common law or whether the status of slavery under colonial law still adhered to him. Different legal authorities had advanced different solutions, but following a judgement of 1749 it was believed that a runaway slave could be legally recaptured. Finally, in Somersett's case of 1772, Lord Chief Justice Mansfield was obliged to pronounce upon a master's power to remove his slave from England to the sphere of colonial law. Mansfield concluded his judgement with the statement: 'The state of slavery is . . . so odious that nothing can support it but positive law . . . I cannot say that this case is allowed or approved by the Law of England and therefore the Black must be discharged' (see Fiddes, 1934). The decision freed no slaves (though some thought it did); it declared that, until Parliament enacted legislation explicitly covering the question, the power in dispute could not be legally exercised. By contrast, the issue of principle was pronounced upon in Scotland six years later (Joseph Knight, a Negro, against John Wedderburn, 15 January 1778). The court found slavery contrary to Scots law: 'the dominion assumed over this Negro, under the laws of Jamaica, being unjust, could not be supported...' (Catterall, 1926, I: 14–19).

Only after Somersett's case did the anti-slavery movement gather strength in Britain. It achieved, in 1807, the abolition of the slave trade, and, in 1833, the abolition of slaveholding in the British West Indies and in other overseas territories of the Crown. For a while, the wrongs of the slave trade became a fashionable subject for impassioned verse from the hand of the accomplished young lady. The flowery style of rhetoric may be judged from one of the sonnets of Robert Southey:

> Hold your mad hands! forever on your plain
> Must the gorged vulture clog his beak with blood?
> Forever must your Niger's tainted flood
> Roll to the ravenous shark his banquet slain?
> Hold your mad hands! and learn at length to know,
> And turn your vengeance on the common foe,
> Yon treacherous vessel and her godless crew!
> Let never traders with false pretext fair
> Set on your shores again their wicked feet:
> With interdict and indignation meet
> Repel them, and with fire and sword pursue!
> Avarice, the white, cadaverous wide and far,
> And for his purveyor calls the demon War.

A surfeit of such sentimentalizing could be a little trying, and it provoked a pardonable protest from Byron:

O Wilberforce! thou man of black renown,
  Whose merit none enough can sing or say,
Thou has struck one immense Colossus down,
  Thou moral Washington of Africa!
But's there's another little thing I own,
  Which you should perpetrate some summer's day,
And set the other half of Earth to rights;
  You have freed the blacks – now pray shut up the whites.

(cf. Dykes, 1942; Sypher, 1942)

For the anti-slavery enthusiasts the Negro was an object of philanthropy, but missionary groups in the churches were inclined to present
him as a benighted rather than a noble savage. Western Europe's sense
of superiority was expressed in the original of the famous hymn 'From
Greenland's icy mountains' by Richard Heber (1783–1826), Bishop of
Calcutta:

What though the spicy breezes
Blow soft o'er Java's isle,
Though every prospect pleases,
And only man is vile . . .
The savage in his blindness
Bows down to wood and stone
Can we whose souls are lighted
With wisdom from on high
Can we to men benighted
The lamp of life deny?

In general, it would seem that late eighteenth-century thought about
the Negro was often diffuse. The issues had not been defined and
people's attitudes were often inconsistent. Certainly it would be misleading to evaluate them from our present-day standpoint. Consider
the following passage from Philip Thicknesse, a former governor of
Jamaica, in which one would detect irony were it not an extract from
one of his letters to Granville Sharp, the abolitionist:

'Having lived in Jamaica when too young to think seriously on any
subject, you have brought to my mind many circumstances which
then struck me with horror. I once saved a beautiful girl from being
soundly whipped! She paid me some time afterwards in a manner I
ought now to blush at, but when I offered to pay her for the kindness
she had shown me she absolutely refused and said: "No massa my
heart beat true for you." But yet surely they ought to be slaves, for

do they not prefer a necklace of glass to one of solid gold? Have they not flatt noses and thick lips, and did they not fire upon me and wound me with glass bottles from an ambush, only for going to hunt them a little in the blue mountains with fifty or sixty soldiers?'

(Lascelles, 1928: 67)

The effect of the abolitionist agitation upon this situation was to clarify and polarize opinion, often, but not always, along the lines of the parties' material interests. As Sir Richard Burton later remarked of the African: 'Before the Wilberforcean age, he was simply a negro. That counteraction of the Asiento Treaty and of other little jobs, which founded Liverpool, and which poured five million pounds of sterling into the national pocket, marked him to the one class a Man and a Brother, to the other a Nigger' (Burton, 1865: 321). During the slave-trading era in West Africa there was little racial tension, but Burton presumably had in mind the fairly rapid development of opinion in England. Following upon the Napoleonic wars there was an upsurge of nationalism in Europe; this, together with the general democratization of society, may have stimulated the search for ways of expressing national distinctiveness (Poliakov, 1967: 228). But in Britain the controversy over slavery probably did more to attract people's attention to questions of racial difference.

An impression of the contending factions and their arguments can be gained from Carlyle's essay 'The Nigger Question', published anonymously in *Frazer's Magazine* for December 1849, and the reply it elicited in the next issue. According to Carlyle, the ex-slaves rejected the good Scots doctrine of the duty of labour. He resented their opportunity – as he imagined it – to live in comfortable idleness: 'To do competent work, to labour honestly according to the ability given them; for that and no other purpose was each one of us sent into this world.' The typical Negro was 'poor Quashee . . . a swift, supple fellow; a merry-hearted, grinning, dancing, singing, affectionate kind of creature, with a great deal of melody and amenability in his composition'. As a result of emancipation 'we have a few black persons rendered extremely "free" indeed. Sitting yonder with their beautiful muzzles up to the ears in pumpkins . . . while the sugar-crops rot round them uncut.' Carlyle railed against 'Exeter-Hallery and other tragic Tomfoolery' – Exeter Hall being where the abolitionist groups held their meetings. The Negroes were the lowest of the human species, and Carlyle's advice to them was: 'I do not wish to see you slaves again: but decidedly you will have to be servants to those that are born *wiser* than you, that are born lords of you; servants to the whites, if they are (as what mortal can doubt they are ?) born wiser than you.' The abolitionist writer in his rejoinder rejected Carlyle's gospel of labour and the appeal to the more brutal features of the natural world; humanitarianism was nobler than strife. He regretted that the essay would give aid and comfort to American slave-owners and stigmatized it 'a true work of the devil'.

RACE AND CULTURE

The Great Chain of Being view of creation in eighteenth-century biology tended to support the monogenetic view of human origins. Controversy between this line of thought and the opposing school came increasingly to turn upon the problem of whether racial classifications should be based upon external characters of colour, body form, etc., or might legitimately also take account of apparent differences in mental characters and culture. John Hunter, who in 1775 submitted an M.D. dissertation at Edinburgh University, *De Hominum Varietatibus*, explicitly rejected Kames's procedure in considering internal characters (see Blumenbach, 1865: 361). Another Edinburgh M.D. candidate in 1808, James Cowles Prichard, chose a similar theme: *De Generis Humani Varietate*. An admirer of Blumenbach, he too insisted 'we must direct our attention to the external characters which distinguish one tribe of men from another'. Such a decision implied that a people's physical constitution and its way of life were independent of one another. In the early nineteenth century it became more and more necessary to look closely at this implication and to consider the possibility that the diversity of human custom and achievement might be traced back to a simple biological source. In 1817 the greatly respected zoologist Cuvier identified culture with race, and the polygenetic view of human origins began to present a really serious challenge. Cuvier held that race determined culture: the Caucasian race had created the most civilized nations and exercised dominion over others; the Mongolian race had formed mighty empires in the East but its civilization was stationary; the hordes of the Negro race had always remained in a state of complete barbarism (Curtin, 1964: 231).

It is interesting to follow Prichard's reactions to the new challenge, for he was the last of the scientific monogenists and had to contend with difficulties on several different fronts (for references, see Banton, 1966). In his 1808 dissertation Prichard maintained, true to his acceptance of the Mosaic story, that the diversities of the human family were not constituted in the beginning but had appeared because living things had a universal tendency to diversification. No physical character acquired by art or circumstance was transmitted to a creature's progeny, so what was the mechanism of change? The answer offered in the dissertation is based on the claim that 'civilized life holds the same relation to the condition of savages in the human race, which the domesticated state holds to the natural or wild condition among the inferior animals'. In other words, there was a process of selection at work comparable to the animal breeder's. Prichard stressed the apparently accidental way in which variations were produced and noted that even whole colonies perished and disappeared in climates for which they were, by peculiarity of constitution, not adapted. In 1897 the Hope Professor of Zoology in the University of Oxford eulogized Prichard's arguments on inheritance and adaptation in an article entitled 'A Remarkable Anticipation of Modern Views on Evolution', in which he testified: 'The main result of Darwin's indefatigable labours on the formation of domestic races could not be more accurately summarized than in these words.' Prichard's anticipations had been overlooked because after 1826 he refrained from restating or developing these evolutionary speculations.

Prichard recognized an association between certain physical traits, such as skin colour, and particular kinds of environment. He also discerned variations in head form associated with hunting, pastoral, and civilized cultures. But instead of believing that anatomical features determined a people's manner of living, he thought that it was changes in culture that led to changes in bodily structure. This opinion is in accordance with the findings of the most modern research, both in respect of genetic adaptation – referred to in the next chapter – and in the field of human palaeontology, where studies indicate that much of human physical structure should be seen as the result of tool manufacture, hunting, and other forms of cultural development. Prichard was on the right lines, and yet he arrived at the hopelessly inaccurate conclusion that race was less stable than culture and that major physical changes could occur in five generations or so. In part, he was misled by some strange scientific reports – such as the 1765 paper in the Royal Society's *Philosophical Transactions* about a Negro who, in Britain, became steadily lighter in complexion – but the major obstacle was Prichard's faith in the Mosaic account as a historical record. He took very seriously the clerical computations which dated the Creation in 3928, 4004, and 5411 BC etc., and went to some trouble to work out his own date by analysing Egyptian genealogies. Believing that the various kinds of man had developed from an original dark-skinned ancestor in the course of some seven thousand years, Prichard was obliged to view physical structure as highly malleable (as did Samuel Stanhope Smith – cf. Smith, 1810: 93–125). This instance illustrates the importance for nineteenth-century anthropology of the great controversy in geology between the Neptunists and the Vulcanists, which ended in the establishment of so much greater a time-scale for the measurement of evolution. It must have been the growing conflict between Genesis and geology that caused the devout Prichard to suppress his early speculations.

The overall impression Prichard's work leaves is unquestionably one of dissociation between race and culture, and of the relative unimportance of physical constitution – an honest conclusion for one who gave so much time and labour to physical anthropology! In his most popular compilation, *The Natural History of Man*, Prichard presented a series of ethnographical summaries with relatively little by way of cumulative argument. The major conclusion was that the same inward and mental nature is to be recognized in all races of man, which strengthened the author's belief that 'we are entitled to draw confidently the conclusion that all human races are of one species and one family'. This was the uneasy quiet before the Darwinian storm.

A few Continental historians had already looked to racial determinism as the key to history, and in the 1840s British scholars began to borrow the thought of the biologists. One of the first and most influential excursions in this direction was by Thomas Arnold in his inaugural lecture as Regius Professor of History at Oxford in 1841. He pictured the force of world history as coming from a series of creative races, reaching its apogee in British leadership; other races either must become followers or, being too inferior, would have to dwindle away. In the years that followed, this theme became increasingly popular (Curtin, 1964: 375–7).

RACISM AT ITS ZENITH

The doubtful honour of composing the first racist treatise has been ascribed to various writers. To Boulainvilliers (Benedict, 1942: 111); to Kames (Bryson, 1945: 64–66); to Herder (Dover, 1952c: 132); and to others. The first author to publish a general argument with a grounding in biological evidence was Robert Knox, an Edinburgh M.D. who began his medical studies a year after Prichard left the university and who was subsequently a highly esteemed lecturer in anatomy there. Knox became a notorious figure when it was discovered that his agent had bought a body from the murderers Burke and Hare at a time when a scandal was developing over the 'resurrectionists' who robbed tombs to provide cadavers for anatomical dissection (Rae, 1964). Knox, who studied in Paris with the great zoologist, was aptly described by Sir Arthur Keith (1917: 17) as 'of the stuff of which Scots Covenanters were made but his religion was made by Cuvier'. He believed that race determined culture, and described his theory, quite appropriately, as 'transcendental anatomy'. Knox wrote (1850: 15–16): 'Whilst still young I readily perceived that the philosophical formula of Blumenbach led to no results: explained nothing: investigated no causes. It was the external-character naturalist trying "his method" on man.' For the same reason, he disagreed completely with Prichard. In 1850 Knox published a series of lectures entitled *The Races of Men*.[1] Though a singularly ill-organized work, this is one of the most articulate and lucid statements of racism ever to appear. 'With me', says Knox (1850: 6), 'race, or hereditary descent is everything; it stamps the man' – a phrasing soon to be echoed by Disraeli and Emerson (Gossett, 1963: 97–98). Literature, science, art – the whole of any civilization was but a manifestation of race. Race determined the course of history and the behaviour of one nation towards another.

But Knox was no chauvinist:

'The placing of the Slavonian and Gothic races foremost among men, first and greatest in philosophy, will much, I believe, astonish the men of other races; the Saxon and the Celt; the Italian and Sarmantian: the inordinate self-esteem of the Saxon will be especially shocked thereby; nor will he listen with composure to a theory which tells him, proves to him, that his race cannot domineer over the earth – cannot even exist permanently on any continent to which he is not indigenous – cannot ever become native, true-born Americans – cannot hold in permanency any portion of any continent but the one on which he *first* originated' (1850: vi).

Each race had its assured habitat: 'No race, however victorious they may be, has ever succeeded in utterly destroying a native population and occupying their place.' But warfare was also inevitable, for varying degrees of antagonism were inbred. He ventured: 'I think there must be a physical and, consequently, a psychological inferiority in the dark races generally'; and asserted of the darker races, 'Further removed by nature from the Saxon race, the antipathy between these races is greater than that between any other: in each other they perceive their direct antagonists.' Believing that races could not acclimatize themselves

---

[1] Notice that whereas the monogenists always wrote 'the races of *man*', the polygenists were careful to refer to 'the races of *men*'.

to other habitats, Knox scorned 'that den of all abuses, the office of the Colonial Secretary' (1850: 67, 222, 224, 449). Knox's influence was considerable, and his biographer states, 'Previous to his time, little or nothing was heard about Race in the medical schools: he changed all this by his Saturday's lectures, and Race became as familiar as household words to his students, through whom some of his novel ideas became disseminated far and wide, both at home and abroad' (Lonsdale, 1870: 292–3).

From 1850 to 1854 was the great period for racist publications: in 1850, Knox; in 1853, Gobineau; in 1854, Nott and Gliddon. Also in 1854, a future Secretary of State for Colonies, Bulwer-Lytton, presented his own racial theory of history. This intellectual current was not necessarily reflected in the attitudes or conduct of the people most involved in dealings with colonial peoples. Sir George Stephen, for example, noted that while there was anti-Negro sentiment among 'good society' in Britain, 'yet men whom business or colonial connection has brought into familiar intercourse with the black or coloured races, know well that the educated among them are not inferior to whites in any of those qualities which acquire esteem for the gentleman or confidence for the merchant' (Curtin, 1964: 381–2).

The volume edited, and largely written, by Nott and Gliddon, was called *Types of Mankind*. It contained little that was novel, but summarized the doctrines of a new American school of ethnology which had grown rapidly in the fifteen years since S. G. Morton, a Philadelphia physician, published *Crania Americana*. Morton had built up a considerable collection of skulls and had developed new techniques of measurement. He stressed the similarity of American Indian skulls from different regions and times, arguing that 'the American race differs essentially from all others, not excepting the Mongolian'. Morton favoured the view of species as immutable and concluded that God must have created each race 'adapted from the beginning to its peculiar local destination'; Genesis described the creation of the Adamic race (Stanton, 1960: 25–34, 142). Morton had requested G. R. Gliddon, the United States vice-consul to Cairo, to collect Egyptian crania, and in this way he gained a bumptious disciple with some knowledge of Egyptology and a flair for publicity. In his *Crania Aegyptica* of 1844 Morton reported on his new skulls, emphasizing the relative permanence of racial characters and drawing attention to the evidence that slavery was 'among the earliest of the social institutions of Egypt'. Such conclusions awakened the interest of Southerners not otherwise curious about scientific research.

One with a more serious interest was J. C. Nott, a physician in Mobile, Alabama, who had earlier published observations maintaining that mulattoes were shorter-lived and less prolific than pure Whites or pure Negroes, but that persons with any Negro heredity possessed an immunity to yellow fever. Nott was soon drawn into the debate and displayed a peculiar pleasure in attacking religious dogma. Archaeological research entered the picture with new evidence of the antiquity of the American Indian. Expeditions and contacts overseas brought further support to Morton's school. Charles Pickering, a botanist on the United States Exploring Expedition of 1838–42, was so impressed by the variety of races and the adaptation of each to its habitat that he moved over to the minority view. But the reports of governmental expeditions had to be wary of a public opinion that was very touchy on issues of this kind, so the author was obliged to bury his own conclusions in a rambling work which was given the title *The Races of Man and their Geographical Distribution* (1848). Another recruit was the notable zoologist Louis Agassiz, but recently come to America, who became a spokesman for the theory that species were immutable and the races separately created. Morton himself could not break away from the idea of purpose in nature, nor from a time-scale which reckoned the age of man in a few thousand years; he was reluctant to maintain the diversity of races in public discussion. Events forced his hand, and in his last years he defended the polygenetic view on one of its weakest points. Species were conventionally identified as categories which did not inter-breed, or, if they did so, produced only sterile hybrids. Man was a notorious inter-breeder. But Morton could find good authority (Prichard among others) for other criteria of species more congenial to his position (Stanton, 1960).

After Morton's death in 1851, Nott and Gliddon planned their commemorative volume *Types of Mankind*. It brought together Nott's conclusions on comparative anatomy, Gliddon's criticisms of biblical chronology from an Egyptological viewpoint, and several other pieces, one by Agassiz. Nott had studied Prichard diligently, and was respectful of his learning, but from much the same material he drew different inferences:

'Human progress has arisen mainly from the war of races. All the great impulses which have been given to it from time to time have been the results of conquests and colonizations. . . those groups of races heretofore comprehended under the generic term Caucasian, have in all ages been the rulers; and it requires no prophet's eye to see that they are destined eventually to conquer and hold every foot of the globe where climate does not impose an impenetrable barrier. . . . *Dark*-skinned races, history attests, are only fit for military governments . . . the superior races ought to be kept free from all adulterations, otherwise the world will retrograde, instead of advancing, in civilization' (Nott & Gliddon, 1854: 53, 79, 404, 405).

This volume was followed three years later by another of similar sort entitled *Indigenous Races of the Earth*.

The theory of race advanced by the French Count de Gobineau was a highly individual production, more complex than some commentators have thought. He was primarily interested in the decline of civilizations and found in race-mixing the key to this problem. But mixture also had a positive side. Civilization in historic times had equally been the product of race-mixing. Art and government were the signs of civilization and no civilization could produce these by itself. The civilizing races, as they brought others within their sway, were especially prone to mix their blood, so that there was a cyclical movement of rise and fall. As the upward tendency gained hold, an elite would be formed whose members could lay claim to the old prerogative of feudal families, and this only by asserting that they *felt* like noblemen; the acceptance of the race ideology as such could become conclusive proof that an individual was 'well bred', that through his veins ran 'blue blood', and that a superior origin claimed superior rights. From an identical political event, the decline of the nobility, Gobineau therefore drew two contradictory consequences – the decay of the human race and the formation of a natural aristocracy (Arendt, 1958: 173). Interwoven with the cyclical theme was a more straightforward assertion of the superiority of the white race and of aristocratic descent: 'a society is great and brilliant only as far as it preserves the blood of the noble group that created it, provided that this group itself belongs to the most illustrious branch of our species'. And: 'The white race originally possessed the monopoly of beauty, intelligence and strength. By its union with other varieties, hybrids were created, which were beautiful without strength, strong without intelligence, or, if intelligent, both weak and ugly' (Gobineau, 1915: 209, 210). In stressing the importance of the aristocratic heritage threatened by a bastardized proletariat, the Count was no nationalist but a continuator of Boulainvilliers's politically motivated philosophy of history.

By applying the polygenetic thesis to the history of civilizations, Gobineau opened a Pandora's box for the coming generation. His ideas exercised a pervasive influence over Western (especially German and French) politics, literature, history, and intellectual culture. His critics have often derided his work on account of inconsistencies, which might be expected in an *œuvre* of some forty volumes of essays, plays, novels, and travel books; and certainly some quite fundamental discrepancies are displayed. Other critics, however, maintain that responsibility for subsequent distortions should not be charged entirely to their originator's personal account and that much can be said in his defence. Lévi-Strauss described Gobineau's identification of race and culture as 'an honest intellectual error' (Lévi-Strauss, 1952: 5). Even the contradictions, it is said, 'as with greater dialecticians than he, always have their explanation in circumstance. They must be held signs of honesty, rather than weakness, of mind' (Barzun, 1965: 54; cf. Toynbee 1934, I: 218; Biddiss, 1966).

RACE AND THE LEARNED SOCIETIES

With the growth of scientific societies in the nineteenth century, interest in and opinions about racial differences were expressed in institutional form. In 1838 Thomas Hodgkin (who had been a classmate of Morton's in the medical school at Edinburgh) formed in London the Aborigines Protection Society, with the dual purpose of saving aboriginal groups in the colonies from possible extinction and of studying such peoples. Communication with interested persons in Paris led to the establishment in the following year of the Ethnological Society of Paris as a purely scientific society. In 1843 the London group divided, and those who wished to pursue scientific interests separately from the activities of the political pressure group formed in that year the Ethnological Society. Shortly afterwards, a society in New York adopted the same name. With the increasing importance of slavery as a political issue, anthropological debates acquired a significance that stretched far beyond the scientific world. The controversy so consumed the Paris society that, having no balancing interests, it dissolved in 1847. Twelve years later Paris savants founded the Anthropological Society of Paris. They had difficulty in obtaining authority: their leader was bound over to keep the discussions within legitimate and orthodox limits, and a police agent attended its sittings for two years to enforce this stipulation. The Society of Anthropology in Madrid was suppressed by the authorities after a short life, its projected investigation of the aboriginal races of the peninsula being considered offensive (Cunningham, 1908: 11).

With disputes about the American Civil War to stoke the flames, dissension in the Ethnological Society increased as the polygenetic view gained favour. The young and energetic Dr James Hunt, but recently its Honorary Secretary, broke away to found, in 1863, the Anthropological Society of London (Beddoe, 1870: lxxx–lxxxiv). Its members believed that anthropology should make its contribution to political discussion by popularizing its discoveries. This they did with vigour (Reining, 1962: 594–5). The new society got off to a noisy start with Hunt's pro-slavery presidential address 'On the Negro's Place in Nature', in which he concluded:

'1. That there is as good reason for classifying the Negro as a distinct species from the Europeans, as there is for making the ass a distinct species from the zebra; and if, in classification, we take intelligence into consideration, there is a far greater difference between the Negro and the European than between the gorilla and the chimpanzee. 2. That the analogies are far more numerous between the Negro and the ape, than between the European and the ape. 3. That the Negro is inferior intellectually to Europeans. 4. That the Negro becomes more humanized when in his natural subordination to the European than under any other circumstances. 5. That the Negro race can only be humanized and civilized by Europeans. 6. That European civilization is not suited to the Negro's requirements or character' (Hunt, 1865: 51–52).

After this address, discussion and recrimination continued far into the night.

It will be noted that Hunt did not restrict himself to the external characters by which racial groups may be distinguished, but judged them according to their intelligence and the extent to which they were 'humanized' and 'civilized'. This was a doctrine of race which was also a theory of race relations in that it offered a ready explanation of the relative power and position of racial groups in different parts of the world. Unlike Knox (whose line of argument he tended to follow), Hunt did not suggest that racial antipathy was inbred, but, like Aristotle, he held that the slave was happiest in servitude. Though doubting the capacity of races to acclimatize themselves in new environments, Hunt did not follow Knox in believing colonization doomed to failure: 'The merest novice in the study of race characteristics ought to know that we English can only successfully rule either Jamaica, New Zealand, the Cape, China, or India, by such men as Governor Eyre' (Hunt, 1866: lxxviii). Hunt died in 1869 at the age of thirty-six. Two years later the Anthropological Society and the Ethnological Society joined as the

Anthropological Institute of Great Britain and Ireland (see also Burrow, 1966: 118–36). The universities first recognized anthropology as a distinct subject when, in 1883, Oxford appointed E. B. Tylor to a teaching post. By this time, the tradition of scientific research in the anthropological field could contain the passions generated by differing views about race.

CHAPTER THREE

Race and Natural Selection

The threatened showdown between the monogenists and polygenists never came to a head, for in 1859 Charles Darwin published his epochal work *On the Origin of Species by Means of Natural Selection; or, The Preservation of Favoured Races in the Struggle for Life*, which demonstrated the part played by the selection of the fittest in the process of natural development. Ultimately, Darwin's theory favoured the monogenists, for it held that all the races of man were descended from a single primitive stock; but it upset any belief in particular creation and, by denying purpose or design in the development of species, seemed to threaten the authority of the Christian revelation which was a fundamental assumption for many monogenists. The polygenists – who had all along put more stress upon present racial differences than upon the question of their origin – were less troubled, for they could claim that the operation of natural selection would create and reinforce racial differences. More important, though, was the effect of Darwin's work in shifting attention from conjectures about origins to aspects of evolution that could be studied in the field or in the laboratory. In 1871, in his book *The Descent of Man*, Darwin turned to selection in the human species. The races of man presented him with a problem he found baffling, for, as he shows, they differ in every physical character in regard to which individuals are known to vary. He made no attempt to classify races, observing that the naturalist has no right to give names to objects which he cannot define. Nevertheless, he recognized considerable differences that had been 'nearly constant for very long periods of time' and thought that they could not be the product of environmental factors. Finally, he came to the conclusion that human differentiation was due to sexual selection, the choice by men and women of partners whom they found most to their taste.

SOCIAL DARWINISM

Darwin's discoveries were given to a world already prepared for them by developments in geology and kindred sciences, and by the writings of Herbert Spencer, 'the great expounder of the principle of Evolution', as Darwin called him. The doctrine of natural selection as the driving force behind development supplied the missing foundation stone for the theory of evolution. The first edition of Darwin's book sold out on the day of publication and had an instantaneous effect. Its theory accorded with the temper of the age in several respects. Darwin's inspiration came from Malthus; applied in the biological field, the postulate of continual struggle fitted the facts better than it had done in the sphere of population studies. In the early decades of the industrial era, when some made fortunes and many starved, life must often have seemed an extended combat. Years before the *Origin of Species* Tennyson had described nature as 'red in tooth and claw'. Thus the extent to which the new ideas upset religious susceptibilities should not be allowed to obscure how much they harmonized with other tendencies. The more progressive writers on social questions soon saw their problems in a new light and promptly began trying to translate Darwin's formulations into a law of social development. This gave rise to the line of thought known as social Darwinism: the key element in it was the idea of variations transmitted by heredity, which were subject to a process of selection. In popular usage this process was described by Spencer's phrase 'the survival of the fittest', but it was often based on a circular argument: The fittest were those who survived; how did one know they were the fittest? Because they had survived!

The early social Darwinists were enthusiasts who thought they had discovered a new key to the interpretation of social changes, and tackled their subject without the scientific caution usually shown by their master. One of the first was Walter Bagehot, who published in 1873 a book entitled *Physics and Politics, or Thoughts on the Application of Principles of 'Natural Selection' and 'Inheritance' to Political Society*, in which he argued that 'those nations which are strongest tend to prevail over the others; and in certain marked peculiarities the strongest tend to be the best'. The forces of imitation and elimination were the main ones in the formation of national character. Shortly afterwards, the Austrian sociologist Gumplowicz applied similar arguments to the struggle for survival between races; and the tide of similar writing flowed in such spate that Benjamin Kidd's *Social Evolution* (1894), a work of slender merit, sold a quarter of a million copies. Three aspects of this trend of thought deserve particular attention: the search for the unit of social development, which many found in the concepts of nation or race; the attempt to apply to this unit the theory of the selection of the fittest; and the impact of evolutionary teaching upon the political scene.

The belief that the unit of development was the nation is found in the work of Bagehot already referred to. The argument that the unit must be racial and physiological characterizes the work of the anthropo-sociological school. Reacting against the earlier view (as in Prichard) of physical type as easily modified, the anthropo-sociologists stressed the permanence of racial characters, borrowing from Darwin the idea that natural selection would ensure the continuance of the best-adapted types. What features were they to study in order to examine the process of natural selection among humans? They wanted to use the 'numerical method', so they needed to concentrate on relatively objective features. This led them, not surprisingly, to pay most attention to measurements of stature, eye colour, hair colour, shape of skull, etc. In France, Paul Broca developed the 'cephalic index', by which the lengthwise diameter of the skull was divided into the crosswise diameter and the result multiplied by a hundred. This was used to distinguish dolicho-cephalic (long-headed) populations from brachy-cephalic (broad-headed) ones. A nasal index was constructed to separate the leptorrhines (narrow-nosed) and platyrrhines (flat-nosed). When the average indices of samples from different populations were markedly different, this was taken as evidence of racial difference.

The two writers who developed anthropo-sociological ideas furthest were O. Ammon in Germany and G. V. de Lapouge in France, but they had their equivalents in other countries, such as C. C. Closson in the United States and J. Beddoe in England. The anthropo-sociologists usually pictured the dolicho-cephalic peoples (Nordics) as the blond, adventurous, aggressive race, and the brachy-cephalics (Alpines, Celts) as the darker, timid, submissive, subject race. Their investigations showed that there tended to be a higher proportion of dolicho-cephalics in the cities. What did this mean? Ammon and Lapouge thought it indicated that the dolicho-cephalics were of greater ability and had been favoured in the selective process. But the same investigations showed that brachy-cephalics were becoming more numerous, so that, unless special steps were taken, the superior race might be eliminated because of its members numerical rather than individual weaknesses. Beddoe, faced with similar figures, stated his conclusions in a more matter of fact manner in referring to 'the undoubted fact that the

Gaelic and Iberian races of the West, mostly dark-haired, are tending to swamp the blond Teutons of England by a reflux migration. At the same time, the possible effects of conjugal selection, of selection through disease, and the relative increase of the darker types through the more rapid multiplication of the artizan class, who are in England generally darker than the upper classes, should be kept in view' (Beddoe, 1885: 270). Those who did not believe that the blond Teutons were destined to inherit the earth could make just as much use of this material. Broca held that France was a nation of Gallic (i.e. Alpine or Celtic) brachy-cephalics and that *they* were the superior race. In the era of nationalistic fervour that followed the defeat of 1870, Broca's exaltation of the broad-heads was inflated into a cult of Celticism that influenced the whole cultural scene (Barzun, 1965: 115–27, 158–62; Benedict, 1942; 118–22, 129–30; Stark, 1961).

In the brief history of the anthropo-sociological school is seen a mixture of racist bias and ordinary bad luck. The features the anthropo-sociologists chose to measure were, in their day, the obvious ones, and they could not know in advance that their examination would prove so unrewarding. To cite one of the more minor investigations, Beddoe recorded the hair colour of 524 married and single women patients at the Bristol Infirmary, but the results demonstrated little more than that there was some truth in the belief that gentlemen prefer blondes (Beddoe, 1885: 226). Even the supposed universality of the prepon-derance of dolicho-cephalics in cities was disproved. Comparative analysis established that city populations were usually drawn from a wider area than rural populations, and therefore showed greater variation. The inferiority or superiority of the racial stocks was in no way involved. The element of racist bias in the work of the members of this school was, however, more serious. An American authority's judgement in this respect is unequivocal. At the end of a detailed review he says that their work 'contained many profound observations. Their emphasis on the operation of selection is of permanent importance', but

'they seemed to themselves to have placed the doctrine of the social superiority of the long-headed blonds among the statistically demon-strated facts of social anthropology. If they had deceived themselves only little harm would have resulted. But they greatly strengthened doctrines upon which have been based pernicious forms of racial arrogance in Germany, England and the United States. They assisted in the inflation of Teutonic chauvinists and Pan-Germanists; they lent aid and comfort to Anglo-Saxon imperialists; they gave a sense of moral righteousness to the spirit of racial intolerance' (Hankins, 1931: 137, 139–40).

At the same time, developments in genetics led to a growing emphasis upon the stability and continuity of races and species as opposed to earlier views of their mutability and change. In Germany, August Weismann developed his theory of 'the continuity of the germ plasm', according to which the characteristics of a race or species derived from an immortal germ plasm handed on from generation to generation. This theory, it has been said, harmonized very well with the claims of Prussia and the German aristocracy, and reinforced political theories of racial hegemony.

The original social Darwinist thesis was that members of human societies competed with each other, resulting in what was termed intrasocial selection. This doctrine, which was accepted by T. H. Huxley and survived in the work of Benjamin Kidd, was soon abandoned by the majority of scholars. Spencer gave it up, and adopted the alternative view, known as intersocial selection, according to which different societies struggle against one another for survival. Prince Peter Kropotkin, in his book *Mutual Aid as a Factor in Evolution* (1902), reminded the public that Darwin himself had said that in numerous animal societies the struggle between separate individuals is replaced by co-operation in order that the community may survive. The same was true of human societies, and those of his followers who ignored co-operation within species had failed to understand either animal or human society. Sir Francis Galton and Karl Pearson, both influential writers, inclined to the same view and opposed the intrasocial theory of selection. Where Spencer, the pacifist and internationalist, shrank from applying his intersocial analysis of selection to international relations, Karl Pearson knew no such inhibitions. A fiery controversialist, pupil of Galton and professor at London University, Pearson held that 'the nation was a unity evolved by the struggle of one living type under the same laws as applied to other phases of life' and that thus 'the theory of the state became biological'. In a booklet called *National Life from the Standpoint of Science*, published in 1901 and reprinted several times, he stated that from a genetic standpoint Negroes were poor stock, and, 'if you want to know whether the lower races of man can evolve a higher type, I fear the only course is to leave them to fight it out among themselves'. Moral principles might be no guide, for 'when the struggle for existence between races is suspended, the solution of great problems may be unnaturally postponed'. Speaking with the authority of a

Fellow of the Royal Society he assured his listeners that 'the scientific view of a nation is that of an organized whole kept up to a high pitch of internal efficiency by insuring that its numbers are substantially recruited from the better stocks, and kept up to a high pitch of external efficiency by contest, chiefly by way of war with inferior races. . . .' He asserted that the 'continual progress of mankind is the scarcely recognized outcome of the bitter struggle of race with race' and developed an ingenious defence of colonialism. According to Pearson, it was advisable to prepare for times of national crisis a reserve of brain and physique: 'such a reserve can always be formed by filling up with men of our own kith and kin the waste lands of the earth, even at the expense of an inferior race of inhabitants'.

Pearson's mentor, Sir Francis Galton, was a man of very different temper. It was he who first provided statistical evidence for the theory that abilities often run in families. Galton went further, and argued that heredity must be taken into account in social policy. Just as horse-breeders achieve the best results by mating horses of good stock, so people should encourage the best elements in the population to have large families and sterilize defectives to prevent their passing on undesirable traits. He became the founder of what has been termed, perhaps a little kindly, the science of eugenics. The acceptance by a man of Galton's intellect and eminence of the thesis that different races could be distinguished and compared with one another, and his use of a mock statistical technique to this end, must have assisted considerably the propagation of racist theories. Galton confidently proposed that couples of 'worthy' genetic qualities should be given special allowances to help them at the start of their married life and to enable them to have many children. Today, the naïveté of such a proposal is startling: could any acceptable procedure ever be devised for selecting such persons?

The course of social Darwinist thought is complicated. Some writers who at first espoused this approach, such as L. Gumplowicz, J. Novicow, and B. Kidd, later went over to the critics and played an important part in exposing its inadequacies (Stark, 1961). They, and others, showed that the naturalistic theory of human inequality – whether Darwinist or Aristotelian – was based on a circular argument: 'fitness' and 'survival' always coincided because the former was defined in terms of the latter. The social Darwinist line of thought was particularly influential in America, and early sociological theory there was for the most part formulated either in conformity with or in reaction against Darwinist ideas. The leading spokesman for a biologically determined conception of society was William Graham Sumner, with his belief that the only choice was between 'liberty, inequality, and survival of the fittest' and 'not-liberty, equality, and survival of the unfittest'. Later sociologists like A. G. Keller and F. H. Giddings followed the Spencer-Sumner line of argument; Albion Small, Lester F. Ward, C. H. Cooley, and E. A. Ross were its active critics (Hofstadter, 1955 edn: 156). But, as a recent writer has shown, the American liberals of the latter part of the nineteenth century and the first part of the twentieth were not at all 'liberal' on the subject of race. They feared that as long as hundreds of thousands of immigrants arrived every year from southern and eastern Europe it would be impossible to protect the native workers from exploitation. In attacking the ideas of intrasocial competition then widespread in the United States, they actually encouraged theories of society based upon racial conflict (Gossett, 1963: 173–5). The Darwinian influence was also apparent in the literary naturalism of contemporary novelists. Thus the best-selling author Jack London was both a socialist and a racist, a man for whom pride of race substituted for pride of family: his heroes were given an appropriate racial ancestry; Jews and half-breeds were represented as inferior beings. Explaining his political beliefs, he asserted: 'Socialism . . . is devised so as to give more strength to these certain kindred favoured races so that they may survive and inherit the earth to the extinction of the lesser, weaker races' (Gossett, 1963: 198–227). In writings about race relations, social Darwinism has remained a periodically important influence down to the present day. Arguments that derive from it are advocated every now and then; some critics acknowledge its former influence by exaggerating the extent to which social patterns are independent of biological factors; for the student of race relations, therefore, it is useful both to understand the arguments of this school and to be able to place them in historical perspective.

Darwin had destroyed the view of races as immutable units. To maintain that an original set of pure races was degenerating because of miscegenation was becoming increasingly difficult. But it was possible to rescue the racist position by arguing that races were in the process of formation and that separateness was therefore to be encouraged. This latter-day version of social Darwinism was elegantly expounded by Sir Arthur Keith. In a booklet *Ethnos* (1931a) he claimed: 'the essential potency of race lies not in outward characters, but in the manifestation of these inward feelings known as "national spirit". Give the inhabitants of any land a national spirit, let that land be preserved intact over many generations, and a race which answers Huxley's definition will certainly appear under the working of the law of evolution. A nation always represents an attempt to become a race; nation and race are but different degrees of the same evolutionary movement.' In this process, prejudice played an important part. Nature, he told the students at Aberdeen in a rectorial address, had arranged national and tribal organization on a competitive basis; each tribe was a team engaged in the eternal struggle to obtain promotion and avoid relegation. Nature's League also had its divisions – racial divisions – white, yellow, brown, and black.

'No transfers for her; each member of the team had to be home-born and home-bred. She did not trust her players or their managers farther than she could see them! To make certain they would play the great game of life as she intended it should be played she put them into colours – not of transferable jerseys, but liveries of living flesh, such liveries as the races of the modern world now wear. She made certain that no player could leave his team without being recognized as a deserter. To make doubly certain she did an almost unbelievable thing. She invaded the human heart and organized it so that her tribal teams would play *her* game – not *theirs*. She tuned the heart of her teams for her own ends. She not only imbued her opposing teams with an innate love of competition and of "team-work"; she did much more. What modern football team could face the goal-posts unless it developed as it took the field a spirit of antagonism towards the players wearing opposing colours? Nature endowed her tribal teams with this spirit of antagonism for her own purposes. It has come down to us and creeps out from our modern life in many shapes, as national rivalries and jealousies and as racial hatreds. The modern name for this spirit of antagonism is race-prejudice' (1931b: 34–35; cf. Keith, 1948: 72).

There are several objections to this thesis. It is far too speculative to justify the inferences asserted as to the function of prejudice. That intergroup hostility might have been an inherited trait in early stages of primate evolution is possible, though recent studies of primate groups in natural conditions underline the importance of effective group organization rather than that of solidarity against other groups. To claim that in the present day it is genetically transmitted strains credulity too far. (It should be remembered that while natural selection continually eliminates certain characters it can select in favour of only a limited number at any one time, so that doubt attaches to whether genes carrying potentialities for high intergroup antagonism could have

continued to be favoured over so many generations when other characters were being selected.) All the evidence indicates that group hostilities
are socially transmitted. Even if this criticism be set aside and Keith's
argument be held to state only the course of long-term trends, it fails to
fit the facts. Racial antagonism does not correlate with emergent
demographic isolates; as this book will show, it correlates much better
with other variables.

It is now time to attempt a general criticism of the approach to the
study of race relations advocated by such writers as Knox, Hunt, and
Keith. Their approach is characterized by the very title of Hunt's
notorious address: 'The Negro's Place in Nature'. It assumes that his
place in society is completely determined by his place in the natural
order. Complementary to this is the idea of racial antipathy as a natural,
not a social, phenomenon. Contemporary critics were quick to point
out the weaknesses of social Darwinism if it were offered as an explanation of the existing state of relations between races, and to emphasize
that moral principles were independent of natural laws: the fact that
an event is likely or even inevitable does not mean that it is to be
regarded as good. Analogies from the natural world are dangerous
because there is only one universe, which is thought of as a more or less
perfectly functioning whole; everything has its 'place' in nature, and,
no matter how reprehensible it may appear, a defence can be found for
it. The naturalist view of racial antipathy as an inherited character
independent of individual volition was completely dependent on the
organic analogy. It saw races as organisms, the different components
of which were inescapably linked to the parent body and governed by
it. The individual man was but a pawn – a specimen of a particular
species bound to behave in accordance with the laws governing his
species's position in the order of life. In social life there is more than one
universe. Man does not have to live in the future as he has lived in the
past, and he can use his moral beliefs as a standard of judgement in the
way that the biologist interpreting animal behaviour cannot.

It has sometimes been argued that the naturalist approach is valid up
to a certain point and invalid thereafter. This is the claim that Society is
not part of Nature. Biological laws, so the argument goes, fix the
framework within which Culture – the realm of freedom governed by
the spirit – operates (Stark, 1961: 56). There have been several futile
controversies over this false dichotomy, which springs from an unreal
fear of the application of scientific methods to the study of human
relations. Those who advance this objection regularly reveal an inexcus-
able ignorance of the nature and the limitations of scientific inference.

The claim that Society is not part of Nature, far from preserving the sphere of human free will, concedes far too much to the vulgar conception of natural sciences as a body of knowledge concerning the forces determining the nature of phenomena. It implies, as has been pointed out by Lancelot Hogben (Banton, 1961: 168), that the social Darwinists' science was right but their error lay in trespassing in an alien territory. (Where any boundary could be drawn it is difficult to see, for biological factors are clearly of the utmost importance in explaining the course of human affairs even if they are irrelevant to the moral judgement.) But, in fact, the social Darwinists' science was wrong. The objection to arguments such as those of Sir Arthur Keith is not that they necessarily commit a methodological error but that they simply do not fit the facts.

IMPERIALISM AND RACIAL CONCEIT

Before social Darwinism took hold, a mystique of Anglo-Saxonism had already developed from the earlier interest in race as an explanatory factor in history, nourished by the climate of nationalism and romanticism in contemporary Britain. Charles Kingsley, the writer of historical novels, sometime Professor of History at Cambridge and supporter of the Anthropological Society, made new use of the idea of race and stressed the contribution of the Teutons to the Anglo-Saxon stock. He was followed by E. A. Freeman, Regius Professor at Oxford, who believed in the permanence of Anglo-Saxon elements in English history, by other professors of history at Oxford including J. A. Foude and W. Stubbs, and by a flock of less gifted writers, until the whole culture was saturated with racial explanations (Williams, 1966). Mathew Arnold, for example, wrote at length about Celts and Teutons, Hellenism and Hebraism, and though he did not subscribe to any racist philosophy, such use of racial categories must have helped to make racist ideas respectable. Nor was racism only a European belief. Edward W. Blyden, the West Indian spokesman for Sierra Leone and Liberia, believed that Blacks and Whites each had their inherited cultural specialities.

Because it justified the evolutionary view of life and revealed an underlying law, the theory of natural selection reinforced these tendencies in historical writing. The suggestion of social Darwinists that nations and races could be understood as organisms introduced a further theme that appealed to anyone who would generalize from historical experience. For if evolutionary processes were at work in the rise and decline of nations, then an understanding of the foreordained course would give man greater control over his condition and a new realization of how far he could change his circumstances. Thus Sir J. R. Seeley, Regius Professor of Modern History in the University of Cambridge, concluded that the key to the understanding of modern times was the expansion of England decreed by 'a Providence which is greater than all Statesmanship'. Summing up his argument, he wrote:

'The peculiarly English movement, I have urged, has been an unparalleled expansion. Grasp this fact, and you have the clue to both the eighteenth and the nineteenth centuries . . . this formula binds together the past of England and her future, and leaves us, when we close the history of our country, not with minds fatigued and bewildered as though from reading a story that has been too much spun out, but enlightened and more deeply interested than ever, because partly prepared for what is to come next.'

The strength of his insistence upon the inevitability of the process expressed in his 'formula' (itself a term scarcely beloved of historians) may be seen from his statement: 'so decided is the drift of our destiny that after we had created one Empire and lost it, a second grew up almost in our own despite' (Seeley, 1883: 357–8).

Another book by an authority on English fourteenth-century history – and a man with governmental experience in Australia – was Charles H. Pearson's *National Life and Character*. This attracted much attention at the time of publication (1893). Pearson believed that it was possible to indicate in a general way the direction of political and social affairs: 'We are bound, wherever we go, to establish peace and order; to make roads, and open up rivers to commerce; to familiarize other nations with a self-government which one day will make them independent of ourselves.' To the expansion of the higher races unchangeable limits were set and the burden of the book became the inevitability of the rise of the prolific black and yellow races (the former 'very little raised above the level of brutes', the latter for the most part 'of such secondary intelligence as to have added nothing permanent to our stock of ideas' (Pearson, 1893: 13, 341). Were Pearson alive today he would claim that his predictions have been faithfully fulfilled: after making their unique contribution the Aryan races are 'even thrust aside by peoples whom we looked down upon as servile'. This pessimism and racial fear comple-mented the more dominant belief in racial superiority, justifying the claim that white privileges had to be actively defended. At the beginning of the twentieth century there was, in fact, a de-Africanization pro-gramme in the West African government services. African doctors were made auxiliaries or prevented from rising to higher posts; other Africans were removed from office on the grounds that Europeans were inherently more competent (Fyfe, 1962: 614–20).

Belief in the inevitability of evolutionary processes coloured many political arguments of the time. It led Herbert Spencer to deny the possibility of securing social progress by direct remedial legislation and to assert that society must wait for the automatic working of the general laws of development. It led another history professor, John Adam Cramb, to argue that big wars were better than small wars. In a series of lectures given in London during the South African war, Cramb pictured the state as 'the embodiment in living immaterial substance of the creative purpose of the race, of the individual and ultimately of the Divine'. From this it was but a short step to pronounce that imperialism 'is patriotism transfigured by a light from the aspirations of universal humanity . . . in a race dowered with the genius for empire. Imperialism is the supreme, the crowning form, which in this process of evolution it attains.' War was therefore, according to Cramb, 'a phase in the life-effort of the State towards completer self-realization, the perpetual omnipresent strife of all being towards self-fulfilment' (Cramb, 1915: 13, 91, 179). In the South African war, two principles equally lofty and impressive were at stake, 'the dying principle of Nationality and the principle which, for weal or woe, is that of the future, the principle of Imperialism'. This struggle was 'the first war waged by the completely constituted democracy of 1884', and its end 'the larger freedom, the higher justice, a war whose aim is not merely peace, but the full, the living development of those conditions of man's being without which peace is but an empty name'. In the professor's system of doublespeak war was peace, and there were many listeners only too ready to adopt his casuistry. But this was not the end of the lecture-room Vulcan's revelation; he went on – 'looming already on the horizon, the wars of races rise portentous, which will touch to purposes yet higher and more mystic the wars of empires' (1915: 90, 96, 136, 147).

The views of Pearson, Seeley, and Cramb may have been extreme, but they are not to be discounted, for they represent the strongly nationalist sentiment of an arrogant generation. The arguments of the liberal writers who pleaded for internationalism seem almost self-evident today; their force and significance can be appreciated only when set against such a background.

The trains of thought that sprang from the writings of Darwin and Spencer combined to elevate the jingo spirit that lasted from the late 1870s for over twenty years – 'We don't want to fight, but by jingo! if we do! We've got the ships, we've got the men, we've got the money too!' This attitude reached its peak in the orgiastic exuberance of Mafeking night, a display that shocked people who were not otherwise prudish. Englishmen began to take a vicarious pride in the achievements of their colonial heroes, and there grew up a new literature of military adventure. This movement was evident in the popularity of Rudyard Kipling's works, with their glorification of action, and in the elevation of the author to a popular idol of prodigious influence. The rise of a popular electorate underlined the crudity of such trends and called forth the cheap newspaper press. Harmsworth's *Daily Mail*, founded as 'the embodiment and mouthpiece of the imperial idea', reached the unprecedented circulation of a million copies within five years. A similar appeal to racialism was made by Horatio Bottomley's *John Bull*. The subjugation of colonial peoples was held to be justified by the natural superiority of the colonizers. If Whites and Coloureds were bound by a higher fate to fight for survival, and if success was to be proof that the winning side was the one that had been most fit to continue its course, what else was to be done but to take over control of the coloured races' lands on behalf of Destiny? And if success justified all things, what did the methods matter by which it was obtained? Nature was not squeamish: the hand of a humanitarian was scarcely to be discerned in the way one species preyed upon another. If such were Nature's methods, would not humanitarian policies upset the natural course of events without delaying the inevitable for more than a short space? As Belloc wrote:

> *Whatever happens, we have got*
> *The maxim gun*
> *And they have not.*

The influence of biological thinking in this era was such that one critic suggested that a new beatitude had been incorporated in the national religion: 'Blessed are the strong, for they shall prey upon the weak.' An authority upon the history of the period concludes that, though economic factors were important in the growth of imperialism, 'the prevalence of evolutionary teaching was perhaps crucial. It not only justified competition and struggle but introduced an element of ruthlessness and immorality that was most characteristic of the whole movement' (Langer, 1951: 95).

In Britain theoretical racism declined with the emergence of Germany as Britain's great rival. Liberal writers attacked imperialist racism vehemently and effectively. In the United States racism gave thrust to the expansionist appetites of men such as A. J. Beveridge who, in 1900, lectured his colleagues in the United States Senate: 'God has not been preparing the English-speaking and Teutonic peoples for a thousand years for nothing but vain and idle self-contemplation and self-admiration. No! He has made us the master organizers of the world to establish system where chaos reigns. . . . He has made us adept in government that we may administer government among savage and servile peoples.' Later American racism expressed the fear that the country was admitting immigrants of poor stock whose assimilation into the population would lead to a general deterioration. This was the pessimistic, eugenist strand in racist thought. Its leading spokesman was H. F. Osborn, but most of the publicity went to Madison Grant, author of *The Passing of the Great Race* (1916), and to another lawyer, Lothrop Stoddard, who wrote several popular surveys. Grant maintained that 'the result of the mixture of two races, in the long run, gives us a race reverting to the more ancient, generalized and lower type. The cross between a white man and a negro is a negro; the cross between a white man and a Hindu is a Hindu; and the cross between any of the three European races and a Jew is a Jew' (Gossett, 1963:353–63, 390–8; Alexander, 1962). Many sensible and serious people, however, were influenced by alarmist talk that America was receiving only Europe's cast-outs and by fear of the 'yellow peril' in the Pacific. When, in 1921, legislation was enacted to restrict immigration, it employed a quota system designed to preserve the existing balance of national groups in the United States, reflecting the influence of the idea of race upon the popular mind.

After World War I scientific racism faltered, unable to furnish the evidence it had so extravagantly promised. An American commentator states: 'What chiefly happened in the 1920s to stem the tide of racism was that one man, Franz Boas, who was an authority in several fields which had been the strongest sources of racism, quietly asked for proof that race determines mentality and temperament' (Gossett, 1963: 429). In Britain, the opposition of opinion was less clear cut; the country was recovering from the conflict with 'fellow Teutons' and was not faced by an immigration problem; imperial claims were being consolidated, not extended. Greater experience of pre-industrial peoples revealed the intricacies of cultural variation and made simple theories seem less satisfactory. The writings of social anthropologists such as Bronislaw Malinowski brought new questions to the forefront.

The 1950s saw the re-emergence of old controversies about race. The report of the settlement of Action for Damages for Libel brought by the editors of the review *Mankind Quarterly* against the Royal

Anthropological Institute and the editor of *Man* has a familiar ring
(*Man*, 1965: 104). The chief difference from the position a hundred
years before is that the school which would now emphasize racial
differences as the primary clue to an understanding of social relations
is a relatively small one, with little support from reputable scientists
(cf. *Current Anthropology*, Vol. 2, 1961: 303–41; Vol. 3, 1962: 154–8,
279–81, 284–302; Vol. 4, 1963: 119–21, 189–209, 313–20).

It is never easy to be sure about the influence of scholarly writing
upon the popular mind, but the author obtained some confirmation when
conducting research in England in the early 1950s. He heard it asserted
several times that if a white woman has intercourse with a coloured
man there is always the possibility that any baby she might bear,
perhaps years after that incident in question, may prove to be coloured.
The presence of a similar belief among Oxbridge students and in a
family welfare clinic (*New Society*, 18 March 1965: 30) has been
independently reported, and it probably has some general currency. In
books on race relations it sometimes appears as the 'black baby myth'.
Here, surely, is an irrational piece of folklore? Yet we find that Darwin
in *The Variation of Plants under Domestication* (1868) gave countenance
to this reputed mode of inheritance, which was named telegony. It was
supported by the case of a mare that had been mated with a zebra-like
animal, giving birth to a hybrid with faint stripes. Later, the mare
was mated with a black Arab stallion and bore three foals which had
the same stripes as the hybrid, though more markedly. Their colouring
was thought to have been due to the first mating, though biologists
now know that the stripes were inherited from one of the mare's remote
ancestors (Ewart, 1911). Nevertheless, the belief persists. English
sheep-breeders will not allow a pure-bred ewe that has once been mated
with a ram of another breed to remain in the Flock Book. The prevalence
of such an idea long after it has been disproved in biology is but one
example of the tenacity of the scientific myth when it appears to lend
authority to a socially convenient belief – convenient in so far as it
discourages women from associating with coloured strangers. Much of
today's racial folklore is in fact the science of a century ago. Contemporary discussions of the 'half-caste' often echo the faulty generalizations of the Anthropological Society of 1863 or the American debate on
slavery (on telegony, cf. Nott & Gliddon, 1854: 396–7).

THE GENETIC SYSTEM

The single most important thing Charles Darwin did, it has been said,
was to force biologists to find a unit of inheritance (Bronowski, 1961:

xv). Once the doctrine of immutability had been overthrown, the source of the variation had to be located. This was the contribution of Gregor Johann Mendel and the early twentieth-century pioneers of genetics. But the elucidation of the modes of genetic transmission did not solve the question of racial classification because there are relatively few physiological features that can be linked unequivocally with particular genes. In the first half of the twentieth century, biological research into racial differences did not result in any striking discoveries. After 1945, with the extension of blood-group analysis, the prospects brightened. The analysis of human proteins such as haemoglobin by paper electrophoresis and paper chromotography revealed varieties which appeared to originate in single genes. The first of these to be discovered was the sickle-cell gene, which appeared to serve as a marker of the racial origins of the Negro group. But when, after a time, appreciable frequencies of this gene were found in India, Arabia, and many Mediterranean countries, the pattern could not be explained by theories of Negro admixture. Furthermore, the identification of new genes contributed new ideas as to racial groupings, until possible racial classifications became so numerous and diverse as to call into question the whole procedure and to make many scientists doubt the utility of these classifications for the purposes of modern research.

All this time there had been a latent conflict between the traditional type of racial theory as applied to human affairs and an explanation in terms of natural selection. Much human variability had been explained by hypotheses about the migration of races, as in the belief that the inhabitants of certain regions were darker skinned because darkskinned races had migrated there. The possibility that the environment had exercised a selective influence in favour of certain traits was not taken so seriously. Just why so many people assumed that the traits or genes used to trace racial heritage were non-adaptive is not easy to answer. It may have been a carry-over of nineteenth-century racist thought which, in this respect, was pre-Darwinian in origin. Thus Knox asserted:

'The Saxon is fair, not because he lives in a temperate or cold climate, but because he is a Saxon. The Esquimaux are nearly black, yet they live amidst eternal snows; the Tasmanian is, if possible, darker than the negro, under a climate as mild as England. Climate has no influence in permanently altering the varieties or races of men; destroy them it may and does, but it cannot convert them into any other race' (Knox, 1850: 52–53).

If it were shown that the sickle-cell trait in fact contributed a selective advantage in a certain environment, this outlook would have to be abandoned.

In the early 1950s Dr A. C. Allison and his co-workers in London showed that inheritance of the sickle-cell trait from one parent conferred protection from *falciparum malaria* and thus opened a new chapter in the understanding of race as a biological phenomenon (Allison, 1954). A simple explanation of the genetic mechanisms involved may be of use. The red cells of the blood are minute in size (several million could be spread on a small coin) and they are normally shaped like discs. They contain a haemoglobin which conveys oxygen, but may also serve as food for malaria parasites. A kind of cell that assumes the shape of a sickle is occasionally produced by mutations arising from a single gene. If children inherit this gene from both parents, their bodies do not manufacture normal haemoglobin and unless, in their early years, they are given frequent blood transfusions they die of sickle-cell anaemia. Those who inherit the sickle-cell gene from one parent only are referred to, in this context, as heterozygotes, and they show a high resistance to malaria. Those who inherit this gene from neither parent are much more likely to die of malaria. If two heterozygotes mate they produce some children with no sickle-cell gene, some with it from one parent only, and some with it from both. As those with anaemia die, their sickle-cell genes are lost to the population. A high frequency of the gene (e.g. 20 to 40 per cent among many West African peoples) is, however, maintained by the selective advantage the heterozygotes possess over other people. With modern methods of malaria control this advantage is now of little value and so frequencies may be expected to fall.

This discovery meant that the distribution of the sickle-cell trait in West Africa could be understood as the product of natural selection acting upon a gene flow which was related to migration and population mixture. Nowadays it makes no sense in human genetics to think of races as discrete units. Human variation is thought of in statistical terms as a series of differences of degree in different measures, often called 'clines'. Population groups are usually heterogeneous from this standpoint; their unity is political rather than genetical, so that there is force in the suggestion that they be referred to as *ethnic groups* rather than races (Huxley & Haddon, 1935). Geneticists examine the variations in different clines and look for ways in which natural selection could have produced the differences. This kind of analysis can produce results of great interest to the social scientist. In the case of West Africa, it was only when peoples migrating towards the coast started cutting down the high forest that breeding-places for the malaria-carrying mosquito *Anopheles gambiae* became widespread, and only after this did selection for the sickle-cell heterozygote begin to operate. Previously, food supply had been the major factor limiting the size of the populations, but the development of agriculture, which had occasioned the cutting down of the forest, increased the food supply very greatly. The new land use increased the incidence of malaria, and disease then took over as the principal population limiter. The spread of the sickle-cell trait can therefore be seen as the first known genetic response to the agricultural revolution (Livingstone, 1958, 1964b).

Natural selection operates through differential fertility and mortality but variations in the death rate are affected by cultural differences. One culture may be better than another at providing people with food. Thus the replacement of Bushman genes by Bantu genes over most of East and South Africa was not due to the superiority of Bantu genes, but to their association with a culture which could support higher population densities. In the competition with the hunting and gathering culture of the Bushmen, the agricultural and pastoral culture of the Bantu proved superior and the population density of the area increased at least tenfold. In the Kalahari Desert, where agriculture is impossible, the Bushmen have not had to contend with this competition (Livingstone, 1964a). The study of how natural selection operates upon human populations has therefore provided an answer to the old question about the relations between race and culture. Race does not determine culture, as the racists thought. Culture does not determine physical type. The two interact, though the interaction is not always the important feature. As an eminent geneticist oberves:

'The salient feature about man – perhaps one might say that it is his defining characteristic – is that he has developed, to an enormously higher degree than is found in any other species, a method of passing information from one generation to the next which is alternative to the biological mechanism depending on genes. This human-information transmitting system is, of course, the process of social learning. This gives man a second evolutionary system imposed on top of the biological one, and functioning by means of a different system of information transmission' (Waddington, 1961: 70).

A particular environment and its various problems result in the selection of particular genes. Men and women with a particular biological inheritance may then develop their environment and create a culture, which influences the course of natural selection. The social heritage passed to their children may confer on them a far greater advantage than any distinctive physical trait.

It may be easier to appreciate the continuing significance of non-interacting elements in race and culture if, in accordance with recent studies, a distinction is drawn between two types of biological adaptation in evolution. On the one hand, adaptation may proceed by genetic specialization, developing special traits; on the other hand, it may proceed by developing plasticity and the abilities of the all-rounder as opposed to the specialist. For example, it is known that the composition of the blood which is most favourable for life at high altitudes is somewhat different from that which suffices at sea level. A species living at different levels from the coast up a mountainside may either (a) become differentiated into several altitudinal races, each having a characteristic blood composition favoured by natural selection; or (b) develop an ability in individuals to adjust their blood composition in accordance with the altitude. Among humans, differences in skin colour, hair form, nose shape, and body structure are almost certainly evidence of natural selection producing genetic specialization as a response to variations in the physical environment. But the evidence suggests very strongly that in the realm of mental traits the course of adaptation has been the alternative one of developing plasticity. A successful human response to the physical environment demands in individuals wisdom, maturity of judgement, social skill, and the ability to adjust to changing circumstances. These are distinctively human characteristics, contrasting with the rigidity of the otherwise marvellously organized societies of insects (Dobzhansky & Montagu, 1962: 149–53). Because this plasticity of mental traits has everywhere been advantageous it has everywhere been favoured – especially as the course of evolution has come to depend more and more upon the transmission of behavioural instructions by learning instead of by genetic inheritance. This explains why the differences in mental traits of human races are of negligible significance. Furthermore, it shows that there is no inconsistency in asserting the need to explain physical characteristics in biological terms and mental characteristics in cultural terms.

CHAPTER FOUR

Race as a Role Sign

PHYSICAL AND SOCIAL DEFINITIONS OF RACIAL GROUPS

The word 'race' is applied to both physical and social classifications. The two classifications overlap, but, because they are designed to serve different ends and are based upon different criteria, they can never be identical. One of the most striking figures of modern American society is the man who to outward appearance is white but socially is defined as a Negro. Throughout the world there are people whose social characteristics are not what other members of their societies expect of people with their racial characteristics. One of the most general reactions to this sort of situation is for a society to distort the physical classification to make it fit its social conceptions. From a biological standpoint, only persons with more than 50 per cent Negro descent would, could this be measured, be counted as Negro, but in many parts of the United States any person with any known Negro ancestry whatsoever is so counted. Such a definition can at times result in what are felt to be absurdities or injustices. Thus a court in Maine in 1852 held that a person having only one-sixteenth African blood (i.e. one great-great-grandparent) was not a Negro where the question of intermarriage was concerned. It is worthy of remark that a court decision should have been necessary to establish this. The possibility that people of white appearance may be of Negro status can cause severe disturbance in a society founded upon distinctions of racial status. For a functionary to demand proof of people's racial status before serving them – like a hotel clerk asking to see the marriage lines of would-be guests – would seriously disrupt the conventional pattern of everyday relations. And if, in error, he extends first-class privileges to a second-class citizen, is he to be accountable at law? A Louisiana court in 1910 handed down a decision that the word 'Negro' did not *of necessity* include persons 'in whom the admixture is so slight that even a scientific expert could not be positive of its presence', but it declared that the term 'coloured' applied 'no matter what may be the proportion of the admixture, so long as the negro blood is traceable'. Most of the Southern states define as a Negro anyone with 'any ascertainable trace' of Negro descent (Cohen, 1948). Though social practice is often less strict than legal definition, it has followed a similar course. The tendency has been not only to classify mulattoes as Negroes but to think of them as fully Negroes, as if a fraction of Negro heredity were more powerful a determinant of individuality than a much larger portion of white heredity. The popular understanding of genetic inheritance is distorted to reinforce and harmonize with the social categories.

A famous example of the same kind of distortion in a different kind of society is that vouched for by Henry Koster, an English traveller in early nineteenth-century Brazil. He inquired of a coloured Brazilian who was in his service whether a certain high official was not a mulatto, only to be told, 'He was, but he is not now'. When Koster queried this, his servant turned the tables upon him by posing the rhetorical question, 'Can a *Capitam-mór* be a mulatto?' (Koster, 1816: 391). In this locality, racial and social status were so strongly identified that when a man changed the one the other was also transformed. The conception the local people held of the nature of race must have diverged as much from the biologists' as the pseudo-science of the Georgia 'cracker' – though in the opposite direction.

Would it be possible to close the gap between physical and social classifications of race by moving in the other direction? To base social categories upon scientific assessments of heredity? This would be well-nigh impossible because, quite apart from the difficulties inherent in such assessments, once a physical category became also a social category it would be subject to social pressures and discrepancies would begin to appear.

The apparent independence of race as a social category has led one writer to speak of 'social race' (Wagley, 1952: 14). There are dangers in such a procedure, for it induces others to think of social characteristics as independent of physical characteristics and evades the task of tracing out the patterns by which physical characteristics are vested with social significance. The difference between physical and social classifications may be a small one, but it is not without importance, for it is to be found with respect to the other physical characteristics of mankind. Differences of sex and of age are in all societies given a significance which cannot be completely explained as the outcome of natural properties. Similarly, in social life the biology of kinship is used selectively to develop modes of organizing much larger units than nuclear families: clans and lineages are formed; cross-cousin marriage is often used to link together descent groups; when couples lack children, they adopt them. In these and other ways societies utilize the idea of consanguinity so that its social significance is at times in conflict with the biological facts of life: for example, in societies with patrilineal tendencies, a person may feel that his father's father's father (with whom he may share a common surname) is a more important ancestor than any other great-grandparent, though from a genetic standpoint he is unlikely to be any more important. Yet we cannot legitimately speak of social kinship as independent of physical kinship, for if the former were not an elaboration of the latter we should not recognize it as being kinship; it could equally well be called something different (cf. Gellner, 1963).

Differences of sex, age, race, and relations of consanguinity are used in social organizations as ways of dividing people up and allocating them positions in the division of labour. It would seem that societies can, in certain respects, be more effectively organized when people are conditioned to believe themselves more different from one another than biological and psychological tests would indicate. Paradoxically, it appears that clear distinctions often facilitate co-operation in the simpler forms of society; perhaps by reducing internal competition they help people to concentrate upon winning a livelihood from a harsh environment. Sex, age, race, and descent are chosen as the basis for simpler forms of social organization because they present mankind with relatively immediate ideas for conceptual distinctions. Differences of sex, age, race, and descent are easily observed and ordered in the mind; upon them social roles are founded and the physical variations then come to serve as indicators or signs of the roles (Banton, 1965: 68–92).

ROLES AND ROLE SIGNS

When racial differences are used as a way of dividing up a population and different sets of rights and obligations (roles) are ascribed to the divisions, then these outward differences serve as signs telling others the sorts of privileges and facilities to which the person in question is conventionally entitled. They may be stimuli as well as signs, evoking particular feelings, just as items associated with age or sex categories, such as white hair, babies' rompers, or women's underclothing, may evoke particular reactions; but for sociological analysis it is the sign function of racial characteristics that is usually the more important. It is also advisable to emphasize that many features of individuals, their behaviour and possessions, have sign values which are often, though

not always, incidental to the purpose of the things in question. A man
may buy a big motor car not for show but because he has a big family;
but, whatever the reasons for his buying it, ownership of a large car
will be interpreted as denoting greater wealth than ownership of a
small car. Just as the sign value of material possessions changes from
place to place, so does the social significance of racial variation. Racial
signs tend to be important when they can be used to classify unequivocally a high proportion of the population, marking off social categories
whose members have frequent dealings with one another. If members
of the categories lead separate lives, then there are fewer occasions on
which people have to look for racial differences in order to inform themselves about social differences, and consequently race does not then
have any high sign value. Racial characteristics do not serve as role
signs in places where everyone is classed as belonging to one race, or in
circumstances where the contact between two races has been too fleeting
for ideas to develop about the relative rights and obligations of members
of the two categories. Race is a role sign only in multiracial societies or
in situations of racial contact in which expectations of behaviour have
crystallized into patterns of some sort.

   How race is employed as a sign may vary from one culture to another.
In Europe and North America, complexion tends to be the primary
basis of distinction, but in a community in the Amazon basin, where
there was considerable Indian as well as Negro mixture, an anthropologist found that people regarded the thickness of lips, the height of the
cheek bones, and even skin colour as unreliable criteria, preferring to
give more attention to a person's hair as his deciding trait (Wagley,
1952: 122). In Brazil, circumstances more frequently arise in which the
sign value of racial traits is cancelled by the value of other traits. The
story is told of a tram conductor who sent all the men wearing collars
into the first-class compartment, whether they were white, yellow,
brown, or black. He relegated all the men without collars to the second
class. Thus a black boy with a collar but no boots or shoes was sent into
the first class, and 'a handsome English lad in a low-cut jersey' into the
second-class compartment. An English writer adds to this account by
relating how, in the West Indies, his failure to wear a collar brought
him not only a diminution of status but even suspicion, since on one
occasion he was detained by the police for questioning, and his movements in the interior were notified to the various police stations in
advance (Dingwall, 1946: 184–5).

   But in many regions there is little opportunity for people to manipulate their claims to racial status. The kind of classification effected is

neither trivial nor like the abstract ordering of a statistical table; it determines the allocation of highly important political, economic, and social rights such as voting, employment, and housing, and such distinctions are reinforced in everyday conventions about the respect which inferiors must pay to superiors. In most societies an individual can choose his occupational role; he cannot choose his sex role, and only to a limited extent can he manipulate his age role. Racial roles, like sex roles, are usually ascribed at birth and cannot be varied. An individual in a racially divided society is usually forced to play his racial role whether he will or not, for the sanctions utilized by the dominant group are extremely powerful. A Southern writer has told how he had his head shaven and his skin artificially darkened before making a journey through Mississippi, Alabama, and Georgia (Griffin, 1961). Had he sickened of his experiment and wished to give up the deception, what could he have done? It would have been little use explaining that he wanted to sit in the front of the bus because he was really white. He would soon have been kicked off. Had he stopped to talk to the average white farmer he would have been under pressure to behave in a mildly deferential manner, by doffing his hat, saying 'Sir' frequently, or laughing at any jokes made at his expense, and so on. Had his failure to conform in this respect given offence, he might well have been beaten. Once he had blackened his skin, Griffin *had* to play the Negro role until the colouring had weakened sufficiently for him to try behaving, in carefully selected circumstances, in a less subordinate manner. In the Southern states, deferential behaviour has been required (with minor exceptions) of all Negroes, including fair-skinned men and women who might not elsewhere have been thought of as Negro, but who in their own localities were known to be of partly Negro descent and were therefore classed as Negro. They, too, were obliged to play the social role of the Negro so long as they remained in their districts. Nor are the persons in the lower category the only ones who, in such a system, have to conform to conventional expectations; as later chapters will show, the deviations of people in the upper category also evoke sanctions.

The operation of race as a role sign can be illustrated most easily by reference to the well-known pattern that has prevailed in the Southern region of the United States, but this pattern is only one among several different kinds to be outlined later in this chapter. Race may serve as a role sign even though the role is relevant to behaviour in only a minority of situations. The sign function remains the same, but the kind of role is different. However, reference to race relations in the Southern states does bring out more clearly a point of some importance. Social roles usually have a core of elements of behaviour which are necessary to them and an outer range of elements which are conventional but not strictly essential – professors are often expected to be absent-minded, opera singers temperamental, and so on. Because new situations are legion and cannot be legislated for completely, roles often grow by having new elements added on which are logically separable from the others. Then, because some roles need to be signalized, they acquire additional patterns of behaviour which reinforce the role. Racial roles become important, as in the Southern states, when they combine many and varied patterns of expected behaviour which, in another social order, could be split up or combined differently.

Some studies of colour awareness and colour blindness bear upon this point, for social factors influence the perception of skin-colour differences. The processes by which children are taught that certain qualities are masculine or feminine, or that people of a particular appearance are socially inferior, may not feature in any school curriculum; parents and teachers may not be aware that they transmit such ideas, but they do so none the less effectively because the process is unacknowledged. In a city in the North-east of the United States, intensive study was made of the ideas and behaviour of 103 four-year-old children, roughly half of them white and half coloured. Fifteen per cent of both groups displayed low awareness of racial differences: only erratically were they interested in their own colour; they seldom used racial terms in describing people or tried to generalize on this basis. Sixty-one per cent of the white and 45 per cent of the Negro children showed medium awareness. Twenty-four per cent of the white and 40 per cent of the Negro children revealed high awareness: they already had a clear perception of skin colour as a social attribute and paid consistent attention to it; they used numerous race terms accurately; they thought in terms of racial categories and sensed patterns of racial discrimination (Goodman, 1964: 76–77). Studies of three-year-old Negro children in both Northern and Southern communities have concluded that more than three children in every four were conscious of the difference between 'white' and 'coloured' (Goodman, 1964: 253).

Some comparable information about the genesis of attitudes to Negroes in Britain is becoming available from a study of 172 white children in three north London areas. On doll-choice tests about social situations, 31 per cent of the children were rated consistently unfavourable to the Negro; the age-group proportions of these rose from 22 per cent at age three to 65 per cent at age six. In another test, 25 per cent chose very distant or distant houses for Negro children. The choice patterns, deliberation, and spontaneous comments of many children indicated an awareness of physical attributes and of the inferior social status of the Negro. The mothers of the consistently unfavourable children tended to be very hostile to Negroes, but no general relationship between ethnic attitudes of mothers and their children was found. The mood of the district was important for, as between two areas with fairly large Negro populations, the one more pervaded by tensions and adult hostility to the Negro out-group displayed the greater hostility in its white children (Jahoda, Veness & Pushkin, 1966, pp. 65–67). In some parts of Britain, children show decided colour blindness. A true story is told of a little boy who one day returned home from school and asked his mother whether he could have a friend to tea. It was a mixed racial school in East London and his mother asked him whether his friend was a black boy. 'I don't know, Mummie,' he replied, 'but I'll look tomorrow' (Polack, 1965; cf. Silberman & Spice, 1950). However, such reactions seem not to be typical of the districts in which coloured immigrants settle.

Another English experiment showed that the mildly antipathetic attitudes of children aged twelve to fourteen, based mainly upon the characterizations of the cinema screen, could be decisively modified by favourable personal contact with African schoolteachers. Racial categories were not so firmly embedded in the wider social structure that attitudes could not be transformed in a space of two weeks (James & Tenen, 1951, 1953).

Among the more important social factors influencing the perception of racial traits are ideas about roles. Gunnar Myrdal maintained that Southerners in the United States were so accustomed to seeing Negroes in certain roles that they recognized them as much by their bearing and way of doing things as by their colour. He gave examples from his observations in 1939 to show that a man with unmistakable Negro features who walked, talked, and behaved like an ordinary white man (e.g. walking into a hotel with his hat on and carrying himself with assurance and ease) was, in relatively impersonal contexts, treated as a white man. On the other hand, a white woman associating with Negroes was considered to be a fair-skinned Negro because Southern men could not believe that a real white woman would want to go about with Negroes (Myrdal, 1944: 683–4). Another study shows how, in these relatively impersonal relationships, people may be less concerned about the skin colour of the party playing the other role than about whether he plays it properly. The experiment was conducted in a large department store in New York City. A Negro and a white clerk (shop assistant) served side by side. The customers were followed into the street, and, without knowing that they had been under observation, were interviewed. When asked if they had ever seen any Negroes employed as sales personnel at the store where they had just been, one in four replied 'No'. Five of the 114 shoppers interviewed stated that they would refuse to buy in any store employing Negro sales clerks – although they had just patronized such an establishment, and two of them had been served by a Negro clerk! Among the more prejudiced individuals who recalled having been served by a Negro, there were some who rationalized what had happened. A woman who had just bought three pairs of stockings from the Negro clerk said that Negroes ought not to be employed in the more intimate relations involved in the sale of food. Had the persons interviewed been served in the food department, some would have insisted that Negroes should not be employed in the clothing department (Saenger & Gilbert, 1950). Once something is represented as customary, some of the opposition to it disappears. Recent research has shown that emotive attitudes often influence perception to a considerable extent (Tajfel, 1967).

RACE RELATIONS AND SOCIOLOGICAL THEORY

Sociological studies in the race relations field have contributed an impressive volume of ordered observations and reasoning. From an intellectual standpoint this work compares favourably with that in many other fields of sociology, and yet, from a theoretical standpoint, it appears that the central core of general ideas is insufficiently elaborated to balance the detail of particular observations in particular places. None of the major sociological theorists, Comte, Marx, Spencer, Pareto, Simmel, Durkheim, or Weber, paid much attention to questions of race relations. The theoreticians of more recent times have scarcely shown any greater interest. Consequently, race relations appears to many sociologists as a field of study out of the main stream of intellectual advance; often they recognize the moral and political importance of the issues in question; indeed, they frequently feel deeply on these matters; but they do not see their discipline as having much relevance to the practical problems of the present period. Race relations studies therefore suffer doubly: from being unrelated to major theoretical lines of inquiry, and from being regarded as an ideologist's stamping ground instead of as an area badly needing detached analysis.

In the last decades, by far the most influential sociological theorist has been Talcott Parsons of Harvard University. He sees human societies as characterized by their sharing of common values, rejecting any form of deterministic theory in favour of a focus on the actor as someone who orientates his behaviour by reference to such values. By its very nature, this approach is not well suited to the study of circumstances in which two societies interact or in which social patterns are maintained by force rather than agreement. When Parsons's pupil Pierre L. van den Berghe undertook to analyse relations in the Republic of South Africa to see how they constituted a social system, he had to modify his teacher's approach out of all recognition. Van den Berghe (1965) found no common value system; everywhere he turned there was conflict concerning the appropriate norms. Studies in other regions of racial conflict have lent themselves no better to analysis in terms of Parsons's structural-functionalism.

What are the alternatives? If the student fastens on the element of conflict he might well turn to the ideas developed by Max Gluckman of Manchester University; he will find his way similarly blocked, for Gluckman's conception of conflict relates to dispute within a common moral order. Cases where groups disagree over basic values or are motivated by radically opposed interests are, for Gluckman, illustrations of cleavage and not conflict. Though this conception of cleavage is capable of development, the student will not find any publication in which it has been worked out and its general application to race relations studies explained.

An argument that helps at this juncture is that set forth in Ralf Dahrendorf's critical treatise *Class and Class Conflict in Industrial Society*. Dahrendorf regards Parsons's approach as an illustration of an intellectual tradition which conceptualizes society in terms of the 'integration theory'. This theory looks at social behaviour from the standpoint of its contribution to the functioning of the social system: if the individual accepts his place in the system he is 'adjusted'; if not, he is 'deviant'. To this line of argument Dahrendorf opposes the tradition that sees society as held together by force and constraint: what people do they do, not because they accept their place, but because they have no real alternative. This is the 'coercion theory', which looks at behaviour from the standpoint of how it provokes or stems from change or dissensus, and how it tends to social disintegration. Such an approach must emphasize the way in which behaviour is affected by people's interests and the way in which dominant interest groups exploit their position. Dahrendorf regards the integration and coercion theories of society as alternatives, any choice between them depending upon a student's personal outlook; no general model subsuming them both seems to be possible (Dahrendorf, 1959: 159–64). This may be so, but the relative importance in particular circumstances of consensus and coercion is an empirical question. It may be useful to view the attitudes of miners towards work underground in terms of the coercion theory: they work because they have to, not because they want to. At the same time, it may be more profitable to view their leisure behaviour in the welfare centre from the standpoint of the consensus theory, highlighting their common outlook and values concerning matters outside the employment situation. Some areas of social life are characterized more by coercion than others are, and it is therefore less rewarding to use the integration theory when examining them. Dahrendorf maintains, very reasonably, that the integration approach has been dominant in West European and North American sociology, with the result that the potentialities of the coercion theory have been overlooked. This seems to be a major cause of the tendency to regard race relations studies as lying at the periphery of sociology as a subject. The coercion approach certainly fits more closely than the integrationist one to the example of a racial role instanced in the preceding section. Griffin as a white man with an artificially dark skin did not subscribe to a value system defining all Negroes as subordinates, and no more, it may be suspected, do most Negroes in Mississippi. But once Griffin blacked his skin he was obliged to play Negro roles in that all the alternatives open to him were less attractive. He was part of a social system depending upon force and constraint. Yet no sociologist has linked up race relations studies to the intellectual tradition behind the coercion theory, permitting the lessons learned in this long controversy to be applied to the racial field, or enabling the study of racial cleavages to benefit fully from the many studies of class cleavage. It is too big a task for more than preliminary steps to be attempted in the present work, but, if such a link can be forged, then race relations studies will become of central concern to sociological theorists. These studies reveal the inadequacy of purely integrationist theory and put the spotlight on the empirical shifts from consensus in certain social relations to coercion in others.

Dahrendorf's mode of argument springs from the same source as Lockwood's complementary critique of the Parsonian theory. This points out Parsons's preoccupation with the level of values and maintains that, for an adequate view of social dynamics, it is necessary to conceptualize not only the normative structuring of motives but also the structuring of interests in the substratum underlying social relations. The groups to which people belong have different material interests; these influence the way in which people interpret problem situations and relate them to general values (Lockwood, 1956: 136–7). Societies are not homogeneous units in which shared values influence everyone uniformly, for material interests pull different people in different directions and generate conflicts with the normative structure. Such pressures are not random; they are an outgrowth of the structure of society and their patterns must be studied alongside those of the common value system. Along lines such as these it may be possible to combine in one conceptual framework both the Parsonian conception of the actor's orientation and the evidence about the structure of group interests in circumstances of racial conflict.

The contributions by Dahrendorf and Lockwood might profitably be related to a line of thought which runs through a number of studies in social anthropology. It is evident in Evans-Pritchard's analysis of structural opposition as a feature of political relations among the Nuer of the Southern Sudan, notably in his argument that 'a man is member of a political group of any kind in virtue of his non-membership of other groups of the same kind'. A Nuer belongs to a tribe, a tribal segment, and a village; tribal membership is activated when there is an opposition of tribe to tribe, segment membership when one segment is opposed to another of the same tribe, and village membership when one village is at odds with another of the same segment. If a village of one segment comes into conflict with persons belonging to a different segment, this brings the two segments into opposition. Therefore, 'a man sees himself as a member of a group only in opposition to other groups and he sees a member of another group as a member of a social unity however much it may be split into opposed segments' (Evans-Pritchard, 1940: 136–7). This argument is worked out with reference to a system having a simple structure of political groups. Without, for the present, discussing the distinction between political groups and other groups, it may be more convenient to generalize the main proposition in the following principle: social groups form because, when responding to stimuli, people choose to align themselves in association with certain persons and in opposition to others. In its negative form the principle is even briefer: without stimuli there are no groups.

Different kinds of social system generate different sorts of stimuli. The system of the Deep South has been one that produces such frequent stimuli to alignment on a racial basis that the two inclusive racial aggregations have come to appear permanent groupings; they seem so natural that the stimuli are overlooked. The system is divided into two categories in that Whites and Negroes are accorded different rights and obligations and everyone must be accounted either a White or a Negro.

Moreover, interpersonal relations across the colour line are in many situations categorical (Mitchell, 1966a: 52–54). Whites and Negroes perceive one another as playing racial roles and ignore differences of class, age, demeanour, etc., between people of the category in question. The other party is simply 'a White' or 'a Negro', and such perceptions are related to standardized and impersonal modes of behaviour. The social categories also represent potential groups, for in times of racial friction people who previously kept themselves separate may be drawn together to form a co-operating group; all Negroes may band together, just as among the Nuer a conflict might escalate until a whole tribe was in opposition to another tribe. At other times, both Whites and Negroes act to reinforce the distance between themselves and others of the same complexion but different social class. Groups form only when people are stimulated to align themselves, and in the Deep South there are many stimuli to evoke racial alignment.

The relatively small village community in countries that are not racially divided tends, on the other hand, to show no such pattern of cleavage. People meet each other in a variety of roles, and two persons who oppose one another in one kind of situation may be allies in another. The texture of social relations is closely knit so that deviant behaviour in one relationship is likely to affect a person's relationships with a variety of other people. This has been discussed as an illustration of high social density (Banton, 1965: 203–7). The higher the overall social density in a society or sub-society, the greater the likelihood that the people share the same values. It is because people who dispute with one another are in other relations linked by what Gluckman calls 'cross-cutting ties' that there can be a common value system. In such a community, quarrels are frequent; there are constant stimuli to align-ment, but the stimuli are so varied that there is no line-up of opposed factions, the members of one opposing those of the others in all circum-stances. This explains why social-class differences present different aspects in the small village and in the big city. In the village, a high proportion of people's contacts are contained within face-to-face relationships based upon personal acquaintance, such as farmer-herdsman, parent-teacher, housewife-tradesman, etc. Only when there is an election, a wage dispute, or some general grievance may people line up on a class basis or think in terms of class opposition. Class distinctions are relevant to a smaller proportion of the situations in which they are involved than is usually the case in the cities. There are few stimuli to class alignment (cf. Banton, 1965: 186–7). It is partly for the same reasons that Brazilian villages do not more readily form opposed groups on the basis of colour, but the evidence on this point can be left to a later chapter.

That various kinds of stimuli cause people to form up in groups is fairly evident, but it is still necessary to indicate the ways in which such stimuli may operate upon individuals to bring about the observed consequence. People do not always follow the norms defining a role or conform to the expected pattern of behaviour. In explaining conformity, the consensus theory of society tends to rely upon the process of socialization whereby individuals are brought up to believe that certain behaviour is right and proper. The alternative approach lays greater stress upon the pattern of rewards and punishments as an influence keeping people in line. It enables the student of race relations to examine his concerns in terms of the model of social behaviour as a transaction, which has been developed by George C. Homans (1961). The transactional model sees interaction between persons as an exchange of goods, material and non-material, and assumes that every actor will seek to maximize his net advantages. People continue as parties to a relation only so long as they think it preferable to such alternative courses as they can conceive. They may be unaware of the alternatives or they may be coerced into submission; they may be willing to continue an established relation for a while, even though the benefits it brings them do not equal the trouble it entails, because in the long run it seems likely to be to their advantage. What is one man's gain is not necessarily another's loss, for many social relations resemble an exchange of goods or services advantageous to both parties. In using this model for the analysis of intergroup relations it is necessary to enter many qualifications to account for discrepancies between the balance of advantages as perceived by the parties and as revealed by objective analysis, and to make allowance for differences between short-term and long-term calculations and the influence of uncertainty or violence at various points in the system. It is also necessary to treat psychological satisfaction (the stilling of conscience by the performance of a traditional obligation or the feeling of wellbeing after a virtuous action) on a par with material benefits. It should be noted that this model does not assert that social behaviour is exchange, only that it is possible to discover new things about behaviour by considering it as if it were exchange. A possible weakness is the assumption that people seek to maximize their net advantages for, as has been seen in economics, this proposition is tautologous. Nevertheless, it has been shown that by using such an approach the sociologist can explain some varieties of behaviour more adequately than by any other means (see also Blau, 1964).

To introduce these theoretical questions before discussing race relations in actual situations means that their full significance may not be apparent to the reader. But illustrative material can be presented only in terms of some theoretical preconception, explicit or implicit, straightforward or confused. It is also necessary to outline some typology of kinds of race relations. Already examples have been drawn from the Deep South, but how representative is the Deep South? For what kinds of interpretation can it serve as a prototype? How do multiracial social systems differ in the generation of stimuli to alignment? Any typology should provide some sort of answer to these questions. It should also be constructed so that, along with additional information, it helps to explain what keeps the system of relations in being, indicating what it is that people obtain from the prevailing order that induces them to play their roles instead of emigrating or revolting. The present work also takes the view that the major causal factor underlying those instances of racial contact which are of contemporary interest has been Western European economic expansion. The chain of implications which spreads out from industrial production through world trade is of profound importance as a determinant of the way in which group relations have developed in different regions and are likely to change in the foreseeable future. The scheme advanced in the next section is inevitably crude, but it fits this process more closely than previous typologies of race relations have done.

SIX ORDERS OF RACE RELATIONS

When members of two different societies first have dealings with one another their transactions may be peripheral to their societies, having no influence upon relations within them nor bringing about any change of outlook. The type case of such forms of contact is probably the kind of exchange known as 'silent trade', in which peoples exchange goods without actually meeting. Herodotus describes the practice of this form of trade by the Carthaginians, and it has been reported from all over the world, from Sierra Leone, Guatemala, England, China, Timor, Eskimo regions, etc. (Grierson, 1903). There is always some pricing mechanism. The Pygmies of the Ituri forest of the Congo have been described as exchanging game and forest products for manufactures and fruit produced by neighbouring Negro settlements of agriculturalists. One group places piles of goods at the trading place and retires. The other group places opposite these piles the goods it offers in exchange. The first group returns and, where the terms are acceptable, picks up the proffered exchange items. As the next chapter will explain, such cases of peripheral contact either are short-lived or arise in restricted ecological circumstances. It may be helpful to think of them diagrammatically, as in *Figure 1*.

Figure 1 Peripheral contact

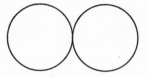

When contact between members of two groups is continuous it may develop along either of two principal courses, institutionalized contact or acculturation. When one of the two groups has a centralized political structure so that a few leaders control the action of other members, these leaders are likely to use their power to try to dominate the other group. When two such societies enter into contact through some of the outlying members and there is no strong competition for resources, a situation arises in which members of each society look inwards towards their own institutions; the people who live on the social boundaries are those most affected by contact and they may make exchanges with the strangers. Such people may come to occupy positions in two social systems, their own society and the new system of interrelations between the societies. They play different roles in the two systems. Frequently, the roles they play in the system of interrelations seem

Figure 2 Institutionalized contact

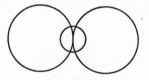

rather crude because the agents of the strangers may not speak the same language or participate in the same cultural universe of shared meanings, but, however undeveloped this system may initially be, it is a system of interrelations in a way that peripheral contact is not. When it is necessary to distinguish these two forms of contact, the adjectives peripheral and institutional will be used. In general, however, the term contact will signify institutional contact, because it is only this variety that constitutes an interracial social order.

In situations of contact, there is no common political order or integral social system. Racial differences serve to signalize roles only in the area of overlap, for in the two major societies pre-contact institutions and customs are maintained with little modification, and the roles related to them have their own signs. If relations between members of the two societies start on a basis of trade and not violence, the first patterns of interrelation are formed by the personal acquaintance of individuals with individuals. Then the expectations a man has of one individual in the other society are extended to a category of people in it or to all members of that society. In so far as these expectations are reinforced by conforming behaviour, roles are created. The people, on both sides, who are involved in the interrelational system develop that system, but, being themselves members of their own societies, they are subject to other pressures. Very frequently, this interrelational system is unable to develop freely because of the power wielded by external interests. When one of the societies is an expanding industrial nation, the balance of power in the contact situation rapidly tips in its favour; to explain the course of events as they affect the participants it is then constantly necessary to refer back to features of the industrial nation's affairs.

When the societies in contact are small in scale and have no centralized power structure, especially when there is little competition and contact is gradual, then change takes the form of acculturation. The people who are in contact can themselves adjust to the strangers, being under little pressure from more distant members of their own society. The two societies and cultures tend to merge, with the weaker making more changes than the stronger. Examples of such change are discussed in the next chapter and they can be represented diagrammatically as in *Figure 3*. Processes of acculturation are also present when one society subordinates the other, but then it is the political balance that most determines the interracial order.

Figure 3 Acculturation

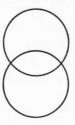

The contact and growth of ties between racially distinguished groups or nations have, in several important instances, resulted in the domination of one by the other and in the constitution of a single society.

The pattern of such an order, both sociologically and historically, can be better appreciated if a distinction is drawn between local and

Figure 4 Domination

national systems of relations. The local system has been the farm or plantation, for example, in which the master exercises a personal domination over members of the subjugated group, many or all of whom he knows as individuals. His power over them is frequently more limited than may appear at first sight, for even slaves have their methods of obtaining retribution when they feel they have been treated with particular injustice. The harshness of subjugation in the local system is therefore often tempered by appreciation of a man's or woman's qualities as an individual and by the need to provide effective incentives if the social arrangements are to work. When the pattern of relations prevailing locally is extended to the national system so that all members of the one category are universally subordinated, then in many of the situations in which members of the two categories meet they are not acquainted with one another; they therefore respond to each other not as individuals, but as representatives of a category. This kind of subordination is far harsher, and it provides the most clear-cut illustration of race as a role sign. Whatever their personal qualities, individuals are ascribed to one or the other category, and those in the lower are prevented from claiming the privileges of those in the upper category. As racial distinctions are drawn in a wide variety of situations (indeed, there is often scarcely a single kind of situation in which they are irrelevant), race is a sign of a basic role like sex or age (cf. Banton, 1965: 33–35). Where race relations show a pattern of domination, the two categories are differentiated by other attributes than those of race: income, education, religion, norms of family relations, etc. Differentiation by these means complicates the picture, but, as will be shown later, is often essential to it, for it makes the gap between the categories greater and more difficult to bridge.

When members of a more powerful nation enter the territory of another and contact is established, a major variable is the political independence of the newcomers. If they are free to determine and enforce their own policy towards the local society, a dominative order is likely to be created (e.g. the 'white settler' society in Africa). If they are subject to control by a home government which formulates its own policy, there is a greater probability of a paternalist order being established. This is a special form of institutionalized contact depending,

Figure 5   Paternalism

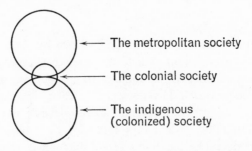

— The metropolitan society

— The colonial society

— The indigenous
  (colonized) society

unlike domination, upon maintaining the distinctiveness of the inter-acting societies. It is exemplified in some forms of colonial rule, such as those that sanctioned and often reinforced the control tribal chiefs exercised over their peoples. In the pure form of paternalism, the only representatives of the metropolitan society who have dealings with the indigenous society are approved agents responsible for their actions to authorities in their homeland. In this case, race serves as a sign of a basic role, relevant whenever members of the two groups meet, but the liberty of the agents to intrude into various spheres of indigenous life is restricted; the development of roles within the colonial society (i.e. the sphere of overlap) is influenced by metropolitan policies, in particular by the regulation of the career structure of the agents. If the agents spend long periods in the territory in question they may identify themselves with groups that do not altogether approve metropolitan policy, and they may acquire interests of their own in the territory. This sort of tendency is stronger when – in a departure from the pure form of paternalism – persons from the metropolitan country other than official agents are allowed to establish relations (as traders or settlers) with the indigenous people. The immigrant section of the colonial society will acquire greater strength from the diversification of its personnel; the tension between its interests and those of the metropolitan society may then become as important as the tension between the colonialists and the colonized. Paternalistic orders of race relations in practice frequently show divergencies in this direction. The essential point is, however, that whereas the relevance and character of roles in a dominative order are determined by the desire of the upper group to maintain control over all significant spheres of activity, in a paternalistic order the relevance and character of the upper group's roles are decided chiefly, or to a considerable extent, by metropolitan policies.

In other circumstances it is possible that much less attention will be paid to racial distinctions, though it seems that they are never ignored completely. The characteristics of a few individuals may be forgotten, but, if such characteristics distinguish a category of people systematically, they are almost certain to acquire social significance (differences, for example, of hair colour, would not be sufficiently systematic because they arise between one brother and another, between parent and child). When minimal attention is paid to racial differences, an integrated order of race relations is constituted. The nearest approach

Figure 6 Integration

to integration is achieved by countries in which there are several different racial groups and many people of mixed descent. Race is then still used as a social sign, though as a sign indicating an individual's background and probable claims to deference. It is one sign among many others, being irrelevant in some sectors (e.g. political rights) but of some account in status-sensitive situations of social acceptance or rejection. For nearly all purposes, race has much less significance than the individual's occupation and his other status-conferring roles. Thus, in a racially integrated social order, race is a sign of an independent role, signalizing rights and obligations in only a few restricted sets of circumstances (cf. Banton, 1965: 33–35).

Equality in political and civic rights may be achieved without dissolution of the boundaries of minority group membership. Some minorities may have to preserve a high solidarity if they are to achieve such equality, and the significance of membership may be enhanced. When minorities compete with one another for jobs and status, they may become identified with particular sectors of the economy and this strengthens their distinctiveness. On the other hand, separation in marriage and leisure-time relations may be entailed by religious differences. Where equal political rights are maintained by minority representation, internal distinctions are reinforced; this kind of social order is better referred to as pluralistic. The balance of power which it presupposes is more likely to develop when there are more than two distinctive groups. In a pluralist order there are no separate racial roles with different political rights and claims to deference: race is not relevant to behaviour in many important situations, so it is not a sign of a basic role. But racial differences do signalize variations in expected behaviour

Figure 7   Pluralism

in far more situations than under an integrated order, so neither is it a sign of an independent role. Elsewhere, roles of an intermediate range of relevance have been identified as general roles (Banton, 1965: 33–35), and in a pluralistic order race will serve as a sign of such a general role.

It will be apparent that there are resemblances and points of difference between certain of these six orders that make it more likely that one order will be transformed into another than into a third. Acculturation leads fairly easily to integration. Initial situations of contact have often been succeeded by either domination or paternalism. In modern circumstances a rapid transition to an integrated or pluralist order is perhaps possible, although, considering the technologically backward position of the relatively isolated peoples, it is not probable. Whether contact gives way to domination or paternalism depends upon the extent to which those who build up relations with the indigenous people can operate as an independent political power. In a paternalist order it is probable that the power of the metropolitan country will be weakened after a time, and that this will be reflected in changes in the skills of the personnel that country sends out and in the definition of their roles. In such ways the transition to an integrated order is facilitated; it may entail the withdrawal of all representatives of the former metropolitan country and the creation of a society without racial minorities. A dominative order is so structured that the pattern of domination is continually reinforced, and fundamental change becomes increasingly difficult. The purest form of domination is one in which there are only two racial categories and the superior one normally resists the entry (by immigration) or creation (by miscegenation) of any additional categories. However, because of economic and political tendencies, the whole society may be absorbed into some larger society; the subordinated racial category may then be accorded political privileges previously denied its members; thus they and their former superiors will become minorities within the larger order, though this does not mean that the inequalities between them will necessarily be reduced rapidly or substantially. It will be argued subsequently that a

Figure 8   Sequence of racial orders

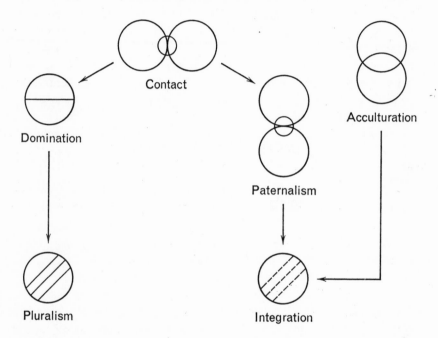

dominative order can be maintained over long periods only if the economic basis of the society is unchanging. Economic development affects a dominative order in such a way that it must either modify some of its fundamentals or explode. If it is to shift from absolute domination, it is more likely to change in the direction of an unequal pluralism than in any other.

This suggestion of typical sequences in changing patterns of race relations is reminiscent of the cyclical theories of race relations elaborated by several authors. R. E. Park maintained that contact is followed by competition, then by accommodation, and finally by assimilation and amalgamation. E. S. Bogardus, who had in mind immigrants to California rather than to the American north-east, outlined a different kind of cycle: curiosity, economic welcome, industrial and social antagonism, legislative antagonism, fair-play tendencies, quiescence, second-generation difficulties. Other American sociologists have proposed variants upon these ideas (cf. Berry, 1965: 129–35). These cyclical theories concern themselves with race relations in a country of immigration and make little allowance for the characteristics of the interacting groups or for the institutional context within which contact occurs. In so far as they posit assimilation as an inevitable conclusion, events of recent years have cast further doubt upon their validity. The sequences outlined here are not cycles of race relations. They are used to draw attention to what seem to be the chief factors relating the use of racial distinctions to economic and political features of the wider social order. They are first approximations, not polished classifications, and will invite further elaboration if they are of use. No assumptions are made about ultimate assimilation or continuing friction, because the future is problematic. It is probable that technological change will continue at an ever-increasing pace and that the substitution of machines for human activity will have important implications for intergroup relations. It is difficult to know whether an age of fully automated pro-duction would generate pressures favouring an integrated or a pluralistic order, or whether it might not give rise to some new pattern.

CHAPTER FIVE

Contact, Symbiosis, and Acculturation

When two societies are brought into contact, influences spread from each to the other. The stronger of the two societies is influenced less than the weaker in this way, and usually has less difficulty in containing any changes that may be initiated. The weaker society is at a disadvantage. Apart from any overt struggles between members of the two societies, contact usually creates a conflict of values within the weaker society. The process of change in the culture of a group of people adjusting to continuing contact with some other group is known as 'acculturation'. Conflict within such a society is a sign that acculturation is taking place.

SYMBIOSIS

Whereas contact normally leads to acculturation, it is conceivable that in certain circumstances the two cultures concerned might be equally balanced and of an inward-looking nature so that a permanent state of peripheral contact could be maintained. Such a state would resemble that known to biologists as symbiosis, in which two different kinds of organism live together to their mutual benefit, each being – as it were – parasitic upon the other. However, examples of friction and imbalance are more common. Early writing about race relations, influenced by social Darwinism, tended to regard conflict as an inescapable feature or phase of contact. Interest was aroused, therefore, when an anthropologist described relations between the Reindeer Tungus and the Cossacks of north-western Manchuria as representing 'culture contact without conflict' (Lindgren, 1938; summarized in Berry, 1965: 99–101). Though the two groups were of distinctive racial appearance they were said to interact without loss of homogeneity or cultural integrity on the part of either; no members of either group were found to 'express fear, contempt, or hatred in relation to the other group as a whole or any individual composing it'; the 'use or threat of force in the relations between these communities' was absent. Other writers have recorded a similar relationship between the Indians and the lower-class agricultural Ladinos in Guatemala (Redfield, 1939, 1962: 210–30; Gillin, 1948; Tumin, 1952) and between Lapps and peasants in northern Norway, Sweden, and Finland (Pehrson, 1950).

In each of these three cases one group is the carrier of a European and literary culture; in the Manchurian and Guatemalan instances this group is also the representative of a universal religion (Christianity) in contact with local, partly Christian, partly traditional, religion; in northern Scandinavia both Lapps and peasants are Christian. It is therefore advisable to open any discussion of cultural symbiosis with the consideration of relations where neither group has the strength of Western industrial culture behind it.

An example is provided by a study of relations between the Mbuti Pygmies and the Negro groups living near them in the Congo. The Pygmies are forest nomads who live by hunting and by gathering fruits, and their culture centres upon the theme of the forest's benevolence. They sing and dance its praises every day, for it provides them with all the necessities of life. An anthropologist who lived with the Mbuti states that any enemy of the forest is an enemy of the Pygmies and that their entire relationship with their Negro neighbours is governed by the opposition between their two worlds. For the Pygmies the world of the forest is sacred; that of the Negro villages is profane (Turnbull, 1965: 81–89, 291–300). A Pygmy comes to a particular village when he wishes, often bringing meat to a Negro who serves as his patron in village matters and who often tries – usually unsuccessfully – to establish control over 'his' Pygmy. When the forest people come to the village it is usually because the hunting is not good, and they feel they would like a change of diet, or because they want to relax, with palm wine to drink, cigarettes to smoke, and drums to dance to. They will not commit the sacrilege of singing forest songs in the village. They leave behind them their whole system of values, even their social customs, and while they are in the village will follow almost any practice pressed upon them by the Negroes. Village customs have no meaning in forest culture and when, for example, the Mbuti return to their hunting camps, the ceremonial initiations of youths so carefully staged by the Negroes are automatically nullified: the initiated boys become children again, going back to their mothers and being excluded from the activities of adult males.

Pygmy-Negro relations at the time Turnbull studied them therefore present an almost pure example of cultural symbiosis. Members of both groups benefit from exchanges but neither culture is altered by them. When Pygmies and Negroes interact they take up new roles which – in the case of the Mbuti at least – are quite independent of their roles within their own society. The continuation of this pattern is facilitated by the small size of the groups involved, the individualistic nature of the Pygmy-patron ties, and the availability of natural resources which means that neither group is really dependent on the other.

The Tungus-Cossack study was based upon the short-period observations of a single ethnographer (cf. Whitaker, 1956: 98n), but it deals with a situation that might well make possible a stable relation in which neither group would dominate the other, yet their mutual dealings would be continued because each group benefited from them. The Tungus group consisted of about 150 nomadic reindeer herders occupying some 7,000 square miles of territory, only the fringes of which have been shared with other groups. Hunting played an important part in their economy, but hunting-grounds were not divided up. The Cossack families numbered about 150 persons; they were agriculturalists, traders, and hunters; literate, speakers of Great Russian; and had the support of other settled Cossack communities not far away. Some two hundred years ago groups of Tungus and Cossacks were in armed conflict; for over a century peaceful relations have obtained.

Members of the two communities meet at markets two or three times each winter (when the Cossacks come to the Tungus) and two or three times each summer (when the Tungus come to the Cossacks). The Tungus trade furs for flour, lead, and gunpowder (which are essentials) and for other products including tea, salt, sugar, tobacco, alcohol, and textiles. Cossacks and Tungus both hunt over the same grounds in the autumn for squirrels and in the spring for wapiti; in this they are rivals, yet the first hunter to arrive in a valley is left in undisturbed possession, and hunters of either group will eagerly seek out the camps of the other for company, sometimes staying overnight. Longer visits occur on occasion, as after an epidemic (which decimated the Tungus' deer) and after the summer markets. Dr Lindgren states that though Tungus and Cossacks will criticize one another they do not generalize one man's failings to blame the whole group: 'Expressions of dislike and distrust with regard to individuals in the other group are of exactly the same type as those applied within itself, and admiration seems to predominate over criticism' (1938: 607). In elaboration, she notes that the Tungus criticize the Cossacks for thieving (within their own communities) but the latter are 'tireless in praising Tungus' honesty'. The Cossacks criticize the Tungus for their random violence when drunk, but the Tungus

themselves acknowledge and deplore this weakness. The Tungus dislike
the Cossack practice of sleeping with a hot stove and closed doors and
windows, but the Cossacks doubtless think no more highly of nights
spent sleeping in partly open Tungus tents. Though Dr Lindgren
heard of no cases of intermarriage between Tungus and Cossacks,
resistance to the idea would be based on differences of custom, not race,
and the possibility of sexual relations between members of the two
groups was apparently not absent from their thoughts. Some Tungus
children had been adopted by Cossacks and brought up in their
community as Cossacks.

Dr Lindgren inferred that the absence of conflict was to be attributed
primarily to: (i) the individualistic type of social and economic organization based on the household unit, with no strong bonds at the village
or regional level (another relevant political consideration was that both
groups suffered from the oppressive taxation policies of the Chinese
administration, which awakened a sense of common interest); (ii) intergroup trade to the benefit of both parties and the relative sufficiency of
natural resources such as hunting-grounds (though it seemed that the
economic balance was beginning to tilt in favour of the Cossacks);
(iii) the continuity of contact, which had led to an interchange of cultural
traits and provided a basis of mutual understanding (this is an important
point for understanding the system of relations). The roles of members
of each group were known and accepted. As in the Pygmy instance, it is
possible to detect an intergroup social sphere separate from the two
intragroup spheres, for the Tungus spoke Russian at the markets and
probably made some concessions to Cossack susceptibilities. But the
Tungus and Cossack cultures were very slowly mingling and there was
not the sharp distinction preserved by the Pygmies.

The contact situation in Guatemala shows similar features, although
much larger groups are involved, their members live in greater daily
intimacy, and the dominance of the Ladino group with its European
literature culture is generally acknowledged. (The Ladinos are rural
agriculturalists of varying skin colour, often poor and shoeless.) In the
locality studied by Redfield it was the Ladinos who were bilingual; they
looked down upon the Indians, but no race prejudice was directed
against them nor was any attempt made to keep them in a position of
social inferiority. Elsewhere – and this is an indication that acculturation
has progressed farther – the Ladinos speak only Spanish and view the
Indians with more contempt. A vital point, to which Redfield draws
attention, is that in this community the actions of individual Ladinos
and Indians have little effect on the reputation of the groups to which

they belong. If an Indian learns to play an accordion, say, that is something which Ladinos will applaud as well as Indians because they
think it a useful accomplishment; his ethnic affiliations make no
difference. The Indian has neither presumed above his station nor
'raised his race' by acquiring the new skill.

The relative harmony of Ladino-Indian relations may be related in
part to the individualistic basis on which contact occurs. Neither group
is organized as a socio-political entity and the whole region is one of
cultural diversity. Individual members of each group are acquainted
with individual members of the other. Many Ladinos have Indian
godchildren. The Indians are also farmers and neither group is seriously
dependent on the other. They do not compete economically. A second
important consideration is that, while many Indians find their traditional way of life preferable, those who are ambitious for the rewards of
the wider Spanish-speaking culture are able to move up the social
scale. If an Indian learns to speak Spanish, to read, and to write, and
assumes the manners of the Ladino, he is commended by Ladinos. If
he moves to another village his ancestry can be concealed. Intermarriage
occurs, though it is less frequent for an Indian man to marry a Ladino
woman. For these various reasons the Ladino and Indian cultures tend
to merge, and there is no distinctive set of social relations linking two
societies which retain their identity.

A comparison may be drawn with the position of the Lapps in
northern Scandinavia. Because their habitat and economy are so
distinct (bolstered by legislation which, in Sweden for example,
prohibits non-Lapps from owning reindeer), the Lapps have been
somewhat more successful in maintaining their separate culture, though
some young people are now lost to the towns and there is the occasional
'tourist Lapp' who exploits the stranger's curiosity and photographic
enthusiasm. Contact between Lapps and peasants used to occur chiefly
at markets and in connection with winter lodgings; it was then possible
to isolate a separate set of social relations interrelating the two societies.
More recently, the economic success of Lapp herders has enabled
Lapps to deal directly with the industrial culture so that they are
a cultural minority within the Scandinavian nations but are not in an
inferior position politically or economically.

For centuries, the Lapps of northern Sweden have grazed their
reindeer on the Norwegian side of the mountain range during the
summer months, herding their deer in the late autumn some 300–400
kilometres south-eastward down the long river valleys for the winter.
The basic social unit is the herding group of several reindeer-owning

households. Towards the end of the year there are markets at which
Lapps sell reindeer for meat and reindeer products such as fur clothing
and skin boots. In exchange, they buy coffee, flour, sugar, salt, and
manufactured goods. Both the Lapps and the local Finnish-speaking
peasants are Christians of the Laestadian persuasion. The Lapps used
to lodge with the peasants during the winter but, more recently,
families have been building their own houses. A study conducted in
1949 reported that the Lapps were occasionally resentful about the
heavy taxes they had to pay on their herds to the Swedish government,
but that they approved governmental policies which, apart from such
matters as health insurance, included good educational facilities
adapted to their pattern of movement and laws that protected their
special interests. There is a measure of mutual respect between the
two cultures, chiefly on a basis of interpersonal ties (Pehrson, 1950;
but cf. Whitaker, 1956: 98n).

Another study based upon a longer period of observation maintained
that there were more occasions for friction:

'Very gradually the settlers' attitudes to the Lapps have changed.
From being their equals they have come to be considered their
definite inferiors. . . . There has been a decline in the hospitality
offered to the nomads, and especially since they received State grants
to enable them to rebuild many of their houses, the peasants have
refused the Lapps accommodation. This has upset all the old
relationships. . . . The peasants still depend upon the Lapps for their
meat supply, but it will be provided against money' (Whitaker,
1955: 100).

The introduction of a money economy and a growing commercialism
have their effect in Lapland much as in other regions. Swedish tourists
in the north – a relatively enlightened group compared with tourists
of many countries – apparently need to be given elementary advice
about courtesy in dealings with Lapps. In the administrative centre of
the region in the earlier years of the century Lapps were disparaged
by the bulk of the population as uncivilized; more recently, an anthropologist recalled that some relatively well-educated people in the north
could, when inquiring about this research, pose the question, 'Do they
let white people stay with them?' (Whitaker, 1955: 121–3).

To claim that relations between Lapp reindeer-herders and Swedish
peasants provide an illustration of 'culture contact without conflict'
seems misleading. To suggest that conflict is characteristic of their

relations would, however, be absurd. The lesson to be drawn from this instance is surely that the power of industrial society is now so over-whelming and uncontrollable that it is no longer possible for a non-industrial society to maintain relations with industrial life without thereby building up great strains for those of its members who wish to continue undisturbed in their traditional ways. They may set little store by the new attractions, but their children are easily seduced. Even reindeer culture can be influenced by industrial processes of production, for some Lapps have taken to chartering an aeroplane to be flown up to the summer grazing-grounds and, instead of using draught reindeer to draw their sleds, now operate snow-scooters.

On the world stage the prospect for traditionalism is overlaid by political forces. Small-scale societies are not left to work out their own relations with industrialism over a period of years, for their very backwardness creates a 'power vacuum'. The big nations are tempted to intervene for political advantage, always fearing that if they do not do so their rivals will. The ideal of cultural coexistence is, in the twentieth century, capable of realization only in so far as the cultures concerned are themselves founded upon industrial production and industrial values.

CASTE

If symbiosis possesses so little relevance now, has there ever been a time when men have been able to operate a series of institutions main-taining separation over many generations with little overt conflict? The closest approximation has been the Indian caste system, which can be examined from this standpoint irrespective of whether it is believed that caste arose as a means of stabilizing groups in contact, or from internal struggle, or from some other cause. It has, in fact, been argued by J. H. Hutton that the original Aryan invaders of India, finding there a society divided by food taboos into exclusive tribal groups, consoli-dated these taboos as a means of maintaining social distance between themselves and the subject population. Were this the case, then social differentiation could well have developed to create a comprehensive caste system. In the literature on race relations a major controversy surrounds the use of the term caste when applied to non-Indian societies. Discussion of this dispute will have to be postponed to a later chapter, but at this stage of the argument it is illuminating to see how caste regulations prescribe and reinforce varied forms of social inequality.

Whether or not inequality in the Indian system presents to an observer features similar to inequality elsewhere, there are good grounds for believing that from the point of view of the people who are members of the society it has highly distinctive features. In the Western democracies the norm is one of equality, which is maintained despite evidence that social differentiation tends to assume a hierarchical character and to be converted into hereditary inequality. Traditional Indian society, on the contrary, can be seen as approving and emphasizing inequality. Ideals of equality are now recognized in the constitution of the Republic of India, but little significance was attached to them in Indians' earlier conceptions of their society.

A caste society is one divided into a large number of permanent groups which are at once specialized, hierarchized, and separated in relation to each other in respect of marriage, food, and physical contact. The common basis of these differentiating features is the opposition of pure and impure, a mode of division which continually and in many spheres repeats itself, so that the reality of the system consists not in the social groups but in the ever-present opposition between higher and lower. In the ideal form of the traditional system, ranking was consistent. The hierarchy was one of religious status, and though status and power were represented in different offices, it was religious virtue that sanctioned the claim to political power. Thus hierarchy integrated Indian society around its values: it expressed the unity of the society while connecting it to what appeared to be universal, namely a conception of the cosmic order (Dumont, 1961: 34–35).

Confusion is caused by the tendency of some writers to identify castes with the category *varna* instead of that known as *jati*, which is sometimes denoted subcaste. The traditional four *varnas* are those of Brahmin (priest), Kshatrya (warrior), Vaishya (trader), and Sudra (cultivator or artisan), with the Untouchable outside the system. These categories provide a national framework for local systems of stratification which vary from place to place. Particular communities can be divided into *jatis*, which are exclusive, ranked, closed, and co-operative rather than competitive. A *jati* can be defined as a group of families whose members can intermarry and can eat in each other's company without believing themselves polluted. Such a system can function only in a relatively small community in which people know one another's status, and control is strong enough to prevent individuals from acquiring roles that conflict with the system (Bailey, 1963; Zinkin, 1962).

Relations between *jatis* were expressed in terms of deference and social distance, which often had an aspect of physical distance also. A South Indian study of 1937 states:

'A Nayar must keep 7 ft. from a Nambudiri Brahman, an Iravan must keep 32, a Cheruman 64 and a Nyadi from 74 to 124. The respective distances between these lower castes are calculated by a simple process of subtraction. . . . The Nyadi when travelling has to avoid not only people of other castes, but dwellings, tanks, temples, and even certain streams when people are bathing in them. . . . Nyadis had to avoid walking over the long bridge over the Ponnāni river and go miles around, because if they walked over it they would pollute it or any at least who might make contact with their foot-prints, while the Andē Koragas of Mangalore District had to carry round their necks a small spittoon since they must not expectorate on the public road for fear of polluting a passer by who might all unknowing tread where they had spat' (Hutton, 1946: 70–71).

Europeans, of course, were outcastes whose contact was polluting:

'The temple of Cottayam had to be reconsecrated because a European passed along the pathway between the temple and the tank attached to it. . . . Thurston records how he touched the ladle in a pot in which an old woman was cooking her meal and later found that she had been outcasted for subsequently touching the cooking pot . . . the reason why it is the general custom in India for Indian gentlemen to call on Europeans at as early an hour in the day as possible is commonly believed to be to enable them to decontaminate themselves so as to take their morning meal in a state of ceremonial purity' (Hutton, 1946: 72, 110; cf. Zinkin, 1962: 48).

These distinctions were maintained by severe sanctions. According to the old Hindu law:

'If a Sudra recites the *Veda* his tongue is to be cut off. If he assumes a position of equality with twice born men, either in sitting, convers-ing, or going along the road, he shall receive corporal punishment. A Sudra committing adultery with women of the first three castes shall suffer capital punishment, or shall be burnt alive tied up with straw . . . if a Sudra intentionally reviles a Brahmin or criminally assaults him, the limb with which he offends shall be cut off' (Ghurye, quoted by Zinkin, 1962: 59).

Through his *jati*, says Hutton, a man is provided with a permanent body of associations which controls almost all his behaviour and contacts:

> 'His caste canalizes his choice in marriage, acts as his trade union, his friendly or benefit society, his slate club and his orphanage; it takes the place for him of health insurance, and if need be provides for his funeral. It frequently determines his occupation . . . often membership will take the place of attachment to a political party . . . the system provides him from birth with a fixed social milieu from which neither wealth nor poverty, success nor disaster can remove him, unless of course he so violate the standards of behaviour laid down by his caste that it spews him forth – temporarily or permanently' (1946: 97).

When learned in childhood, customs centring upon prohibitions, such as food taboos, leave an indelible impression upon people's outlook. A change of intellectual conviction may not be sufficient to bring about a change in observance, for purely physical repulsion may be engendered. Mrs Zinkin, commenting upon the possibility of marriage between the daughter of a Kharaya Khubja cabinet minister and a son of Jawaharlal Nehru, a Kashmiri Pandit, though also a Brahmin and Prime Minister, says that the marriage would have obliged the bride to make adjustments in the running of the home deeper, in some ways, than those necessary for a Daughter of the American Revolution who married a Southern Negro; not only would she have to watch her husband eat meat, but she would have to overcome the inner repulsion which his eating meat would inevitably induce in her (1962: 16). Young, educated, and Westernized people may sometimes break free of such restrictions and inhibitions, but to be expelled from his *jati* is, for the ordinary Indian, a terrible punishment. The person expelled does not move into the group one step lower – he will not be accepted even by his previous inferiors. He is completely boycotted by the kinsfolk on whom he has previously been so dependent, and he may be physically ejected from his village. Such sanctions are used not only against offenders but against the kinsfolk of offenders. A Hindu whose relative breaks the rules may find it difficult to make a satisfactory marriage; his own social standing goes down with his erring kinsman's. Mahatma Gandhi's eldest sister suffered a lifetime of ostracism and humiliation from the people of her community on account of her brother's insistence upon mixing with unclean people. When asked about her brother she exploded into toothless anger and tears, calling him a man so selfish that he had not cared what harm he had done to his family (Zinkin, 1962: 49–56). Expulsion is a punishment which a *jati* directs against any member who lets down the group in its struggle to maintain or increase the respect shown to it by other groups. It must be remembered that there are many distinctions of status between different Brahmin groups and even different groups of Untouchables; moreover, that it is not unusual for a *jati* to divide into two, one section observing stricter ritual restrictions and moving itself up the scale. Because there is no big status gap at any point in the hierarchy, even the lowest groups are motivated to try to improve or maintain their position; to this end they use against some of their own members the same weapons that cause much suffering to themselves when used by the superior groups. The system has moulded all participants to serve its values.

There is much evidence to indicate that the ideology of caste distinction is not forced upon the lower groups but is accepted by them. Religion instructs members of the Sweeper *jati* to do the work that comes to them by birth; if they do it humbly and do not mind being treated as pariahs, they may be reborn as Brahmins. Their hope of the next life depends upon acceptance of their present status whatever temptations may be set before them. Untouchable parents have been known to kill their daughter for running away with a Rajput prince. Nehru tried to bring up in his household with his own daughter a little Untouchable girl. The parents were eager that their daughter be given a good education and sent her willingly to the Nehru mansion; but when they heard that she ate and sat with Brahmins they were so horrified that they took her back (Zinkin, 1962: 22). However, it is equally possible to argue that how people see their social system does not necessarily reflect the interests that make it work. An alternative explanation would stress that high caste position is bolstered by economic, prestige, and sexual gains. The subordination of lower *jatis* assures a ready supply of free service and cheap labour to the superior ones. The deference shown to high-caste people constantly reinforces their feeling of superiority; in the lower castes they have a permanent scapegoat. Sexual gains are evident in that high-caste men can take as brides not only women of their own group, but, in hypergamous marriages, women of a lower *jati*; this is perhaps not a frequently used or important privilege, and resembles less a 'gain' than the freedom that even orthodox Brahmins have to patronize Untouchable prostitutes – always provided they undergo a ceremony of purification afterwards. Brahmins may have to purify themselves even after shaving, and the need to rid themselves of pollution is easily seen simply as a nuisance rather than as the equivalent, in the Western sense, of penance to atone for sin. Thus upper-caste people do have a distinctive interest in the preservation of the system and it could be maintained that Hindu religion is the most complex ideology ever developed in defence of the privileges of a congeries of local ruling classes.

CONQUEST

Intergroup relations are likely to form a symbiotic pattern only where neither group is appreciably more powerful than the other. The origin of the Hindu caste system is in doubt, yet, apart from its intrinsic interest, this system is of some relevance to any consideration of symbiosis for the light it throws upon the social mechanisms necessary to maintain institutionalized inequality. In the more numerous instances where a powerful industrial society is in contact with a pre-industrial one, symbiosis is out of the question, and relations are likely to develop along one of two courses. If the pre-industrial society is fairly large and well organized, and if the might of the industrial society is not brought to bear quickly and comprehensively, then a pattern of institutional contact may develop (this is discussed later in the present chapter). But when the pre-industrial society has been relatively weak, then the conquering society has often made no concessions to the traditions of the defeated people.

Presenting the conclusions of his sober historical review of racial contacts between English-speaking Whites and aboriginal peoples in the United States, Canada, Australia, and New Zealand, Grenfell Price averred that in the majority of regions White–native relations fell into three stages:

'During an opening period of pioneer invasion on moving frontiers the whites decimated the natives with their diseases; occupied their lands by seizure or by pseudo-purchase; slaughtered those who resisted; intensified tribal warfare by supplying white weapons; ridiculed and disrupted native religions, society and culture, and generally reduced the unhappy peoples to a state of despondency under which they neither desired to live, nor to have children under-go similar conditions' (Price, 1950: 1–2).

This severe judgement is fully substantiated by the evidence he adduces. In some cases white–native contacts never developed beyond the first stage because the natives did not survive it. In Tasmania, during the nineteenth century, the two or three thousand aborigines were shot at indiscriminately. Governors and official commissions unhesitatingly censured the Whites. Governor Daly, for example, reported in 1813 that native resentment was almost wholly due to a barbarous and inhuman mode of proceeding, 'under which the whites robbed the aborigines of their children'. But the colonial officials could not or would not punish the aggressors and in the end the aborigines turned on the immigrants. Full-scale war followed, in which capture parties hunted the Tasmanians like wild beasts, using women as decoys. The last full-blooded Tasmanian was a woman who died in 1876; as she was born in 1803, the opening years of the white invasion, her life-span coincided with the period over which her people were exterminated (Price, 1950: 108–9, 124). Early nineteenth-century policy in Australia was often little different.

The second stage described by Grenfell Price was one in which, responding to the philanthropic movements in early nineteenth-century Britain, the Whites gathered some of the survivors onto small and often unsuitable reservations, where government agents and missionaries laboured worthily but ineffectively to impart to them Christianity and an academic education, together with a training in arts such as agriculture which were distasteful to peoples accustomed to making a living from hunting. These policies gave way in the twentieth century to a stage in which greater respect was shown for the peoples' own cultures, and they were given more practical help in establishing them-selves in the wider society. A striking illustration of how some native peoples were able to make a come-back after the period of disorganiza-tion and distress which followed conquest is provided by the Maori of New Zealand. Prior to the European invasions in the early nineteenth century, there may have been about 200,000 Maori; about one-third of them succumbed to disease after the European intrusion, and another third were killed in fighting (mostly with fellow Maori using imported muskets). After a time, the Maori responded eagerly to Christian mis-sion and educational activity, but there were many points of tension, centring chiefly upon European land purchase. In attempting to fix the boundaries of European encroachment, the Maori found war forced upon them. They were defeated by a large army of British and colonial troops. Then reprisals followed. Much Maori land was confiscated and the people became embittered. A wave of alcoholism spread over the Maori and their extinction appeared inevitable. In 1856 a doctor wrote: 'The Maoris are dying out and nothing can save them. Our plain duty, as good compassionate colonists, is to smooth down their dying pillow.' For a further fifty years this belief that the Maori people were 'sick unto death' seemed justified. Mission and educational work during this period met with little success. But then, Maori population figures began to increase. The revival has been attributed to the inspiration of a new generation of Maori leaders who were able to improve the morale of their people and restore some of their own organization. The assumption that the Maori must come to resemble in all respects the Pakeha, or white New Zealanders, was abandoned (Price, 1950: 150–88). The Pakeha began to take pride in Maori culture, especially their songs and dances, as distinctive of New Zealand as a nation.

A similar sequence of three stages can be noted in the dealings of United States settlers with Indians. In New England the Puritans frequently modelled their behaviour upon that of the war bands of the Old Testament. They enslaved Indian women, kidnapped Indian children, and burnt and slaughtered, at times under clerical inspiration and leadership. Bounties were paid for the production of Indian scalps. Policy and opinion sometimes fluctuated. In 1676, for instance, Massachusetts hanged two white men for the wanton killing of Indians. Yet in the following year the women of Marblehead, returning from church, encountered and massacred some captured Indians, after which 'the rough element' went off to kill the women and children of a neighbouring Indian village. This frontier ruthlessness was repeated later as white settlers pushed west to California in the middle of the nineteenth century. The miners, whose temper has often been displayed in Hollywood films, were followed by lumbermen, farmers, and cattlemen who were contemptuous of the peaceful Indians. Those who escaped slaughter or enslavement were ruthlessly pushed up and down the country while state and federal government remained passive. At times, Californian Whites killed Indians 'as a sport to enlive Sundays'; others thought of them as vermin that had to be exterminated. One settler who had been helping in a massacre of male Indians came upon a group of children huddled together in fear; he thought they looked 'cute' and could not bring himself to use the ·56 calibre rifle because 'it tore them up so bad', so he had to take his ·38 calibre revolver to kill them (Price, 1950: 11–18).

By this time a reservation policy was already established in other parts of the United States. Treaties were made with different tribal groups, often in a sincere attempt to protect them in the occupation of desirable country. Then from 1871 to 1887 the federal government concentrated upon segregating the Indians in reservations, supplying them with rations and using government agents to supervise and elevate them. This line of action was succeeded by a policy of merging them in the white community by granting the individual Indian his land together with citizenship of the United States. This determination to ignore cultural differences in turn came to an end in 1932 with the

Roosevelt administration's 'New Day' policy. Though these changes in national policy were reflected in White-Indian relations, there was considerable variation in the pattern of contact from place to place, depending on the circumstances of the group involved and in particular upon the numerical strength of the Indians. In some localities they fought back as fiercely as any Whites. The study of these variations cannot be pursued here, but one feature deserves mention because it forms part of the general pattern of reactions to conquest. This is the development of religious cults centred upon a messianic leader, or upon a belief in an imminent change in which the defeated people will achieve moral and material elevation.

The most notable of such North American Indian cults was the Ghost Dance, which first appeared in 1870 among the Paiute of Nevada, at a time when they were suffering from new diseases and economic restrictions consequent upon the reduction of the buffalo and their confinement to reservations. The movement was led by a prophet who insisted that the Indians' misfortunes were a consequence of their neglect of traditional religion. The dance was designed to bring back the ancestors ('ghosts'), after which there would be a great cataclysm and the golden age of the past would be restored. This message spread to other Indian groups (except those whose traditional religion caused them to fear the dead) and was a major factor in the unrest which culminated in the massacre of more than two hundred Sioux men, women, and children in 1890.

How a policy of absorbing a native minority has in practice affected interpersonal relations can be seen from a study of a small Indian tribe, the Makah, in the extreme north-west of the United States, on the Pacific coast close to the Canadian border (Colson, 1953). Makah experience of white civilization has been more favourable than that of many groups, but the interest in this case lies not in evaluating administrative policies so much as in showing that assimilation can proceed very far and yet a sense of separateness will persist as long as there is a basis for it in a group's interests. The Makah were primarily a seafaring people who fished and hunted whale and seal; they rarely ventured more than a few miles inland. Thus they were less disturbed by white intrusion than land-based peoples. They were a small group, never more than six hundred strong, which also facilitated assimilation. In the old days, membership in the community seems to have been based much more upon residence than descent, but government policy unintentionally changed this. The Makah formerly lived in independent villages with little by way of tribal organization. In 1855 the Makah, by treaty with the United States government, ceded the territory which they claimed to control and received in return a small reservation at the tip of their peninsula. The establishment of this reservation virtually created a tribe, for after 1855 a group of Makah owned the land and needed a tribal organization to regulate the use of their common property. Into the beginning of the twentieth century the local Indian Service administrator still insisted that his work was that of civilizing the Indian by making him adopt white ways. Activities of a ceremonial or ritual character were discouraged; matrimonial irregularities on the part of Indians could invite official intervention; attendance at school was compulsory. Thus, though administrative policy was later loosened, the Makah were for several generations exposed to continuous pressure to accept American customs.

By 1941, when Elizabeth Colson's study was begun, the Makah were in general the propertied class in the village where most of the relatively small population was concentrated (357 Makah, some other Indians, about 100 local Whites, and perhaps another 250 transient Whites associated with the lumber camp or with defence works). The local Whites rented houses from the Makah under a lease system, and, since the village was within the reservation, any minor legal cases in which they were involved went before an Indian court. The Indians could have non-Makah evicted from the reservation if they wished, and consequently the Whites were careful not to give offence. Whereas some of the Indians had a racially distinctive appearance, many were physically indistinguishable from Whites. Their group was defined neither by appearance, nor by social isolation, nor by common culture, nor even by descent, for some persons of partially Makah descent were counted within the group and others were not. Membership was defined by admission to a roll of names maintained under the constitution of the tribe: the roll listed those persons who were descendants of the original inhabitants and whose claims to membership were not in conflict with enrolment in some other tribal group. The shared land rights of those who were on the Makah roll held them together as a group.

As the Whites had no secure standing within the reservation they were in no position to discriminate against the Makah in anything other than private matters such as the choice of friends and associates. In the stores it was 'first come, first served'. Intermarriage was not unusual. The Makah had their own celebrations after weddings and on like occasions, to which Whites were rarely invited. They were well aware that as Indians they were liable to meet discrimination if they went off to the cities elsewhere in the state, but on their own land they enjoyed many privileges: immunity to certain taxes and licences; some extra social services, etc. As long as the Makah had their special economic and legal privileges, they were bound to hold together to maintain traditions which were theirs alone, and to be viewed by others as a special category. They were capable as individuals of acting within the white social world and some of them sporadically did so, but further integration was checked because it was in the interest of the group to utilize the benefits of a special status. This status, therefore, determined the circumstances in which the Makah played a distinctive tribal role either towards Whites or towards one another.

CULT MOVEMENTS

Some anthropologists have interpreted movements such as that of the Ghost Dance as 'nativistic' or backward-looking in that they attempt, by either magical or rational methods, to return to an idealized past or to modify the frustrations of the present by returning to traditional ways. Such movements are widespread and often show quite remarkable similarities (to take a minor example, the prophet's assertion that if the Whites fire on members of the movement their bullets will turn to water); these suggest certain uniformities of a psychological or social character in the response of non-literate peoples to contact with an incomprehensibly richer and more powerful culture. Yet though these movements appear in different regions and times, they have been absent in others, and the pattern is not susceptible of any very simple explanation.

One region that has seen a marked concentration of the 'cargo-cult' variety of such movements is Melanesia. The observable aspect of cargo-cult activity consists in the emergence of a leader from among the local people who persuades them, or many of them, to copy some of the external features of European behaviour. Objects associated with the people's traditional religion may be destroyed. Instead, they may form military-style units and engage in drill. They build jetties or clear landing-strips for the 'cargo' that will be sent to them when they succeed in putting themselves into the right relation with the spiritual world. The cargo will be machines, goods, and material possessions similar to those that are brought to the Whites by ship and aeroplane.

Administrators were initially inclined to interpret cargo-cult movements as nativistic or atavistic crazes worked up by sorcerers. Recent research has shown that, on the contrary, they are forward-looking movements in which the natives, working within the framework of traditional ideas, try constructively to come to terms with their new circumstances. Far from being indigenous to the peoples in question, the movements have been influenced at every point by the prevailing pattern of race relations (Worsley, 1957; Burridge, 1960; Jarvie, 1963; Lawrence, 1964). The most recent of these studies insists that the disparity in the power and wealth of the two groups was the basic factor motivating people to form and support the new cults, for they quickly came to believe that they could have satisfactory dealings with Europeans only if they acquired large assignments of cargo. The native world-view was one which taught that goods so superior to their own products could not be manufactured by human endeavour and skill. Material wealth originated from and was maintained by deities who, with the ancestors, could be manipulated by ritual to man's advantage. With this went a view of society which assumed that a true social relationship existed only when men demonstrated goodwill by reciprocal co-operation and distribution of wealth. To the Melanesians, the activities of Europeans suggested that, for some reason, the newcomers' gods or ancestors were more benevolent than their own. Europeans did not enter into the network of reciprocal exchanges but kept most of their wealth to themselves; sometimes the settlers were arrogant and brutal. The Melanesians therefore represented their subordina-tion to Europeans in the metaphor of a traditional relationship of subordination-with-privileges; one told Japanese officers: 'We natives are like women. First came the Germans and we were married to them. Then came the Australians and we were married to them. Now you Japanese have chased out the Australians – and we are married to you' (Law-rence, 1964: 107).

The native economies were static and the gap between their standards and the Europeans' got no narrower. Prices paid for native products, responding to a volatile world market, fluctuated bewilderingly. At times, the people flocked to the missions and professed Christianity with enthusiasm; then, finding that this brought them no material benefits, they often retreated in disillusion, accusing the missionaries of insincerity (it was sometimes believed that they had removed the first page of the Bible on which the secrets of the cargo were explained). The natives wanted cargo because European goods possessed such obvious advantages over their own products, but it also became for them a matter of self-respect; as long as they were without European goods their spiritual inadequacy was exposed and they felt relegated to a position of inferiority and contempt. So the cult movements were not anti-White: they were attempts to find ways in which to co-operate with white men and to persuade white men to co-operate with them.

A full analysis has recently been presented of a particularly interesting cargo movement in New Guinea after World War II, which was itself in some ways a development from previous movements in the same locality stretching as far back as 1871. Its leader was a man called Yali who had been a sergeant-major in the Australian armed forces (then the highest rank open to a native of New Guinea). In 1945, with the support of the colonial administration, Yali inaugurated a Rehabilitation Scheme which was to help his people to adopt more prosperous ways resembling European practice. Yali believed that, if the people did this, substantial material assistance would be provided by the administration. Over the next few years the movement changed in character, partly because of the tendency of the local people (encouraged by some of Yali's lieutenants) to interpret in terms of cargo beliefs advice that was intended to convey something different. The course of this development defies brief summary but it displayed, with fascinating precision, the blending together in apparently logical fashion of elements which Europeans would regard as mutually inconsistent. Yali had been impressed by the care Australians lavished on seemingly useless pets, by the solicitude with which animals were housed in the Brisbane zoo, by the preservation of prehistoric animal bones in the museum, and by the importance agricultural officers attached to improving native standards of animal husbandry. From these observations Yali inferred that animals were totemic creatures in European religion; some men, missionaries, had Adam and Eve as totems; others belonged to groups who believed in evolution, as a native clan or tribe might have its own particular origin myth; and these other Europeans were organized in groups with distinctive totem animals. Yali concluded that the missionaries were determined to keep the people of his district in ignorance of the Europeans' cargo secret and that, by discouraging ritual performed for the pagan gods and ceremonies in honour of the spirits of the dead, the missionaries prevented the natives from obtaining cargo through the good offices of their own tutelary spirits. Therefore he organized a widespread revival of paganism, not as reversion to more primitive living, but as a possible way of obtaining spiritual favour and becoming civilized. The movement got out of hand and in 1950 Yali was sentenced to imprisonment on charges of depriving certain natives of their liberty and of incitement to the rape of a native woman (Lawrence, 1964: 116–221).

Comparative study of cargo movements shows that, while the pressures of European occupation lead to cult activity, it is not necessary for native culture to be disrupted before they can take hold. Several scholars have reported cults among peoples whose traditional culture has been relatively little affected. Nor are the movements the result of any irrationality in the Melanesian mind or outlook. The various stages in the interpretations of the human condition attempted in the movements displayed logically impeccable deductions from the premisses of traditional epistemology. These premisses may have been false, but they were not incompatible with leading a good life within a pre-industrial order. The work that some cult leaders organized could be seen as the peoples' attempt to prove that their ends were morally right. The work might be useless, but, asks one student, could not the same be said of the building of Rouen Cathedral? 'From this distance we can well argue that the citizens of Rouen were also misapplying their energies. But 800 years ago Europeans were in many respects as ignorant as the primitive natives of today. Only knowledge recently acquired enables us to say that disease is more effectively prevented by improving housing, water supply, and drainage than by holding processions and building cathedrals' (Hogbin, 1958: 219).

A different aspect of cargo movements is that of their political func-tion. Whatever the intention of the leaders of the cults in Madang District, New Guinea, described by Lawrence, one result was to give all the people of this region a sense of unity they had never previously known. The cults provided a setting within which anti-European senti-ment and political activity could easily grow. In one of the movements prior to Yali's, the leaders styled themselves as paramount rulers and began to build up a military organization to expel the Australians. Cargo cults can overcome divisions among and between the native peoples, integrating them into wider social groups opposed to the Whites; to this extent they can be regarded as the first stirrings of nationalism. This interpretation starts from the socio-political function of such movements and works back to a rather different conception of what constitutes their cause than an approach such as Lawrence's, which begins with the study of participants' motivations as they are channelled by traditional culture. But either kind of theory points to the value of locating these movements within the context of White-native race relations. When the same material is looked at from a different angle, there is an equally good case for concluding that these analyses of cargo movements teach the student lessons of general relevance for the study of relations between social groups where one is much more powerful than the other.

INSTITUTIONALIZED CONTACT

To illustrate features of race relations where two societies or large groups are interrelated through the activities of a small number of intermediaries, a single study will be considered. The analysis of relations between Whites and Blacks in Zululand advanced by Max Gluckman (1955, 1958) is of interest not only for the detail it provides about how office-holders may be required to serve as racial go-betweens, but also as exemplifying a method which could usefully be employed by more students of race relations. This method consists in the close analysis of interpersonal relations, looking for logical explanations of the simplest forms of behaviour – such as how a man dresses, where he stands in a gathering, how he greets someone who comes up, and so on. It regards the study of race relations as the study not of relations between groups but of relations between members of groups. The observer notes that a man displays deference towards a member of another group, and asks himself: what would have happened had the man failed to do this ? To explain a simple action the sociologist is led back gradually to consider the power relations between the two groups, the economic and legal systems, the distinctive characters of the groups, and many features of the total social universe. By relating observable behaviour to general social forces, this method makes it possible to test predictions and develop a sociological theory.

The Dutch first established a permanent settlement at the Cape of Good Hope in 1652. It is popularly believed that during the latter part of the seventeenth and throughout the eighteenth century Bantu and Dutch were slowly spreading into the almost empty subcontinent from opposite directions. However, there is good reason to regard this version of the Bantu movement to the south as a political myth, suiting the purposes of white nationalists. Bantu-speaking peoples were established well to the south by the late sixteenth century, from which period the first written records derive (Wilson, 1959). In any case, between 1816 and 1828 the Zulu chief Shaka carried to a high point the process of uniting the Nguni peoples into a single Zulu state. He was master of 80,000 square miles of land, lord over 100,000 people, and commander of a most effective military machine. The British had taken over the Cape colony in 1795, and in 1824 a small English party established a settlement at Port Natal (Durban) to trade in ivory and skins. They were not strong enough to be any threat to the Zulu nation and Shaka tolerated their presence; through them he also gained firearms. Though the culture of neither group was static, the general picture was not one of acculturation. The Zulu were the more powerful as a group but they could see that the Whites possessed weapons and equipment far superior to their own, so that there was a certain balance between the two groups. They were not united in any common political order nor did they interrelate so as to constitute any integral social or economic system. The forces serving to create such interrelations were at work nevertheless. Small Natal tribes that had been scattered by the Zulu regrouped under British protection and Zulu fugitives fled to the settlement. Alarmed that this might incite the Zulu king to attack them, the English sent him an envoy in 1835 to negotiate a treaty endorsing the king's power over refugees. In one sense, then, the English acknowledged Zulu overlordship. They contributed trade goods and medicines, started farming, and introduced missionaries in return for a relatively unmolested existence.

The balance was upset by the arrival, in 1838, of a large party of Boer trekkers. Dingane, Shaka's successor, attacked and killed most of them. The English abandoned their good relations with the Zulu nation and supported the Boers, who later defeated the Zulu army and took possession of Natal. In 1879 there were further hostilities when the British, aided by a dissident Zulu faction, defeated the then king Cetshwayo and divided his people into thirteen independent units. Eight years later the British government decided to occupy Zulu territory and exercise direct control. Struggles between Zulu factions increased the power of the relatively small British administration to control the entire region. With the introduction of taxes and cash trading, with evangelization and the opening of schools, with increased migration by younger Zulu to work for European employers at the time when they would earlier have entered a Zulu regiment, and because of other changes, the Zulu became more and more dependent upon the white group. It was money, says Gluckman, rather than the maxim gun or the telephone, that established a measure of social cohesion by creating common, if dissimilar, interests in what could after a time be regarded as a single economic and political system. The desires of the Boers for land, of the British for trade, and of the Natal colonists for labour, had brought them to absorb Zululand into the expanding industrial and agricultural organization of South Africa.

The manner of Zululand's incorporation, together with other features of South African policy, increased the Zulu's sense of opposition to Whites and of allegiance to their own people, but this should not obscure the way in which the opposition between a much greater variety of groups may be used to resolve conflicts and achieve co-operation. The same Zulu might have different loyalties in respect of his membership of a descent group, as a cattle-owner, as a Christian, as a parent, and so on. The people who opposed one another over one issue might be allies in other circumstances. This point is fairly elementary, but there is originality in Gluckman's demonstration of the significance of links crossing the colour line. It might be in the chief's interest to oppose the government on some matters and to support it on others. It was certainly in the white administrator's interest to win support from the Africans if his district was not to acquire a reputation for being trouble-some (which would reflect on him) and if he was to persuade them to comply with government policies. At the time and place of Gluckman's research, chiefs and native commissioners worked together fairly well. The chiefs and their subordinate officers assisted the commissioners in the enforcement of law; the commissioners were anxious to see their districts progress, and occasionally would oppose other Whites or government departments in advocating the policies they believed correct. It was unusual for Zulus and Whites to form united groups in open confrontation. Anyone who wished to understand how the system of Zulu-White relations worked had therefore to examine how intergroup contacts were institutionalized by analysing particular social situations. Part of the theory underlying this viewpoint is compressed in the state-ment: 'Shifting membership of groups and relationships enables indivi-duals to act by different, even contradictory, values . . . Zulu can act by European values, forming new groups on their basis. For a social system has not consistency in itself: it is systematized by situational selection of individuals' (Gluckman, 1958: 47). Individuals may define apparently similar situations in different ways; by so doing they resolve inconsistencies and establish new social patterns.

To illustrate how the affairs of 2 million whites and $6\frac{1}{2}$ million Africans were interrelated, Gluckman describes a ceremony which brought together twenty-four Europeans and about four hundred Zulu. The occasion was the ceremonial opening, by the chief native commissioner, of a bridge. The proceedings opened with a hymn in English, led by a Swedish missionary; all the Zulu, pagans included, stood and removed their hats for the singing. The local magistrate made the first speech, and he was followed by the chief native commissioner, a representative of the Provincial Roads Department, a local European, and finally the Zulu Regent. The European officials then drove over the bridge in their cars, preceded by Zulu warriors singing a traditional chant. Afterwards, the Europeans retired to take tea and cake; the Zulu – on the opposite bank – prepared a feast; and the missionary led some further hymn-singing. The starting-point for this ceremony was a bridge, planned by European engineers and built by Zulu labourers, which would be used by a European magistrate ruling over Zulu and by Zulu women going to a European hospital. The way in which the participants were brought together represented both their common interests and the various divisions among them. The Whites and the Zulu assembled in different places; though an individual White might talk with an individual Zulu about common interests (as when the veterinary officer exchanged words with a Zulu official about the programme of cattle-dipping), each was bound in other respects to his own group and they could not, for example, sit down to dine together in the local hotel. The pattern of segregation inhibited the growth of social ties across the colour line, but European employment of Africans prevented segregation from becoming complete: for instance, whereas ordinary Zulu did not enter the European shelter, those who were domestic servants to Europeans were required to go in and out. To appreciate the social inequalities between the Whites and the Zulu gathered for the ceremony, it was necessary to understand the subordinate position of Africans in the political and economic structure of South Africa. The extent to which individual Zulu and Europeans were able to enter interpersonal relations with members of the other group was largely determined by their occupational roles. Gluckman, as an anthropologist, was in a position to form more egalitarian and intimate relations with Zulu than were other Europeans. The veterinary officer was brought in touch with Africans more than the Treasury official was. The missionary at the ceremony associated both with the Europeans and with the Christian Zulu. Such contacts continually required members of the opposed groups to adapt their behaviour to one another. The chief native commissioner had elements of Zulu ritual incorporated into the ceremony: he accepted from the Regent a gift of beer in the manner a Zulu chief would use, though he remained apart from the Zulu people as one of their own chiefs would not.

This illustration brings out the way in which the participants all occupied basic racial roles, as Europeans and Africans, but at the same time they had more independent roles to play which brought them together in other respects. Those Europeans most involved with the Zulu alternated between roles permitting association with Zulu and roles requiring distance or segregation. Other Europeans, however, did not have to play as many roles requiring association with Zulu, or did not have to play them so much. Had the political climate been more favourable, ties crossing the colour line might well have become stronger, but South African government policy – as discussed in Chapter Eight – has been to minimize such ties.

CHAPTER SIX

Slavery and the New World

Faced with variations in the pattern of race relations in different times and places, several writers have interpreted the shifting scenes in terms of the relative strength or absence of 'race feeling'. This is conceived as a cultural and historical phenomenon, transmitted from one generation or group to another and reflecting the peculiar features of each individual locality. The more a writer attempts to give full weight to particular sequences of events and to particular circumstances, the less selective he can be; the more he is forced to employ historical explanations, the less easily can he operate within the framework of generalized causal explanations such as are favoured by the social sciences. No reputable scholar now believes that these variations can be explained in terms of any one causal factor; the distinctions are those of emphasis. Nevertheless, the belief that a particular element in a sequence of events is more significant than the others will always lead scholars towards more general statements about the dynamics of change. This has been evinced in several discussions of one of the most important happenings in modern history, the forced transportation of millions of Africans across the Atlantic, and their fate in different countries of the New World.

THE SLAVE TRADE

Slaves were brought northwards across the Sahara in ancient and mediaeval times. Not all of them were Negroes, but it seems possible that the caravans of white Muslim slavers transported over a million Negroes across the desert in every century of the late Middle Ages. The Portuguese started to seek their own slaves in Africa during the fifteenth century. A regular maritime traffic of Negro slaves to Portugal began in the 1450s and increased rapidly (Luttrell, 1965). In West Africa, slaves were acquired by peaceful trading, and relations between Blacks and Whites were comparatively harmonious. In the sixteenth

century the Portuguese began to carry slave cargoes directly from
Angola to Brazil but the cost of transportation was high in proportion
to the value of their labour. With the planting of sugar cane in Brazil
and the West Indies, and the mounting demand for sugar in Europe,
the value of a slave to a planter on the other side of the Atlantic shot
up. Shipments increased in corresponding measure, reaching their
peak in the eighteenth century. Sugar production, it may be noted,
required a great deal of labour relative to the value of land and capital.
England benefited greatly from the 'triangular trade' whereby manufactured goods (rum, brandy, cloth, trinkets, iron bars, and weapons)
were sold in Africa, and slaves were bought for sale on the other side
of the Atlantic, where sugar, tobacco, cotton, and rum were to be
purchased. When Jamaica in 1775 imposed an additional duty on
imported slaves, the Board of Trade in London disallowed the duty
because it 'could not allow the colonies to check or discourage in any
degree a traffic so beneficial'. How many slaves made the journey it is
impossible to calculate with any confidence but possibly 15 million
were shipped from Africa. This figure may be set alongside the calculation that in 1940 there were some 26 million Negroes and 15 million
mulattoes in the Americas; it should be remembered, however, that
in earlier centuries it was primarily males who were imported, and
reproduction rates on some plantations were often quite low.

The main element of the labour force in such North American
colonies as Virginia was made up of white indentured servants: people
who had sold their services for a period of three to six years in exchange
for their passage. The first Negroes reached Virginia in 1619. They
cannot have been indentured and it is difficult to establish precisely
what their status was. Twenty-three Africans were listed as servants
in the muster rolls of 1624 and 1625 and it seems that they were released
after having served their masters for seven years. It is recorded that
the child of one couple was baptized, which, in the circumstances of
the day, may have implied the eventual right to vote. As late as 1651
some Negroes whose period of service had been completed were
assigned land in much the same way as white servants, but Virginian
society was still on a small scale, and little attention appears to have been
paid to questions concerning their legal status. In the course of the
second generation, however, their status definitely deteriorated until
being a Negro became equated in men's minds with being a slave; in
the words of a law passed in neighbouring Maryland in 1663: 'All
negroes or other slaves shall serve *durante vita* . . .' From an early stage
of their settlement in North America, practically all Negroes were

restricted to a status of total subjugation, and even the abolition of slavery does not seem to have led to any very significant diminution of race feeling. This pattern is often contrasted with that which holds, or is believed to hold, in much of Latin America, where Negroes and their descendants have been at a considerable disadvantage but there is less racial exclusion or concern to maintain a colour line.

THE INFLUENCE OF RELIGIOUS BELIEFS

Impressed by this contrast, which he believed to reflect variations in the policies of different European colonial powers in other parts of the world also, the historian Arnold J. Toynbee called attention to its association with two versions of Christianity and two epochs of European history. Toynbee implied that the difference between North and South America in the treatment of the Negro was to be ascribed to the race feeling that characterized the Europeans of the northern colonies but not of the southern; he treated 'race feeling' as if it were a single homogeneous factor which could be explained by being traced back to its antecedents. Toynbee's argument was that 'our modern Western race-feeling' was unknown during the so-called Dark Ages and Middle Ages; he averred that our forefathers, instead of dividing mankind into white and coloured people, divided men into Christians and heathen, and that 'this medieval Western freedom from the prejudice of race-feeling has survived among Western peoples who have remained more or less in the medieval phase of our Western Civilization: for instance, the Spaniards and Portuguese and the descendants of Spanish and Portuguese settlers who have established new Western communities in America'. The French, he said, have retained a similar outlook in a secular state by adopting civilization rather than race as a criterion for classification (Toynbee, 1934, I: 223–5). On the other hand, he detected a vein of ruthlessness in the English method of overseas settlement, which reached far back in time. When the Roman Empire broke up, most of the Barbarian war bands simply stepped into the places of the former Roman soldiers and officials. The English war bands alone more or less exterminated the local people in the provinces they overran, and repopulated the country themselves instead of being content to rule and exploit the population they found there. Moreover, the frontiers of England with Wales and Scotland were the scene of ferocious fighting, and English policy in Ireland embodied an equally disparaging attitude towards the indigenous people (Toynbee, 1934, I: 465–6). This historian believed, further, that race feeling 'springs naturally from the religious background of those Western people who are of the Protestant persuasion'. 'The "Bible Christian" of European origin and race who has settled among peoples of non-European race overseas has', said Toynbee, 'inevitably identified himself with Israel obeying the will of Jehovah and doing the Lord's work by taking possession of the Promised Land, while he has identified the non-Europeans who have crossed his path with the Canaanites whom the Lord has delivered into the Land of his Chosen People to be destroyed or subjugated.' In continental India, where the natives could not be supplanted in this way, 'only a negligible number of the "natives" were converted to the religion of the ruling race or were physically assimilated to it by inter-breeding. For good or evil, the English Protestant rulers of India have distinguished themselves from all other contemporary Western rulers over non-Western peoples by the rigidity with which they have held aloof from their subjects. They took to the Hindu institutions of caste as readily as if they had not found it established in India when they came but had invented it for their own convenience' (Toynbee, 1934, I: 211–13).

Toynbee's argument maintained that the inherited attitudes which characterize a culture are of the greatest importance in shaping the pattern of relations between a dominant and a conquered people. Among the most powerful of these attitudes are those associated with religion. This kind of historical explanation has certain limitations. In objection to Toynbee's particular interpretation, it may be argued that he failed to take account of the variations in racial attitudes in North and South America over the several centuries. In objection to such explanations in general, it may be urged that they do not contribute the kind of understanding that makes it possible to calculate the implications of new developments. But Toynbee's approach, which was original in its time, does have merits, among them being its tying of modern racial sentiment firmly to the religious and economic changes which have been fundamental to the character of Western industrial culture.

Does Protestantism bear a special responsibility for the rise and formulation of modern racial sentiment? Within Protestantism, does not the Calvinist outlook lead to a particularly acute consciousness of racial distinction? Influenced by Max Weber's study *The Protestant Ethic and the Spirit of Capitalism*, some sociologists have been inclined to see as the distinguishing feature of Calvinism a belief that some individuals are predestined to rank among the elect and others to be damned. The incautious have been ready to assume the existence of a reasonably homogeneous doctrine and practice which correspond to the name. This has led them to stress the exclusive character of Calvinism. On closer study, such assumptions break down. Calvin's teachings are susceptible of a number of interpretations, and the various churches that have followed them have differed among themselves and over the centuries in their doctrines, so it is not easy to identify the 'ism'. According to the Rev. Professor T. F. Torrance of the Chair of Christian Dogmatics at Edinburgh University, any account of Calvin's teaching should begin with the universal range of God's grace both in creation and in the redemption of creation, rather than with beliefs about man's fate. When considering the relation between Calvin's ideas and racialism, it is necessary – according to Torrance – to emphasize three key doctrines at the outset. First, that God's purpose is the salvation of all men, and that when damnation overtakes men it is an 'accidental' result arising from unbelief or disobedience (in this respect it is necessary to differentiate the original doctrine from the pietistic and rationalistic modifications to which it was subject at the end of the eighteenth and in the nineteenth century). Second, that Calvin's view was universalistic by contrast with mediaeval thought (e.g. in its conception of God's covenant with man, or, in secular affairs, in its doctrine of resistance to tyrants) and was focused upon God's intentions for humanity. Third, that Calvin's doctrine is one of corporate election. Christ is the head of the whole human race, though by unbelief men may break themselves off from this engrafting into Christ. The idea that election is only of individuals is a later and more corrupt belief. In developing his view of society Calvin took up Stoic notions of 'natural law', 'the right of nations', 'civil right', etc., relating them to 'the order of creation' and 'the course of nature' so as to arrive at a conception of universal law for all peoples and nations.

It would be conceded by all students of this question that there is nothing in Calvin's system of thought which of itself promotes racial discrimination. Rather must attention be directed to the selection of elements from it and to their use in ways which, given the circumstances of their time, have that effect. On the one hand, the Calvinist view of man is highly egalitarian; it makes humanity and charity fundamental virtues, requiring from the civil power the preservation of human rights and from the believer the effort of imagination necessary to put himself in the place of others. But, on the other hand, there are chains of thought which seem, in practice, to have had a contrary effect. The condemnation of paganism rests on its distortion of 'the seed of religion' and 'the sense of divinity' planted in all men, just as much among 'brutal and savage' peoples as among others. The knowledge of God given equally to all men is smothered or corrupted, partly by ignorance and partly by malice. This doctrine may have provided support for any tendency on the part of European settlers to identify native cultures with the work of the devil. Another possible influence may have sprung from the tendency of some Calvinists – rightly or wrongly – to interpret worldly success as a sign of 'justification' in the eyes of God. In North America and South Africa the colonizing ventures of the Puritans and the Dutch were, to outward appearances, successful, whereas the Red Indians, Hottentots, and Bantu resisted the stimuli coming from the European civilizations and remained in a miserable state, just as if God in his inscrutability had confirmed their damnation. In the Calvinist interpretation of peoples' state of grace by means of outward signs, economic activity sometimes acquired a special significance, though such activity was a means of expressing the puritan ethic rather than, at this stage, a mode of racial exploitation. Work was conceived as an ascetic activity independent of material needs, but it seemed to Europeans that the natives, once they had satisfied these needs, handed themselves over to the works of the devil ('idolatrous ceremonies' or 'erotic dances'): in this way, the interpretation of a pre-capitalist mentality in religious terms became a source of tension. The justification of work as something performed to the greater glory of God could be stretched to present as meritorious the expropriation of land that was not being properly cultivated. The parable of the talents and the desirability of putting them to good use is not a rationalization of egoistical interests, but it could become one.

In South Africa, the early Boer church leaders were laymen without theological training, who relied on the Old Testament more than on any knowledge of Calvin's writings. The congregational basis of Afrikaner religion was very strong, so that when, after taking the Cape, Britain supplied Scots missionaries in place of Dutch, the newcomers were obliged to yield to their congregations' views on separate services for Black and White, etc. The Dutch Reformed Church in South Africa has subsequently developed the idea of corporate election. It is believed that God responded to prayer on the eve of battle in 1838 by giving the Afrikaners divine assistance (this is the event commemorated by the Day of the Covenant). God has elected the Afrikaner nation, and it is its special mission to spread Christianity in Africa; but what God has separated man must not bring together, therefore racial identities must be maintained and used to serve God's ends. At other times, it is said that the natural diversity of mankind is not broken down by the Church's unity in Christ but is, instead, restored and sanctified. These doctrines have been resisted by some Afrikaans theologians (Marais, 1952: 290–319).

In the Southern states of North America a modified Calvinism had some influence, and an association between puritanism and racial intolerance can be detected, but these associations are weak (cf. Cash, 1941: 67–68, 91–95). The Puritans of New England cannot be identified unequivocally as Calvinists. It should be remembered that people with a Calvinist background were often among the earliest groups to settle in the frontier regions where the tensions were greatest. In contrast to more evangelical denominations, Calvinists insisted upon an educated Church and an educated ministry, but in frontier situations it was difficult to cater for the education of members of the congregation, let alone that of any possible converts. Moreover, exclusivist tendencies in any denomination are apt to be accentuated where the minister does not have a parish responsibility. In the Southern states, the Calvinists were followed by Baptists, and then Methodists, whose standards for church membership were lower. Initially they pressed great numbers of men into the ministry without very much training, but their policy enabled them to reach much larger numbers of people. However, Baptist and Methodist revivalist activity at the beginning of the nineteenth century proved a stimulus to racialism. The Dutch at the Cape (and in northeastern Brazil during the seventeenth century) started their colonial activity with attitudes favourable towards the local peoples; in the course of time these attitudes were reversed, not because of changes in their understanding of Calvin's teaching but because changes in their own situation caused them to select and emphasize different elements in their theological inheritance. An important contributory to these changes may well have been the pressures of frontier life. A frontier society is one menaced both from outside and from inside. The local cultures are a continual temptation, inviting the colonizer to abandon the demanding requirements of his beleaguered group and to live the easier life of the majority, which is perceived as being erotically exciting. The moral rigidity of the Puritans made this temptation seem a snare of the devil which had to be combated by a refusal to make any concessions towards the other culture. The more forcibly such temptations were repressed, of course, the greater their power became (Bastide, 1959).

Even so, this sort of examination of the religious element in interracial situations can do no more than clear the ground for more detailed studies which go more closely into particular cases. The Protestant-Catholic distinction has involved more than religious differences. The Protestant countries have maintained cultures adapted to more northerly environments and have been more deeply committed to industrial capitalism by comparison with the Catholic countries. There are grounds for believing that the view of the world developed in puritan thought may have encouraged the sort of activity that promoted capitalism. There may then be some factor in capitalist organization which makes racial distinction or discrimination more likely (a question considered again in Chapter Eight). A recent series of investigations has enabled social psychologists to distinguish a particular kind of motivation which is characterized by a need for achievement (as opposed to a need for power, for security, for approval, etc.). Such a motivation is inculcated by child-rearing practices which stress self-reliance and possibly strengthen any sense of guilt and any tendency to direct prejudice upon a convenient scapegoat. A change in a way of life which led to an increase in the proportion of people with a high achievement motivation would therefore inspire the calculating, cumulative activity fundamental to capitalist enterprise and, at the same time, increase the psychological potential for exclusivism and discrimination. Though this factor should not be considered in isolation from particular social and historical circumstances, need for achievement may well prove to be one of the factors in the psychological structure associated with racialism, and a clue to unravel the tangle of observations suggesting a triangular pattern of Protestantism, capitalism, and racialism (McClelland, 1961). A recent study carried out in Brazil showed that mothers there were less likely than their counterparts in the United States to train their sons in self-reliance, personal autonomy, and a high valuation of achievement. The values emphasized in child-rearing were those associated with the authoritarian, father-dominated traditional rural family in which there was a double standard of morality for men and women (Rosen, 1962). This kind of family structure has been identified by historians as contributing to tolerance of racial variation (see p. 258 below).

The northern Protestant cultures also differ from the Mediterranean Catholic ones in folk concepts of sin and morality. The idea of a relapse into primitivism seems to be more tempting (Dingwall, 1946: 231), and a man's work is invested with considerable cultural significance instead of being regarded as an unpleasant and philosophically unimportant necessity. One writer says of the Brazilians:

'Unlike the North American, who seems to live to work, they work to live. . . . After the war of 1914-18, a play was produced in the Brazilian capital which satirized the attitude towards love of a North American business man. In love with the heroine, he is depicted as running on and off the stage, rushing up to the lady and saying, effusively, "I love you", and then getting out his watch and saying, "But I must go to my business: I will return". Work to the North American is often an escape *from* life, and especially from women; to the Brazilian it is a means through which life and love can be enjoyed.'

This author continues: 'The common attitude of the ordinary American tourist, when visiting the Latin countries of Europe, is often one in which can be detected the belief that what he thinks of as "loose living" is being practised there; and it is often obvious that secretly he hopes that he may have the opportunity to "loosen up" himself if occasion offers' (Dingwall, 1946: 236).

THE INFLUENCE OF LEGAL CATEGORIES

In a brief but stimulating essay, Frank Tannenbaum drew attention to the significance of their different legal traditions in accounting for differences between North and South America. The people of the Iberian peninsula were not strangers to slavery, for, because of the wars with the Moors which continued until the very year of the discovery of America, there had long been white and coloured slaves in their homelands. A long tradition of legal determination concerning slavery had been codified in *Las Siete Partidas* of 1263–65. So, when the Negro came upon the scene, no special social category of Negro was created for him; Spanish law and *mores* knew the category of slave, and those placed in it were the beneficiaries of a legal heritage which defined their rights and obligations. Slavery was conceived as a legal not a moral state; it affected only the outer man. Spanish law regulated slavery and with it went the religious doctrine that, in the words of Saint Paul, in the sight of God 'there is neither bond nor free' (Galatians iii. 28). Tannenbaum's summary of this law begins:

'The slave might marry a free person if the slave status was known to the other party. Slaves could marry against the will of their master if they continued serving him as before. Once married, they could not be sold apart, except under conditions permitting them to live as man and wife. If the slave married a free person with the knowledge of his master, and the master did not announce the fact of the existing slave status, then the slave by that mere fact became free. If married slaves owned by separate masters could not live together because of distance, the church should persuade one or the other to sell his slave. If neither of the masters could be persuaded, the church was to buy one of them so that the married slaves could live together. The children followed the status of their mother, and the child of a free mother remained free even if she later became a slave. In spite of his full powers over his slave, the master might neither kill nor injure him unless authorized by the judge, nor abuse him against reason or nature, nor starve him to death. But if the master did any of these things, the slave could complain to the judge, and if the complaint were verified, the judge must sell him, giving the price to the owner, and the slave might never be returned to the original master. Any Jewish or Moorish slave became free upon turning Christian, and even if the master himself later became a Christian, he recovered no rights over his former slave' (Tannenbaum, 1946: 49–50).

Las Siete Partidas defined the conditions under which slaves might be manumitted, and provided avenues by which they could appeal to the courts. A master frequently manumitted slaves as part of some family celebration. Slavery had, for all practical purposes, become a contractual arrangement between the master and the bondsman. The latter's liabilities were limited and the state appointed an official protector of slaves. So well institutionalized were these arrangements that for a long time no new legislation was needed to regulate slavery in the colonies of the New World – though new law was enacted concerning the treatment of Indians. When in 1789 a code of Negro slavery was finally promulgated it only restated Spanish law and custom (Tannenbaum, 1946: 52–56).

The position was quite different in the colonies that were heir to the English legal tradition. Says Tannenbaum: 'In neither tradition, policy, nor law was there room for the slave. The Law did not know him and could not make provision for him when he came upon the scene. . . . He certainly was not a free man. And the law did not know a slave. . . . The fact that the slave was a Negro merely added to the confusion; it did not create it' (1946: 101). This picture of the situation can draw some support from the famous *Commentaries on the Laws of England* by Blackstone who, in the first edition (1765: 127), stated that 'a slave or negro the very moment he lands in England falls under the protection of the laws and with regard to all natural rights becomes *eo instanti* a free man', to which he later added, 'though the master's right to his service may possibly still continue' (Fiddes, 1934: 506). Where was the line to be drawn between natural rights and other rights in which the slave might well be deficient ? There was no case law upon this point, and well after the much-bruited Somersett judgement of

1772 the legal situation was still confused; indeed, in 1778 several noted abolitionists in London joined to purchase the freedom of an African they wished to liberate! If the law did not recognize and define the status of slave, one alternative was to treat him as property. This was not a perfect solution. As a commentator upon the legal situation in the Southern states of the early nineteenth century observes: 'Legislators and magistrates were caught in a dilemma whenever they found that the slave's status as property was incompatible with his status as a person' (Stampp, 1956: 189). Lord Mansfield himself instructed the jury in the Lewis case of 1771 that whether masters 'have this kind of property or not in England has never been solemnly determined'. After the jury had considered their verdict the foreman said, 'We don't find he was the defendant's property' and 'there arose at the same instance a general voice of "No property, no property"'. This cry implies that there was popular concern about the question of whether there could be property in people, though it is possible that the decision turned simply upon the master's failure to provide satisfactory evidence of how he had originally acquired the slave in the West Indies (Fiddes, 1934: 503).

The differences in the legal situation in the English-speaking and Spanish- or Portuguese-speaking parts of the New World were paralleled by differences in the religious outlook upon slavery. In the Spanish view the slave had a right to become a Christian, to be baptized, and to be considered a member of the Christian community. Slave and master must both recognize their relationship to each other as moral beings and as brothers in Christ. When, in 1685, there was some question of the Dutch being allowed to supply slaves to the Spanish Caribbean colonies, the Inquisition urged the King: 'In case any contract is made with the Dutch, you will please to ordain that necessary orders be provided and issued for the utmost care of the conservation and purity of our Holy Catholic Faith, because one can very justly fear that if the negroes come by way of the Dutch, they may be greatly imbued with doctrines and errors. . . .' The Dutchman who received the contract was forced to take ten Capuchin monks to his African factories for the religious instruction of the Negroes, to support them, and to allow them to preach in public. Every slave was to receive baptism and religious instruction before being put on board, and upon reaching port every ship was to be boarded by a friar charged to examine the conscience, faith, and religion of the new arrivals (Elkins, 1959: 70–71).

In the British West Indies, by contrast, slaves were almost completely

denied the privileges of Christianity. The plantation-owners opposed
the preaching of the gospel on the grounds that the slaves 'would be less
attentive to labour, less inclined to obey their overseers and other
deputies, and would be more anxious to throw off the yoke of slavery
altogether'. The Church acquiesced in this view. In the United States
there was no systematic opposition to Christian instruction for the
slaves, but little mission work was undertaken by white ministers of
religion relative to the number of slaves. When Christianity spread
among Negroes in the Southern States it was largely through the
leadership of Negro preachers. The Negro Church took root under
slavery but it is significant that in this phase of its development it
should be referred to as 'the invisible institution' (Tannenbaum, 1946:
82–88; Frazier, 1964: 16–19).

CHANGES IN THE CHARACTER OF NEW WORLD SLAVERY

Closer examination reveals that the contrast between North and South
America from the seventeenth to the nineteenth centuries in respect
of the status of the Negro is less marked than Toynbee believed or than
Tannenbaum's argument would imply. The Portuguese have not been
free from 'race feeling'. What seems to be the last surviving copy of a
pamphlet published in Lisbon in 1764 was recently discovered by C. R.
Boxer (1964). It suggests strongly what other research would indicate:
namely, that while in Portugal there was at this time an enlightened
minority, for most of the contemporary population it was an article
of faith that the black man was born to serve the white. The pamphlet
is cast in the form of a dialogue, one of the parties being a slave-owner
who seems to acknowledge no moral obligation to keep the promise
he made to his slave to free him if he worked well for ten years. The
argument runs over familiar ground, such as the belief that Negroes
are descended from Cain, their peculiar blackness, the even worse
treatment they would receive elsewhere (Brazil is cited), the difficulty
of supervising slave labour, and the rights of property. The treatment
of slaves in Portugal was doubtless much better than in the overseas
territories, but there is plenty of evidence to indicate that the development of systematic racialism was not prevented by a difference of
psychological make-up.

A similar criticism can be directed against any explanation of Spanish
policies in purely humanitarian and individualistic terms. Indian slaves,
lacking immunity to measles, smallpox, and respiratory infections
introduced by Europeans, and unadapted to regular field labour, died
by hundreds of thousands. Were this process to have continued it

would have threatened the power of the Church (which was based to some extent on its missionary function) and then the very existence of the colonies. Marvin Harris concludes: 'The laws of 1542 were passed because slavery of the highland Indians was a political and economic threat to the sovereignty of the Spanish Crown in the New World. There is no other way to explain the benevolent, pious concern exhibited on behalf of the Indians in contrast to the indifference displayed toward the Negroes.' This author's examination of differences between North American and Latin American slavery leads him to the view that, contrary to the Toynbee–Tannenbaum arguments, 'what we call prejudices are merely the rationalizations which we acquire in order to prove to ourselves that the human beings whom we harm are not worthy of better treatment. . . . Negroes came to be the object of virulent prejudices because they and they alone could be enslaved' (Harris, 1964: 16–17, 68, 70).

Whatever view of non-European peoples prevailed in the metropolitan countries, their colonial policies were heavily influenced by the stage of economic development attained and by the extent to which planters or colonial interests could determine the manner in which imperial measures were actually implemented. It is important to note that sugar and cotton production, wherever carried on, required large-scale plantation organization and led to the degradation of labour. Coffee and cocoa – the crops initially favoured in much of Latin America – could be grown by the small farmer and favoured a different pattern of labour relations. But when production in these colonies became oriented to the world market, they took over chattel slavery. Eric Williams observes that in 1789 there was no greater hell on earth than Saint-Domingue (1966: 225–7). Cuban slavery had at one stage been very mild. Spain's humanitarian laws may have hindered the maturation of slave-based agricultural capitalism, but they could not prevent it. In the mid-nineteenth century, the Cuban sugar plantations dehumanized the slaves as viciously as did any other system (Mintz, 1961: 582). The exploitation of slaves in the English colonies was facilitated by a tradition of representative government which meant that slave laws would be made in the colony by the slave-owners. In the Spanish colonies, such laws were made in the mother country. But when Cuba's slave-owners became politically powerful the legal rights of slaves were so many dead letters. Though slaves were supposed to be able to maintain their own families, seek new masters, own property, and buy their freedom, the production of sugar overrode legal provisions (Harris, 1964: 76–77). Similarly, in the case of Puerto Rico, when a planter

representative was named to the central governing council of the
Spanish Empire in 1808, his first objective was to seek greater freedom
of action for the island's merchant and landed classes. New forced
labour laws drove freemen squatters onto the plantations. A series of
repressive laws was passed, increasingly limiting the slaves' legal,
social, and economic status, and provoking a parallel series of slave
revolts. Landless Creoles suffered equally (Mintz, 1961: 283–4). The
doctrines of Catholic religion could be forgotten when they were inconvenient.

The slave plantation producing some basic commodity for the mother
country was a special, emergent capitalist form of industrial organization
which appeared earlier, and with more intensity, in the colonies of the
north European powers than in the colonies of Spain. Variations in the
growth of the slave plantations are to be understood, says Mintz, as
resulting from different ecologies, differential maturation of metropolitan markets and industries, and different political relationships
between Creole governing bodies and the metropolitan authorities. The
rate of growth of the slave plantation, he is sure, did not hinge on matters
of race, civil liberties, protection of the rights of individuals, slave or
free, nor on the presence or absence of any particular religious code.
Moreover, he recalls that the south European countries and their
colonies gave up slavery later than did those of northern Europe
(Spain's Antillean colonies, Cuba and Puerto Rico, declared emancipation in 1880 and 1873 respectively). But priority in emancipation is
not an index of moral enlightenment. Much of the existing conception
of slavery in Brazil is derived from Freyre's studies of domestic slavery,
whereas on the sugar plantations and in the mines of colonial Brazil
conditions were more like those obtaining in the United States. The
most lucrative phase of the sugar plantation was over by the end of the
seventeenth century, and thereafter the expense of maintaining a slave
compared with his relatively low capital value must have stimulated
the rate of manumission. In the Northern states of America, where
slavery was unprofitable it was eliminated, despite these states' sharing
in the ethical and religious heritage stressed by Tannenbaum as a cause
of Anglo-Saxon severity (Wagley & Harris, 1958: 127–8). In the
Southern states, Negroes were forced into a more subordinate position
with the passage of time, but this – as the next section will demonstrate
– was a response to social and economic forces at work in that region.
Where slavery came to an end in conditions of labour shortage, it was
succeeded by massive importations of indentured labourers who were
treated not very differently from slaves. British Guiana and Trinidad

imported Indians; Cuba and Trinidad imported Chinese. Recently, a Dutch scholar, in the course of a broader survey of compulsory labour, has reviewed H. J. Nieboer's thesis of 1900 that the occurrence or non-occurrence of slavery depends upon the economic state of society. He concludes: 'Although ethical considerations can be seen to have played a role in the abolition of compulsory labour, this influence has been only secondary. The most important motives have always been of an economico-commercial nature' (Kloosterboer, 1960: 215).

THE LOGIC OF THE TWO-CATEGORY SYSTEM IN THE DEEP SOUTH

If, as in a society practising enslavement, some men are people and some men are property, a great variety of other institutions and patterns have to be organized to take account of, and support, this distinction. There must be a strain towards consistency among the institutions of a society, or it will disintegrate. At the same time, no society ever quite succeeds in treating men as chattels; the attempt to do so creates stresses which grow in strength as opposition becomes more extreme. In Brazil, the pattern of harsh subjugation in the mines and plantations never spread throughout the society as it was able to do in the more compact and densely settled states in the Southern region of the United States. Referring to the way in which slavery affected other institutions, Tannenbaum remarked:

'. . . slavery had a logic of its own. Wherever it existed in this hemisphere it worked its way into the social structure and modified the total society . . . so inclusive was the influence of slavery that it might be better to speak, not of a system of slavery in Brazil, Cuba, or the United States, but of the total pattern as a slave society. Slavery was not something apart from the world in which it existed. It was merely one facet of the world and cannot, in its influence, be separated from or described apart from the total community. Wherever we had slavery, we had a slave society, not merely for the blacks, but for the whites, not merely for the law, but for the family, not merely for the labor system, but for the culture – the total culture. Nothing escaped . . .' (1946: 116–17).

Slavery attained its greatest importance as a means of organizing labour on plantations. The way in which it spread from the plantation to the wider society depended on how the plantation fitted into the social, economic, and political structure. It may be helpful here to follow E. T. Thompson in comparing the plantation with the manor.

Both are relatively large landed estates, based on agricultural economies and governing numbers of people through the exercise of personal authority. Both lord and planter exercise judicial functions and tend eventually to become officials of state. But the manor sought to be independent of the state and emphasized self-sufficiency as a cultural ideal. Prince Kropotkin is quoted as writing that under the old régime in Russia 'the ambition of every landed proprietor was that everything required for his household should be made at home, by his own men'.

> '"How nicely your piano is always tuned! I suppose Herr Schimmel must be your tuner?" perhaps a visitor would remark. To be able to answer "I have my own piano-tuner," was in those times the correct thing. "What beautiful pastry," the guests would exclaim, when a work of art, composed of ices and pastry, appeared at the end of the dinner. "Confess, Prince, that it comes from Tremblé" (the fashionable pastry-cook). "It is made by my own confectioner, a pupil of Tremblé, whom I have allowed to show what he can do", was a reply which elicited general admiration' (Thompson, 1959: 29, 35).

This ideal of self-sufficiency would have appealed to the masters of the Brazilian big houses described by Freyre (1946).

The manor arises in a world which is discontinuous economically, politically, and culturally. Its guiding principle is the pursuit of diversified agriculture directed to local consumption. The plantation, on the other hand, gains strength in a world characterized by a continuous, relatively integrated, economic, political, and cultural system. It is based not upon self-sufficiency but upon the market. It needs good communications, a staple crop, and new resources to exploit. In America the plantation system took form only as particular plantations became articulated with the larger society. Control of the state was a matter of crucial importance. To bolster the power of the planters, an intermediary group was required of free persons who were persuaded that their interests lay with the planters rather than with the unfree. Authority within particular plantations could be based upon personal acquaintance, but these relations needed to be generalized and rendered more abstract in some way if the pattern of the plantations was to be repeated in the larger society. In the South this could be done by adopting race as an overriding principle of organization.

The plantation was a little society in itself: every member could know every other member not only as someone of a particular status but as an individual. Everyone had a certain interest in the economic

success of the whole. This was not the case in some of the large plantations established later, nor was it the case in the wider society of the
South. There is a close parallel with the reckoning of social status in
modern industrial societies, for, in the small community or work group
today, a man's social standing can be accurately determined because
his fellows know well his various roles and how competently he plays
them; in the city or nation at large such intimate knowledge is impossible and people tend to be lumped into general categories (especially
those based on social class) and treated as representatives of a category
rather than as individuals. This was the contrast between the plantation
as a social system and the wider system of colour-caste, with the
qualification that the distinction between slave and free was far more
fundamental than any modern class division. Extreme subordination
could not be maintained on the plantation if the slaves could easily
escape or could be instigated to disobedience by rebellious teachings
outside. But the slaves and employees could not be isolated from local
life outside the plantation. Therefore the planters – who held the
political power – were obliged to see that similar principles of racial
subordination obtained outside. The status distinctions on the plantation (which coincided with the colour line) were generalized to the
wider society where the criterion of colour did not fit so well (because
of the overlap in the worthiness of respectable free coloured people
and disreputable poor Whites). This generalization of colour as a status
sign, besides having the effect of stressing categories at the expense of
personal judgement, introduced a new element of rigidity.

Once the expectation took hold that a white complexion designated
the status of freeman and a dark complexion that of slave, a special
logic was established which, in the circumstances of the time, made it
almost inevitable that the social system would develop in particular
ways. Political power was reserved to the Whites. The planters needed
the support of the non-slaveholders (for there was a continual fear of
slave revolts) and the price of this support was the elevation of the
meanest White over the worthiest Negro. This doctrine was later stated
with precision by Jefferson Davis, the Southern leader, when, just
before the outbreak of the Civil War, he told the Senate: 'One of the
reconciling features of the existence [of Negro slavery] is the fact that
it raises white men to the same general level, that it dignifies and exalts
every white man by the presence of a lower race.' White supremacy
and solidarity became a political doctrine, sometimes overlooked in
private relations but never in public matters. Part of the price of the
support of the non-slaveholding Whites was the maintenance of the

status gap between White and Black. If the equation of status with race was to be enforced, intermediate groups who fitted in neither of the major categories were troublesome anomalies whose very existence called into question the basic assumptions of the system; therefore they could not be tolerated. Free Negroes appeared dangerous so they had to be reduced to subjugation wherever possible. Children of mixed parentage could not be accepted as intermediates, but had to be assigned to the lower category. These tendencies were already implicit in the social system but they were given much additional force by the increasing value of slaves.

In the eighteenth century, Negro slavery acquired a new and more extensive significance on the tobacco plantations of the South-eastern states. After the invention of the cotton gin in 1793 and the expansion of cotton production, there was a boom in the price of slaves as the new crop spread westwards, until people over most of the South could assent to the popular expression 'cotton is king'. The big profits from slave-breeding and slave-dealing were made in Virginia in the seventeenth century, in South Carolina in the eighteenth century, and in Alabama and Mississippi in the early nineteenth century. A 'prime field-hand' of twenty-five years was worth $500 in 1832 and, after the recession of the 1840s, more than three times this sum on the eve of the Civil War. In the 1850s in the Mississippi delta, the Louisiana bayous, the Red River and Arkansas River valleys, and the Texas prairies, fabulous profits were to be made. On the new cotton plantations a good slave might be worth $250 per annum, though in the older cotton, sugar, and rice areas of the Deep South profits were much lower (Stampp, 1956: 385).

Of the tendencies implicit in a two-category system of the Southern variety, one became apparent long before the rise in the price of slaves: this concerned the status ascribed to the children of slave women. The Maryland law of 1663, already quoted, held that 'all children born of any negro or other slave, shall be slaves as their fathers were for the term of their lives'. Stating that 'divers free-born English women, forgetful of their free condition and to the disgrace of our nation, do intermarry with negro slaves', it went on to provide that their issue should be slaves and that the women in question should serve the masters of their slave husbands during the lifetime of their husbands. This law restates the common law doctrine of *partus sequitur patrem* (the status of a child follows that of the father) in order to make slavery inheritable; according to this principle, however, the illegitimate offspring of a white freeman and a Negro slave woman would be free.

Virginia from 1662 adopted the contrary civil law principle of *partus sequitur ventrem*, and Maryland changed over in 1715 to make slavery inherited through the mother. In Jamaica the condition of slavery ceased, by express law, to attach upon the fourth degree of distance from a Negro ancestor, but in the South there was no such restriction: if *any* maternal ancestor of a man was a slave, this made him one too. These laws were intended to define the legal status of slavery, but one of their consequences was that the interracial sexual unions of white men thereafter served to reinforce the distinction between White and Negro rather than to weaken it.

A second tendency also became apparent quite early and was accelerated by the rise in the price of slaves, namely the attempted suppression of free Negroes. In seventeenth-century Virginia there were Negro slave-owners who possessed Negro slaves, and up to 1723 free persons of colour had the vote. But the South was a region of 'open resources' in which labour was more scarce than land so that employers were induced to strengthen their hold over their workers. Whites sought to help one another in discouraging runaways by checking on any unknown Negro who claimed to be free. As long as free Negroes were an acknowledged element in the population their very presence represented a threat to the planter's control over his slaves. The sign value that racial appearance had acquired was epitomized in the recognition that a fair complexion decreased the value of a slave: he or she, or a child of him or her, stood a better chance of escaping or establishing freedom before the courts (Moore, 1941: 190–1). For harbouring a runaway, any South Carolina Negro was in 1740 made liable to a very heavy fine, and failing payment he was 'to be sold at public outcry'. In Maryland in 1717 a free Negro was to be enslaved if he 'intermarry with any white woman'. It was not only serious offences against the colour-caste order that were penalized in this way. In Florida a free Negro could be reduced to slavery for the smallest debt executed against him. In Mississippi any Negro 'not having the ability to show himself entitled to freedom' could be sold into slavery by the court. The trend of *ante-bellum* legislation was to prohibit the movement of free Negroes from one state to another and to deny them the right to return as freemen if they left a state. In Virginia the law provided that any emancipated slave who remained in the state for twelve months after manumission might be 'sold by the overseers of the poor for the benefit of the literary fund', so that the former President Thomas Jefferson had in his will to 'humbly and earnestly request of the legislature of Virginia' permission for five slaves he was manumitting to remain in the state. In South Carolina and the Gulf states Negro seamen were arrested and kept in custody while their ships were in port. Many Southerners desired the complete expulsion of all free Negroes (Stampp, 1956: 210–11, 227). A similar sentiment added impetus to the schemes for sending Negroes as colonists to Liberia.

Slave-owners who had Negro concubines were often inclined to manumit their children so that the free Negro population included a high proportion of fair-skinned persons who had *sub rosa* ties with the white group. This increased the danger of their becoming established as an intermediate category. Some Southerners welcomed the idea, believing that they would ally themselves with the Whites, but the majority disagreed and, from the early eighteenth century, laws were passed to restrict manumission. No slave-owner could liberate a slave if he lacked sufficient money to pay his creditors or to provide an estate for his widow. In South Carolina, Georgia, Alabama, and Mississippi no act of manumission was valid without the specific ratification of the legislature, and the last-named state also required evidence of meritorious action on the slave's part to the benefit of his master or the state. Policy with respect to manumission nevertheless varied from state to state and from one era to another. At one time the anti-slavery movement was strong and the slave states contained a great many more anti-slavery societies than the free states did. Between 1780 and 1810 the free Negro population of Virginia increased from 3,000 to 30,000 (McColley, 1964:141). The movement reached a brilliant climax in the free and full debates over emancipation in the Virginia legislature during the session of 1831–32 when the motion for a programme of emancipation was lost by only one vote. But, in response to Northern pressure, loyalty to the South came to be defined in terms of conformity in thought about its characteristic institution, and by 1837 there was not a single anti-slavery society remaining in the whole South (Woodward, 1960: 178–9). In any event, manumission was no alternative to abolition, for it entailed only the withdrawal of rights by the master and conferred no rights of citizenship.

Further legislation systematized the Negro's subjugation. An American author who reviewed this legislation in 1856 summarized the slave's legal status in twelve propositions (Stroud, 1856: 12–13). They are worth careful consideration, for each legislative provision was dictated by the logic of the social order. It is a useful exercise to calculate what the implications might have been had any one of these propositions been reversed. They run:

'1. The master may determine the kind, and degree, and time of labour to which the slave shall be subjected.

2. The master may supply the slave with such food and clothing only, both as to quantity and quality, as he may think proper or find convenient.

3. The master may, at his discretion, inflict any punishment upon the person of his slave.

4. All the power of the master over his slave may be exercised not by himself only in person, but by any one whom he may depute as his agent.

5. Slaves have no legal rights of property in things, real or personal; but whatever they may acquire belongs, in *point of law*, to their masters.

6. The slave, being a *personal chattel*, is at all times liable to be sold absolutely, or mortgaged or leased, at the will of his master.

7. He may also be sold by process of law for the satisfaction of the debts of a living or the debts and bequests of a deceased master, at the suit of creditors or legatees.

8. A slave cannot be a party before a judicial tribunal, in any species of action against his master, no matter how atrocious may have been the injury received from him.

9. Slaves cannot redeem themselves, nor obtain a change of masters, though cruel treatment may have rendered such change necessary for their personal safety.

10. Slaves being objects of *property*, if injured by third persons, their owners may bring suit, and recover damages, for the injury.

11. Slaves can make no contract.

12. Slavery is hereditary and perpetual.'

These propositions state the relation of the master and the slave but do not touch upon the slave's position as a member of civil society or in relation to other slaves. In this latter respect the author came to seven conclusions, viz.:

'1. A slave cannot be a witness against a white person, either in a civil or criminal cause.

2. He cannot be a party to a civil suit.

3. The benefits of education are withheld from the slave.

4. The means for moral and religious instruction are not granted to the slave; on the contrary, the efforts of the humane and charitable to supply these wants are discountenanced by the law.

5. Submission is required of the slave, not to the will of his master only, but to that of all other white persons.
6. The penal codes of the slaveholding states bear much more severely upon slaves than upon white persons.
7. Trial of slaves upon criminal accusations is in most of the slave states different from that which is observed in respect to free white persons, and the difference is injurious to the slave and inconsistent with the rights of humanity.'

It was part of the record that, according to the attorney-general of Maryland, 'A slave has never maintained an action against the violator of his bed. A slave is not admonished for incontinence, or punished for fornication or adultery; never prosecuted for bigamy, or petty treason, for killing a husband being a slave, any more than admitted to an appeal for murder.'

Indeed, it is the punishment visited upon Negro offenders that best illustrates the logic of a slave system. On a Mississippi plantation, a Negro savaged an overseer almost to the point of death but was never punished. If he had been executed his master would have lost a slave as well as an overseer, and what would be the point of that? Why destroy a man's property? Some states compensated the owners of any slaves condemned to death, but not all. Special courts for the trial of Negroes – on which the slave-owners were well represented – were particularly lenient (Stampp, 1956: 222). The slave-owners were concerned not with reinforcing morality in the slave quarters but with protecting their own interests.

The question of punishment shows how enforcement of the legal definition of the slave's status could lead to results at variance with moral ideas. The need to buttress this status when threatened by outside influences is seen in legislation affecting the freedom of the press. Thus in Louisiana it was enacted that any author, printer, or publisher using language with the intent 'to diminish that respect which is commanded to free people of colour for the whites by law, or to destroy that line of distinction which the law has established between the several classes of this community' was subject to severe fines and imprisonment (Stroud, 1856: 104). Thus slavery worked its way into the total structure.

The simplicity of the legal position could be quite ruthless. It was summarized with bitter clarity by Chief Justice Ruffin from the North Carolina Supreme Court bench in 1829. He said:

'The end (of slavery) is the profit of the master, his security, and the public safety; the subject, one doomed in his own person and his posterity to live without knowledge and without the capacity to make anything of his own, and to toil that another may reap the fruits. What moral consideration shall be addressed to such a being to convince him, what it is impossible but that the most stupid must feel and know can never be true – that he is thus to labour upon the principle of natural duty, or for the sake of his own personal happiness. Such services can only be expected from one who has no will of his own, who surrenders his will in implicit obedience to that of another. Such obedience is the consequence only of uncontrolled authority over the body. There is nothing else which can operate to produce the effect. The power of the master must be absolute to render the submission of the slave perfect. I freely confess my sense of the harshness of this proposition. I feel it as deeply as any one can and as a principle of right every person in his retirement must repudiate it. But in the actual condition of things it must be so; there is no remedy. This discipline belongs to the state of slavery. It constitutes the curse of slavery both to the bond and free portion of our population' (Park, 1950: 177–9, referring to *The State* v. *Mann*, 2 *Devereux Rep.* 263, 266).

In social terms it created a situation in which a humane master's impulse to be kind to his slaves was thwarted by the inescapable problems of control. The chief justice's recognition of slavery as a curse to the free portion of the population was very apposite. For a system that inured Whites to the harsh treatment of other human beings and gave them an exaggerated sense of their own importance could not but have a harmful effect upon the masters also. A historian concludes: 'Slavery, by its nature and influence, rendered the master class unfit to live easily in a society of free men . . . the slave holder could gratify with little restraint man's "natural lust for authority": he could not endure an employee who made demands upon him, who could legally refuse to obey him, and who cherished his self respect and personal dignity' (Stampp, 1956: 398). The disproportionate power bred what has been termed 'the Prospero complex' (see pp. 310–11 below): the desire to manipulate others in terms of the Superman's conception of what would be best.

Legislative controls over the Negro reached their apogee with the Supreme Court decision of 1857 in the case of *Dred Scott* v. *Sandford*. The reasoning behind the decision was sound, but the chief justice's *obiter dicta* when delivering the judgement have become notorious. He declared that Negroes 'are not included, and were not intended to be included, under the word "citizens" in the Constitution, and can there-fore claim none of the rights and privileges which that instrument provides and serves to citizens of the United States'. Dred Scott was not a citizen of Missouri within the meaning of the Constitution of the United States, and not entitled as such to sue in its courts. The chief justice saw this judgement as confirming earlier custom according to which Negroes 'had no rights which the white man was bound to respect'. Between 1856 and 1860 seven Southern states passed laws to permit free Negroes voluntarily to enter slavery; there is no evidence that many Negroes utilized these provisions but their enactment does suggest that by this time the freedom of the free Negro may have been little greater than that of the slave (Moore, 1941: 194n).

COUNTER-CURRENTS

Some acquaintance with the legal position is of central importance to the sociological study of a system like that of slavery, but it is far from sufficient for an understanding of how social relations were actually conducted. Legal penalties were of chief relevance in the wider system of colour-caste. On the plantation they were much less effective, for the slaves had their own means of restricting output, of embarrassing over-seers in their relations with the plantation-owner, and of retaliating against their subordination. At cotton-picking time they might carry cotton from the gin house back to the field in the morning to make their day's harvest seem the greater. They would put stones among the cot-ton, damage property, work slowly, abuse the mules, and plough or hoe so as to spoil the crop. Sometimes they cultivated their own plots far better than they tended their masters' fields. One Negro, says Stampp, shammed blindness so successfully that he avoided practically all work, but after emancipation he produced eighteen good crops on his own account. Another convinced his owner that he was totally disabled by rheumatism until one day he was discovered vigorously rowing a boat (1956: 104–9). Much Negro ingenuity went into attempts to beat the system. If the owner or overseer was too benevolent it was the slaves who took advantage of him. On the white side there were contrary pressures. To be counted a true Southern gentleman a master had to be humane to his bondsmen, to exercise self-control in dealing with them, to know how to give commands without raising his voice. Slave-mongering was reprobated and the dealer was scorned. But masters wanted profits also, and frequently the troublesome or sickly slaves were sold off first (Stampp, 1956: 176, 235–6, 256).

Race relations on the smaller and middle-sized plantations, and to a certain extent even on the largest, must have been based on personal acquaintance rather than on categoric responses. In many situations, tensions must have been contained within interpersonal relationships and the slaves' discontent directed against incidental wrongs rather than against their common subordination. On the plantation, masters could afford to be indulgent towards particular slaves to an extent that would be impracticable with strange Negroes. It was this aspect of Southern life, and the privileged position of the household slaves, that was foremost in the minds of those who defended the South's 'peculiar institution'. Possibly it is this, too, that explains a strand in the legislation about slavery which was inconsistent with the account that has so far been given here. Some judges could not go along with Chief Justice Ruffin's logic, and affirmed that for certain purposes a slave must be treated as a person and not as property. Thus in an Alabama decision of 1861 it was held: 'Because they are rational *human beings*, they are capable of committing crimes; and in reference to acts which are crimes, are regarded as *persons*. Because they are *slaves*, they are . . . incapable of performing civil acts; and in reference to all such, they are *things*, not persons . . .' (quoted Moore, 1941: 198). The same state's code of 1853 described a master's obligation to be humane to his slaves and to provide them with adequate food, clothing, and care during illness and old age. As a person, the slave was more frequently charged with obligations than endowed with privileges, but he was entitled to protection from malicious injury to his life and limb. In several other forms of legislation also there can be detected an implicit ethical norm, vague though it may have been, a norm attributing value to the human individual, free or in bondage (Moore, 1941: 195–202; Sio, 1965: 299–306).

Only a minority of Southern Whites were directly involved in the system of interracial relations based upon the plantation. In 1790 slaveholders constituted only 35·3 per cent of the total free population of the South, and some of these would have owned only domestic slaves. By 1860 this figure had declined to 26·1 per cent. The total of slaves and slaveholders combined rose only to 57 per cent of the Southern population in 1790 and to 50 per cent in 1860. But the whole status and prestige system was dominated by the planter and by the image of the life of the Southern gentleman. Among slaveholders, rank was heavily influenced by the number of slaves a man possessed. Among non-slaveholders, the immediacy of a man's relationship to domination over slaves or the extent of his progress towards the goal of slaveholding were the chief considerations. Even slaves might benefit from a sort of reflected prestige stemming from the rank of their masters. The poorer non-slaveholders were effectively held in check by the dominant class's use of the colour line, for if particular Negroes under the protection of the planters were allowed to encroach upon white occupations the implications could be far-reaching. Once a few Negroes were able to establish themselves in a certain trade there was the possibility that it would become typed as a black man's occupation, and Whites would be obliged either to vacate it or to accept a role which had degrading associations. Southern Whites were continually protesting against the intrusion of free Negroes and slaves into skilled work; they were usually successful in resisting it, but the threat was kept alive and the political loyalty of the lower-class Whites reinforced (Moore & Williams, 1942). The pattern of race relations in the Southern cities of this period was in some ways quite different. Instead of a two-category pattern with considerable social distance between members of the two categories, the white and Negro categories tended to fragment into smaller interest groups, distance was reduced, an overlap in status was sometimes apparent, and more mixing occurred. Slave workers were hired out by their masters. Free Negroes were concentrated in the cities and had a disturbing effect on the slaves. Public policy was to segregate the races so that the distinction between free and slave Negroes was minimized and colour-caste became the chief principle of social relations in many situations. Slave-owners, finding how much their control both over their slaves and over the whole social order was loosened, moved their bondsmen back to the country, and urban Negro populations declined. With the influx of European immigrants before the Civil War, Negroes were driven out of some of their better occupations (Wade, 1964: 243–86). Thus, while plantation slavery was only one element in the pattern of stratification in the *ante-bellum* South, it was the critical one and influenced all other parts of that pattern, urban as well as rural. As Tannenbaum wrote: 'Wherever we had slavery, we had a slave society, not merely for the blacks, but for the whites. . . .'

It is scarcely surprising, therefore, that the slave society should also have influenced the way in which its publicists defended that society against Northern criticism. Most Southerners were reluctant to utilize the ethnological theories of polygenesis (discussed in Chapter Two) although they could be made to justify slavery by showing Negroes as an inferior species. They were uncomfortable over polygenesis because it seemed to contradict the Bible, which was much revered in the Protestant South and offered, after all, its own justification of slavery. The Southern way of life embodied gross differences of rank within the white population as well as the subordination of slaves and therefore required a more elaborate philosophy than simple racism. The ablest of the Southern apologists, George Fitzhugh, laid the foundations of such an outlook in his polemical *Cannibals All!*, where he maintained:

'We do not agree with the authors of the Declaration of Independence that Governments "derive their just powers from the consent of the governed". [None of] the women, the children, the negroes, and but few of the non-property holders were consulted, or consented to the Revolution or the governments that ensued from its success. As to these, the new governments were self-elected despotisms, and the governing class self-elected despots. Those governments originated in force, and have been continued by force. All governments must originate in force, and be continued in force. The very term, government, implies that it is carried on against the consent of the governed. Fathers do not derive their authority, as heads of families, from the consent of wife and children . . . masters dare not take the role of slaves. . . . Captains of ships are not appointed by consent of the crew . . .' (Fitzhugh, 1857: 243).

Fitzhugh did not merely defend the South; he attacked the North and claimed that, in any comparison with it, the South came out better. Holding that 'equality begets universal envy, meanness and uncharitableness – slavery elevates and purifies the sentiments of master and slave', Fitzhugh believed that the South had actually realized the most happy political, social, and economic conditions ever seen on earth. In particular, these conditions were superior to the deplorable state of affairs in the North: 'We are better husbands, better fathers, better friends, and better neighbors than our Northern brethren' (1854: 248, 289). An essential part of his thesis was the claim that 'the unrestricted exploitation of so-called free society is more oppressive to the laborer than domestic slavery'. The white slave trade of Northern industry was far more cruel than the black slave trade of the South, for the masters of wage-slaves recognized no obligations towards them. Convinced that free society had failed, Fitzhugh saw the rise of socialism as a recognition of this failure and a misguided attempt to substitute a better system. 'As modern civilization advances', he claimed, 'slavery becomes daily more necessary . . . it is impossible to place labor and capital in harmonious or friendly relations, except by the means of slavery, which identifies their interests' (1857: 30–31). Slavery and socialism are alike in their opposition to *laissez-faire* economics and their attempt to mould society in terms of independent values.

Among the critics of Southern society, one of the most effective – apart, of course, from the author of *Uncle Tom's Cabin* – was Hinton Rowan Helper, with his book *The Impending Crisis of the South* (1857). Helper was no friend of the Negro but a spokesman for the non-slave-holding Whites. These people, he said,

> 'have never yet had any part or lot in framing the laws under which they live. There is no legislation except for the benefit of slavery, and slaveholders. As a general rule, poor white persons are regarded with less esteem and attention than negroes. . . . The lords of the lash are not only absolute masters of the blacks, who are bought and sold, and driven about like so many cattle, but they are also the oracles and arbiters of all non-slaveholding whites, whose freedom is merely nominal, and whose unparalleled illiteracy and degradation is purposely and fiendishly perpetuated' (1857: 48–49).

Helper charged that 'all slaveholders are under the shield of a perpetual license to murder'. He asserted that, because of the slaveholders' commitment to plantation agriculture, the South lagged behind the North in economic growth, to the particular disadvantage of the poor Whites. He assembled a mass of new statistics from the recent census to support his point. The non-slaveholding Whites failed to rally to the views of their self-appointed champion. Despite his vehemence against the Negro, Helper was regarded as a notorious renegade and dared not return to the South. The alliance between rich and poor Whites proved stronger than he had calculated.

In considering Fitzhugh's defence of the South it is illuminating to notice how he coupled his ideas to an older tradition. Writing of a journey in which he noted the deficiencies of Northern society, Fitzhugh observes: 'We procured in New York a copy of Aristotle's "Politics and Economics". To our surprise we found that our theory of the origin of society was identical with his. . . We saw at once that the true vindication of slavery must be founded on his theory of man's social nature, as opposed to Locke's theory of the Social Contract on which latter Free Society rests for support' (1857: 12–13). It is appropriate that a discussion of slavery in the United States should have led back to the views of Aristotle, for it can scarcely be contended that Southern planters developed an authoritarian pattern of living because they believed in Aristotle's philosophy. Slavery came first; an intellectual justification was discovered afterwards. What came before slavery? What explains the differences in the development of North and South

America? The preceding discussion should make it clear that there is no simple answer and that a historical explanation is likely to be of a different character from the analyses employed in the social sciences. Historical sequences consist of unique interactions of particular forces – economic, military, psychological, etc. They cannot be isolated and compared accurately with one another to see which is the more important, because the interaction is an essential part of their nature. Therefore to assert that, say, economic factors are more important than others is to express a philosophy of history rather than to offer an explanation. Historical explanation, in the stricter sense, is limited to the elucidation of particular events by discovering and interrelating the various relevant factors. Many different sorts of things may turn out to have exercised an influence so that the historian can never disregard certain kinds of evidence from the outset. The social scientist can. His task is not to explain particular events but to solve the problems that events pose to anyone with his theoretical orientation. For the sociologist this means uncovering the logic of social relationships, which forms part of the pattern of particular sequences but has also to be studied comparatively.

A good example of how a social science perspective can contribute to the analysis of historical problems is provided by Elkins's book *Slavery*. The author shows how the historians who have written on slavery in the United States have been unable to escape from the opposition between two value standpoints: the pro-Southern outlook and the anti-slavery one. The contrasting starting-points of the two schools cause them to place differing emphases upon the various bodies of available evidence, and to make different assumptions. Kenneth Stampp, the latest and most notable anti-slavery writer, begins with the statement: 'I have been able to assume (unlike historians of a half-century ago) that innately American slaves were merely ordinary human beings, that innately Negroes are, after all, only white men with black skins, nothing more, nothing less' (1956: 8). Elkins shows that this assumption is a dangerous one to make in the study of the nineteenth-century South. He calls attention to the widespread stereotype of 'Sambo . . . docile but irresponsible, loyal but lazy, humble but chronically given to lying and stealing, his behaviour was full of infantile silliness and his talk inflated with childish exaggeration', etc. (1959: 82). This stereotype had a basis in fact, and the observation of a considerable proportion of childish, dependent Sambos profoundly influenced the Southerners' view of slavery. Stampp's assumption would deny the relevance of such data. Elkins, the social scientist, looks around for evidence of other situations in which a similar personality type has been produced. He finds it, not in traditional Africa, but among the inmates of Nazi concentration camps. The brutal Gestapo treatment of their prisoners broke down their personalities and produced a similar infantilism and even idealization of the guards. The circumstances under which Africans were sold into slavery, transported across the Atlantic, split up so that there was hardly any one with whom they might talk in their mother tongues, and subjected to the slave-owners' discipline must have had a similar effect. This argument will doubtless stimulate the re-examination of a number of questions and it has its weaknesses, not least in respect of the differences between the experiences of the United States and of Brazil, but it does bring a new dimension to the study of slavery and illustrates how the social scientist's focus of interests may differ from, but complement, the historian's.

CHAPTER SEVEN

White Supremacy in the United States

Once a society has adopted the assumptions of a two-category social order, many forces are mobilized to maintain the 'status gap' between the categories or to restore it if some development tends to upset the pattern. Slavery had a logic of its own, but it was only a special variety of the more general logic governing any social system based upon a single fundamental form of inequality. The strength of the forces supporting or reinforcing inequality once it has been institutionalized can be seen from the trend of events in the United States. Slavery was abolished, the foundations of inequality were severely shaken, yet the two-category system reasserted itself in new forms. Economic changes reduced the central significance of the plantation and the power of the planters, urbanization continued, yet, contrary to the general trend of social change, characteristic features of the old order were re-established with a new kind of harshness.

THE AFTERMATH OF SLAVERY

The Civil War began in 1861 when the Southern forces opened fire on Fort Sumter, a Federal arsenal on an island in the harbour of Charleston, South Carolina. It ended in 1865 after the surrender of the Confederate armies. When President Lincoln in 1862 issued the Emancipation Proclamation to free the slaves, he had already declared: 'My paramount object in this struggle is to save the Union, and is not either to save or destroy Slavery. If I could save the Union without freeing any slaves, I would do it.' In 1865 the thirteenth amendment to the federal Constitution was adopted, declaring, 'Neither slavery nor involuntary servitude . . . shall exist within the United States.' Three years later came the fourteenth amendment to remedy the Dred Scott decision: 'All persons born or naturalized in the United States, and subject to the jurisdiction thereof, are citizens of the United States and of the State wherein they reside. No State shall make or enforce any law which shall abridge the

privileges or immunities of citizens of the United States. . . .' In 1870
this was made more explicit by the fifteenth amendment: 'The right
of citizens of the United States to vote shall not be denied or abridged
by the United States or by any State on account of race, colour, or
previous condition of servitude.'

Table 1   U.S.A.: the states of the South[1]

States	Slave States 1861	Seceded in Civil War
DEEP SOUTH		
South Carolina	South Carolina	South Carolina
Georgia	Georgia	Georgia
Florida	Florida	Florida
Alabama	Alabama	Alabama
Arkansas	Arkansas	Arkansas
Oklahoma		
Mississippi	Mississippi	Mississippi
Louisiana	Louisiana	Louisiana
Texas	Texas	Texas
UPPER SOUTH		
Virginia	Virginia	Virginia
North Carolina	North Carolina	North Carolina
Tennessee	Tennessee	Tennessee
BORDER STATES		
Kentucky	Kentucky	
West Virginia		
Maryland	Maryland	
Delaware	Delaware	
Missouri	Missouri	
District of Columbia	District of Columbia	

[1] See map of the United States at p. 350.

Immediately after the war, eight Southern states responded to the
emancipation of the Negroes by enacting what were termed the Black
Codes, which, in devious ways, returned the Negroes to a condition
of servitude. These laws were among the factors which induced
Congress to take a more active part in the reconstruction of Southern
government. Initially, Congress had been more concerned to establish
Republican government in the South than to intervene directly in civil
affairs. Whatever may be thought of slavery, there is no doubt that
before the war there were powerful pressures upon the slaveholders
to use their slaves in the economically most advantageous manner. The
war caused a serious economic recession. The Whites lost the capital
they had invested in their slaves, they had to bear the war debts of the
Confederacy, they had lost many of their own sons and brothers, and

they had no incentive to help the Negro to establish himself as a freed man. On the other hand, the Negroes were inclined to utilize their new freedom to leave their plantations and to work in a more leisurely fashion. Gunnar Myrdal – who can speak on such questions with the authority of an economist – has listed the steps that were needed for a rational reform of the Southern economy. It is instructive to consider his statement, for it enables the reader to understand the better why it was that, in default of such a reform, the subsequent trend of events was so unfavourable to the Negro. Myrdal argues that a proper reform would have entailed the expropriation of the plantations and full monetary compensation of all persons who lost lands or slaves. (Slave-holders in the British West Indies were compensated when the British government emancipated the slaves there.) Compensation would have provided the capital needed for the development of the region, but the federal government – having shouldered a heavy war debt of its own – was ill-disposed towards such schemes. The expropriated plantations, says Myrdal, should have been used for distribution in small units to cultivators against mortgage claims on their new property, to be paid off in yearly instalments. The freed men should have been subject to close supervision, and taxation should have been instituted to meet some of the expropriation costs. The cheapness of land in America would have made land reform easier than in most countries, and a programme along these lines would have cost the nation a lot less than the policy actually followed (1944: 225–6).

Congress and President fell out over Reconstruction policies, and in 1867 Congress took charge. Subject to military rule, the Southern states had to hold new elections on the basis of Negro suffrage and to adopt new constitutions acceptable to Congress, upon which they might be readmitted to the Union. Reconstruction was supervised by Northern politicians ('carpetbaggers') and Southern Whites ('scala-wags') who co-operated with them. The latter were vilified as renegades, but many were poor Whites trying to break the power of the plantation-owners, and others were men who had long opposed slavery. The period of Reconstruction has been described in lurid terms which it never merited. Thus the author of a history of the United States, pub-lished in a standard English library, avers:

'Under the control of this ill-omened trinity of Carpet-Bagger, Scallywag, and Negro adventurer grew up a series of Governments the like of which the sun has hardly looked upon before or since. The Negro is hardly to be blamed for his share in the ghastly business . . .

Governments presided over by Negroes, or white courtiers of the
Negro, and defended by the bayonets of an armed black militia,
gave no protection to the persons or property of the whites' (Chesterton, 1919: 244–5).

In fact, there was no 'black domination' or 'black terror'. None of the
Reconstruction governments was Negro-controlled, and their political
corruption was not particularly striking when compared with that of
contemporary New York. Political privileges which the agricultural
labourers of England did not obtain until 1885 were, in Reconstruction,
thrust upon almost a million Negro men. At the same time, one hundred
thousand white men were disfranchised and an additional like number
(including many of the most able) were both disfranchised and dis-
qualified from holding office. It was not surprising that such a situation
should have produced weak and venal governments. It is nevertheless
important to recognize that a myth of the horrors of the Reconstruction has been perpetuated. For Southerners, this myth serves a
ritual defensive function justifying the illegal violence employed
by the Whites to re-establish their control. Northerners have
been inclined to accept this version of the period's history because
it enables them to make up to their Southern fellow citizens and thus
to heal some of the wounds of the Civil War (Myrdal, 1944: 446–8,
1314–16).
    There is a tendency to see the post-Reconstruction pattern of race
relations as simply a reassertion of traditional Southern norms on a
somewhat milder basis, constituting a stage in the steady improvement
of the Negro's position from the beginning of the nineteenth century
to the present day. This idea is fundamentally misleading: first, in its
contrast of North and South prior to 1867; second, in its neglect of the
way in which race relations deteriorated towards the end of the century
and its failure to explain the factors underlying the change. On the first
count it should be noted that there has never, in modern American
history, been a period when Negro voters have been totally absent
from the polls. At the time the Constitution was drawn up, free Negroes
had the vote in all the original states except South Carolina and Georgia,
whereas even by 1861 they could not vote in several of the states of the
North-east. Slavery had been recognized in the North. There were
'Jim Crow' cars for Negroes on three Massachusetts railroads as late
as 1843; in parts of the North, schools were segregated and laws against
intermarriage were on the statute books; whereas in 1831 (as has been
mentioned) the Virginia legislature nearly approved a motion for the

gradual emancipation of the slaves (Woodward, 1957: xiii–xiv; Myrdal, 1944; 429).

The Southern Whites responded powerfully to Reconstruction. The last of the seceded states returned to the Union in 1870, but before then the reaction had begun. The Ku Klux Klan and similar secret societies took the law into their own hands. They flogged, intimidated, and murdered Negroes for offences real, trivial, or imagined. Negroes were kept from the polls. By 1876 the Southern Democrats had regained control over their state governments and Reconstruction was at an end. The leading historian of the period, discussing 'the Redemption' or 'the Compromise of 1876', says:

'The phase that began in 1877 was inaugurated by the withdrawal of federal troops from the South, the abandonment of the Negro as a ward of the nation, the giving up of the attempt to guarantee the freedman his civil and political equality, and the acquiescence of the rest of the country in the South's demand that the whole problem be left to the disposition of the dominant Southern white people' (Woodward, 1957: 6).

But, remarkable though it sounds, the decade of the 1880s was a time when Whites and Negroes in the South mixed together harmoniously on terms of equality. A series of visitors contrasted the position very favourably with that obtaining in the North. For example, a Negro journalist who returned to his native South Carolina on a race relations muck-raking expedition returned an astonished man. He watched a Negro policeman arrest a white man 'under circumstances requiring coolness, prompt decision, and courage'. Testimony about mixing in restaurants, places of entertainment, and cemeteries was reported even from Mississippi (Woodward, 1957: 17–24).

The second count against the idea of Reconstruction as a mere interruption of Southern ways is that it stresses customary behaviour and overlooks the extent to which changes in race relations were the outcome of a struggle for power in which the Negro lost all the important encounters. The milestones in this sequence are the Supreme Court decisions which deprived the Negroes of the rights they had secured under the fourteenth amendment: notably, the 1873 judgement in the *Slaughter House Cases*, which curtailed the privileges recognized as being under federal protection; the 1883 declaration that the Civil Rights Bill of 1875 was unconstitutional; and the 1896 affirmation in the vital case *Plessy* v. *Ferguson*. This case determined the constitutionality of the Louisiana Act of 1890 providing for separate railway carriages for

White and Coloured. Plessy petitioned that he was seven-eighths Caucasian and one-eighth African blood; that the mixture of coloured blood was not discernible in him, and that, possessed of the rights of a United States citizen, he had lawfully occupied a vacant seat in a white car until forcibly removed. The court recognized that the conductor, in assigning passengers to coaches, acted at his peril, for someone wrongly assigned had a remedy at law. It rejected any argument that the enforced separation of races stamped the coloured man with a badge of inferiority or that equal rights could be secured by an enforced commingling. This was the crucial decision, upholding the 'separate but equal' provisions and denying that they were 'unreasonable'. After the compromise of 1876 Northern liberals abated their criticism of the South, so that Woodward can comment: 'The court, like the liberals, was engaged in a bit of reconciliation – reconciliation between federal and state jurisdiction, as well as between North and South, reconciliation also achieved at the Negro's expense.' Soon afterwards, the federal government plunged into imperialistic adventures in the Pacific and Caribbean, which suddenly brought under its jurisdiction another 8 million coloured people. As America shouldered the White Man's Burden, she at the same time took up many Southern attitudes on the subject of race (Woodward, 1957: 53–56). This tendency was quite marked, for example, in the response of Northern Protestants. Though there were many individual exceptions, the denominations gradually moved towards an acceptance of Southern practices, until eleven o'clock on Sunday morning became the most segregated hour in American life (Reimers, 1965: 51–83).

The Redemption of 1876 was achieved under the leadership of the Southern upper-class Conservatives who were able to establish the relatively harmonious race relations of the 1880s in public contacts. Lower-class white attitudes were much less favourable. Before the decade was out, the Conservatives were losing their grip over Southern politics and the storm of discontent aroused by agrarian impoverishment expressed itself in a new political movement: Populism. Initially the Populist white farmers espoused the cause of the Negroes. Their leader, Tom Watson, told the two races: 'You are made to hate each other because upon that hatred is rested the keystone of the arch of financial despotism which enslaves you both.' For a time, Negroes and Southern poor Whites knew a degree of fellowship. But the Conservatives were willing to use any weapons to defeat their new opponents. They made common cause with the Negro-haters. They bought Negro votes or, in the Negro sections, recorded Negro voters as polling on their side whether or not these voters went near the polls. In the Georgia election of 1894 Tom Watson was defeated by brazen fraud in the urban part of the constituency, where his opponent was given a majority of 13,780 though the total possible poll was 11,240! Because the Negro was used by the bosses of the Democratic party to defeat the reformers, Watson in 1904 supported Negro disfranchisement in order that the Whites should be able to divide on the political issues; in this way a reform candidate got to the governor's chair (Woodward, 1938: 220, 270, 370–1). Though there were occasional gains of this kind, the Populist movement was thwarted by unscrupulous machine politicians and the support of the rural counties won for a policy of white supremacy with the Negro as a scapegoat: conflicting class interests were reconciled at the Negro's expense. The disfranchisement of the Negro prevented either party from ever going back on the agreement and seeking Negro votes in support of its own policies. Henry W. Grady, the Georgian prophet of a 'New South', had said: 'The whites understand that the slightest division on their part will revive those desperate days (of Reconstruction). . . . So that the whites have agreed everywhere to sink their differences on moral and economic issues, and present solid and unbroken ranks to this alien and dangerous element' (quoted Myrdal, 1944: 453–4).

There have always been political divisions within the South that could not be fought out within a cramped one-party framework. There is justification for W. E. B. DuBois's statement that 'the white primary system in the South is simply a system which compels the white man to disenfranchise himself in order to take the vote away from the Negro'. The suppression of political divisions within the ruling group tended in the South, as elsewhere, to favour right-wing ideologies and to put restraints upon reform movements of all kinds. Any reformer was apt to find that because he opposed the existing order on one point he was suspected of opposing it on all others, and that people wondered whether he was not an atheist, communist, and labour organizer to boot.

The new alliance set about reinforcing white supremacy by a multitude of tricks which entrenched a pattern of illegality deep in Southern politics and public morals. Negro disfranchisement was achieved by limiting the vote to people who could, *to the satisfaction of the local registrar*, prove that they could 'understand' the Constitution, or were of 'good character', or qualified under the 'grandfather clause' which restricted polling to those persons who had voted prior to 1867 and to their descendants (this last clause, first introduced by Louisiana in

1898, was declared unconstitutional in 1915, but once the Negroes had been removed from the voting register informal pressures were enough to keep them off). In Louisiana in 1896 there were 130,334 registered Negro voters; in 1904 there were 1,342.

Under the slavery régime, individual Whites had been allowed to exploit individual Negroes in any way they wished provided it did not threaten the social system. In the Deep South, most of the slaves spent practically all their time on the plantations of their owners, and had few contacts with the mass of the white population. Yet a historian of Mississippi observes of the new era following upon slavery that, by 1890:

> 'In all of the daily contacts of life, the Negro had come to recognize and comply with a code that was stronger than the law, stronger than the Slave Code of 1857 or the Black Code of 1865 . . . this new code . . . established a ritual of behaviour for the Negro in his relations with the white man. It marked the completion of the transition from slavery to caste as a method of social control' (Wharton, 1947: 216, 274).

In seeking to legitimize itself the new system appealed rather less to power and custom and more to the ideology of social distance and racial difference, which was progressively elaborated. Whites might continue to exploit Negroes provided they did not threaten the system, but it was a new system, and previously permissible action on the part of Whites might now be more dangerous. It was in this context that disapproval of miscegenation and of senseless violence against Negroes began to grow. As Harris observes: 'In general, when human beings have the power, the opportunity and the need, they will mate with members of the opposite sex regardless of colour. . . . Whenever free breeding in a human population is restricted, it is because a larger system of social relations is menaced by such freedom' (1964: 68–69). This issue draws attention to a problem of central importance in theories of society. It may be in the collective interest of members of a group to behave in one way (as by showing restraint towards subordinates) but to the advantage of individual members to behave otherwise (as by using subordinates as objects of their passions). How is collective interest comprehended? By what mechanisms may a group prevent individuals from infringing collective interests? A sociological analysis in these terms of Southern white behaviour and policy since Reconstruction has still to be undertaken. In general, it would seem that white policies have been framed so as to extract maximum collective short-run advantage out of changing circumstances and that this has created tensions between different interest groups within the white social category which have not benefited equally from these policies. Such an interpretation, however, necessitates qualification. The pattern of countervailing checks and balances characteristic of community relations is distorted where there are cleavages and one category of people cannot adequately press its claims. When this happens, those who gain most immediately from their rivals' weakness (in this case the Southern poor Whites) acquire a strategically advantageous position. They press their short-term sectional interests at the expense of the long-run interests of their social category, and, indeed, of the whole regional society.

This process is evident in that the Southern Conservatives, having purchased the support of the lower-class rural Whites, were now prisoners of their own policies. The Jim Crow laws bore most heavily upon the better educated and more responsible Negroes. This suited the poor Whites, who were most opposed to any Negroes whose accomplishments refuted the idea of a natural status gap. It did not suit the upper-class Whites, who feared nothing from the Negro but were alarmed by the way in which some poorer members of their own racial group were prepared to use their power. They thought it only just to deny the suffrage to uneducated Whites as well as to Negroes, but the political difficulties were considerable. Most of these men must have found the demands for solidarity on racial lines too imperious to be opposed.

The history of these times is reflected in the controversy surrounding a man recognized as the Negroes' national leader: Booker Taliaferro Washington (c. 1859–1915), author of the best-selling *Up from Slavery* (1901), who was born a slave and rose to be one of the most influential men of the South. 'Booker T.' attracted attention as principal of the Tuskegee Institute in Alabama, a Negro school which concentrated upon teaching its pupils industrial skills. In 1895 he gave an address at a gathering of national importance, the Atlanta Cotton States and International Exposition, and his statement became known as 'the Atlanta Compromise', 'a platform on which blacks and whites can stand with full justice to each other'. In it he advised the Whites that were they to help and encourage Negro effort they would be 'surrounded by the most patient, faithful, law-abiding, and unresentful people that the world has seen. . . . In all things that are purely social we can be as separate as the fingers, yet one as the hand in all things essential to mutual progress.' When Washington became a Negro national leader, a policy of intransigence would have been useless: the times demanded a fox rather than a lion. Washington's puritan regard for the virtue of industry and thrift made him acceptable to the merchant princes of his day, who responded with funds for Tuskegee and Negro causes. He assured Southern industrialists 'that you are in debt to the black man for furnishing you with labour that is almost a stranger to strikes' and condemned trade unionism. Other Negro leaders, who sympathized with the difficulties of anyone in Washington's position, became increasingly anxious as white support enabled the 'Tuskegee machine' to dominate Negro affairs. The virtues of alternative policies could not be properly discussed. Opposition came into the open in 1903 when, in *The Souls of Black Folk,* W. E. Burghardt DuBois, a Negro Harvard graduate, maintained, without venom or rancour, that Washington's programme was 'becoming a gospel of Work and Money to such an extent as apparently almost completely to overshadow the higher aims of life'. This programme of submission practically accepted the alleged inferiority of the Negro and took from him 'that manly self-respect [which] is worth more than lands and houses'. The results of Washington's conciliation had been: '1. The disfranchisement of the Negro. 2. The legal creation of a distinct status of civil inferiority for the Negro. 3. The steady withdrawal of aid from institutions for the higher training of the Negro.' DuBois favoured the training of a 'talented tenth' who could lead their race to better things, and stressed the obligation to protest when justice was left undone.

There is room for dispute as to the factors underlying the growing hostility of the Whites. Lynchings in the South increased rapidly from 1882 up to 1890, and showed a further sharp rise in the early nineties when the white South began to legislate the subordination of the Negro; the downward trend thereafter coincided with the growing tendency on his part to accept, at least outwardly, the status forced upon him (Frazier, 1949: 159–62). The more defenceless the Negro became, the more he was subjected to the ruthless aggression of white mobs. The ultra-conservative ex-Governor Oakes told the Alabama constitutional convention of 1901 that he was shocked at the change in public opinion: 'Now, when the Negro is doing no harm, why, the people want to kill him and wipe him from the face of the earth!' Others wrote in 1903 that 'there is more hatred of whites for blacks than ever before' that 'the races are wider apart than in 1865', and that 'the rights of the Negroes are at a lower ebb than at any time during the thirty-five years of their freedom, and the race prejudice more intense and uncompromising'. Negroes had less incentive to work hard than ever before. Under slavery, as DuBois acknowledged, the two races sometimes 'lived in the same house, shared in the family life, often attended the same church, and talked and conversed with each other', whereas under the new system they were sundered from each other. Crowding into the slums, the Negro population of Southern urban communities increased 32 per cent between 1890 and 1900 and 36 per cent in the following decade. The proportion of crimes for which Negroes were imprisoned rose even faster. As the walls went up between the races, so the Negroes built on their side a copy of white society, its schools, banks, theatres, professions, and so on. Beginning as a largely undifferentiated mass of former slaves, Negro society soon developed all the social and economic classes of the white capitalistic society upon which it was modelled (Woodward, 1951: 350–60; 1957: 70–72, 80–81).

The edifice of white supremacy was virtually completed by 1906. Did the white Southerners behind their legislative ramparts now enjoy the social security they had sought to obtain by this policy? The evidence indicates that matters were in some respects worse than ever before. This was the time when Ray Stannard Baker began the travels and inquiries that, in 1908, were published under the title *Following the Color Line*. The author displayed a particular interest in problems of lawlessness and violence. From his study it clearly emerges that, while Negroes were sometimes responsible for violent crimes, the riots injured the responsible elements in the Negro community more than others, and that, though lynch mobs were ostensibly concerned with the maintenance of order, in fact they were a major threat to it. Once the mob found that they could break the law to kill one Negro they were disposed to kill others when there was less cause to think the accused guilty of a culpable offence (Baker, 1908: 22, 197–8, 215). Lynching never prevented further crime, but it was important to the Whites as a sanction reinforcing all sorts of everyday exploitation and intimidation.

Another lesson of legislated segregation in the Southern states (equally evident in South Africa, too) is that the walls between the races are never so high or so thick that people cannot find nooks and crannies that they think should be filled. Some smaller Southern towns excluded Negro residents completely; others confined them to particular quarters. In 1909 Mobile passed a curfew law applying exclusively to Negroes and requiring them to be off the streets by 10 p.m. In 1930 Birmingham legislated to prevent Whites and Negroes playing at dominoes or checkers together. In 1935 Oklahoma separated the races while fishing or boating. Such tendencies, once established, do not readily collapse because of any lack of public support; on the contrary, the ideas of superordination and segregation become ever more deeply rooted in the value system of the dominant group. What stops this vicious circle is a change in the balance of social power. World War I and the northern migration it stimulated brought Negroes new hopes and greater power. Some twenty-five race riots erupted in American cities during the last six months of 1919. Mobs took over whole cities for days at a time. Even Negroes in the uniform of the country's armed forces were lynched. Nevertheless, the Negro community made important gains. World War II and the continuing shift in the distribution and economic status of the Negro community brought further major challenges to the prevailing order: these changes laid the foundations for the more radical movements of recent years (Woodward, 1957: 86–87, 100, 104).

A SYSTEM OF COLOUR-CASTE?

The new pattern of interracial relations was obviously different from that either of slavery or of social equality. What was it to be called? Even before the Civil War there was a tendency to refer to racial separation as exemplifying caste, and many writers have followed this usage. Their practice has been vehemently criticized by both Indologists and Negro American sociologists, who characterize the Hindu caste system as a stable system in which social distinctions are validated by religious beliefs and are accepted by all members of the society.

On the one hand, it is urged that the caste system is not a simple societal trait that may be universalized by cross-cultural comparison, but that it constitutes the social and institutional structure of a distinct pattern of culture. The essence of the caste system is a hierarchy of groups based upon the principle of inequality; it is not a two-category system (Cox, 1948, 1961; Dumont, 1961: 30). From this standpoint it is necessary to decide first of all whether the case for analysis is one of 'race relations' or 'caste relations' and to examine it accordingly. On the other hand, it is said by those who think the use of 'caste' appropriate that the White Southerner in the United States believes the Negro to be happy in his place and may quote science and Scripture as justifying the system. He does not subscribe to Myrdal's conception of American culture as based upon a belief in equality. The critic of the Indologist's view goes further to maintain that Hindu caste operates in practice in a fashion different from that which a scholarly analysis of the documents would imply. He stresses that the idea of caste traditional in academic circles does not account for 'the recurrent grass-roots attempts, long endemic in India, to raise caste status; for the state of mind which has often led to low-caste defections from Hinduism when the opportunity to do so without fear of major reprisals has presented itself; nor for the chronic resentment and tension which characterizes inter-caste relations' (Berreman, 1960: 124). This approach does not claim to constitute a method for analysing caste as a system, but it offers a means of analysing intergroup relations where the subdivisions are based on hereditary membership, are endogamous, and are hierarchically related.

The term 'caste' has been employed to describe the social system in the South by W. Lloyd Warner, who refers to this system as exemplifying 'colour-caste'. The addition of the adjective indicates that his use of the word caste is not intended to imply an identity between the two systems. He writes:

'Our attention was brought to this complex problem in the state of Mississippi in the Deep South where in some respects certain Negroes out ranked many whites or, to state the obverse, certain whites were, for given purposes, inferior to many Negroes, despite the fact that colour caste operates strongly and is backed by very severe sanctions. Further inspection and analysis of this problem led us to the conclusion that, while all Negroes are socially inferior and categorically subordinate to all whites in colour caste, many of them are superior and superordinate by social class position to many, if not most, whites' (Warner, 1952: 17).

Within the two colour-castes, class differences were found. Relations between members of the same colour-caste were conducted on a basis of class position. Relations between members of different colour-castes were conducted on a basis of caste position when they touched upon sexual relations and certain other sensitive areas, but might follow class norms when it was economic relationships that were in question.

Myrdal used the concept of caste to stress the rigidity of the line between Whites and Negroes in the United States (the 'status gap') and did not use the term for comparative analysis; nevertheless, he doubted whether the Hindu system had the stable equilibrium that American sociologists sometimes attributed to it, and thought that caste – with its socially static connotation – was a less dangerous and inaccurate term than race – with its biologically static connotation. Myrdal believed the United States caste system to be 'fundamentally a system of disabilities forced by the whites upon the Negroes'. He saw caste as the extreme case of absolutely rigid class, preventing movement between the groups (1944: 667–76, 1375).

It would seem, therefore, that the term caste may reasonably be used in the analysis of social systems other than the Hindu one. Caution is necessary, but then caution is needed in any comparison of interracial social patterns.

THE COLOUR LINE

To express the difference between distinctions based on class and distinctions based on colour-caste as they were revealed in a study of Natchez, Mississippi, in the late 1930s, Lloyd Warner presented a diagram, which is reproduced as *Figure 9*. The diagonal lines A–B

Figure 9 Warner's representation of colour-caste

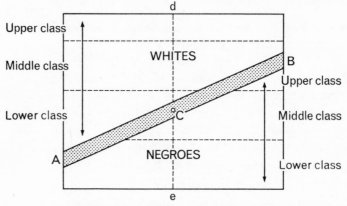

Source: Davis, Gardner & Gardner (1941).
This kind of diagram represents the relative positions
of racial and class categories, not their relative size.

incorporate the status gap and divide the Whites from the Negroes. The two double-headed vertical arrows indicate that movement up and down the class ladders within each caste can and does take place, but that there is no movement across what Warner calls the caste line but which here will be termed the colour line (to minimize any confusion that might be caused by excessive reliance upon analogies with the Hindu system). Warner refers to the diagonal slant of the colour line, saying that this expresses the essential skewness created by the conflict of caste and class in the South. At the end of the Civil War it was almost horizontal, but since then a Negro class system has evolved which has pushed the line round its axis (C) so that the top Negro group is higher in class traits than the lower white group and is so recognized. If this process continues, he says, the line might move round to the vertical (d–e) which would be a system of combined equality and separation; theoretically, it could even move farther round towards the other diagonal. At the time of writing the skewness appeared well established, but it imposed strains on certain groups, such as the upper-class Negroes; it seemed possible that some of the emotional instability of persons in this group might be attributed to the conflicts between their class and caste roles (Davis, Gardner & Gardner, 1941: 10–13; Warner, 1952: 17–19).

Warner's method of conceptualizing relations in a two-category social system of racial dominance is of considerable interest and merits a more systematic analysis than he attempts. Three features of the diagram draw attention to important characteristics of such social systems: namely, the sharpness of the line A–B as a boundary, its angle, and the framework within which it is placed. These will be considered in turn.

In a two-category social system, everyone belongs on either one side or the other of the line, and for many purposes it does not matter how near to or far from the line a person is, because everyone on the same side is treated in similar fashion. There is one sharp line, not a blurred intermediate zone in which one category shades into another. Illustrations of this principle can be found in the description of Southern communities that follows later in this chapter, but a critical test of the chief idea can be obtained by examining the placement of persons who are anomalous in respect of racial signs. The previous chapter has shown that Southern society would not recognize free Negroes as an intermediate category. They were free of exploitation within the plantation system, but in the wider system of colour-caste the roles they had to play were the Negro roles; within this system little distinction was made between the subordination of free and unfree Negroes. A person with any known measure of Negro descent was socially a Negro. Children of white fathers and Negro mothers might receive favours on the plantation, but in the wider system they were as much Negroes as men and women of the darkest complexion. Indeed, Whites were on the watch lest free Negroes or fair-skinned Negroes might claim favoured treatment as of right, and were more inclined to punish any presumption on their part. (It will be remembered that the appellant in the *Plessy* case said that the mixture of coloured blood was not discernible in him.) Sometimes, however, the Whites were presented with a potentially intermediate group established in the locality by prior settlement (as with the Indians) or by immigration (as with the Chinese in Mississippi, see Cox, 1948: 349n, 365n). In Mississippi the Indians have been entitled to sit in the front of the bus, to go to white schools, and to use white waiting-rooms, lavatories, and water fountains. Though they have

suffered some racial discrimination, socially they have been counted as
Whites. Why ? Presumably it was more appropriate to class them with
Whites than with Negroes and there was no third alternative. The
author is ignorant of the historical circumstances surrounding the incorporation of Indians into colour-caste systems, but probably the main
factor was that, though the Indians were regarded as inferior, they were
not slaves on the same scale as were Negroes. Why they were counted as
Whites instead of being ascribed to a special third category can
be worked out on general principles. To build a third set of schools,
waiting-rooms, etc., would be expensive and might make the whole
system of distinctions seem less logical, but a more important aspect is
that of power relations. In a two-category system the upper category
must display solidarity if it is to remain on top. The upper members of
the superordinate category need the support of the lower members of it.
These last are concerned to keep themselves above the upper members
of the lower category and they oblige the upper members of their category to help them to maintain their position. If there were three categories, there would be a continual danger of two categories' forming a
coalition against the third and changing the character of the system.
Whereas all members of the top category would have a common interest
in maintaining the status gap between themselves and the second category, it would be difficult to arrange things so that they had an equal
interest in maintaining the status gap between the second and third
categories.

The need to keep the line distinct may perhaps explain the venom
with which members of the upper category often regard anomalous
persons. People who fit in no category upset any simple unreasoning
view of social distinctions. The writer J. H. Griffin reported that, when
it became known in his part of Texas that he had blacked his skin and
passed as a Negro in other Southern states, local feeling towards him
and his family was so hostile that they had to leave the state. His action
was a reminder that the social distinctions between races in the South
are conventional, not a straightforward product of natural distinctions.
Such reminders can be unwelcome. A two-category system of this kind
cannot function easily unless it is possible to assign individuals to one
or other category at sight, on the basis either of outward appearance,
or, in a very small community, of personal knowledge. It would be
possible for all persons who appeared to have any white ancestry to be
treated as white within this kind of system, but only provided that they
stopped associating with other coloured people and behaved in every
way as Whites. People who might otherwise have been thought inter-

mediate must be allocated unequivocally to one or the other category; among any people, and especially among those who inherit little property from their parents, it is more difficult to divide a person socially from his mother than from his father, so it is not surprising that the children of a white male and a Negro female in the South follow the condition of the mother. Cases of children of white mothers and Negro fathers pose a more difficult problem because the baby is a sign of the mother's transgression, lowering the status of the woman, and her kin and associates. Such a woman must be forced to leave the community or to place the child elsewhere, or, if she refuses to do either of these, to become herself socially a Negro.

The basic racial roles above and below the colour line have an obligatory character. Whites must behave like Whites: if they act so as to reduce white prestige or to weaken the system, they are subject to sanctions. Negroes are obliged to assume Negro roles whether they like them or not. To maintain such forms of institutionalized inequality it is necessary to develop some ceremonial expression of superordination and subordination which is regularly re-enacted. In the army, a salute expresses deference. In societies in which one group holds supremacy, a whole etiquette of deference is imposed on members of the lower group. Every salute, every 'yes massa', is an acknowledgement of subordination, and a failure to pay formal respect is a symbolic rejection of a basic role and must be punished accordingly. The salute itself is nothing, but if the organization is to function satisfactorily it must each and every day impress upon the participants its definition of their roles. The more the social hierarchy is out of line with the objective distribution of talent, the more firmly the ceremonial must be enforced. The salute is then everything. It is by such forms of interpersonal control that the status gap is maintained in daily life.

In the South (at least up to World War II and in the rural areas for two decades after it) the pattern of interracial etiquette limited serious conversations to shared business interests. Talk of politics or of the struggle for existence, other than in a context of Negro subordination, was frowned upon. The Negro was expected to address the white person as 'Mr', 'Mrs', or 'Miss', or perhaps by a title such as 'Cap'n' or 'Judge' even though the White was not entitled to it. The white man would address the Negro by his first name, even if they hardly knew one another, or by an epithet such as 'boy' or 'uncle'. The Negro was expected to be humble and self-deprecatory in his demeanour; if he addressed an ordinary white man in correct 'college' English this was tantamount to an insult, for it constituted a claim to equality or superiority (Cox, 1948: 366). A Negro was not allowed to contradict a white man and was expected to give way to him, even when driving an automobile (Powdermaker, 1939: 49; Myrdal, 1944: 1368; Johnson, 1943: 125). When visiting a white house he was supposed to stand, hat in hand, at the back door. A white person might return a greeting from a Negro but would never touch his hat, and hardly ever shake hands; he was supposed to speak in a condescending manner, but if he got angry, the Negro could not reply in like kind (on etiquette, see Johnson, 1943: 117–38; Myrdal, 1944: 610–12; Doyle, 1937).

These forms of deference were observed across the colour line; a Negro employer could not demand them of a Negro employee and to this extent was at a disadvantage (Powdermaker, 1939: 127). Yet they could be exploited by Negroes to their own advantage. There is a famous story in Richard Wright's *Black Boy* of how a Negro lift attendant would allow Whites to insult and kick him in return for a generous tip. Lower-class Negroes were – probably still are – expert at managing white people through their vanity. The 'Sambo' or 'Rastus' type of Negro takes off his hat, grins, and touches the boss for half-a-dollar, as a reward for submissiveness. It was an odd thing, thought Dollard, but Southern Whites often seemed to be completely taken in by such behaviour. For the Negro to maintain a continuous affirmation of the white man's wishes and ideas was very flattering and white people got so accustomed to it that they felt in some way deprived if it was withdrawn (Dollard, 1937: 179–80, 302–3). Negroes, on the other hand, might be unwilling to pay more deference than was strictly necessary and in practice there was an important element of flexibility. The use of one of the traditional forms of deference might cause a White to define the situation quite differently. This is evident from a story related by St Clair Drake, bearing upon the conflict of class and colour-caste symbols:

'A Negro was driving through the Deep South; his car went dead in a small town late one afternoon. The white constable came up and said: "Boy, why you stoppin' traffic? You better get a move on; no niggers allowed in this town at night." The Negro replied, "My motor died; I'm having trouble getting it started again." At this point the constable noticed some books in the back seat, and asked: "You a communist or agitator?" "No." "Preacher?" "No." "Teacher?" "Yes, a college teacher." Then the constable said: "Boy, I ain't heard you say 'sir' to me yet." The Negro replied: "Well, sir, I'm just trying to get my car started so I can move on."

At that point the constable hollered to two Negroes sitting on the curb in front of a gas station: "Hey, you niggers, come help this coloured gentleman get his car started!"' (quoted Kahl, 1957: 246–7).

Technological changes reduce the personal element in many contacts and restrict the utilization of controls based upon patterns of deference. In a telephone conversation, the colour of a person's skin is not visible. Many urban dwellings have no back doors. When driving at a normal speed all motor vehicles must obey a single code; it is simply impossible to follow a code of social precedence on the highway without a great loss of efficiency.

To keep the colour line distinct everyone must belong on one side of it or the other. Permanent exceptions or anomalies cannot be tolerated, but temporary ones may be permitted if they do not threaten the long-term working of the system. Negroes who live in the local community cannot be allowed to deny the roles accorded to them but visiting coloured persons can be given a tacit exemption from the requirements of caste. James Weldon Johnson, the Negro writer, described in his autobiography *Along this Way* how, when a boy, he was travelling in Florida in a first-class rail car with a Spanish-speaking companion. The conductor of the train doubted Johnson's right to be in the car. The other boy asked, 'Que dici?'; then, 'as soon as the conductor heard us speaking in a foreign language, his attitude changed; he punched our tickets and gave them back, and treated us just as he did other passengers in the car' (Johnson, 1933: 34). Booker T. Washington similarly relates how a dark-skinned Indian boy accompanying him was served when he was not. He tells of an occasion when the presence of a coloured man in a hotel caused great indignation; later it transpired that he was a Morroccan: 'as soon as it was learned that he was not an American Negro, all the signs of indignation disappeared' (1901: 131). Negroes in America have found that if they bind a scarf round their heads turban-fashion, wear African costume, or even sometimes just behave confidently and differently they are exempted from the norms of colour-caste (though African diplomats in ordinary dress have often suffered discrimination – much to the distress of the United States State Department). Such exemptions permit the two-category system to deal with cases that might otherwise be embarrassing and are a sign of the strength and flexibility of the system, not of any weakness or inconsistency.

A second property of Warner's diagram is the angle of the colour line. This line affects not only relations between the groups, but also relations within each group. Many writers have noted the harmful effects of slaveholding upon the masters. Initially, there are usually different interest groups within the upper category, but, as has been shown in the case of the South, these groups come to feel that white solidarity is an overriding priority and they suppress such divisions. The upper members of the upper category, in return for the political support of the lower members of that category, defend their interests against those of the upper members of the lower category. A racist South must be a 'solid South'. The upper members of the upper category are therefore prisoners of the system like everyone else. It was this phenomenon that underlay Myrdal's observation: 'The colour line has taken on a mystical significance: sophisticated Southern Whites, for example, will often speak with compassionate regret of the sacrifices the Negroes "have to" make and the discriminations to which the Negroes "have to" submit – "have to" in order to preserve the colour line as an end in itself' (1944: 677). As the forces tending to fill the status gap grow stronger, so must more energetic attempts be made to preserve it. Control over the lower category has to stretch to more and more sectors of social life. The gap between the categories in respect of political rights is transferred to new spheres so that the initial differences are overlaid by others, reinforcing colour-caste as a principle and at the same time confusing the source of inequality. These tendencies are increased by the action of many members of the lower category who deflect their energies to the construction of an independent parallel structure under their leadership; contacts across the colour line tend to be depersonalized and communication is impaired. Members of each category hold false beliefs about members of the other, and the forces of sexual attraction and repression add their quota to the tendencies making for separation. A vicious circle is set up: discrimination depresses the standards of members of the lower group in respect of health, education, manners, and morals; this then seems to justify the discrimination. Once they have been built into the social order, social distance and mutual resentment between the groups will grow until there is either interference from outside or a revolt within.

From the analysis so far offered it is impossible to understand why, in Mississippi, the colour line should have tilted to any extent at all. Warner noted that it had moved round, regarding this as a historical process outside the realm of sociological analysis. He did not inquire into the structural conditions necessary for tilting to be possible. This question belongs not with an examination of the angle of the line at any particular moment of time, but with a third property of the diagram, its framework. Warner stated that while all Negroes were socially inferior and categorically subordinate to all Whites in colour-caste, a growing number were superordinate by social-class criteria to many, if not most, Whites. At times, white men had to decide whether to interpret their relations to a Negro in caste terms and treat him as a subordinate, or in class terms and treat him as a social superior. Close study of the book reveals that the circumstances in which such a choice can present itself arise in urban rather than rural communities, and in business relationships not sociable ones (Davis *et al.*, 1941: 53–56, 457–67). Many of them, such as the relationship between a Negro doctor in his car and a white filling-station attendant, are circumstances that never arose in the society of 1863. The higher posts to which Negroes have attained tend to be in new enterprises, to entail only impersonal relations with Whites, or to be positions catering to a coloured clientele which therefore have no implications for the white community. Where a Negro attained a higher position in the sector governed by traditional interpretations, the caste norms might apply. Thus a coloured man who rented houses to white tenants in Natchez had to go to the back door when collecting his rents, and to behave meekly, or his tenants might have been able to utilize their caste status to repel him. (This situation, too, has doubtless changed. The author was told that in a similar Mississippi city in the early 1960s a Negro landlord with white tenants drove round rent-collecting in an air-conditioned Cadillac, tooting his horn outside each of his houses, whereupon the white housewife would come out to the car with the rent and the landlord would reply, 'Thank you, Mam'. The landlord would not normally enter one of his own houses alone with a female white tenant since this might expose him to an accusation of attempted rape; any sexual allegation would force him into a caste role.) These examples show that the colour line has been able to swing round towards the diagonal only because economic development has changed certain sectors of social life. Mississippi society in 1939 was not the same as it was in 1863, and the same diagram cannot accurately represent both societies; to represent the later society the framework would need to be enlarged in some way (scarcely possible in a two-dimensional figure) to take account of the new situations that could by that time arise within it. Even so, on Warner's evidence it would be more accurate to represent the position in 1939 by a line turning up from the horizontal rather than tilting – as in *Figure 10* – for it seems that the Negro upper class has been able to establish itself in the cities *because* it has not in any significant respect forced the white lower class farther down.

Figure 10   Changes in the colour line

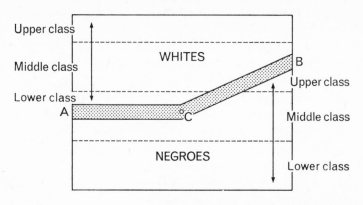

To sound a warning about the implications in the framework to a diagram such as Warner's is only to rephrase the widely accepted view that (with the possible exception of peoples like the Australian aborigines in previous generations) societies are never completely closed systems. Their development over time introduces a flexibility which may thwart a predicted explosion. Yet the degree of closure is an empirical question and will vary from one society to another. In the Southern states the various social elements have been drawn into an inclusive political system so that Myrdal (1944: 75) was justified in treating the various forces contributing to the racial problem as interdependent. In recent years the pattern of interdependence has changed. As the isolation of the South has been steadily reduced, so conflicts between Southern norms and national norms have been less tolerable. Herbert Blumer, in asserting that the significant agents of change in the South have been located outside the region, emphasizes the part played by the various divisions of the federal government – administrative acts of the executive branch, desegregation decisions in the armed services, judicial interpretation by the federal courts, legislation by Congress, and enforcement acts by appropriate federal agencies; he also attaches weight to the influence of national institutions and associations such as trade unions, churches, civil rights organizations, political parties, and the mass media of communication (Blumer, 1965a: 325–6). As the South has been increasingly incorporated into the nation in respect of political, economic, and social relations, so the Southern colour line is no longer part of a well-integrated system. The framework within which it is contained has been greatly expanded. Indeed, it would seem that the very idea of a 'line' is justified only with reference to interpersonal relations in the small, segregated community. In the analysis of local social systems, the notion of a colour line suggests questions to the investigator which may help him to design his inquiry, but it has later to be discarded for lack of precision. In the study of regional or national social systems, the idea of a colour line is at best a suggestive metaphor.

Examination of Warner's diagram draws attention to certain elements in the development of two-category systems which were implicit in the historical summary of the Southern states and are encountered again in accounts of white supremacy societies in other parts of the world. The study of deference behaviour shows how the social distinction between Whites and Negroes stretches to all sorts of interaction so that racial roles are relevant to behaviour in almost every conceivable situation. Consideration of the placement of children of mixed parentage can serve as a reminder that an individual's role cannot be decided on a basis of his own circumstances but must fit with the roles and status of those persons with whom he is necessarily identified and to whom he is bound by other ties. This helps to explain why it is so difficult for the person who would rebel against racial discrimination to get round the requirements of the colour line. One important question raised by Warner's diagram, which, rather surprisingly, has not hitherto been discussed, is whether changes in the angle of the colour line are associated with tendencies for the line to get sharper or become blurred. When Warner mentions the possibility of its moving to the vertical he assumes that the line will remain distinct, and, indeed, there is much in the history of Southern race relations to encourage the view that, as long as the structure of power is fundamentally unaltered, the line will become sharper whenever this is feasible. In other countries, however, colour lines have been blurred and even dissolved; these cases will be reviewed later, but their existence should suggest to the reader questions that may be used to extend and deepen the colour-caste analysis of Southern race relations.

THE SOCIAL STRUCTURE OF DOMINATION

The system of social relations in Mississippi in the 1930s was one of white domination and the exploitation of Negroes (as it was in the South generally, but three of the best sociological studies were those conducted in Mississippi – Dollard, 1937; Powdermaker, 1939; Davis et al., 1941). As Dollard noted in detail, their privileged position brought the Whites economic, sexual, and status gains. But an analysis that quite properly emphasizes the elements of exploitation and oppression may, nevertheless, convey a false impression to the reader unacquainted with such kinds of society. Any society in which one category exercises domination over another must present a harsh and grim-faced aspect at moments when domination is being reasserted. At other times, relations may seem genial and harmonious. If a study of a dominative social order concentrates so much on the means of repression that it fails to indicate this variation of moods, then it does not seem to constitute a true picture to those who know the society from the inside. Sometimes the research worker disapproves so strongly of the subordination of the lower category that he attributes too much significance to the modes of repression and does not notice examples of co-operation across the colour line. Some studies present an unreal idea of white supremacy societies in that, if the societies were actually as they are described, then they would break down immediately. The subordinated people would revolt or flee. The people on top would never be able to keep any servants or employees from the lower category because, to judge from these accounts, there are no forces other than fear and habit to keep them at work. It is possible to suppress all of the people some of the time, and some of the people all of the time, but not all of the people all of the time. If a society is to maintain itself there must be some give-and-take between the groups that make it up.

To understand the social structure of white domination in the American South it is therefore necessary to appreciate that, though the social order depends on occasional spells in which Negroes are violently reminded of white supremacy, the weapon of violence is blunted by over-use and, in the longer periods of outward quiet, social relations depend upon positive incentives to work and co-operate. In the second place, it is necessary to appreciate that colour-caste is only one element in the social system and that it is not relevant to behaviour in all situations. Members of the same racial category may interact with one another on the basis of their relative class rank. Members of different colour-castes may interact not as White and Black but as landlord and tenant, buyer and seller, motorist and mechanic, etc. The institution of colour-caste embodies a set of norms regulating behaviour, not all behaviour, but only that which is regarded as subject to these norms. This means that there may be dispute as to how far the boundaries of the colour-caste norms may stretch; the individuals concerned may define the situation differently, and other people may have to judge which is the correct definition. Thus a lower-class white woman in Natchez pointed a pistol at a respectable Negro professional man; he knocked it from her hand. She ran down one of the main business streets shouting, 'That nigger struck me' (i.e. she represented it as an offence against caste norms). The woman had the Negro arrested but the judge, refusing to regard it as a matter of caste, threw the case out of court (Davis *et al.*, 1941: 477). Though the colour-caste distinction separates a white person from a Negro in certain circumstances, there may be other occasions when those two people are linked by ties of common interest. These cross-cutting ties are essential to the continued functioning of white supremacy societies.

Another aspect sometimes misunderstood by outsiders is that white supremacy groups usually have their distinctive moral values. Outsiders may believe these values to be immoral rather than moral, but they have the same binding power for the insider as the values of his own society have for the outsider. When Hucklebury Finn was drifting on a raft down the Mississippi with his friend, the Negro Jim, Huck's conscience was troubled. Jim had saved his life, but Huck knew that he ought to hand Jim over as a runaway nevertheless; he did not question the morality of slavery – that was something taken for granted by the ordinary boy who grew up in a slave state. In the Deep South of the 1930s the Whites generally believed Negroes to be inherently inferior, childlike, impulsive, and intended by God to be subordinate to the Whites who were responsible for them. The educated Negro had arguments with which to counter each one of these ideas but the ordinary Negro field-hand usually had a less systematic conception of society, and, within the context of particular relationships, might concede that he lacked the capacity of better-educated Whites.

As part of a wider social system the system of colour-caste was organized round the control of sexual relations and reproduction. Intermarriage was prohibited by law (and still is in many states both inside and outside the South). No Negro might make sexual advances to any white woman and, if a woman's fevered imagination led her to allege that he did, little or no attempt was made to discover whether there was any substance in the charge. White men were not denied access to Negro women. Casual relations were not infrequent, but permanent liaisons were rare and marriage was impossible. The critical issue was not that of sexual contact but the extent to which society was called upon to acknowledge the relationship. Davis, Gardner, and Gardner mention a number of permanent liaisons and observe that Negro informants regarded the relation between the white man and his mistress as essentially a family relation. Outside the home they could not appear as a family group or participate as such. The more the white man was attached to his family the more he was isolated from ordinary relations with Whites, but the woman's status in Negro society might be enhanced. It is possible that such liaisons were more frequent in the Deep South, where white control was most secure, than in other regions where the Whites could less afford to permit such deviations. In any two-category system, the superior power of the upper category is likely to be utilized by its males to obtain access to the women of the lower category. They can use their position to offer these women favours they could get from few men of their own category. This is also a way of humiliating the men of the lower category and reminding them of their subordination. The extent to which the men use their power in this way must depend upon the extent to which the women of the upper category can mobilize sanctions against interracial libertinage. In Natchez, the privileged position of the white male was recognized by a Negro (probably a woman) who remarked: 'Oh, well, if she's got a white man, she mus' be sumpin', 'cause if yo' gotta white man, yo' got evahting. Yes, indeed, yo' got evahting' (Davis *et al.*, 1941: 37). Males and females, white and coloured, stood in different positions in respect to the maintenance of segregation. This was epitomized in the saying that the only free people were the white man and the coloured woman, for their colour-caste roles did not inhibit their sex roles. The idealized white woman was restrained by strict norms of propriety yet often tormented by the knowledge that her menfolk were familiar with Negro women. The Negro male was in one sense emasculated by his powerlessness when Whites took 'his' women. Both the white man and the Negro woman, however, could obtain sexual partners from either race.

In most cultures certain sexual desires are repressed as incompatible with the social pattern. In the South there is reason to believe that evangelical religion, belief in Negro inferiority, and the warm relationship many white infants had with a Negro nurse, all combined with the unconscious symbolism of blackness to make the sexual elements especially important to race relations. White women who had learned that sex was not respectable often saw their men going to Negro women (or feared they might be) and became themselves less responsive sexually. If the men did go to Negro women they felt guilty and were more inclined to place their own women on a pedestal, which, in turn, inhibited relations within their own colour-caste (on the idealization of white womanhood, see Cash, 1941: 95–98, 332–3). Later, perhaps, the white man began unconsciously to suspect white women of committing the same sins as he did. The question 'Would you want your daughter to marry a coloured man?' betrays an assumption that this daughter might want to make such a marriage. A vicious circle of guilt and suspicion made the white man more ready to project his own sins onto the Negro male; finding greater pleasure in sexual relations with Negroes he came to regard them as possessed of greater sexual vitality, an idea which, in respect of Negro males, implied also a threat to his own position (Smith, 1949: 98–108). Dollard stated that there was a widespread belief that the genitalia of Negro males were larger than those of Whites (1937: 160). Such a belief may appear a straightforward example of the projection of unconscious fears. The notion that a white women might be injured by sexual relations with a Negro could be interpreted both as grounds for punishing Negro rapists more severely and as a means of making white women afraid of any idea of sexual relations with Negroes. These may be relevant arguments, but the belief itself should be seen in historical context. In 1795 J. F. Blumenbach, the physical anthropologist, wrote, 'it is generally said that the penis of the Negro is very large', and added a footnote: 'the same was said of the northern Scotch who do not wear trousers . . . I have shown, however, on the weightiest testimony that this assertion is incorrect' (Bendyshe, 1865: 249). In 1799 Charles White, apparently unaware of Blumenbach's evidence, affirmed the earlier view as having been demonstrated in every anatomical school in London. Half a century later anthropologists inferred, for the same reason, that it was dangerous for a white woman to have relations with a Negro, and that genital incompatibility might hinder the growth of hybrid populations (Broca, 1864: 28). Doubtless the opinion about the genitalia is no more correct for the Negro than for the kilted Highlander, but a historical perspective does serve to show that a seemingly irrational belief reflects what once was considered an established scientific fact. Much racial folklore stems from the scientific speculations and researches of an earlier period.

Colour-caste divides the races; class, in certain circumstances, unites them and creates divisions within the colour-castes. Davis, Gardner, and Gardner were confident that the evidence at hand left no doubt that a strong solidarity existed between the leading white and coloured business and professional men with regard to the manipulation of the caste sanctions (1941: 474). At lower levels, cross-caste class ties were formed less frequently, though it was noticeable that lower-class Whites living in Negro neighbourhoods treated their Negro neighbours in much the same way as they did their white neighbours. Antagonisms between economic groups within the white category could be noted in such situations as when white landlords would not accept white tenants but preferred Negro tenants. Within the Negro category, antagonisms between landlords and tenants were equally evident. Interracial sexual liaisons might also create cross-caste ties. A Negro is quoted as saying, 'if any violence starts, a white man who has a coloured son or daughter will think about this coloured child of his, and he'll be against violence' (1941: 39). Many occupational relations, especially the employer-servant, permitted considerable variations from formal caste behaviour. A Negro servant travelling with a white child on a bus would sit with that child in the front, showing that it was not contact with Negroes as Negroes that the Whites disliked, but behaviour inconsistent with their subordination. The Whites had no objection to intimacy, but they feared equality, which strengthens the view of segregation as a question of roles rather than of races. In the rural areas the Whites were primarily middle- and upper-class planters, the Negroes predominantly lower-class tenant-farmers. The planter generally exercised close control over his tenants' activities and, while he would himself punish 'his' Negroes, he would resent any attempt by lower-class Whites to exercise such controls in other than extreme cases. In the country, then, race relations exhibited a uniform pattern of caste-like subordination. But in the cities class factors exercised considerable influence over White-Negro relations. The white upper class was not in control to the same extent. The urban Negroes often crowded Whites in the stores, ignored them on the streets and sidewalks, and behaved so freely that they were frequently accused by Whites of 'seeing how far they can go'. (Later, it was suggested that Negroes agreed upon one day each week as 'shove and push day'!) In the city the informal controls of the landlord were replaced by the police and the courts, which took over responsibility for punishing Negroes. Thus while city-living brought some Whites and Negroes together in new ways, creating new bonds, it also divided Whites and Negroes in other respects, creating new antagonisms.

Dollard's study underlined the importance of white patronage for Negroes but, being more concerned with the urban end of the scale, it did not bring out the full significance of the pattern of race relations associated with the farming structure, particularly the 'furnish' system whereby tenants were given credit. Landlords took pains to protect and help 'their' Negroes when they thought they deserved it; without this kind of benevolence the social system would never have worked – and, of course, it encouraged the Negro to behave in a less responsible way than he might otherwise have done. An upper-class white man might be accustomed to return home a little earlier on a Saturday night because he expected to be telephoned to ask if he would stand bail for any of 'his' Negroes who had been arrested; since his relations with them have become more impersonal he is less inclined to bother about playing the role of the Negro's 'angel' or patron.

In Mississippi in the 1930s there was extensive intimidation of Negro labour to maintain the landlord's exploitative position, to make tenants work, to punish stealing, etc. This violence was exacerbated by the depression, which brought white men to compete for Negro jobs and reduced the Negro's bargaining position. Occasional whippings were administered for breaches of the caste roles, but, say Davis *et al.*, periodically there developed situations in which several Negroes seemed to lead a revolt against the caste restrictions, expressed not openly but by gradual pressure. The Whites felt that the Negroes were getting 'uppity' and resentment increased until a small infraction led to violence and a Negro victim became both a scapegoat and, after punishment, a warning to other Negroes. After such an outburst Negro pressures abated and the tension relaxed (1941: 48–49). At times, when a Negro was accused of a sexual offence against a white woman and a feeling had been building up among the Whites that the Negroes needed a lesson, a lynch mob was more likely to form. If the white upper class and the local officials were determined to thwart the mob they usually could, otherwise the offender might be 'sprung' from the gaol, or, if caught by the mob, would not be surrendered to a law officer. A recurrent pattern in many lynchings was that rabble-rousers brought in lower-class Whites from other districts who were not acquainted with the victim as an individual and were more merciless. This is not to say that a Negro might not be lynched by men who knew him personally – hysteria can turn close acquaintances into foes – but the severest sanctions can be wielded more easily by strangers (for a psychological study of a lynching, showing how members of a mob stimulated one another to perform as a crowd actions they none of them could have performed as individuals, see Miller & Dollard, 1941: 196–210).

In the towns, the control of Negroes was to a greater extent the responsibility of the police, who, like the Whites in general, tended to believe that fighting, drinking, and gambling among Negroes were inevitable and not to be treated as crimes as long as they did not involve Whites and were kept out of the limelight. One upper-middle-class white woman said: 'We have very little crime. Of course, Negroes knife each other occasionally but there is little *real* crime. I mean Negroes against whites or whites against each other' (Davis *et al.*, 1941: 499). By neglecting to enforce the law within Negro neighbourhoods, white policemen permitted criminal Negroes to terrorize the Negro community. There was a humorous saying among policemen: 'If a nigger kills a white man, that's murder. If a white man kills a nigger, that's justifiable homicide. If a nigger kills another nigger, give him some more ammunition and turn him loose.' This attitude had the effect of keeping Negroes as a category more firmly subjugated. Later on, as middle- and upper-class Negroes gained more influence, they argued that they were not getting proper police protection and were able to secure the appointment of Negro police officers. Since World War II the political strength of the Negro community and the representations of liberal Whites have led to the hiring of appreciable numbers of Negro policemen in many Southern towns and cities. Having a greater identification with the cause of law in the Negro community, these officers have been able to bring order in neighbourhoods that were previously lawless, and in some cities a Negro policeman can now arrest even a white offender without occasioning any racial friction (Banton, 1964: 173–4).

One element in the Southern pattern – so obvious that it invites no elaboration, yet crucial to the maintenance of white supremacy – was the exclusion of the Negro from the polls. This was generally achieved by the device of the 'white primary'. The selection of candidates was decided by local political parties which claimed to be private bodies and therefore able to follow private rules. Such tactics were supported by constitutional clauses which left to local registrars the decision as to whether a would-be voter could interpret the state Constitution. Registrars regularly deemed Negro applicants to have failed the test. The more recent federal legislation which has led to increased Negro registration will give Negroes more effective political power and should help to transform the social order.

Some American students of race relations speak of 'the advantages of the disadvantages'. This phrase draws attention to the ways in which segregation has compensations for some members of the subordinated category. In the Southern situation, Negro professional men and entrepreneurs could often acquire a clientele from within their own category more easily than if they had been exposed to competition from Whites. Plans for school desegregation have not been welcome to Negro teachers whose qualifications were insufficient to ensure them posts in a reorganized school system. The development of class groupings within the Negro group aided the maintenance of caste distinctions because the upper-class Negro made status gains from his class position; benefiting to some degree from the prevailing order, he was less inclined to challenge it. Some Negroes – especially in the Northern cities – have extensive vested interests in segregation and this helps to explain the tenacity of racial divisions.

Studies of race relations in the South demonstrated also that Negro religion could be better understood if it was seen in a social context. Evangelical religion encouraged Negroes to look for a happier time in the next world instead of in the present, displacing their discontents from more logical targets. This view of the matter may have underlain the outlook of planters who welcomed the building of churches but were much less enthusiastic about schools. On the other hand, religious activity was a sphere in which the Whites could interfere with less justification than in most others. Church organizations gave Negroes one of the few opportunities – in the Deep South usually the only opportunity – to build an institution of their own with their own leaders. Their doctrine and services provided members with consolation and a sense of racial solidarity. Churches have fostered the appreciation of education and a Negro philosophy of social reform.

A subordinated group may initially accept its subordination because the benefits it receives seem sufficient compensation compared with the prospects elsewhere. It should be remembered that many Negroes have left Mississippi and other parts of the South to study at the University of Chicago or some other Northern centre, and have then returned to their home state. They can lead what seems to them a tolerable existence in a colour-caste society. A student who served as a civil rights worker in Mississippi in 1963 and 1965 wrote that the resources in the Negro community which made possible the success of his group were, first, the existence of an institutional structure based on the churches and, second, a 'faith in the possibilities of political action and co-operation, which has amazingly survived the pressures of the white world on the Negro community . . . the Mississippi way of life has not damaged the personality structure or dislocated the family system of Negroes in the same way that life in the Northern cities has' (Bosanquet, 1965: 173). People do not judge their status by reference to an absolute scale, but by comparison with significant others. For instance, a research group which studied adjustments to military life in the United States armed forces during World War II found that Negro troops from the Northern states who were stationed in the Southern states and subjected to the local conventions of social segregation outside their camps complained about this, about the Jim Crow transport, the Southern police, and so on. They said that they would sooner be stationed in the North. Yet when the research group investigated personal adjustment to army life, its data indicated that these dissatisfied Northern Negroes in Southern camps were adjusted as well as or better than Negro soldiers in Northern camps. The group concluded: 'Relative to most Negro civilians whom he saw in Southern towns, the Negro soldier had a position of comparative wealth and dignity. His income was high, at least by general Southern standards . . . [and he] received treatment more nearly on an equality with the white soldier than the treatment of the Negro civilian in the South as compared with the white civilian' (Stouffer *et al.*, 1949: 563). This finding has stimulated further work on the reference groups people employ, consciously or unconsciously, in evaluating their own position.

In calculating how much a subordinated group will tolerate, it is important to take into consideration that influences from outside may raise its expectations. As members of the group become aware of new comparisons – for example, as Negro Americans have watched the progress to independence of new African nations – so the price of social inferiority to the people's pride grows heavier. Earlier, in Chapter Four, it was suggested that interracial behaviour may be viewed as a transaction and that people follow a particular course only if the anticipated gains (material and psychological) outweigh the anticipated costs (material and psychological). The metaphor of trading relations can be extended to cover change in a dominative social order as the subordinated group comes to set a higher price on its pride. If its members come to feel that they are no longer getting a fair deal the effect is as if this group refuses to continue trading with the other group on the old terms. The superordinate group may reply by offering better terms. Alternatively, it may be so indignant over what seems to it an abrogation of a hallowed understanding that it tries to bully the subordinated group into trading on terms it would reject in a free market. This reaction is also to be expected when the superior group's position is such that it cannot afford to offer better terms. Aggression may therefore be seen as the introduction of power or violence to change the terms of exchange. The Negro who moves into a white residential area in some American cities has to reckon with the possibility of having his windows broken and his life made miserable. If the risk of unhappiness outweighs the anticipated psychological gains from the move, he is unlikely to take any chances.

AN AMERICAN DILEMMA?

In a justly famous study of race relations in the United States, Gunnar Myrdal stressed the contradiction between certain of America's national ideals and the norms implicit in life at the local level. He characterized 'the Negro problem' in the United States as a dilemma, an

'ever-raging conflict between, on the one hand, the valuations preserved on the general plane which we shall call the "American

Creed", where the American thinks, talks and acts under the influence of high national and Christian precepts, and, on the other hand, the valuations on specific planes of individual and group living, where personal and local interests; economic, social and sexual jealousies; consideration of community prestige and conformity . . . dominate his outlook' (1944: xlvii).

The American dilemma in this analysis is a dilemma for Whites: Negroes are only spectators and the Negro community is merely a pathological growth caused by white discrimination. Myrdal's argument was over-rationalistic in assuming that people find it difficult to live with such contradictions, while it tended to underestimate the strength of the parochialism that characterizes so many American communities. The analysis implied that American culture was a reasonably consistent whole and maintained that changes would operate so as to reduce inconsistency. It is understandable that an outsider should have been more impressed with the peculiar attributes of the American way of life and inclined to see it as a whole. In the light of hindsight, however, it can be maintained that Myrdal should have looked more closely at the discontinuities. He could have benefited from studies which demonstrate that social life may be built up from multitudinous situations defined in mutually inconsistent ways. For example, Evans-Pritchard's celebrated analysis of Zande witchcraft beliefs (1937) showed that in each isolated situation people's behaviour could be considered rational, though the system as a whole was not logically coherent. The contradictions were suppressed by beliefs that particular criteria were relevant in certain situations but not in others. In just this way, the Dixie politician might be worried about how he could resist federal power without perceiving Negroes' moral claims within the same set of categories as those he used when thinking of white society. When, in 1962, Governor Barnett spoke about 'the people of Mississippi' he was inclined to refer only to the white people of his state. Social life is full of distinctions that may appear illogical or inconsistent to the outsider but seem quite reasonable to the people who have grown up to take them for granted. The critic of the Myrdal diagnosis observes that there are other value premises sanctioned by American culture and other less idealistic American creeds which are not given their due weight. He argues that social change does not uniformly reduce inconsistency but in many respects divides up social domains, making situational discontinuity even more important (Medalia, 1962: 223–7; Campbell, 1961: 228–34). This aspect of the matter will be considered in Chapter Fourteen.

CHAPTER EIGHT

White Supremacy in South Africa

The rise of racist doctrine has been described: it started in the 1850s and climbed quite quickly to a dominant place in man's thinking about himself. But since World War I there have been no significant elaborations of the racist philosophy and, except for Southern Africa, it now seems everywhere in retreat. Social intolerance seeks less systematic forms of expression and justification. Even the new nations which have suffered from racial discrimination in the past show little inclination to soothe their bruises by imputing innate deficiencies to their former masters.

THE POLITICAL FUNCTIONS OF RACIST IDEOLOGY

The effects of racist doctrine will persist for some time, and there will be occasional revivals, but future historians may fix the period 1850–1950 as the century of racism. This prompts two questions. Why did racism suddenly appear in several different but independent countries and fields of study at about the same time? There are certain patterns in the development of racism: do they reflect the logic of the ideas themselves or are they created by the action of society in moulding the ideas to particular ends? To both of these questions persuasive answers have been offered by writers influenced by Marxist thought; to appreciate the character of these answers it is necessary first of all to outline the assumptions from which the Marxist school takes its departure.

In a famous passage in the preface to his *A Contribution to the Critique of Political Economy* (1859) Marx states that the foundation of social life consists in the material productive forces (the way in which man wins a living from nature) and in the relations of production necessary to the harnessing of these forces (e.g. the lineage-based herding groups among pastoralists or the recognition of private property in land among agriculturalists involved in a cash economy). Upon this infrastructure arises a legal and political superstructure conditioned by the mode of production. People's thoughts about their society reflect its institutions and ideologies, but in fact the categories in which they organize their thoughts are determined by the economic base of the society. It is men's social being that determines their consciousness. All ideological forms – racism among others – are to be seen from this standpoint. They reveal man's subjective consciousness of social relations, not the objective conditions which underlie them and which in due course will change them in a predictable manner.

The Marxist sees technological development as a fairly continuous process which constantly renders existing relations of production obsolete and creates tensions within the infrastructure that in turn bring about the transformation of the superstructure. Modern history begins with a situation in which there are no clear lines of class stratification: the journeyman is bound to his master rather than to his fellow journeymen. Society is subdivided in multifarious ways. The rise of capitalism simplifies the picture stage by stage. First, the bourgeoisie, pursuing the advantages brought about by the creation of new markets overseas and by technical improvements in manufacturing, is brought increasingly into conflict with the aristocracy. The bourgeoisie needs political power to facilitate the pursuit of gain and to ensure that it can utilize the fruits of its own activity. To reduce the power of the aristocracy, and to compete with the bourgeoisie of other countries, the bourgeoisie is obliged to solicit the support of the proletariat; in bringing the proletariat into the political arena it takes a big step towards its own undoing. The cohesion of the proletariat gradually increases. The opposition between capital and labour sharpens. Sections of the ruling class are precipitated into the proletariat. The lower-middle class of small traders, etc. discovers that in the long run its interests lie in joining the proletariat. The cross-cutting ties that bring together diverse groups are gradually stripped away until society has been polarized into two opposed blocks related only by the cash nexus; as the *Communist Manifesto* says: 'The bourgeoisie . . . has ruthlessly torn asunder the motley feudal ties that bound men to their "natural superiors"; it has left no other bond betwixt man and man but crude self-interest and unfeeling "cash payment".' This process cannot be halted. The individual bourgeois may be opposed to measures that further the political education of the proletariat, but this is to no avail. The bourgeois class has no alternative but to try to utilize proletarian power in its dynamic drive which 'drags all the nations, even the most barbarian, into the orbit of civilization'. If the individual manufacturer does not adopt the methods taken up by his competitors then his profits will decline and he will be forced out of business. The logic of the system overpowers subjective attitudes.

The bourgeoisie is urged onward by the need for an ever-expanding market. One of the contradictions of the capitalist social system is that, because the employers appropriate some of the rewards due to the workers, home consumption can never keep up with home production. J. A. Hobson, the English liberal who preceded Keynes in expounding an under-consumptionist theory of the trade cycle, argued in his book *Imperialism* (1902) that a country's acquisition of colonies was due principally to the demand of its exporting and financial classes for new markets and fields of investment. Other classes had to be persuaded that imperialism was in their interests, too, by false doctrines about the necessity of colonial outposts for purposes of national defence or about the need to secure food imports. Above all, an ideology of imperialism was developed, which caused even the underpaid day labourer to feel elevated by his membership in a ruling race. The themes of 'Land of Hope and Glory' still strike a responsive chord in many of the hearts of the Queen's poorer subjects. Hobson believed that this process of uniting the nation behind the interests of a class affected most institutions of national life. The industrial and financial groups ultimately controlled the political party, the press, the Church, and the school.

'For these business politicians biology and sociology weave thin convenient theories of a race struggle for the subjugation of the inferior peoples, in order that we, the Anglo-Saxon, may take their lands and live upon their labours; while economics buttresses the argument by representing our work in conquering and ruling them as our share in the division of labour among nations, and history devises reasons why the lessons of past empires do not apply to ours while social ethics paints the motive of "imperialism" as the desire to bear the "burden" of educating and elevating races of "children"' (Hobson, 1902: 221).

Racism, therefore, presented the bourgeoisie of the imperial countries with a tool they could use in manipulating the home society. Lenin reiterated this argument, underlining one point with a quotation from a letter of Engels, which asserts, 'The English workers gaily share the feast of England's monopoly of the world market and the colonies.' Lenin maintained that imperialist policies were calculated to divide the working-class movement and to buy off opportunist workers by offering them some of the fruits of colonial exploitation (Lenin, 1916: 98). It has since been argued that the capitalists spread racialist propaganda in the home country to prevent the white proletarians from realizing that their interests are identical with those of the coloured workers and to postpone the day of reckoning on which they will unite against their oppressors.

According to Marxists, the capitalist economic system requires that entrepreneurs shall treat land, labour, and capital as abstract purchasable qualities. Labour has to be bought and sold in the market like the other factors of production, with a view to profit. To do this, the concept of labour has to be depersonalized; the fact that 'labour' consists of human beings with families and political desires must be ignored if it is to be treated as a commodity and exploited like other economic resources. In capitalist countries the industrialists must proletarianize the masses. In dealing with colonial labour they go a stage farther and deny that the coloured workers are entitled to the status even of white proletarians. Thus the Marxist writer, like Oliver Cromwell Cox, views 'race prejudice' as 'a social attitude propagated among the public by an exploiting class for the purpose of stigmatizing some group as inferior, so that the exploitation of either the group itself or its resources or both may be justified' (Cox, 1948: 393). The motivations of those who spread such a doctrine are irrelevant; what matters is the effect it has upon social relations. By branding a group as inhuman or inferior, racist doctrines help the capitalist to exploit this group and its resources.

One consequence of the thesis that racist ideologies are a response to the requirements of capitalists in an era of imperialism – the highest stage of capitalism according to Lenin – is the conclusion that race prejudice, in the Marxist sense, is the product of a particular historical epoch. It was not found until capitalism developed overseas interests and it will disappear with the coming collapse of capitalism. This is the argument of what Maurice Freedman has called 'the 1492 School of Race Relations', which has found an echo in the UNESCO series of publications (Little, 1952: 9–15, 51–52). This view identifies as situations of race relations only those where groups conceive of themselves as racially different, whereas to a strict Marxist such conceptions are only ideological epiphenomena. It also avoids mention of the many authenticated cases of interracial brutality in situations untouched by racist philosophies and fails to prove that they differ from the others in important respects. The Marxist does not regard judgements of value as independent of judgements of fact. For him, value is decided by fact, by the place of the thing in question in the historical process.

Therefore it is necessary for him to establish at the outset the sort of phenomenon with which he has to deal. Cox goes to tortuous lengths to make this sort of distinction when he argues that race prejudice is not to be confused with anti-semitism. Anti-semitism, he says, is a form of social intolerance, 'an unwillingness on the part of a dominant group to tolerate the beliefs or practices of a subordinate group because it considers these beliefs and practices to be either inimical to group solidarity or a threat to the continuity of the status quo'. Whereas race prejudice facilitates exploitation, intolerance is directed towards the conversion, expulsion, or eradication of the minority. 'The dominant group or ruling class does not like the Jew at all, but it likes the Negro in his place . . . the condition of its liking the Jew is that he ceases being a Jew and voluntarily become like the generality of society, while the condition of its liking the Negro is that he cease trying to become like the generality of society and remain contentedly a Negro.'

There is a certain truth in what Cox says, but clearly, from other standpoints, the two have much in common. Racism may, in certain cases, have the political and economic functions he ascribes to it, but racial hostility is not only this: it is also a psychological, sociological, geographical, historical phenomenon – and much else besides. Orthodox Marxists are apt to imply that once the student has understood that racism is essentially a cover for exploitation this is enough. It only remains for him to trace out the way in which the economic factors have done their work. The view of the 'bourgeois' Western social scientist is that this approach leads to the caricature of society as a giant conspiracy and that the other aspects must be studied in their own right; the political functions of racism are then seen to be the main focus of interest only for the student of political science. Arguments about what prejudice 'really is' are futile. If prejudice against Negroes fulfils the same personality functions as prejudice against Jews, then the psychologist may treat them as similar for his purposes. Historically viewed, hostility against either of these groups serves different political ends at different times and in different places. Thus it is the social scientist's selective interest in particular problems that decides which aspects of events he will concentrate upon and how he will conceptualize them.

Racism attained its greatest influence just after the rise of capitalism but this does not prove that there is any logical connection between the two. Their association might be to some degree coincidental. To what other developments, then, can the rise of racism be related? Chapter Two has shown that our understanding of it is enhanced if we see it as in part an error within a particular branch of science that was associated both with the antecedent ideas and with the increased factual evidence that was becoming available about racial and cultural variation. The suggestion that Marxism provides a sufficient explanation of the appearance of racism in the middle of the nineteenth century can be rejected, but the claim that Marxism explains how the initial errors were utilized is a much stronger one.

Some elements in Marxist analyses of social relations are not acceptable to non-Marxist sociologists so that the Marxist approach remains distinct. The student of race relations therefore needs to understand the bases of such disagreements and the special characteristics of Marxist interpretations in the disputed areas. Yet other elements in Marxist analyses have not been open to objection and have been assimilated in the general development of sociological theory so that it is no longer possible to unravel the Marxist from the non-Marxist strands of thought. Some of the Marxist interpretation concerning the political functions of ideology and the pattern of group alliances in societies split by a fundamental cleavage has in this way been incorporated into sociological theory. To the model of racial friction as the product of individual sentiments (foreshadowed in Chapter One and expounded in Chapter Twelve), and the model of racial friction as characteristic of certain kinds of social relationship (the theme of several chapters), it is possible to add a third model which conceives of racial friction as the outcome of racist ideology and the manipulations of exploiting classes. How far this is still a specifically Marxist line of analysis is open to dispute. It can be argued that it is now part of any sociologist's intellectual armoury, useful for answering certain sorts of questions and useless for others. In so far as questions concerning the influence of ideology and the pattern of group alliances are of particular interest in the study of race relations in South Africa, so the third model has special explanatory value in the review of trends there. For the same reason it has been appropriate to mention the intellectual antecedents of this model (important to any understanding of how the scientific analysis of race relations has been built up) before summarizing salient aspects of South Africa's experience of racial friction.

ETHNIC AND CLASS ALLIANCES AMONG THE WHITES

The situation in South Africa in the 1880s was comparable to the pre-capitalist phase, described by Marx as patriarchal, in which many workers were bound to the existing order by individual interests. The two political poles were the Afrikaans-speaking Transvaal Republic (one clause in its original Constitution declared, 'There shall be no equality between black and white either in church or state') and the English-dominated Cape Colony. In the Boer republic of the Orange Free State and the Transvaal were to be found scattered, largely self-governing, communities of farmers. Many Africans lived on practically undisturbed. The labour required by trek-Boers was, says Macmillan (1949: 117), easy paced and, though the African farmers were defined as squatters and required on occasion to pay rent in kind, their use of their land was possibly less disturbed than it had been in earlier days of inter-tribal warfare. Diamonds were discovered in Kimberley in 1869, and gold near present-day Johannesburg in 1884. Until this time agriculture was unprofitable and transport costly. Farming necessarily took the form of ranching rather than of intensive cultivation, and the lonely existence this forced upon the Afrikaans-speaking rural population gave them their independent democratic character. With the growth of the gold-mining industry the political leaders began to feel that the distinctive character of their republic was threatened, but it was for some time difficult to guess whether the economic cleavage between farmers and miners would dominate public life or whether the ethnic opposition between the British and the Boers would transcend other divisions.

In the Cape Colony the government was for many years controlled by an alliance between Cecil Rhodes and the Afrikaner leader, Hofmeyer. Even the policy of the 'Cape franchise', the enrolment of qualified Africans as electors, was generally accepted. Local life, says Macmillan, who was there as a child (1949: 306), was without the fundamentals even of organized agricultural industry: home-produced butter, cheese, bacon, and biscuits were in short supply and of poor quality; like canned fish and bully-beef, these were among the staple imports. The great export trade in fruit had not begun. No one dreamed of manufacturing boots or shoes or blankets, let alone steel or heavy arms; the mines were far away and the politicians were concerned with them only as contributing to railway and customs revenues.

Relations between the British and the Boers had been aggravated by British interventions in the Transvaal, but the situation was transformed when Rhodes's friend, Jameson, in 1895 led an unsuccessful attack on the republic. In the Cape the Rhodes–Hofmeyer alliance broke up immediately. Ever since, it has been the British–Boer opposition that has cut deepest in social relations among Whites. In 1899 it could not longer be contained: a war broke out that was to last for two and a half years, and to leave the Afrikaners for the first time a united people. But it also uprooted many of the rural population. The

South African Native Commission of 1903–5, which had been appointed by Lord Milner (nine out of the eleven members were British), recommended the abolition of the practice whereby Africans lived as squatters on European lands and the separation of Black and White by limiting native purchase of lands to certain defined areas. The Commission also wanted to see a limited number of native constituencies created to give Africans an avenue of political expression. This last idea was dropped when, in 1913, the government suddenly introduced the Native Land Act. The Act made it illegal for natives to rent or lease land from Europeans except in return for labour service; it prohibited Africans from acquiring land in areas other than the 12 per cent of the country already secured to them by treaty or other measures. Macmillan describes the Act as 'a hasty and ill-prepared measure' and comments:

'Looking back from this distance of time it becomes perfectly clear that the South African Parliament had not the faintest idea of the dimensions of the upheaval this Act was bound to initiate. The Natives of the provinces chiefly affected were totally unrepresented. . . . To penalize squatting was, in fact, to sit on the safety valve. Parliament was guilty of a further enormity. The one-sided prohibitions of the Act took effect immediately: the express promise to make "further provision" of land remained unfulfilled for over twenty years' (1949: 315).

A writer influenced by Marxist thought, Julius Lewin, prefers to regard the Act as the deliberate implementation of a conscious policy: 'A more substantial reason was no doubt the serious difficulties that the mine owners of the Rand had long faced in their unending quest for a veritable army of unskilled labourers willing to work for very low wages. . . . If the Africans were free to acquire more land, they would be reluctant to leave the reserves to work for low wages in the mines' (Lewin, 1963: 99). Lewin sees the Act as an implementation of the 1903–5 Commission's report, which later was described even by a conservative imperial journal as 'mainly the natural product of well-to-do land and mine owners, representatives of an acquisitive society hardened by pioneering experience and eager for economic development'. In support of this interpretation it is possible to urge that, from the ending of the war, the British were ready to make political concessions to the Afrikaners if they could thereby strengthen their economic interests. Thus, rather than try to extend the principle of allowing non-Whites to vote, the British in 1905 themselves proposed that the Union franchise should be limited to white men. Keir Hardie, then

Labour leader at Westminster, observed: 'It is ridiculous to say that the great trading and commercial interests whom the Act of Union will benefit – the customs and railway interests and the whole of the property interests – are going to throw away the benefits they anticipate because the House of Commons insists that the Union Parliament shall remain open to Africans, as the Cape Parliament was open.'

Developing this line of argument, Lewin presents the contemporary political situation in South Africa as the result, first, of a 'deal' between the English-speaking ethnic group and the Afrikaners; and, second, of a 'deal' between the white bourgeoisie and the white proletariat. On the first point he writes:

'Here is a curious phenomenon: the economic power wielded by the English is divorced from political power, which is entirely in Afrikaner hands. At bottom this is explicable by the satisfaction that the giant mine owners feel with a government that guarantees them a supply of cheap, migrant black labour. Moreover, the English group is influenced by the interests of Britain and the United States which have in the past provided a large part of all the non-agricultural capital invested in the country . . . [A major factor in political development has been] the basic desire of the English to carry on their mining, manufacturing, and commercial business as usual, regardless of the political consequences of their attitude' (1963: 11, 16).

This sharing of power, the one group taking the economic power and the other the political power, is quite striking. Though 59 per cent of the white population have Afrikaans as a mother-tongue and only 39 per cent English, in 1954 the Afrikaner share of the total national income (now over £2,000 million) was one-quarter. In mining, the Afrikaner share was only ½ per cent, and in retail trade only 6 per cent of the annual turnover. In 1957 the average Afrikaner earned £260 a year in comparison with £435 earned by the non-Afrikaans White. Compare this with Afrikaner strength in political institutions. Afrikaners staff all the public services, including the police force, and all government departments from top to bottom. The contrast is eloquent, and Lewin's argument carries conviction as an explanation of why the English-speaking group has never made common cause with the Africans against the anti-democratic aims and methods of Afrikaner nationalism.

The war of 1899–1902 uprooted many of the rural population and, after the cessation of hostilities, there was a steady drift of 'poor Whites' to the towns. The outbreak of world war in 1914 created new employment opportunities and, attracted by the rising wages, Afrikaners moved into the mining industry to take over the underground jobs that had previously been held by English, Scots, and Australian workers. The new men were not as skilled as those they replaced, and they were not in a position to defend the high levels of payment that prevailed. The Afrikaners feared the competition of African labourers only slightly less skilled and very much cheaper than themselves. The position of the African workers, however, was not very strong owing to their lack of organization and the surplus of rural workers. In 1913 an 'African Congress' had been formed to fight the Land Act but it was only a beginning. During the war, landless and displaced rural Africans competed for employment, which kept their wages low although wartime conditions caused a rise in prices. In 1919 'native unrest' became serious. The Industrial and Commercial Workers' Union led by the Nyasalander Clements Kadalie rapidly built up a following among landless farm servants. With the end of the war, the return of the soldiers, and the effect of many countries' domestic economic difficulties upon international trade, the mine managements were forced to modify their policies. The Transvaal Supreme Court held the regulation embodying the colour bar in mining employment to be *ultra vires*. This opened the way for the engagement of African workers for semi-skilled work. When the Chamber of Mines announced that its members would change the ratio of white to black labour and retrench 2,000 white miners, they provoked the revolutionary strike of 1922. The white miners lost the decisive battles but in the end they won the political campaign that followed.

The strike was a struggle between white workers and white employers, but those labour leaders who attempted to keep it on this basis were swamped in the rising tide of anti-African feeling, for the strikers' objective was to exclude Africans from the more desirable jobs (Roux, 1948: 157–9). The eight-week strike culminated in a further two weeks of armed revolt; this was brought to a sanguinary end by the troops that Smuts's government called in. At the polls in 1924 the government fell to an alliance of the Labour and Nationalist parties. Hertzog's government then implemented its 'civilized labour policy' by which many Africans were dismissed from government employment. One result of this policy was the 1925 Mines and Works (Colour Bar) Act, which provided legal support for the white miners' claim to all jobs classed as skilled. In Lewin's interpretation, this policy represents a second 'deal'. It was a bargain between the white financial interests and the white workers, which split the proletariat in the fashion foreshadowed by Lenin's argument:

'What was really decided by the explosion of 1922 was that white public opinion would never tolerate the replacement of white labour by black labour at a lower wage. The crisis made a deep impact not only on the public mind but on the mine owners. They learnt the lesson that a permanent part of the cost of mining in South Africa was the acceptance of the colour bar. Never again did they attempt to abolish, or even to lower, racial barriers on the mines. From that time the mine owners and the white miners entered a kind of partnership based on a common attitude [of] denying advancement to Africans in the industry' (Lewin, 1963: 101).

The bourgeoisie split the proletariat by buying the loyalty of the white workers. This meant that it denied itself the support it could later have expected from an African bourgeoisie. Thus the process was started which, on the Marxist pattern, might be expected gradually to exacerbate the tensions between the two blocs, stripping away all ties except those of material interest until they were related only by the cash nexus.

The way in which different groups in the upper category of the South African social system were forced into alliance shows marked similarities with the process already found in the history of the United States. There, the North and the South made peace after Reconstruction at the expense of the Negro; then, when the poorer Whites challenged the Southern ruling class, those two groups entered into an alliance based upon the more rigorous suppression of the Negro. In South Africa, first Afrikaners and English, and then industrialists and white workers came to terms on policies of mutual support in opposition to the claims anticipated from the African majority. As in the Deep South, the South African Whites were influenced by a belief in their inherent racial superiority; they enacted legislation to keep the colour line distinct, forcing anomalies down into the lower category; they took steps to create and enforce a status gap between the lower members of the upper category and the upper members of the lower; they extended the pattern of segregation to new kinds of situation, and, unwillingly, by all these measures stimulated the opposition of the dominated group to the whole social order. Yet there are important differences between the Deep South and South Africa, for in the latter country the various social groups were and are more distant and the system as a whole is less integrated (e.g. in South Africa there have been many languages instead of one, and the people of the subordinated groups have been influenced by membership in their own political and social units – such as tribal communities). Material incentives bring separate groups together and regulate or resolve conflicts between them. This process has gone further in the American South than in South Africa. Mississippi is being integrated into a national society, the character of which is determined by a multitude of interlocking and opposed political and economic pressures. The pattern of race relations in South Africa is being tailored to fit into a national society based on an ideological blueprint; this society utilizes governmental power to reduce the influence of sectional interests which are not committed to the politically dominant ideal. Though the South African economy is heavily industrialized in certain respects, the racial position there can be said to resemble that obtaining in the American South in the years prior to World War I more closely than it resembles the current phase. When a spokesman for South African Nationalist policy refers to friction between the English- and Afrikaans-speaking groups to argue that 'the introduction of a third partner at this stage of precarious political balance would inevitably result in a ganging up of two partners against the third' (Pienaar & Sampson, 1960: 8), there is an echo of what has been said about the reasons for the disfranchisement of Negro voters in the South at the beginning of the century. But any attempt to develop this kind of historical comparison must depend upon a variety of assumptions as to the kind of cycle that is at work – a question that will be considered in a later section of this chapter.

THE INHIBITION OF ALLIANCES BETWEEN SUBORDINATE GROUPS

In 1960 the population of the Republic of South Africa consisted of some 3 million Whites, 11 million Africans, $\frac{1}{2}$ million Asians, and $1\frac{1}{2}$ million Coloureds, making a total of almost 16 million. The proportions living in urban areas were: Africans, 32 per cent; Whites, 84 per cent; Coloureds, 68 per cent; and Asians, 83 per cent. A 1957 estimate of the linguistic distribution of 9·54 million Bantu-speaking Africans listed the following totals: Xhosa, 2·77; Zulu, 2·46; Northern Sotho, 1·05; Southern Sotho, 1·02; Tswana, 0·78; Tsonga, 0·45; Swazi, 0·33; Ndebele, 0·24; Venda, 0·16; others, 0·28 (three of the above linguistic groups may be familiar to readers under the names Basuto, Bechuana, and Matabele). In 1958 only 3·2 per cent of all African children were in secondary schooling, compared with 22·7 per cent of white children; some 35 per cent of Africans over ten years of age were reckoned to be literate (van den Berghe, 1965: 47, 288–91).

The non-white population is divided into three principal groups; both the Indians and the Coloureds have regarded themselves as differing radically from the Africans and being in many respects more like the Whites. The Africans have not seen the Indians and the Coloureds as their allies and they have themselves been divided by linguistic and cultural differences. The territories of different tribal groups are separated by considerable distances; the workers in industry may be grouped on a tribal basis and may associate on the same basis in the locations; relatively few of the Africans have won through to the educational level at which people come to possess a common non-racial culture. Therefore, members of the superordinate category have not been threatened by the prospect that the subordinate groups would make common cause in the immediate future. It has not hitherto been necessary to elaborate any Macchiavellian policy of 'divide and rule' because the groups ruled have already been divided and have not been coming together very fast. Nevertheless, South African policy does reveal the intention to maintain these differences so far as is possible.

Though South African governments since the Union have been unchanging in their insistence upon white supremacy, policies for the implementation of this ideal have undergone several slow transformations: from racial separation (apartheid) to separate development and, more recently, to limited self-government in 'Bantustans', with talk about possible partition. Since 1948, when the Nationalist party came to power, a major factor in the formulation of such policies has been Afrikaner nationalism. Conscious of their own identity as a nation, the Afrikaners have looked at other groups in like manner. A spokesman for their view has insisted that the Bantu is neither a backward black Englishman, nor a backward black Afrikaner, nor even a backward black Bantu. He is a Zulu, or a Xhosa, or a Sotho, or a member of some other African nation. It should not be government policy to try to denationalize him (surveying their own history, Afrikaners believe denationalization to be not only undesirable but almost impossible). Government policy must be based on the Bantu authorities in the Bantu areas, upon the traditional system of tribal chiefs, and not upon the denationalized Africans of the towns. So, 'once this idea is grasped that the South African Government is handling this issue not upon the basis of westernizing individuals but on the basis of civilizing nations, a great many things and a great many laws that must from the outside at first blush seem to be not only incomprehensible but also reprehensible, fall into pattern' (Pienaar & Sampson, 1960: 9, 11, 21). Whether South African government policy is as consistent as this implies is doubtful. The Nationalist bloc is a close alliance of separate power bases – industrial trade unions, the farmers, the churches, the intellectuals, etc. – but it is by no means monolithic, as was shown briefly when the problem arose of finding a successor to Dr Verwoerd in 1966.

Criticisms of South African government policy are of two kinds. The first kind questions not the end, but the means of its implementation. If the Africans are to be encouraged to develop separately they need land that will repay careful cultivation. Though they constitute almost 70 per cent of the population, the Bantu Self-Government Act of 1959 allots them 13 per cent of land in the regions where the tribal reserves have been situated. If the three British High Commission territories of Basutoland, Swaziland, and Bechuanaland are counted in – as the South African government maintains they should be – the percentage is raised to 47, but much of this is made up by the arid wastes of the Kalahari Desert. Opponents of Nationalist policy site discrepancies of this sort in their attacks. The second kind of criticism questions the end to which policy is directed. It is urged that civilization is not a national attribute but something common to people of every nation who attain to a certain level of understanding. The idea that, because African organization a hundred years ago was based on the tribal unit, it must be tied to the same unit today is condemned: 'Throughout its fifty years, the sense of African nationhood has been expanding, from the tribe, to the city, to the nation, to the continent' (Pienaar & Sampson, 1960: 74). The two kinds of criticism unite with respect to urban policies. White industry in the towns is dependent upon black labour and will remain so; to evade recognition of this by stressing rural development is said to be hypocritical. Urban Africans are harried by pass laws and other legal restrictions, by the vesting of extensive powers in policemen and administrators inadequately controlled by due process of law, and so on. The manner in which urban policy is administered may fall into pattern in the context of the Afrikaner outlook, but this does not stop its appearing reprehensible to many observers.

For the Nationalist policy-maker, acute problems are posed by the claims of the better-educated and wealthier Africans. Afrikaner ideology envisages a series of changes such that the colour line in Warner's diagram will move round to the vertical and the two cultures and the various nations will thereby retain their distinctiveness. White society will be able to offer temporary employment in menial positions to Africans, who will return to their own society having benefited from the discipline of employment in an industrial culture (see *Figure 11*, to which further columns would need to be added if it were also to represent provision for the Indians and Coloureds). If this is to happen, the colour line must be allowed to swing round and a separate niche found for the upper members of the African group so that Whites will not find themselves subordinate to them. If Africans are not allowed to rise in this way, the sincerity of the policy-makers must be as dubious as their critics suspect. As the South African government is troubled by the country's international isolation, its public relations officers like to use stories of 'Bantu millionaires' (whose capital is exaggerated) to show an aspect of their policies which may mollify a critical overseas

Figure 11   The colour line as envisaged in separate development

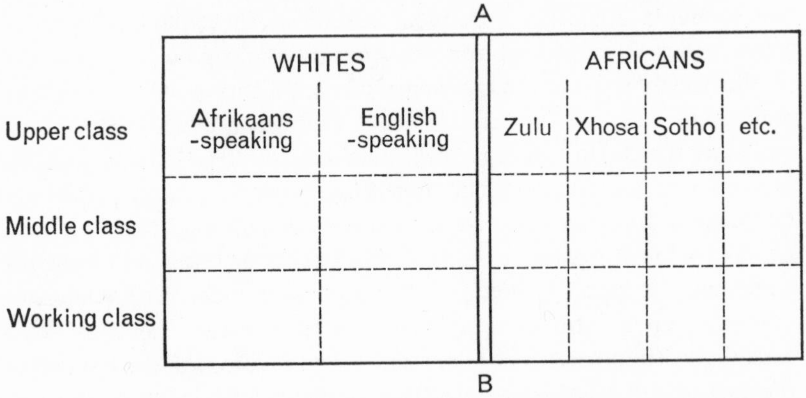

	WHITES		AFRICANS			
Upper class	Afrikaans-speaking	English-speaking	Zulu	Xhosa	Sotho	etc.
Middle class						
Working class						

opinion. But from an internal standpoint the position of this group presents problems. Can concessions to an African bourgeoisie serve as a political safety-valve, offering energetic Africans a prospect of material success if they concentrate upon their occupations? Would these same men otherwise be inclined to use their energies and talents trying to frustrate government policies? Or, by making concessions to those Africans who press upwards, is the government allowing potential opponents to consolidate a position from which they will later launch attacks upon them and upon the interests of their supporters?

The economic interests at stake are almost as significant as the political ones. In 1958 the Minister of Bantu Administration told an Afrikaans Chamber of Commerce that African purchasing power was estimated at £365 million per year. Africans spent nearly all of it (98 per cent) themselves, and their rate of acquisition of goods was rising more steeply than the Europeans'. How was this purchasing power to be serviced? By free competition? That possibility was ruled out by ideological considerations. By reserving African retailing to African traders ? That was what apartheid seemed to promise. Or was the power of the state to be used to channel most of the consumer demand to white commercial interests ? Such a practice would have been in accordance with the way in which apartheid policies were often implemented, and this course was advocated by Afrikaner spokesman who claimed that their nation should now be compensated because other groups had been entrenching themselves in commerce and industry while the Afrikaners were opening up the country and making it safe for white civilization. They claimed that the grant of a monopoly to African leaders would not earn the government the gratitude of Africans but would instead enable them to divert any economic benefits into anti-government agitation. The urban locations were in white areas and the Africans must not be allowed to acquire permanent interests there. The Minister responded to this dilemma by recommending Afrikaners to enter the African consumer market as wholesalers; at the same time, he promised to set a ceiling to African commercial expansion by stating that the more successful African traders would be directed to invest their capital in the Bantu homelands. When discussing the question of retail trade in his study of the African 'middle class', Leo Kuper observed that a rising commercial class frequently becomes voracious. Recruited from low-income strata, successful traders suddenly find that they have broken through the horizons of near-subsistence living and that the future offers them a prospect of ever-increasing wealth if they can maintain the momentum of their advance. The Afrikaans Chamber of Commerce, with almost unlimited opportunities in the country as a whole, was not prepared to forgo the chance of profit from the impoverished urban areas. For the same reason, it is unlikely that African traders will scruple to exploit racial antagonism, first for the rewards offered by apartheid, and then later, as they gain strength, for the rewards of the larger society (Kuper, 1965: 288).

The African elite (it is not really a bourgeoisie, as Kuper acknowledges) does not have much choice in the question of whether it is to be a safety-valve or a nucleus of leaders against the government. For the political issue impinges on the occupational roles of the elite in quite different ways. The African medical practitioner can avoid political involvement; he is at the top of the prestige ladder in his own community and if he goes into private practice he is subject to relatively little government interference. Openings in medical education may therefore present Africans with the picture of a career that meets many of their immediate aspirations without drawing them into the political vortex. A lawyer is professionally well fitted to be a political leader but there are other avenues open to him. By the type of practice he builds, an African lawyer chooses the extent of his political involvement. A teacher does not have quite the same choice, for he is forced into a political role. His professional status has been downgraded by the government and the school system reorganized to make him teach what the Whites hire him to teach and nothing more. The Minister of Bantu Education has made clear what this is: '. . . our aim is to keep the Bantu child a Bantu child. The Bantu must be so educated that they do not want to become imitators of the Whites, but that they will remain essentially Bantu.' In similar vein, the Prime Minister asked the House of Assembly: 'What is the use of teaching the Bantu child mathematics when it cannot use it in practice? That is quite absurd. . . .' The African teacher cannot but be regularly reminded of the political implications of his duties: every day he acts either as a servant or as an opponent of apartheid and there is no neutrality.

Similarly, the African minister of religion, whether he receives a salary from one of the larger churches, such as the Methodist, Anglican, Catholic, Lutheran, or Congregational churches, or is a spiritual entrepreneur in charge of his own enterprise, is forced into a political role; to express no opposition to the régime is as political a stance as protest. The part played by the churches in the growth of African protest has often attracted attention. The missions were, in many parts of Africa, the first providers of education, especially secondary education, and so they trained many of the men who afterwards became political leaders. Some Africans took up posts of religious leadership but leaned over towards political expression without making a clean break – as was to be expected, since the issues were, to them, intertwined. Sometimes African congregations separated from mission bodies and developed new doctrines reflecting a rejection of racial subordination. Because of this, there has been a general tendency to interpret separatism in political terms without making sufficient allowance for variations of time and place. This issue will be taken up in the next chapter. For the present, however, it is relevant to note that in the 1951 census 1·6 million Africans were enumerated as members of 'Native Separatist Churches'. The larger separatist or independent churches are limited to single linguistic groups and the majority are very small. Though these churches reflect their members' frustrations under the rule of white supremacists, they no longer have much political content. The remedies for the present situation are seen in the next world, not in this one. The leading authority on the South African independent churches states explicitly: 'the politically awake and active, if still subscribing to "Christianity" at all, are found in other churches, and not among "the Native Separatists"' (Sundkler, 1961: 305). Political opposition to the Whites is now sufficiently self-conscious for its organizers to dispense with any religious cloak or vehicle.

Though there are considerable differences within the African elite related to occupational roles, the common elements in their general social status may prove of equal or greater significance for the political outlook. All Africans, irrespective of occupation, are subjected to regulations and controls based upon race, which are imposed by rulers of another race in the interests of their people. Moreover, South African economic development has been very rapid so that many Africans enjoy a material standard of living much higher than that of Africans in other countries. But the greater the advance, the greater the impatience with arbitrary restraint. The drive to revolutionary change does not come from the poorest people; it comes from groups which have been advancing and raising their standards but feel that they are deprived relative to groups which have greater influence in the structure of power. Apartheid heightens the tension between anticipation and reality. 'The Government is driven, by the need for moral justification and for African acceptance, to boost the rewards of separate development. But it dare not grant these rewards, lest African advancement undermine Afrikaner power or diminish Afrikaner profit' (Kuper, 1965: 404). Though occupation affects the involvement of Africans in political protest, it is unlikely that any particular occupation will provide an undue proportion of leaders, because government surveillance is close; much will depend upon the personal commitment of individuals, but, given its existing position of social leadership, the 'middle class' elite is bound to provide many of the African political leaders also. Having the regard of other Africans, the elite is less flattered by social patronage on the part of Whites. A research worker who studied *Manyanos* (women's church groups) reported: 'the higher the social class of a Church or a *Manyano*, the less inclined the members are to welcome a European woman visitor' (Brandel-Syrier, 1962: 31).

Hitherto, the South African government has not needed to modify its ideological perspectives in order to keep the subordinate groups divided. The Hertzog governments of 1924–39 eliminated Africans from the common electoral roll in the Cape and instituted a system whereby qualified Africans, on a separate voting list, elected three white representatives in Parliament. But, although Hertzog was opposed to miscegenation, he saw in the coloured group a 'natural ally' of the Whites against the 'Black menace' and favoured its economic, cultural, and political assimilation. Since World War II this view of the coloured group has been abandoned. Many amenities are *Net Vir Blankes*, for Whites only. All non-Whites are barred, and there is no favoured treatment for any intermediate category. Racial segregation on a two-category basis is the rule in respect of restaurants, hotels, cinemas, hospitals, schools, waiting-rooms, park benches, beaches, cemeteries, residential areas, ambulances, blood transfusion, taxis, trains, buses, picnic areas, airports, entrances to public buildings, swimming baths, sports grounds, post offices, lifts, banks, toilets, bars, national parks, and many other places, though, as in the Deep South, non-white servants accompanying their employers may be allowed to use facilities restricted to Whites. The Reservation of Separate Amenities Act of 1953 provides that these amenities shall be not only separate but also unequal (van den Berghe, 1965: 126–7, 57–58). By subjecting the Indians and the Coloureds to the same disabilities as the Africans, the government encourages these groups to enter into political alliance, but Indian leaders have not found much enthusiasm for such a policy among their people and the leaders of the Coloureds have only recently started looking in this direction. (Though the Indians are being forced into the general non-white category, it appears that some Whites may regard them as anomalies in the racial structure; this seems the most charitable explanation of the finding that in a social-distance test one-fourth of Afrikaner and one-fifth of English-speaking students indicated that they wished 'someone would kill all Indians' – Pettigrew, 1960: 248. Historical evidence for such an interpretation is implicit in an 1884 Transvaal petition against Asian immigration, which declared: 'Our constitution recognizes only two races of men, white and coloured.') Non-white solidarity has been growing slowly, being subject to periodic setbacks. In 1949 the Zulus in Durban rioted, looting Indian shops and houses, and killing and wounding several hundreds of Indians. At first the police seemed to be attracted to the 'give him some more ammuni-tion and turn him loose' outlook, but later they intervened and their own indiscriminate gunfire greatly added to the casualty figures. In all, 142 persons were killed and 1,087 injured. Yet, after the event, Indian leaders reiterated their desire for friendship with the Africans.

In March 1960 a crowd of Africans who had converged upon the police station at Sharpeville in the Transvaal, as part of a peaceful protest against the pass laws, were fired on by the police. On the same day there was a similar scene at Langa, in Cape Province. Altogether that day 72 Africans were reported killed and 180 wounded (many of them shot in the back). Events of this kind – apart from their effect on world opinion – mark the steps by which the sentiment of solidarity is built up in an oppressed category of persons. Even such violence, however, cannot prevent the internal divisions among Africans opening up when the situation is not felt to be one of crisis. Policies of apartheid work along lines of natural cleavage in appealing to the traditionally oriented Africans as opposed to the modernizing ones, and to the middle classes rather than the workers. The principle of 'the advantages of the disadvantages' applies here too. African ministers in the Dutch Reformed Church may support government policy because of the opportunity it gives them to build up their own congregations. At times it becomes difficult to determine whether the more effective opponent of white supremacy is the multiracialist or the Black racialist. In the Transkei, the first of the Bantustans, Paramount Chief Victor Poto stood for representative government on a non-racial basis and obtained a majority of votes, but he could not command a majority in the new assembly because his opponent, Chief Kaiser Mantanzima, obtained more support from the appointed members (mostly chiefs sitting *ex officio*). Mantanzima has learned the vocabulary of apartheid and uses it to press for an extension of territory and greater powers. He might well prove a more serious embarrassment to the government than his opponent.

The way in which the growing African sense of solidarity has to compromise with other ties, giving particular Africans competing interests, is illustrated in the employment of Africans in the lower reaches of the white bureaucracy. There is great competition for clerical posts. In discussions with educated Africans in Durban, Kuper found much tolerance for the African civil servant. They tended to judge him not so much by his position and its duties, as by his attitude to the work and his identification with his own people; even men in the more notorious sections of the administration gave help when they could. Studies of work relations in Western industry have shown that an organization can never be so perfected that it can be made to function adequately simply by penalizing the people who fail to observe the regulations. Something more positive is needed. Employees can hamstring any organization by 'working to rule'. The African employee in South Africa is more vulnerable than most – even Marx never envisaged so complete a system of control over the lives of the proletariat – but some measure of co-operation from him is still needed and can be withheld. There is some give-and-take in the social system. Thus a police chief may have difficulty using African constables for raids on African dwellings when the people are especially indignant and the policemen sympathize with them. One deputy commissioner of police explained his intention to reduce the frequency of liquor raids by saying that the raids were becoming too great a strain on his force; the force was becoming identified with the city council and was losing prestige and popularity with the African population on account of such raids. An African lawyer does not necessarily experience difficulty in relations with white court officials who are less educated than he. One of them testified: 'The average civil servant here who is Afrikaans feels oppressed by the English. He is anxious to show how anti-English he is by attending to me before an English attorney. This happens also in the Police Force, and they tend to give you better treatment. Also, they like to tell you that I am not well treated by the English. I speak to them in Afrikaans.' This observation supports the claim that the idea of a political alliance between the Africans and one of the white groups against the other white group was a serious possibility. Though the government has tried to strip away ties that cross the colour line, it has not been altogether successful; new ones are continually created by the interests of the employer and the common sentiments of people who share the same industrial culture. It is the tenacity of such ties that explains why 'daily life is characterized by innumerable acts of co-operation between persons of different race in every sphere of life, vastly in excess of the violent encounters' (Kuper, 1965: 256, 343, 237, 408).

Though various groups in the non-white population are still far from making common cause, and though the legislative foundations of separate development have been laid in a long sequence of enactments and regulations, there is little to suggest that group relations are becoming more peaceable. On the contrary, there seems to be on all sides a resigned acceptance of the inevitability of violence. In Marxist terms, the Africans constitute a class 'in itself' rather than a class 'for itself' because they lack consciousness of their shared place in the system. Not until they have acquired such a consciousness will there be a 'revolutionary situation' in the Republic (Lewin, 1963: 107–15). An ideology of revolution has been formulated by the nationalistic Pan-African Congress in its struggle with the originally multiracialist African Nationalist Congress. The basic assumptions of the Pan-Africanists' political theory are Marxist, but its conclusions are non-Marxist in that it holds the conflict to be a racial and not a class conflict (Kuper, 1965: 371–87). African organization has not developed in very close accord with the Marxist prediction and there are indications that the Afrikaner outlook is flexible enough to modify a system of race relations once it ceases to be profitable. There are still few signs of a confrontation between a homogeneous proletariat and a homogeneous bourgeoisie.

INTERPERSONAL RELATIONS

When South African Whites and Africans are directly involved with one another, the two may interpret similar events in quite different ways. As many Whites do not respect African cultures or seek to understand them, they may fail to see that the Africans' view of the situation is a reflection of a different culture and regard it simply as an indication of childishness or stupidity. How frequent and important these misunderstandings may be depends upon the nature of the association. The relation between an employer and an employee does not necessarily require mutual understanding in any depth. But the missionary who seeks to preach the Gospel effectively may wish to understand the African outlook on a great variety of fundamental matters.

In some respects the cultural gap is wide and deep. It has been argued by the Rev. Placide Tempels that there is a recognizable Bantu philosophy in much of Southern Africa. Instead of basing itself, as Cartesian thought does, on the idea of 'being', this Bantu philosophy is said to have as its central concept an idea of 'essence' expressed as 'life-strength' or 'power'. This force is ethically neutral, so that ideas of good and evil have social rather than natural roots. Man is seen as part of nature, not as a being who has to master nature either without or within. There is no dualism of body and soul, mind and matter, God and man (Tempels, 1945). This theory is not easy to substantiate in a scientific manner and it has not met with complete acceptance, but to many people who have tried to translate European ideas into African cultural terms it carries conviction. There are many instances of urban Africans' interpreting events in their lives in a way that accords with the theory and illustrates the relevance of cultural differences to interpersonal relations. A man's success is attributed not to the logic of his actions but to his personal power. Ideas originating in the traditional ancestor cult are absorbed into the observance of Christian ritual. Mia Brandel-Syrier, who investigated these questions in Johannesburg, stresses the frequent identification of Christianity and civilization. She is convinced that the urge to become Christian, civilized, educated, and 'modern' is much more pressing for the women than the men. For the women, change in this direction means an expansion of personality and opportunity whereas, for the men, the adoption of Western norms means a restriction upon their traditional domestic authority and a yet more ambivalent relation with the institutions of the white employers. The same writer maintains that in traditional culture knowledge of sexual matters was incorporated into a consistent outlook. Christian missionaries forbade the initiation schools in which such knowledge was imparted, and provided no substitute. Consequently, Africans have come to see Christianity as having no bearing upon sexual behaviour. When asked to give reasons for disapproving of premarital childbirth, only two out of forty-nine nurses suggested that it was sinful. This is just one example of how the missionaries' doctrines have been mistaught or misunderstood. Others could be cited, and they exemplify a serious obstacle to interracial communication (Brandel–Syrier, 1962: 110–64).

There is an interesting implication that, in a white supremacy society, the Negro women gain a relative advantage because they suffer less from racial subordination than their men, and because the subordination of the men permits their women to seize greater authority in domestic matters. This was the case in the United States and the West Indies. It resulted in a matrifocal pattern of family living which devalued masculine activities and, by affecting the personalities of those who grew up within it, made it harder for the Negro community to climb up from the bottom of the economic scale. On the western side of the Atlantic the Negro women often made status gains through being sought as wives or concubines by white men. Reports from South Africa suggest that even without miscegenation a similar tendency may set in, for the Johannesburg conclusions are borne out by a much more comprehensive study in East London, Cape Province. This investigation shows how complex the picture can be. East London is a city with over 43,000 white residents and nearly 70,000 others. Almost all the non-white residents are drawn from the Xhosa-speaking peoples – a Bantu group centred upon the nearby Ciskeian and Transkeian reserves. The Xhosa have responded to contact with Whites in two contrasting ways. One group, the 'School' people, are at least nominal church adherents, send their children to school, and adopt many European standards. The other group, the 'Red' people, wear the old-fashioned red blanket and try to maintain the traditional style of rural life; they spend any savings upon establishing a homestead and stocking it with cattle and sheep. But in modern conditions Xhosa cannot make much of a living from the land alone. It is essential that some members of a family should obtain wage-earning employment in one of the towns if the others are to live above subsistence level (Mayer, 1961). In East London the distinction between the School and the Red migrants is maintained, but it is overlaid by another. Not every African now has rights to land in the reserves. There is a significant number of landless rural labourers who must seek a rural employer if they cannot obtain official permission to remain in the town. With the growth of the urban population there is, therefore, a considerable number of Africans who, either because of choice or because of land shortage, become 'real townsmen' in the sense of living their lives in an urban menial environment as well as an urban physical environment. Fourteen per cent of the present adult population of East London have been born in the city – most of them the children of School parents.

Unable to deploy effective sanctions against erring members, the second generation shows many of the features that conventionally indicate social disorganization. The majority of the town Bantu girls have at least one baby before they get married. Over 60 per cent of the unmarried town-born females over the age of fifteen years in a sample were mothers (Pauw, 1963: 118). There is a further tendency for unmarried mothers to continue to have children as they grow older. Extramarital sexual relations are common and marriage is unstable. But the evidence shows that the urban Xhosa women can, if necessary, support children by their own efforts. The social price such a household pays for the absence of a legitimate husband and father is one of lowered esteem; economically the household can be quite viable (Pauw, 1963: viii). This suggests that, though the differences are still considerable, an enforced colour line in the second and subsequent generations brings African household structure closer to that reported for Negro American communities.

This same study stresses that African clubs, churches, and other associations in the town are highly 'Western' in their organization and activities. Those who engage fully in town life are convinced of the preferability of 'civilized' to 'tribal' ways in modern circumstances, and in an urban industrial social system they must organize along lines compatible with the other pressures in that system. The cultural differences mentioned earlier may persist, but that is not to claim that they are relevant in every social situation. To the Red Xhosa the Whites remain first and foremost a foreign 'tribe' which has vanquished them; the principal political grievance is that they have continued to exploit their victory in a 'cruel' manner, perpetuating their own domination by force. Xhosa complain, 'They hate anyone who preaches unity to us'. Or, 'I have nothing in particular against the white way of life. As a different race from us their way of life ought to be different too. It's their bad attitude towards us that I don't like. I don't care how they live, if they don't offend others.' The attitudes of School people hold a strong element of ambivalence. When they complain of 'being kept

down' they do not mean that they wish to escape from Whites but that
the Whites are 'cruel' not to let Xhosa share in the fruits of civilization.
In other respects, common incidents of town life breed deep resentment
among both Red and School people: 'White people humiliate a Native
father in the presence of his family.' 'A young white foreman will clap
a much older Native on the face with his open hand.' 'I hate the foolish
names white people give us.' 'White people do not want us to stay with
them in town. Why? Have we got an offensive smell? What about
our womenfolk who do their domestic work?' 'They are all united
against the Africans.' The better educated School migrants expressed
their attitudes in more general terms, for example: 'We Xhosa are not
employed in the better posts, under the false pretence that we are
incompetent. . . . We lack opportunities. We have been prevented from
prosperity.' Contact between Whites and Xhosa is affected by the
segregation of the Native locations and the white town. Few Whites
are ever seen in the locations but many Africans come into the white
town (where they are allowed between the hours of 5 a.m. and 11 p.m.,
provided they have special passes). They come to work in white enterprises or households, or for shopping or sightseeing. Pay and conditions
of employment are determined by the white employer alone, for African
trade unions have not been allowed effective powers. Economic and
social discrimination are ubiquitous, but pleasant relations at an individual level are not unusual. A Xhosa may fulminate against white
people's 'cruelty' or 'arrogance' in general, but praise a given employer
or foreman as being kind and understanding. At work, a kind of
camaraderie sometimes develops: the foreman cracks a joke with his
'boys', the housewife receives confidences from her 'girl'. But personal
appreciation, where it does occur, has to be contained within the limits
of the formal master-servant relation (Mayer, 1961: 32–33, 50–51).
Non-Whites are expected to behave in a subservient manner and address
Whites as 'Sir', 'Madam', 'Master', or *baas*. The Whites address
Africans by their first names (real or imagined), or as 'boy' or 'girl'.

Interpersonal relations between Whites and non-Whites have been
restricted to those of the master-servant type by a battery of legislation,
much of which dates from the Nationalist political victory of 1948. It
has been reviewed by the International Commission of Jurists, whose
report (1960) has been used for the following summary. A fundamental
provision is the Population Registration Act of 1950, which empowers
the Director of Census to allocate all persons to racial categories. Some
flexibility is permitted in its operation. Japanese diplomats and trade
representatives have been counted 'honorary' Whites. A white man

lived with a coloured woman whom he considered his wife and refused to leave; he was told by the magistrate that he would have to ask the population registrar to reclassify him as coloured; though this would entail leaving his job and forgoing association with Whites, he was apparently willing to follow the course suggested. But the effect of the Act is to prevent 'passing' and to keep the colour line sharp. In 1952 the pass laws were consolidated and extended to women. All adult Africans are required to carry a 'reference book'; failure to produce it immediately on the demand of a policeman is an offence punishable by a fine or imprisonment. This law, together with others that give magistrates power to regulate the movement and employment of Africans in or about the urban areas, enables the government to control African activities very closely. If a native commissioner or magistrate declares an African 'to be an idle or undesirable person' he may order him to be removed from the urban area or to be sent to a work colony or farm for employment. In a number of cases, Africans have literally no right to live anywhere in their own country; quite frequently women have no right to live with their husbands, and unmarried daughters may not be permitted to reside with their parents (cf. *The Guardian*, 30 November 1965, reporting on cases investigated by the Institute of Race Relations – Black Sash Advice Office at Cape Town). The Group Areas Act of 1950 has been used to drive African workers out to locations many miles from their place of work. It was amended in 1956 in a way that permits African freehold areas to be declared group areas for other races.

Occasionally, such rules and regulations operate to the disadvantage of individual Whites and to the advantage of individual non-Whites. Thus a commentator upon life in the spacious suburbs of modern Johannesburg remarked:

'I was present when a consignment of drinks was delivered at a friend's front door. She asked her male cook to help her carry the bottles to the wine closet. As he did not appear, she called out a second time: "Maiko, will you please help me?" He replied: "If the madam wants a porter, she better send for one. Any more wrong orders and I leave." My friend went very red in the face and turned on her heel without a word. Later she explained that owing to the difficulty Africans had in getting permits to work in white areas, servants were at a premium. Only very rich people could afford white servants, but it was being made increasingly difficult to employ non-white domestics in the city' (Listowel, 1966: 745).

Africans cannot present much threat to the government's desire to keep White-African relations on a master-servant basis. Dissident Whites are a greater threat. They have been checked by other laws. The Suppression of Communism Act (1950) enables the Minister to name as a communist anyone who has ever 'advocated, advised, defended or encouraged the achievement of any of the objects of communism' either actively or even by any 'omission which is calculated to further the achievement of any such object', etc. An Immorality Act of 1927 had prohibited extramarital sexual relations between Europeans and Africans; further legislation in the 1950s was used to make an offence of what might be termed 'statutory immorality', by which any white person associating with non-Whites could be brought to court and, even if acquitted, would probably suffer serious damage to his or her reputation. Control is further increased by laws inhibiting peaceful assembly and association when they involve members of different racial groups, and laws regulating freedom of opinion and expression. The list of barred books includes the UNESCO booklets on race and extends to anti-Nazi literature, such as Edward Crankshaw's book, *Gestapo*. As has been shown in the case of the American South, the maintenance of a colour line means less freedom for those above the line as well as for those below it.

THE ECONOMIC DYSFUNCTIONS OF RACISM

Afrikaner nationalism tends to be almost consciously anti-capitalistic. A recent *laissez-faire* critic complains: 'the survival of *apartheid* is, indeed, the survival of a kind of socialism', recapitulating unawares the views of mid-nineteenth-century American writers like Fitzhugh who saw slavery and socialism as alternatives to the ravages of capitalism (see Chapter Six, p. 127). The South African critic maintains that 'disinterested market pressures, under the profit-seeking inducement, provide the only objective, systematic discipline that would dissolve traditional barriers and offer opportunities irrespective or race or colour' (Hutt, 1964: 73). The plight of the Negro in the northern cities of the United States and the unwanted consequences of individual profit-seeking in the plural societies of South-East Asia suggest that this proposition holds only in certain circumstances – which its advocate does not explore – but in contemporary South Africa at least there are hundreds of ready examples of how the businessman's interests are frustrated by the legislation of apartheid.

The tensions between the political and the economic systems of South Africa have been concisely analysed by Pierre L. van den Berghe

(1965: 183–216), and the concluding section of this chapter needs only to summarize his statement with a little extra supporting evidence. In the first place, the South African economy reflects the imbalances inherent in any economic system with an extensive subsistence sector that is undergoing rapid industrialization. In the second place, it is affected by a variety of economic dysfunctions arising from private and official discrimination and prejudice. The outstanding example of such dysfunctions is provided by the reliance upon migratory labour, which increases the social disorganization of the African community, adds to labour costs, and results in a gigantic waste of the labour force's potential. Migratory labour is maintained, first, because of the high initial capital investment that would be needed were even rudimentary housing for the workers' families to be substituted for single men's barracks; second, because the Chamber of Mines has a vested interest in the migratory pattern: gold-mining would become unprofitable if wages were substantially raised; third, the government sees a political interest in a system that facilitates segregation and control over the labourers, even though all the measures it has framed have not prevented the permanent settlement of increasing numbers of Africans in towns. Other forms of discrimination have economic consequences similar to those of dependence upon migratory labour. A wide range of occupations is reserved to white labour, and Africans are prevented from competing for them in a way that would raise efficiency (cf. Hutt, 1964: 117–20). Whereas Whites are free to form trade unions and to strike, Africans are not; with the result that white workers are able to push up their wages at the expense of non-union labour. Since their wage levels are not fixed by the balancing actions of a free market, Africans do not have the incentive to work which would increase their consumer demand and the output of the industries that cater to it (cf. also van den Berghe, 1965: 166–7; van der Horst, 1965: 130–3, 137). As each racial group is expected to finance its own amenities, including schools and hospitals, the African labour force is less healthy and skilled than it might be. Segregated facilities cost more, and the transport costs entailed by the distant siting of African locations are considerable. Schemes to rehabilitate the native reserves and to establish institutions of higher education away from the main urban centres run counter to the principles of economic location. Foreign indignation over apartheid policies has at times made overseas financiers reluctant to invest in South African enterprises.

In the third place are the economic dysfunctions springing from the conflict between capitalist interests and the demands of political

ideology. The English-speaking business class looks on the Afrikaner
Nationalists with disdain but fears that government policy is restricting
their privileges, threatening their language and way of life, and contra-
vening almost every rational principle of economic development. Apartheid is seen as impractical, costly, economically harmful, and politically
dangerous rather than as morally objectionable. Nationalist intellectuals,
in a fashion unanticipated in the Marxist theory, developed economic
power for ideological ends. Their government, since its accession to
power, has done much to channel contracts to Afrikaner business.
An indication of how valuable state aid may be in this connection is
provided by figures concerning Sanlam, the biggest Afrikaner insurance
company. Its assets amounted to £3½ million in 1939, to £10 million
in 1949, and to £90 million in 1961. It is impossible for the Nationalists
fully to implement their policy of apartheid so long as a major sector
of the economy lies beyond their control. They aim, therefore, to
create a corporate state in which the interests of capital and labour
will be co-ordinated by state bodies directed by members of the
Afrikaner political elite (Bunting, 1964: 279–94).

If the dysfunctions of racism are so extensive, why, then, does the
South African economy continue to expand so rapidly? The answer
must be that a country of open resources, with natural wealth, an
abundance of one of the factors of production (in this case, labour),
and a loosely knit overall social structure, can tolerate contradictions
that would be impossible in a mature and highly integrated economy
such as that of Great Britain. In addition, the high level of technological skills in the population, white and non-white, puts South Africa
at an advantage compared with other African countries; also, the
rigorous style of government planning is often modified by compromise
and negotiations between the parties concerned. How far such com-
promises will bring about changes in the fundamentals of the present
system of racial division it is impossible to predict. The major opposition
to the government policies is unrepresented in the House of Assembly,
and the groups above the colour line are forced to coalesce whenever
the Africans seem to be mobilizing their political potential. Many of
the social scientists who know South Africa from the inside seem to
feel that, although the immediate future will be a time of violence and
bitterness, the white population's interest in security and prosperity is so
great that over the years the power structure and its policies may
change enough to avert the ultimate conflagration.

CHAPTER NINE

Colonial Africa: Religious Rejections

In Chapter Five mention was made of cult movements arising among peoples subject to influences from much stronger European civilizations. They are of interest for the light they shed on the tensions in such contact situations. Comparable movements have arisen in Africa and have attracted the attention of scholars interested in their possible political significance. There has been a tendency to stress the extent to which the new African churches serve as vehicles for the expression of political protest and to neglect the nature of their religious appeal (e.g. Lantenari, 1963). Yet much of the evidence fits more closely Max Weber's conclusion that, 'however incisive the social influences, economically and politically determined, may have been upon a religious ethic in a particular case, it receives its stamp primarily from religious sources, and, first of all, from the content of its annunciation and promise' (1947: 270). Those who favour a political interpretation often represent these movements and their teachings as more coherent than the evidence warrants. Proceeding, therefore, from an examination of one of the more instructive cases, this chapter will explore some of the interrelations between political and religious factors in the growth of prophetic cults.

AFRICAN PROPHETS

On 18 March 1921, a Mukongo named Simon Kimbangu was, so he said, 'touched by the grace of God'. He claimed an ability to cure the sick and raise the dead. Disposed either to believe such claims or to give them a trial, people came flocking to him. Some were cured and so his fame spread. Simon Kimbangu had been a catechist of the English Baptist mission in the Belgian Congo and was, according to reliable accounts, a diligent and enthusiastic student of the Bible. He read his Bible and preached it to his followers, presenting himself as a messenger of God.

The news that the despised Blacks now had a prophet of their own swept over the land like a tidal wave. As economic conditions at the time were unfavourable, the people were even more willing to listen than they might otherwise have been. At first they believed that Kimbangu had put himself at the head of a Protestant movement, so they massed in the Protestant churches both in the Belgian Congo and in French Equatorial Africa. Then the tide turned and the churches were emptied. Everyone rallied to the prophet. One Protestant hospital which had been badly overcrowded emptied completely. Even Catholic churches lost their congregations. Natives employed by local firms left their jobs to take part in pilgrimages to Kimbangu's village, Nkamba, which his adherents renamed Jerusalem.

The colonial administration was quickly informed of these developments and was soon under pressure from commercial interests to take repressive action. But the local administrator was not convinced that this was any more than a religious movement. There seemed no good grounds for arresting the prophet or for interfering with the religious liberties of the people. On 11 May he went to see Kimbangu, but the latter refused to talk with him, saying that God had commanded him and his followers to sing, dance, and read the Bible without interruption for ten days and ten nights. That he was able to ignore the administrator's advances contributed considerably to Kimbangu's prestige. 'We have found the God of the blacks', the Africans said, and came to him in ever greater numbers, until he may have had some 10,000 followers. To help him with his burgeoning movement, Kimbangu selected a group of apostles from among his adherents and sent them out to preach the word. The demand for leaders was so great, and Kimbangu's control so weak, that soon many self-appointed prophets built up local followings. The movement started to acquire a nationalistic and anti-European aspect; therefore, after attempting to mediate through one of the missions, the government decided to intervene. On 26 June Kimbangu was arrested in Nkamba, but later that day he escaped and went into hiding. To have evaded the Belgian soldiery enhanced his reputation still further. More and more workers fled from their employment on the railway and in European enterprises; the economic life of the whole region was seriously disorganized.

Accounts differ as to how Kimbangu was eventually caught. According to one version he was betrayed by the African catechist of a Catholic mission (Chomé, 1959: 49–51). According to some African informants, Kimbangu returned voluntarily to Nkamba, emulating the surrender of Jesus to the Temple (Andersson, 1958: 66). At all events, he was arrested on either 14 or 15 September 1921, and brought to trial immediately. The movement had not been responsible for any violation of the peace; nor had it been directly responsible for the death of any person. The judgement of the court on 16 October did not hold Kimbangu guilty of any specific offence, but decided that, in as much as he had disturbed the native population, had spread false religious notions among the natives and instigated them against the established powers, had posed as the saviour of the Blacks, and had created a state of affairs in which anti-white sentiment was rapidly increasing, he should be sentenced to death and his eleven principal followers to life imprisonment. Appeals were made to the king on Kimbangu's behalf. The local colonists submitted a petition urging his immediate execution. However, in the following month his sentence was remitted to life imprisonment and Kimbangu was banished to Elizabethville gaol in Katanga.

At the trial, one of the defendants, according to a newspaper account, had the impudence to question the judge himself and ask him why the Africans were forbidden to have their God, their prophet, and their Bible, seeing that the Whites had theirs. The judge was so indignant at such a question that he suspended the sitting. This incident demonstrates very well how the Kimbangu movement must have developed. Kimbangu himself was a relatively modest man with no delusions of grandeur, but his followers wanted him to be something more and his lieutenants doubtless helped to build up myths of his near-divinity. The people frankly regarded Kimbangu as their Jesus and awaited his second coming which was to usher in the millennium. The movement had to go underground before any central organization or agreed doctrine had been established. Minor prophets maintained clandestine followings in many parts of the lower Congo, preaching a mixture of evangelical Christianity, millenarian hope, and traditional belief. At times Kimbangist beliefs found legal expression in new cult movements such as the Mission des Noirs, which borrowed heavily from the Salvation Army and in whose creed Kimbangu becomes the 'Saviour and King of the Blacks', a part of the person of Christ. 'God', the cult says, 'has not wished that we should hear his word without our being tested. He has sent us Simon Kimbangu who is for us the Moses of the Jews, the Christ of the strangers, and the Mohammed of the Arabs.'

Notice that Kimbangu was at liberty as a prophet only from 18 March to 14 September – a period of less than six months, half of which he had to spend in hiding. Notice that he spent the remaining thirty years of his life in Elizabethville gaol, where he worked as a cook, completely out of contact with his followers and doing nothing further to support the image of himself as a national or religious leader. Yet, despite this, his fame extended. The Belgian authorities had, from 1921 well into the 1950s, to exile from their home districts appreciable numbers of religious enthusiasts, many of whom were identified in some degree with Kimbangu.

At the end of 1958 about 60,000 people belonged to this illegal organization, by then known as the 'Church of Jesus Christ on Earth according to Simon Kimbangu'. After the riots of January 1959, many people abandoned the Catholic and Protestant churches for the Kimbangists, whose numbers rose to about 100,000. Then, in December of that year, less than six months before the Congo became independent, the Belgians lifted their ban on the movement. It is interesting to note in passing that during the riots many people believed that Kimbangu had returned in the flesh. Once the movement was legalized, the church had Kimbangu's remains brought to Leopoldville, and reinterred in April 1960 at a ceremony patronized by leading political figures – for Kimbangism was playing an open political role allied to Abako, the Bakongo nationalist party.

During the time it was proscribed the Kimbangist movement seems to have split: on the one hand, there were many local cults which venerated the prophet's name but were under the control of their own leaders (Raymaeckers, 1959: 679–87; Gilis, 1960: 84–90); on the other hand, a group led by Kimbangu's sons and mother began, in the second half of the 1950s, to organize a church on more orthodox lines and to seek European approval. The latter group, the 'Church of Jesus Christ on Earth according to Simon Kimbangu', led by the third of the prophet's sons, resembles the Protestant churches in belief and practice except that its members believe Kimbangu to have been the messenger of Jesus Christ to the Blacks, and that one day he will return again. The prophet's charisma has been routinized, the element of political protest has been shed and, though the beliefs of the members vary greatly, the theology disseminated by the leading group resembles that of the Protestant missions in everything except the view of the founder. He, be it noted, is not claimed as the equal of Christ but is held to be the other comforter whom Christ said he would send later (Raymaeckers, 1959: 737–8; cf. The Gospel according to St John xiv. 12–18).

Few other African movements reflect quite so well as Kimbangism how political forces may mould religious beliefs and activities, but there have been a host of comparable movements which have shown similar features. The Amicalist movement in the neighbouring

French Congo is a case in point. Its founder, André Matswa, was brought back from Paris to Brazzaville to stand trial for irregularities in the conduct of a society that had been formed to aid Africans in distress, but was acquiring a political character. The Bakongo people saw hardly anything of Matswa except when he appeared as the opponent and victim of the colonial administration, which made it easier for him to become a symbol of every sort of political resistance (Balandier, 1955: 398–400). Matswa was banished, and later died in prison in 1942. Many followers refused to believe that he was dead, and his name was put up, successfully, for election to the legislative assembly in 1947. A popular view was that 'the whites may perhaps have killed him, but he has risen again, and one day he will return to power and majesty to drive away the whites and their black troops'. Though the movement had started as a secular one, its leader had become Jésus Matswa and a messiah in the minds of his fellow tribesmen. Andersson, in his admirable book on messianic movements in the lower Congo, shows that they date back to the early eighteenth century and have been both numerous and influential. Van Wing adds the names of more such cults to the list, such as Mvungism, Tonsi, Les Dieudonnés, and Tokism; it is clear that the roll call for the lower Congo is lengthy but by no means complete.

Farther inland in the Congo and over the Rhodesian border, the Watch Tower movement, known as Kitawala, has been very active among some peoples and appears to have had political content at times (Kaufmann, 1964: 69–101; Taylor & Lehmann, 1961: 227–47). In Northern Rhodesia in the middle 1950s there was alarm over what was known as the 'Alice Movement'. Two years previously a Bemba woman, Alice Lenshina Mulenga, had a revelation from the Almighty, who instructed her to preach. She reported her vision to the local Presbyterian mission and, without any encouragement from that quarter, started baptizing, laying hands on the sick, and exhorting Africans to lead a life according to biblical teaching. She, too, was a modest leader, in no way anti-European, but the movement became identified in the eyes of many Whites and Africans with the Nationalist cause. Mission schools in some localities were emptied in consequence of the attraction her movement had for her fellow Africans (Rotberg, 1961; Taylor & Lehmann, 1961: 248–68). Some two years before Zambia's independence in January 1964, members of the 'Lumpa Church' (as the movement had become known) were instructed to take no part in political activities. This injunction seems to have been part of a tendency to make the church more exclusive and pietistical. When they refused to join the dominant Nationalist party Lumpa members were attacked by some political activists. Feeling encircled, members of the church responded with apparent desperation, attacking police and villages of non-members. At least 500 persons were killed in the disorders of July and August 1964 before Alice Lenshina surrendered to the government. After being kept in protective custody for some months, she was released.

Religious movements of this kind are no new development in Africa; as in the Pacific, they go back to the early days of colonial rule, and religious elements have been present in very many African rebellions. Some of the rebellions aimed simply at recovering the traditional way of life, but the prophetic cults have mostly been forward-looking, seeking to institutionalize a creative response to the new influences. Not all the new religious movements have centred upon a prophet. John Chilembwe, the African clergyman who founded an independent church in Nyasaland, claimed no prophetic vision and did not display any messianic faith in his power to deliver his people. Like some other African leaders, Chilembwe and his immediate adherents were 'marginal men', seeking to preserve some elements of the old and mix in others of the new, but, caught in the opposition between African and European society, they lost control over the forces they unleashed. In 1915 Chilembwe's followers embarked upon a bloody but short-lived revolt which has been made the subject of a detailed historical analysis (Shepperson & Price, 1958). In other parts of the continent, in South Africa, Uganda, Kenya, Ivory Coast, Nigeria, etc., independent churches have attracted the attention of scholars because of the light they throw upon racial and cultural contacts. Though each of these movements has its own character, it is remarkable how some features are recapitulated and how many common themes serve to unite them both with one another and with others outside Africa (Thrupp, 1962; Talmon, 1962; Köbben, 1960).

It has been noted by many commentators that movements of this kind serve as a medium for the expression of social protest, both the inarticulate protest of people subject to a new order they cannot understand or master, and the more clear-cut opposition of peoples prevented from expressing themselves in direct political action. On these lines it has been claimed that there is an association between the large-scale messianic movements of the Kimbangu type, which can spread like a bush fire, and the relative oppressiveness of a colonial social order in which the gulf between Africans and Europeans seems unbridgeable. This general thesis obviously contains an essential element of truth but it is subject to many limitations. The extent to which any religious movement expresses protest varies from time to time, and one cannot easily be compared with another. To take a key example: it has been demonstrated that the Kikuyu independent schools in Kenya – which had links with independent churches – did not produce any higher proportion of Mau Mau adherents than did those under mission management (cf. Welbourn, 1961: 160). At times it is impossible to establish that the element of protest is of any significance at all.

Very soon the student of these movements is brought face to face with the problem encountered by anyone concerned with the sociology of religion: the explanation of faith. At first there was little pressure to treat prophet movements or cargo cults as religious phenomena meriting the same respect as the observer might accord a group representing a major world religion. But this is no longer the case. The problem has been pointed up in respect of Kimbangism by Jules Chomé, a European lawyer, whose book *La Passion de Simon Kimbangu* is written in such a way as to emphasize the similarities between the life of Kimbangu and that of Jesus: curing the sick, appointing disciples, running foul of the established religious authorities, becoming a nuisance to the colonial administration, being betrayed, arrested, tried, and condemned. The author claims, in effect, that the one story is as credible as the other.

A similar lesson is taught by a very different volume, the study *East African Rebels*, by F. B. Welbourn, then (1961) a Protestant chaplain at the University College of East Africa. Other writers have been inclined to draw attention to ways in which separatist movements embody elements of traditional practice; to show, for example, how a prophet may play a part similar to that of the diviner in traditional custom; and in this way they have implied that the new movements remain partly pagan and therefore less worthy. Welbourn, however, is prepared to recognize that much that Westerners regard as belonging to Christian practice is pagan in origin, and that a more serious attempt will have to be made to separate what are necessary requirements of faith from what are only elements of Western culture. To take a rather different illustration: it is probable that most people of any religion would find it strange to participate in a service planned according to their own faith but arranged for deaf and dumb people. To strip away the cultural idiom of religious expression and concentrate upon the core of belief would be quite impossible for most believers. Building upon the work of earlier missionary authors, Welbourn is able to go beyond them and face up to the argument of East African independent churches that

female circumcision and polygamy are simply African customs and no
more opposed to Christian belief than male circumcision or the tolera-
tion of involuntary spinsterhood. The evaluation of the ethic of these
movements from a theological standpoint must be an agonizing task;
but independently of this there is a need for sociological examination.
The African peasant leaves no personal documents about how the new
changes affect him, and the best evidence available about the social and
psychological concomitants of change is often that implicit in the new
institutions characteristic of the situation. The range of institutional
innovation is not so very great and religious organizations are in many
ways as useful an indicator of change as the new voluntary associations
or political institutions.

THE PROPHETIC ROLE AND THE SOCIAL ORDER

A striking feature of many new cults is that religious leaders who, by
conventional standards, were undistinguished figures, and whose period
of activity was very short, should have been judged so significant by
their contemporaries and by later generations. Kimbangu, who played
the role of prophet for six months out of a life of about sixty-two years,
is regarded as the messiah of his people, the door through which the
black race may enter heaven. According to others, the Kingdom will
come when André Matswa returns to judge the missions. Of Chilembwe,
we are told: 'Many Africans deny that he is dead. To the simple, he is a
liberator who will come again.' To the enlightened, he is a hero (Shepperson & Price, 1958: 415; cf. Wishlade, 1965: 139). The important
thing about these leaders seems to be not what they were but what they
symbolized.

There is a parallel here with the legend of the honourable robber as
it developed in Europe in early modern times. One of the best examples
of this legend is the figure of Robin Hood (Hirn, 1941; cf. Hobsbawm,
1959: 22–23). Nothing certain is known about him, but there is no
reason for thinking that, as an outlaw, he would have been a particularly
estimable sort of person. He was popularly believed to have robbed the
rich to give to the poor and, like the highwaymen of a later age, he
evoked wide sympathy among ordinary folk; indeed, Robin Hood has
been called the ideal of the people, as King Arthur is that of the upper
classes. Is it too far-fetched to wonder if Hood represented the old
English values denied by the Norman occupation, or if the legend
asserts the legitimacy of the old order in opposition to the new one of the
invading power? Certainly there is an element of this in Kimbangu's
success: he remains a historical figure rather than a legend, but what

he symbolized seems to have been more important than any charisma he may have possessed. A French writer has concluded that the African messiah is, in the first place, the man who can bring back the lands where there will be no more servitude. The promised land will come from the ancestors; the land in which, in Bakongo territory, the crowned chief holds sway as the defender of its integrity and the intermediary between the men of the lineage and the community of ancestors (Balandier, 1958: 92; cf. Welbourn, 1961: 189–90).

The issue is not a simple one, for Kimbangu did not stand for a return to pre-colonial beliefs, but for a mixture of some of those beliefs with biblical doctrines. Van Wing states that Kimbangu, very early in his prophetic career, promulgated three laws: the destruction of fetishes; the abandonment of the erotic *ngoma* dances; the banning of polygamy. Then, later on, three more. When interviewed late in life, Kimbangu denied responsibility for the first two of the second group of edicts, namely, that the people should not pay tax or plant any more manioc, and perhaps these are to be attributed to the growing power of his new lieutenants. The last law was that they should clean the graveyards and the paths leading to them, for the ancestors were going to return the moment the Whites had left the country. They would bring everything the heart could desire and the people would live with them in abundance and peace. By the perfect cleaning of the graveyards and the paths, the people could show the ancestors that they were anxious to have them back (Van Wing, 1958: 572; note the striking similarity with cargo cult beliefs).

While considerable evidence has been assembled about elements in the thought of the prophetic leaders, there is little information on their actual teaching or on the important question of the beliefs and motivations of their followers. The popular understanding of the new doctrines probably varied somewhat, and it should be noted that many Protestant missionaries found much good in the movements, seeing in them traces of Christian revival. For many of Kimbangu's followers, his movement must have represented a return to a purified practice of the ancestral cult supplemented by lessons learned from the white man's Bible. In traditional life, the ancestral cult was the source and sanction of morality in dealings between kinsfolk, and the epitome of all that was good in human life. But, whereas each clan had its own ancestors responsible just for their own descendants, the Kimbangists held their ancestors in common (Köbben, 1960: 137 – the authority for this statement is uncertain, but cf. Balandier, 1955: 469).

Why should they have destroyed the fetishes ? This was Kimbangu's first command and it was obeyed with startling fidelity for many miles by people who had never met the prophet. Van Wing's view is that the ancestral cult was inadequate to protect the Bakongo from witchcraft accusations even from fellow clansmen and that the *minkisi* fetishes were a supplementary defence that frequently turned upon themselves and only increased people's anxieties. Kimbangu banished the fetishes which the people themselves were periodically apt to discard as ineffective, and in their place he put baptism. In this way, according to Van Wing, he split clans into the elect and the damned; his adherents thought in terms of 'us, the saved, good people' and 'the others, the damned, witches, Whites'.

Most authorities are convinced that the fear of witchcraft was a potent factor in the spread of the prophetic movements. In pre-colonial times the Bakongo had protected themselves with various devices for detecting witches, who could then be subjected to ordeal by poison. But the administration had outlawed these practices, leaving the people defenceless against their worst enemies. The leaders were afraid that their clans and nation would die out; from their point of view, the colonial laws against the smelling-out of witches were but a subtle policy of genocide. When, in 1935, the Salvation Army started preaching in the Congo, two ideas got about. First, that the 'S' in the 'AS' on members' collars signified 'Simon' and that they were the emissaries of Kimbangu himself. Second, that anyone who shook hands with a Salvation Army man or stood beneath the Army's banner, and survived, was innocent of witchcraft. The fantastic crowds that flocked to Salvation Army meetings were convincing testimony to the concern with witchcraft anxieties.

In discussing traditional beliefs it is necessary to emphasize how greatly the social context of traditional African religion differs from that of the post-Reformation West. Traditional religion was not a separate category of thought. It penetrated every aspect of everyday life and could only with difficulty be considered apart from the mundane round. The distinctions between politics and religion, between the sphere of government and the sphere of the individual conscience – which Westerners take for granted – are, in fact, relatively late developments. One consequence of this involvement of traditional religion in all aspects of social life is what has been called its 'totalitarian' character: because it is so little differentiated, the ideas of causality which it supports cannot be tested or disproved within this universe of meaning. The first step necessary to the introduction of secular political activity is therefore a change in popular cosmology.

In the colonial situations that have thrown up the more politically inclined prophetic movements, a similar pattern of subordination has obtained equally in the Africans' relations with European administrators, merchants, and missionaries. These aspects of European power are easily identified with one another. The Congolese said that in the crisis of the early 1930s all 'companies' except three were forced to leave the country; the only ones to survive were the state, the Catholic Church, and the Protestant mission. Earlier, an independent African religious leader in Nyasaland had written: 'the three combined bodies, Missionaries, Government and Companies, or gainers of money – do form the same rule . . . we would advise them not to call themselves "Christendom" but "Europeandom". Therefore the life of the three combined bodies is altogether too cheaty, too thefty, too mockery' (Shepperson & Price, 1958: 163–4). The identification of the organs of European power did not depend so much upon African perceptions as on the logic of the situation itself, in particular upon the ties of common interest which forced state, merchants, and missions to co-ordinate their policies. Only in the last phases of colonial rule in central Africa have cross-cutting ties developed such that the missions have sided with their African congregations against the government.

In the early phases, opposition to any one of the European institutions rapidly became opposition to the others, frequently in spite of the attempts of the original leader to confine the struggle to the initial area of disagreement. This is clearly shown in Kimbangu's case. When the people asked him if they should stop worshipping with the Europeans, Kimbangu answered them with an allegory: 'We are like wives to our Whites . . . for they have come here and have given us the Gospel; they suffered many hardships in order to come to us; they have bought us for a great price, and so they are wedded to us. If we leave them, they will be sorely afflicted. Therefore, you should not break away from your Whites.' He also warned them to give to Caesar the things that were Caesar's, and to pay their taxes (Andersson, 1958: 61; cf. Lawrence, 1964: 107, quoted in Chapter Five, p. 94 above). Kimbangu's effort to confine the conflict to the question of increased ecclesiastical flexibility was in vain. Popular discontent over the changes that had occurred in recent years (Andersson, 1958: 235–8) could find no outlet and was easily displaced into the prophet's movement. A group of radically minded Africans seem to have used Kimbangu's doctrines and works for their own ends so that the movement was given an anti-European character and propaganda for the establishment of a native church was disseminated. When they found that this sort of appeal was well received, Kimbangu's lieutenants would tend to respond to what the people wanted. However, the evidence concerning these lieutenants is not very reliable. It seems probable that any movement providing an opportunity for the expression of dissent would have been moulded by the structure of the colonial order into a similar form. The character of the original innovator was much less influential. The analysis of the succeeding events is therefore likely to centre upon the unintended political consequences of an initially religious activity. It is easy to see that with the arrest of the prophet and the vicious reaction of the Whites, culminating in the unmerited sentence, the movement was bound to become more nationalistic.

Andersson suggested that the climate of native opinion at the time of the arrest is reflected in a newspaper interview with an African, who said:

'Our messenger from God is now a prisoner, but he won't stay long in your hands, for if he doesn't himself decide to leave we will seize him ourselves . . . you had Jesus who was sold for forty [sic] pieces of silver by one of his brothers; he was killed, but he went to heaven just the same and though he is no longer here, you've made a pope and priests; he has been replaced millions of times. Well, it's the same here. If Kibango goes we'll have others to take his place.'

It does not seem unreasonable to claim that in such an atmosphere Africans were led to identify the realization of the religious ideal with the termination of their political and economic subordination (Chomé, 1959: 98). Certainly, local groups of Kimbangist persuasion demonstrated clearly anti-government and anti-European sentiment on many occasions in the 1920s. But recently this has not been the case. Even though some of these religious movements represent a rejection of white superordination more clearly than other popular institutions do, the members themselves are extremely well disposed towards any European who approaches them on an equal footing; indeed, they often seem more friendly than comparable groups (Gilis, 1960: 66–69). This has, indeed, been the general experience of European students of the new churches.

If opposition to European rule is to find institutional expression under a paternalist colonial order, it is more likely to appear in the ecclesiastical sphere than any other. It is easier to organize a charismatic movement centring upon the revelations of a single leader, than a bureaucratic political party acting on majority decisions. It is also more difficult for a colonial régime to feel justified in suppressing a movement which seems basically to belong in the sphere of its subjects' private concerns. Yet there appear to be more fundamental factors on the cultural and intellectual planes that explain the priority of changes in the religious sphere. Religious beliefs provide an answer to the question all people ask: 'How did we get this way'? For colonial peoples this can be an acute problem. Why should the Europeans be so powerful? What had they done to deserve the machines and other goods that outclassed anything the Africans had ever conceived of? Because, in traditional African belief, the spirit world is usually regarded as controlling human fortune, it was logical for the Africans to suspect that the secret of the white man's power lay in his religion. The white men had received *their* messiah. If only the Africans were to have theirs, too, they would soon be on an equal footing with the Whites. The search for a secret might possibly have been an element in the story (from the Congo) of a priest, just arrived from Europe, who lost his breviary and found that a newly ordained African had borrowed it to compare it page by page with his own and make sure he had not been provided with a second-rate version (Slade, 1960: 35). Furthermore, Africans who have grown up in a pre-industrial environment often do not fully adopt the impersonal scientific conception of causality because their way of life does not support such a conception in the way that an industrial culture does. The new ideas that would lead people in this direction had themselves to be simple at first; the believer's interpretation of his Bible served admirably as a means of encouraging the spread and development of new conceptions of the universe.

It would seem, therefore, that these prophetic movements, based though they were on a personal faith, had the paradoxical effect of playing a secularizing part in the development of African thought. They helped to break the old cosmology by answering it in terms of a new religion, some of which was not difficult for the villager to grasp. They assisted the first step in the politicization of local groupings by presenting religion as a personal affair separate from the things that belonged to Caesar, and in this way differentiating the political sphere as an independent realm of activity. New religious movements have been of prime importance in the spread of many new ideas, not least the realization that new ways could be found of combining against the colonialists (Hodgkin, 1956: 113–14). In regions where the administrators, merchants, and missions were aligned, the colonial power perceived prophetic cults as posing a threat to its dominance, but it was rarely more than momentarily alarmed by them, and independence, when it came, was the fruit of secular struggle. It has been argued that both the messianic movements and the independent churches of the South African type transcend village and tribal particularism, providing a broader basis for political action, but the evidence for such a conclusion is slender; many of the African movements have remained predominantly of a single tribe or have been side-tracked once secular politics have emerged.

RACIAL AND CLASS SUBORDINATION

Max Weber held that the cults of dominant social groups tend to emphasize *being* rather than *becoming*: because the rich man wishes to be assured that he deserves his good fortune, his religious institutions are inclined to stress the present world and their members' rights and responsibilities in it. The cults of subordinate groups help their members to come to terms with their position by developing a theodicy of suffering: they rehearse the vanities of this world and the rewards of the next (Weber, 1947: 269–88, 1965: 106–7). This formulation seems inapplicable to traditional African beliefs but it is very relevant to an examination of the new movements. They reflect political reactions, but in varying degree. In some of the new churches there is little emphasis upon a condition of racial subordination and there is no reason to believe that, with political independence, the new churches in West Africa have undergone any perceptible change. When reading an account such as that of Lantenari (1963), it is necessary to remember that in most regions the membership of the independent churches is only a fraction of that of the mission churches or of their orthodox successors. If the political element were as important elsewhere as it seems to have been in the Kimbangu movement, far more spectacular consequences would have resulted. Therefore, if the new churches are to be seen as the cults of subordinated peoples, it is necessary to look into other forms of subordination as well as those that follow racial lines. In the cities, large numbers of Africans may be assembled and, since the European group lives at a distance, it may be divisions within the African population that appear most immediate. The study of African voluntary associations on the Copperbelt suggests that the pantomime element in their activities represented in the 1920s a vicarious participation in European social life, but that by the 1950s similar activities represented a form of vicarious participation in the life-style of the upper levels of African society (Mitchell, 1956: 12, 15). From what is known of similar movements elsewhere, it is highly probable that the people drawn to independent churches value highly the customary forms of respectability and would like to move up the social scale. This may help to explain the remarks of two missionary students of Zambian churches, who say of one of the independent groups: 'Both in the urban and the rural district there seemed to be an eagerness not only to be on friendly terms with the members of the "orthodox" mission churches, but also really to co-operate with them and with their missionaries. This was remarkable at a time in which an all-African congregation might be tempted to exploit the widespread anti-white feeling. . . .' (Taylor & Lehmann, 1961: 216).

It seems unlikely that many of the Africans who trekked to hear Kimbangu did so because they were converts to Christianity, or to a more compelling version of it. It is more reasonable to conclude that they were looking towards a time of justice in this world; that they were responding to racial subordination and seeking earthly improvement. The Mission des Noirs hoped for a Second Coming in the near future when the Whites would be expelled, though in its theology there was also the suggestion that Kimbangu might bring justice and recompense in the next world. In the 'Zionist' churches of South Africa occurs the doctrine of a reversed colour bar as the entrance to heaven: 'Shembe at the gate turns away the Whites, because they, as the rich man, have already in their lifetime received their good things' (Sundkler, 1961: 291). These sentiments reflect the pattern of political relations between Black and White but do not prove that the motivation of the individuals who join these churches is consciously or unconsciously political. The leading authority states: 'Claims that "political" reasons are behind the Separatist Church movement miss the mark . . . even admitting the existence of much outspoken anti-White propaganda in most Independent Churches, one should not forget that the attitude of the leaders and masses of these Ethiopians and Zionists has on the whole been loyal, not least during the trying experiences of war' (Sundkler, 1961: 295).

The evidence on this point is not as clear as might be desired, but it seems that there are significant variations between the churches based on congregations in the reserves and those based on congregations in the cities. The syncretistic, prophetic groups – which Sundkler calls 'Zionist', and which, he says, lean to the idea of a reversed colour bar in heaven – are based on the reserves and seem to respond to the pattern of racial subordination there. They also separate themselves from the traditional Bantu political structure. The breakaway churches, which Sundkler calls 'Ethiopian', reject European church leadership but nevertheless follow the organizational pattern of the Protestant mission churches. They are active in the reserves, and, like members of the Church of England, think it appropriate for the head of the state to be the head of the church. Ethiopian churches are more strongly supported than Zionist ones in the cities. Little systematic information is available on the part played by independent churches within the African community, but it would appear that the urban churches appeal more to women than to men, offer appreciable material assistance to members in distress, and serve to some extent as channels of upward social mobility. Many have an elaborate structure of ranks and offices. They help the first generation of townswomen to adapt their ways of life to the new surroundings. That Bantu leaders secede from their own churches shows that the oppositions are not only political. Many commentators refer to the struggle for leadership positions, for prestige and power; this, it may be observed, is a struggle for advantage in a system of social status differentiation, and those who contend accept the system within which they compete. Many religious leaders have become successful businessmen. Groups that initially renounced the world now show greater interest in their children's schooling. In the town, new criteria of social status are replacing traditional systems of rank; status distinctions appear between congregations, some of the Ethiopian churches attracting Bantu doctors, lawyers, editors, and teachers while, at the other end of the scale, Zionist sects take care of the uneducated (Sundkler, 1961: 80–99, 140–1, 296–7, 302–10; cf. Brandel-Syrier, 1962). In South Africa, sectarianism seems to be more of an urban than a rural phenomenon (cf. Pauw, 1960: 105). The urban churches reflect their members' position in the *African* social universe to an important extent and are less directly concerned with racial subordination.

How closely do the independent churches of West Africa correspond to the urban congregations of South Africa ? The most striking feature of the West African churches is their literal acceptance of the Bible and their belief in its efficacy. They resemble the 'fundamentalist' sects of Britain and America in their attitude towards the Bible and in their reproach of the orthodox for not really believing the message of their own holy book. 'Not a few Christian Zulus', says Sundkler (1961: 275), 'when asked why they have left the parent Church, reply "I left because of the book".' There is a greater, if simpler, faith in the breakaway African churches than in those they have left. Their moral code is usually puritanical, reviving many of the prohibitions of Leviticus, as if to strengthen their faith. 'The *direct* healing of man's physical and mental illnesses by Almighty God, often without the use of any medicine, either European or traditional, is proclaimed as of the essence of the Gospel and is perhaps the most universal characteristic of the Aladura or Zionist type of Independent African Church ... African religion is deeply concerned with the problem of good health *in this world*' (Mitchell, 1963: 47–48).

In strict logic the doctrine of these groups is that, without grace, man is inescapably evil so that political action is of no avail. In practice, their members are probably as much or as little involved in politics as other people of the same socio-economic level. In some parts of West Africa the congregations of the Aladura churches (corresponding doctrinally to Sundkler's Zionist sects) are, by comparison with other congregations, drawn more than proportionately from the lower classes. Church organization reflects the members' subordination in the system of social status, but, on present evidence, it does not seem that their doctrine promises heavenly recompense in the way that some evangelical preachers in early nineteenth-century England drew their hearers' attention to the rewards of another world, distracting them from the problems of the present one (Parrinder, 1952: 107–32; *Nigeria Magazine*, Vol. 53, 1957: 119–34; Banton, 1956; Turner, 1959, 1960, 1962).

It should be recognized that all religious institutions, and especially these new ones, serve many functions. A striking illustration is provided by the film *Les Maîtres fous*, made by Dr Jean Rouch of the Musée de l'Homme. In it he shows how immigrant workers from the Upper Volta, who are not fully adjusted to life in urban Accra, go out at weekends to a centre where they enter into possession states; this practice apparently helps their adjustment the rest of the time. These psychological functions – even though rarely as striking as in the cult Rouch discovered – are probably important for many adherents of the African movements, as they also seem to be for members of some of the more demonstrative European and American sects.

Equally, it is necessary to give separate attention to the use of religious forms and media by secular movements. Mau Mau utilized hymns and crypto-creeds to build up mass support and to provide an unexceptionable cover for political activity (Leakey, 1954: 41–76). In a somewhat different fashion, the National Church of Nigeria and the Cameroons – with its prayers to the God of Africa, its hymns to freedom, and its litany beseeching deliverance from imperialism – has functioned, to borrow Hodgkin's words, as 'a kind of ecclesiastical instrument of radical nationalism in eastern Nigeria' (cf. Coleman, 1958: 302–3). Unless the new African governments exercise rigid control over all forms of political expression, it is improbable that this utilization of religious forms will be much developed; it is more likely that religious imagery will be employed to bolster the claims of the political party in power.

This chapter has suggested that, while prophetic movements in Africa may undoubtedly serve political functions, these are not so immediate as some writers have implied; that there are significant circumstantial variations between the different movements which make it impossible to consider them as manifestations of a single type; and that other sociological aspects of the movements have been neglected. They cannot be adequately understood if the student does not at some point view them as popular attempts to come to terms with new and troubling situations; to provide moral justifications for the new kind of life that is demanded. The importance attributed to the leaders may derive less from any charismatic authority than from the values they symbolize in the context of the social order. In so far as these prophetic movements reflect racial sentiment this is incidental and temporary. Observers have often underestimated the extent to which a protesting people – be they Nigerian or Congolese – can be opposed to British or Belgian rule without being against the British or Belgian people. Yet the difficulty of adjusting to a rapidly changing scene full of contradictory elements often precipitates moments of unexpected violence. The African prophetic movements have served as active agents in differentiating the spheres of religion and politics; in freeing the religious element in Christianity from its association with colonial subordination; and in diffusing new ideas through the countryside. But, though they may at first reassert elements of the old order, the likely course of development, once secular political activity has been established, will follow the lines of national or class pressures. In the later stages these prophetic cults may be, indeed, not stimuli to political activity but substitutes for or sublimations of it.

CHAPTER TEN

Colonial Africa: Industrialization

A distinction was drawn in Chapter Four between a dominative racial order and a paternalistic one. In the former, a colour line is maintained by members of the upper category who act in defence of their own interests as they see them. In the latter, there may be important racial distinctions, but there is not a colour line in the same sense, because members of the upper group take orders from their homeland and do not have the same interest in the local system of relations. It was pointed out that whether a situation of contact gives way to one of domination or of paternalism depends upon the extent to which the more powerful incomers can organize as an independent political power. Chapters Seven and Eight showed that, once a colour line is established, a social logic operates such that members of the upper category are obliged to try to keep the line distinct and horizontal; this entails the repression of members of the lower category who would otherwise have moved up the social scale and it therefore causes increased resentment in the subordinate category; in such a society the colour line can tilt and move round towards the diagonal only if the social and economic system provides a niche for the upper members of the lower group, permitting them to occupy a higher position without making any members of the upper category directly subordinate to them.

When the members of a superior category are the agents of a metro-politan power responsible for the government of the country, a different logic obtains. It should be noted that in this case the expression 'patern-alist' is used to describe the racial order, not the way in which people in that order tend to see their actions. In societies characterized by racial domination, members of the upper category often believe that they stand in a paternal relation to members of the lower category, but the paternalistic elements in the relation are a product of the distribution of power relatively untouched by any quasi-familial ties. If the master regards his relation to his servant as paternalistic this provides a justification for the authority he claims, but the pattern of behaviour is unlikely to resemble closely that of a father to his child. In some societies fathers claim the labour of their sons until the time comes when their sons' independence can no longer be denied. The period at which this change must occur is known to those affected by it. In most modern societies fathers do not exploit their sons but help to establish them in their careers. Members of the dominant group in a white supremacy society do not behave like fathers: the time at which their wards will achieve independence is pushed into an indeterminate future or subject to varied qualifications. Segregation and unwillingness to enter relations that do not conform to the master-servant pattern are not signs of paternal behaviour.

The justification for using the expression paternalist in the present connection may be questioned as the selection of a high-minded label to classify policies which were often the outcome of expediency, but British African territories in which white administrators were the dominant influence followed policies more congenial to the interests of the native peoples than did those territories where European settlers were powerful. A distinction was drawn early between a 'tropical dependency' and a true colony or settler colony. Sir Harry Johnston, for example, believed that tropical Africa between the Zambesi and the Atlas must be ruled by Whites, developed by Indians, and worked by Blacks. In 1897 he held that in such regions where 'we merely impose our rule to secure a fair field and no favour for all races, and inferentially for our own trade, there the local government must depend directly on London'. This policy was contrasted with that for 'districts where . . . climatic considerations encourage true colonization, [for] there undoubtedly the weakest must go to the wall and the black man must pay for the unprogressive turn his ancestors took some thousands of years ago' (Mason, 1958: 214). In a tropical dependency the behaviour of European administrators might be relatively altruistic because there was a double division: between Africans and Europeans; and between the Europeans in the dependency and the officials in Whitehall. The administrators were employed in a colonial bureaucracy and, according to their success in implementing the policy formulated by their superiors, they might be either transferred to another territory on promotion or moved away from a district in which they had built up local ties and interests. Their primary allegiance was owing to the Crown and they were not allowed to let other loyalties interfere. Paternalism was evident in legislation prohibiting aliens from acquiring permanent land rights and preventing competition between Europeans and Africans (Hailey,

Africa: political boundaries

1938: 825–7). In the settler colony, however, the majority of Europeans could not look to any postings to other territories or any civil service pension. They had invested their capital in their farms, their enterprises, and their homes, and, without the power to defend their interests, they could lose everything. Political relations within the ruling minority, therefore, put local interests before imperial ones and minority interests before majority ones. In the early stages of the growth of some colonies the European minority was united more by a sense of opposition to the metropolitan power than by any conflict with the indigenous peoples (the Dutch at Cape Colony often exemplified this proposition). The colonists demanded liberty from rule by officials without envisaging any comparable liberty for the indigenes. When, under colonial rule, a settler community became numerous and well established, its outlook often influenced the views of the officials.

Table 2 Africa south of the Sahara: population by country

Country	Date	Total population	African population	Percentage African	Other ethnic groups	
Angola	1960	4,830,449	4,604,362	95·3	White	172,529
					Mixed	53,392
					Other	166
Botswana (formerly Bechuanaland Protectorate)	1964	543,105	535,587	98·6	European	3,492
					Asian	375
					Other	3,291
Burundi (formerly part of Ruanda-Urundi)	1958			99·7	White	4,639
					Asian	1,211
					Other	294
	1959	2,213,280				
	1965	3,000,000*	2,207,780		European	3,500
					Asian	2,000
Cameroon Republic (incl. former Southern Cameroons)	1956	3,187,000	3,171,000	99·5	European	16,000
	1961		4,126,000		European	17,000
	1965	5,210,000*				
Central African Republic	1962	1,352,000*	1,279,642		European	5,000
	1965					

Country	Year			%	Group	Number
Chad	1962		2,750,000		European	5,000*
	1964		3,300,000			
The Congo (formerly Belgian Congo)	1957		12,768,706	99·2	White	109,457
	1958				Asian	1,233
					Other	5,114
	1965		15,627,000*			
Congo Republic (formerly French Middle Congo)	1960	826,000*			European	10,000*
	1964		581,600*			
Dahomey	1961		2,106,000		European	5,000*
	1964		2,300,000*			
French Somaliland	1956	62,892	58,532	93·1	Non-African	4,360
					European	7,000
					Arab	3,000
					Other	16,500
	1963	86,000*	54,500			
Gabon	1961	447,880	442,000	98·7	Non-African	6,000
	1965	462,000*				
Gambia	1963	315,486	314,869	99·8	Non-African	617
Ghana	1960	6,726,815	6,710,850	99·8	Other	15,965

Table 2—cont.

Country	Date	Total population	African population	Percentage African	Other ethnic groups	
Guinea	1955		2,570,219			
	1964	3,500,000*			European	2,000*
Ivory Coast	1958		3,100,000			
	1964	3,750,000*			European	15,000*
Kenya	1962	8,636,263	8,365,942	96·9	European	55,759
					Arab	34,048
					Asian	176,613
					Other	3,901
	1965	9,365,000*				
Lesotho (formerly Basutoland)	1956	641,674	638,857	99·6	European	1,926
					Asian	247
					Mixed	644
	1965	745,000*				
Liberia	1962	1,016,443				
	1965	1,066,000*			European	5,000*
Madagascar	1956		4,846,000		European	72,000

	Year					
	1963	5,862,258	5,752,624	98·1	French	46,009
					Fr. Community	536
					Comorian	33,795
					Alien	29,294
Malawi (formerly Nyasaland)	1961	3,990,890*			European	8,750
	1962				Asian	10,630
	1963		3,970,000*	99·2	Coloured	1,490
Mali	1961	4,100,000				
	1965	4,576,000*			Non-African	7,500*
Mauritania	1956	900,000*				
	1964				Non-African	1,616
Mozambique	1955			98·1	White	65,798
					Indian	15,235
					Mixed	29,873
					Other (incl. assimilated Africans)	6,499
	1960	6,578,604				
	1965	6,956,000*				

Table 2—cont.

Country	Date	Total population	African population	Percentage African	Other ethnic groups	
Niger	1960	2,501,800				
	1962		3,100,000*			
	1965	3,328,000*			European	2,700*
Nigeria (incl. former Northern Cameroons)	1956	31,834,000	31,824,000		European	10,000
	1963	55,653,821			Non-African	27,000
Portuguese Guinea	1960	521,336				
	1964	525,000*	60,000*		European	7,000*
Rhodesia (formerly Southern Rhodesia)	1965	4,259,700	4,020,000	94·4	European	219,000
					Coloured	12,700
					Asian	8,000
Rwanda (formerly part of Ruanda-Urundi)	1958			99·9	White	2,470
					Asian	1,109
					Mixed	131
	1964		3,018,000*		European	1,200
					Asian	750

	Year				
Senegal	1961	3,109,840	98·1	European	37,800
				Asian	14,780
				Eurafrican	6,760
				Other	920
Sierra Leone	1963	2,180,355		European	2,000
				Asian	3,000
Somali Republic (formed by union of British Somaliland Protectorate and Italian Trust Territory of Somalia)	1965	2,500,000*			
South Africa	1960	16,002,797	10,927,922 (Bantu)	68·3 (Bantu)	White 3,088,492
				Asian	477,125
				Coloured	1,509,258
	1965	17,867,000*			
South-West Africa	1960	526,004	428,575 (Bantu)	81·5 (Bantu)	White 73,464
				Asian	2
				Coloured	23,963
	1965	574,000*			
Spanish Guinea	1960	246,000*		European	7,084

Table 2—cont.

Country	Date	Total population	African population	Percentage African	Other ethnic groups	
Swaziland	1962	280,300	270,000	96·3	European	8,040
	1965	292,000*			Eurafrican	2,260
Tanzania (the United Republic of Tanganyika and Zanzibar)	1965	10,179,000*				
Tanganyika	1962		9,285,600 (incl. Arab)		European	21,400
					Indian, Pakistani, Goan	92,100
Zanzibar	1958	299,111	230,066		European	507
					Arab	46,989
					Asian	18,334
					Comorian	2,880
					Somali	263
					Other	72
Togo	1960	1,439,772			Non-African	34
	1965	1,642,000*				

Country	Year			%	Group	Number
Uganda	1963	7,189,600	7,093,000	98·7	European	9,800
					Arab	2,200
					Indian and Goan	82,100
					Other	2,500
Upper Volta	1961		4,293,000			
	1963	4,600,000		99·8	European (incl. assimilated Africans)	
	1965	4,882,000*				3,500
Zambia (formerly Northern Rhodesia)	1961				European	74,540
					Asian	7,790
					Coloured	2,050
	1962			97·5		
	1963		3,409,110			
	1965	3,780,000*				

* Estimates or provisional figures.

Sources: Demographic Yearbook for the years 1963, 1964, and 1965 (published by United Nations Department of Economic and Social Affairs, New York); Population and Vital Statistics Report (United Nations Statistical Papers Series A, Vol. XVIII, No. 2, New York, 1966); Economic Survey of Africa since 1950 (United Nations Department of Economic and Social Affairs, New York, 1959); Economic Bulletin for Africa (Vol. V, January 1965, United Nations, New York); Africa: a Handbook, edited by Colin Legum (London: Anthony Blond, 1965 edn.); the Statesman's Year-Book 1966-67, edited by S. H. Steinberg (London: Macmillan, 1966).

In Southern Rhodesia imperial control in the sphere of 'native administration' was never as strong as elsewhere and the tendency was for the administrators to become the agents of the white minority.

THE COLOUR LINE IN RHODESIA

Southern Rhodesia provides the clearest example among the British African colonies of a society in which there was a definite colour line from the beginning. Some colonies, like Kenya and Zambia, seemed at times to be heading in the same direction but were drawn back by the tide of African nationalism. Yet other colonies, like Uganda and much of British West Africa, approximated to the idea of the tropical dependency: they were governed by officials, admitted very few people who could be counted as white settlers, and, though they displayed varied forms of racial discrimination, never developed the two-category social system of the dominative order.

It is possible to speak of Southern Rhodesia as a single society comprising both Europeans and Africans from the 1890s onwards. In 1893 Jameson entered Bulawayo at the head of a military force. In 1898 Her Majesty's government established a legislative council in Southern Rhodesia on which the European settlers were represented, serving with officials appointed by the Crown. But the territory was not directly subject to the Crown: it was under the control of the British South Africa Company, a private company operating under a royal charter of 1889, and did not become a Crown colony until 1923 (when the Whites voted against incorporation into the Union of South Africa, and in favour of the ending of company rule in exchange for the status of a partially independent colony). At the birth of Southern Rhodesia as a distinctive society, the Whites and the Africans had little in common. The status gap between them was not the result of social contrivance but a reflection of the greater military power of the Whites and of their command of skills with a much higher market value.

In all the African territories there were, from the earliest periods of contact, changes that made for a filling-in of the gap between the groups. Like nature, society abhors a vacuum. Some Africans adopted European ways; they were often encouraged to do so, for there was a pressing demand for interpreters, clerks, policemen, telegraphists, catechists, craftsmen, and other trained personnel whose assistance might enable European skills to be more economically deployed (Gann, 1958: 39–40). Some Europeans took native wives or concubines. Some intermediate groups grew by immigration, like the Lebanese in West Africa, the Arabs on the East coast, and the Indians in several territories that were at one time under British administration. In Rhodesia there was a demand for native auxiliaries and there was miscegenation, but the relative separateness of the white and African populations, the pattern of settlement, and the absence of any significant intermediate group meant that the gap was not rapidly filled in.

The maintenance of a colour line depends upon the transmission of status from one generation to another, so that a child remains in the category into which he was born. When a child's parents belong to different categories an anomalous situation arises; all such children need to be allocated unequivocally to one category or the other and, as the analysis of racial status in the Deep South has shown, the logic of domination favours their ascription to the lower category. In Rhodesia, though the children of white fathers and African mothers have received many privileges, their place has been on the African side of the colour line, and their very presence causes some Europeans to feel uneasy (Keatley, 1963: 259). Another possible threat to a pattern of inherited racial status is posed by an economic overlap. Commenting on Rhodesian politics before World War I, Philip Mason writes: 'This was one strand of argument in the continuous debate. "Preserve the gap – and to preserve it, make sure the native does not advance."' He refers to a report from 1918 which describes white farmers' disapproval of the selling to Africans of European cattle as breeding stock: at a meeting it was pointed out that such sales were not in violation of the law – as if the farmers thought that they should be (Mason, 1958: 253, 265). From the same standpoint, an educated African was a social anomaly. In 1903 a Rhodesian legislator asserted that 'the uneducated native was the most honest, trustworthy and useful', and this sentiment has been echoed by many settlers over the decades. The way in which the status gap in a two-category social system is reinforced by an etiquette of subordination has already been explained. In this respect, too, practice in Southern Rhodesia resembles that in the Deep South and in South Africa. Whites have generally withheld the titles of 'Mr' and 'Mrs' from Africans, preferring to say 'boy' or to use first names (for a general review, cf. Rogers & Frantz, 1962: 208–22). An earlier law making punishable any 'contemptuous behaviour' on the part of an African towards a native commissioner has recently been extended to authorize imprisonment for any African who says or does anything likely to bring an official or a government department into disrepute or contempt. What constitutes actionable behaviour is not easy to define and the effect of such legislation is often more extensive than was originally intended (cf. Franck, 1960: 105). Southern Rhodesian Whites seem to watch carefully lest educated Africans should secure exemption from the racial etiquette. Commenting upon the Europeans' 'preference for the uneducated African', one author testifies that many civil servants go as far as they can to avoid making any concession to the better-educated African. He states that the chief native comissioner told him in 1949 that it was his policy to make no distinction between educated and uneducated Africans. If any of them wanted to sit down in his office they sat on the floor (Gussman, 1962: 102).

The forces that operate to keep the colour line distinct also tend to keep it horizontal. As Chapter Seven demonstrated, the angle of a colour line affects and is affected by relations within each category as well as relations between the categories. White supremacy is dependent upon white solidarity, and this can be achieved only at a price paid by one or more of the conflicting interests within the white category. Whereas the Deep South and South Africa show in many circumstances a clear opposition between Black and White, Southern Rhodesia for many years could not afford so deep a cleavage and sought to avoid it. The metropolitan connection, with its liberal strands, was cultivated the more because of the apprehensions aroused by Afrikaner nationalism and the strength of the Afrikaner element within the white population. Yet since World War II the logic of the two-category system has forced events to follow the path taken by the other white supremacy societies. To further the interests of the ruling minority it has been thought necessary to subsidize European immigration very heavily indeed relative to the country's budget. To induce Europeans to come in sufficient numbers it has been necessary to pay men with little skill at artificially high wage rates, thus giving them as strong an interest as any other European in the existing order. Because the electorate has been virtually confined to Europeans, the real opposition has been excluded from political bargaining. Thus the only electoral tactic that offers any prospect of success is the claim to be the most effective champion of European interests against the real, if suppressed, threat of an African takeover (Leys, 1959: 292). British immigrants, whatever their previous politics, have adopted with alacrity the intransigent attitude towards the Africans, and their numbers have swamped the influence of men from established Rhodesian families, men economically and socially more secure. This growing pressure from the right has been reflected in the governing party for many years and, since the defeat of Garfield Todd as premier and the rapid succession to that office of Sir Edgar Whitehead, Winston Field, and Ian Smith (who made the illegal declaration of independence in November 1965), it has been clear that white solidarity is to be founded on right-wing extremism. Yet further changes in the power structure are possible: it may be that, reacting to external pressure, Rhodesian settler groups will seek more actively to divide the African opposition and to detach groups willing to collaborate with them.

The etiquette that regulates race relations controls the behaviour of members of the upper category as well as of the lower. To preserve their privileged position, members of the ruling minority must be able to exercise supervision over their own number. The immigrant who comes out to a position of power in a new society has the opportunity to behave in a despotic and libertine fashion which can be in accord with powerful unconscious desires (Mannoni, 1956). The group therefore elaborates informal controls, chief among them being self-segregation, which not only protects its monopoly of power, but makes the immigrant more dependent upon the approval of the other members of his racial category. The standardization of relations with members of the lower category makes it more difficult for superordinates – as well as subordinates – to deviate from the expected pattern. Though sexual relations between members of the two categories may be tolerated at first, disapproval grows. A ruling minority often needs a mystique of being different, and this may be destroyed by a proclivity for sexual liaisons with native women. In Kipling's story, *The Man who would be King*, a European rules over people in a distant region who believe him to be a god, until he takes a wife from among them, when they recognize him for a man and revolt. The Southern Rhodesian Nationalist leader, the Rev. Ndabaningi Sithole, has said (1959: 152–3) that Europeans' liaisons with African women in his country had this sort of effect. Yet it may be doubted whether the controls imposed by the European community are motivated by a concern for their racial mystique. The objection is more likely to stem from the undesired social consequences of such unions: the anomalous children, and the difficulty Europeans would have in maintaining an impersonal distance in relations with Africans if, in between times, they were on such familiar terms with their sisters. Once there is a fair proportion of women in the minority community they increase the social pressures upon non-conforming males.

In two-category racial systems, skin colour acquires tremendous significance as a guarantee of the social order, and further associations are added to it. A bare statement about the white use of political power to maintain privileges is therefore insufficient in that it does not throw enough light upon the motivations of the Whites in the use of their power. They would represent their actions as guided by a desire to establish high standards of individual performance and integrity ('civilized values'), and this element is not to be dismissed as a simple rationalization. Moreover, the Whites are subject to powerful cultural conditioning from their exposed political position and this conditioning represents their objectives in an idiom that makes them seem more acceptable morally. They interpret their shared determination to defend the prevailing order as evidence of a collective 'will to survive' or 'instinct of self-preservation' – a mode of expression that sounds the more reasonable in a post-Darwinian culture.

The desire to preserve its privileged position induces the minority to impose controls upon those of its number whose actions might lead to a diminution in the prestige attaching to a 'white' complexion. Thus, in the early days of Northern Rhodesia, licences were refused to white traders who had insufficient capital (Gann, 1958: 153). Elsewhere, immigrants who could not live in the expected manner were repatriated by their fellows. The same consideration may affect even the cinema: in Southern Rhodesia the quality of the films shown to Africans, almost always cowboy epics, has been very poor, and the stories are often difficult to follow since the films themselves may be heavily cut. Africans are not supposed to see Europeans behaving in a disreputable fashion and this sometimes eliminates much of the plot! (Gussman, 1962: 85.) Within the upper category of a society threatened by an encircling majority there is often more social equality and good fellowship than in a society based on a class hierarchy, for this is but one mode of reinforcing group solidarity. From the beginning, Europeans needed to stand by each other. A traveller observed in 1881: 'A Kafir who is owed money by one Englishman, perhaps the wages for a year's work, will take a letter without a murmur to another Englishman hundreds of miles away, if he is told by his master that, upon delivering the letter, he will receive his payment' (Gann, 1965: 47). Another aspect of the same feature is the pressure for conformity (Rogers & Frantz, 1962: 121–4). This is highlighted by the popular objections to investigations by social scientists whether they examine the Africans' social life or the attitudes of Europeans. Thus a leading article in the *Central African Post* in 1953 complained:

'In the name of science certain Englishmen enter this country to make exhaustive studies of the customs and habits of African tribes and in the process they conduct themselves in such a way that they lose the deference traditionally accorded to White men by Africans. . . .

The so-called scientists . . . who, from the very nature of their studies are usually advanced politicians, like to live as closely to the African way of life as they can. . . . Frankly we think that much of this anthropological or sociological study is "hooey". . . . When Africans see European scientific men, who are considered by them to be a better type of European, behaving as if they were Africans, then they lose their respect and deference for all Europeans. . . . Moreover, such sociologists can disturb the political atmosphere of the country. They can give Africans "wrong ideas". They treat them as if they were a grown-up responsible community when they are not. . . . We do not ask sociologists to be Tories. They can be Communists if they like, but they should behave like responsible Europeans during their investigations' (quoted Richmond, 1961b: 152–3).

When two social psychologists (one an American) commenced a highly sophisticated study of European attitudes, a Rhodesian M.P. and news-paper leader-writers and correspondents were quick to condemn it as unscientific, to tell Americans to solve their own racial problems first, and to insist that the money would be better spent 'in more practical directions' (Rogers & Frantz, 1962: 366–74). The criticism experienced by teachers at the University College of Rhodesia and Nyasaland, who sought the sort of freedom of expression taken for granted in industrial democracies, is further evidence of the pressure to conformity on social and political issues. Outside the College, men and women who else-where would be leaders of opinion have kept silent when silly and unscientific theories of racial superiority have been voiced because these rationalizations were needed by the less secure people in the lower reaches of the European group and their political power has been pivotal.

To defend their own position, the lower members of the upper category mobilize as much pressure as possible upon any of the upper members of the lower category whose actions appear to push the colour line away from the horizontal. In Rhodesia the claims – or alleged claims – of African political leaders were vehemently disparaged by the lower Whites, and it became quite common for all Whites to dismiss the opposition of African leaders to Federation as the agitations of self-seekers who thought their prospects of office would be worse under that political order. In November 1956 one of the two African representatives of Southern Rhodesia in the Federal Parliament 'called at the Post Office for a parcel and was told by a clerk that he must "show his *situpa* (certificate) like all the other boys"' (Mason, 1960: 180). This incident, at a time when Southern Rhodesians hoped that the Africans would accept Federation, provoked shock and concern. A new scheme was introduced to mitigate the operation of the pass laws for the African graduate though it remained an offence for even the African Federal M.P. to be without his comprehensive document. Subsequently there were further attempts to reduce what were called the 'pinpricks' of segregation. The pass laws were repealed. Yet the etiquette governing interpersonal relations between members of the two categories is not just a matter of individual goodwill; it is a part of a system of relations and cannot be modified unless other factors are changed too. An interracial etiquette is necessary to the maintenance of a status gap.

It is right to recognize that 'race relations' in Africa are relations between categories of people distinguished by more points of difference than race, being economic relations, cultural relations, and class relations as well. Yet the Southern Rhodesian case shows that it is also necessary to appreciate that the significance attributed to racial background in a two-category social order introduces elements of much greater social rigidity than is characteristic of these other kinds of social relations. The sequence of events in Southern Rhodesia, and the attitudes of the ruling minority, are illuminated by comparisons with the Southern United States and with South Africa. In Rhodesia, Indians have been able to establish themselves as an intermediary group only by confining their activities quite closely to trading. Structurally, it is a simpler pattern than that of South Africa, and more closely resembles the Deep South. Developmentally, the illegal declaration of independence corresponds not with 1772 but with the assertion of white supremacy in the South after the era of Reconstruction.

URBANIZATION AND WHITE SUPREMACY

Chapter Seven showed that in the Deep South urbanization provided a niche in which upper members of the lower category could establish themselves in a class position superior to that of the lower members of the upper category. The towns of rural Mississippi are small; both inside them and outside, white supremacy has been tempered by the flexibility in interpersonal behaviour that personal acquaintance makes possible, but, and for the same reasons, white control of Negro behaviour has been very close. The growth of larger towns has permitted the division of social life into relatively independent compartments, segments, or spheres within which Negroes can attain higher positions because they climb at the expense of other Negroes and are not placed in a master-servant relationship to Whites. This can happen because the norms of racial subordination are defined as regulating only certain kinds of contact between Whites and Negroes, and the proportion of contacts exempt from them (e.g. when driving automobiles) has been increasing. Chapter Eight showed that in South Africa urbanization has not had this result. Blacks and Whites start off from separate communities with different languages and cultures. Urbanization brings the two groups together on a segregated basis; it entails a considerable measure of economic integration and a smaller one of social integration. The more productive economic system brings the urban African a higher standard of living in material terms, but there is no tilting of the colour line, which remains firmly horizontal. The concentration of Africans in urban locations has hitherto enabled the Whites to exercise a closer control over their behaviour than has been possible or thought desirable in the country districts. Possibly the segmental character of urban living in South Africa, with its almost separate white and black towns, will after a time make governmental control of African life more difficult, but the position does not yet show any resemblance to that described for the Deep South.

Urbanization in Southern Rhodesia has followed the South African pattern in its course and effects. It should also be noted that British colonial theory was never well adapted to the problems of urban administration. British suzerainty in Africa was represented as being for the Africans' good, therefore it was obliged to profess respect for the subject peoples' cultural integrity and to disclaim any intention of making black Englishmen of them. Hannah Arendt has observed: 'The imperialist-minded business men were followed by civil servants who wanted "the African to be left an African", while quite a few, who had not yet grown out of what Harold Nicholson once called their "boyhood ideals" wanted them to become "a better African" – whatever that may mean' (1958: 130–1). A modern psychological study of racial attitudes also found, upon factorial analysis, that a belief in 'fair play' or legal justice for all races was second only to 'general conservatism' as a characteristic of the European outlook there (Rogers & Frantz, 1962: 110–11).

The ideal of preserving Africans' cultural integrity inspired an anti-acculturation policy in administration. When Africans congregated in the towns, this was interpreted as a threat to the policy, for in the towns they became 'detribalized', giving up their distinctive cultures for the less colourful pursuits of an urban proletariat. As Lord Hailey noted, in South Africa and Southern Rhodesia the urban native was regarded as an anomaly because 'he breaks into the symmetry of a scheme which would divide the European and native populations into two separate spheres of activity' (1938: 543-4). The twin objectives of economic development and cultural non-interference were mutually incompatible, but in Central Africa a compromise along South African lines was attempted by regarding Africans as only temporary town-dwellers and housing them in locations separate from the permanent settlements of the Whites. Urban life was to be a feature of the white way of life, not of the African. In Southern Rhodesia the fundamental legislation putting this conception into effect was the Land Apportionment Act of 1930, which divided the country into a sort of chess board of black native reserves and white European areas. Of 96 million acres, 40 were placed in tribal trust, 36 were allotted to European farmers and 10 to national parks and reserves, and 10 were left unallocated, though subsequently 4 of these were set aside for African purchase. The remaining unreserved land is of poor quality and can be developed only by heavy investment of capital. The Morris Carter Commission which preceded the Act believed that for practical and psychological reasons 'the points of contact between the races should be reduced', but this has not been achieved: nearly a quarter of a million Africans are employed as labourers on European farms. In Salisbury today, the Africans whose economic contribution to the city is so important live in satellite townships about two to five miles out. Another aspect of Rhodesian policy which restricts African participation in the urban economy is that regulating African education. In 1965, 628,000 African pupils were due to be enrolled in primary schools – an increase of about 40 per cent over the last ten years. But only a tiny percentage gets beyond the primary grades. Only 12,000 were due to go to secondary school, and there are but four sixth forms for Africans in the whole of the country. Those getting to universities have been just a handful. African demand for education is at present insatiable, but government policy provides Africans with the training for subordinate posts only.

In Rhodesia, as in other parts of Africa, there appears to be a surplus of African labour relative to the number of jobs available. The appearance is deceptive. Rhodesia, like South Africa, attracts workers from other territories who travel long distances to obtain wage-earning employment. In 1956, 48 per cent of the Rhodesian labour force came from outside the country – chiefly from Nyasaland (now Malawi) and Mozambique (on the distribution of immigrant labour in Rhodesia, see Mitchell, 1961a: 212–31). Partly because the indigenous labour is not used economically, Rhodesia has been dependent upon these migrant workers. Paradoxically, the urban situation is exacerbated by the retrograde state of subsistence farming. Capital investment which might help native agriculture has been slight. Roads and railways have been built only to serve areas that produce export crops or minerals. Wage-earning employment in the cities appears the more attractive when income from subsistence farming is low. In the towns, migrant workers, because they are numerous, have been in a weak bargaining position with respect to wages, and employers have had less incentive to economize on the numbers employed or to promote the potential capabilities of their workers. Effective industrial growth depends, in the long run, upon the development of the rural areas which produce the food and can expand the consumer market. At present, the young and vigorous men are drawn away from the farming districts and the remaining women and children may be scarcely able to maintain the farming economy. The shortage of such men in the villages and the excess of them in the towns both have undesirable social consequences (Mitchell, 1961b: 81-82).

The urban locations in which the Africans live are governed by officials, and the African has little direct influence over their decisions. In one Salisbury location there are government-built quarters for married people; in another, about 50,000 single or separated males are crowded together. If an African loses his job he may lose his house. A recent study states that if he went into the white town the African had to take his food with him; furthermore, unless he was careful in choosing where to eat it, he might give offence. Service in the shops was provided by white assistants and the African would usually have to wait until every white customer had been served and was then fortunate if he was treated with civility. Wherever he went, he had to carry a pass; it was an offence to be without it and a policeman could demand to see it at any time. It was against the law for him to be given European beer, wine, or spirits; he was allowed only 'Kaffir beer', and that – with some exceptions – he was permitted to drink only at a municipal beer hall (Mason, 1960: 169). The spatial segregation of Black and White was regarded as vital. Proposals to build a government house for a leading African in a white area and to admit the son of a Pakistani diplomatic official to a white school both excited forceful protests. Some white schools run by missions and private bodies admitted small numbers of African pupils, but the government has invoked the Land Apportionment Act to discourage this. Segregation enters into all institutions in which both races participate. In general, African priests have not been allowed to administer Holy Communion to Europeans and there has been a substantial status gap between African and European ministers of religion.

In industry, men of the two races have to work together so segregation has been based upon the reservation of certain occupations to Europeans. Such practices have not necessarily been reflected in legislation.

'When a European wants to build a house in Southern Rhodesia he will, if he wants the bricklaying done cheaply and well, employ an African to do the work. It will cost him five or six times less than if he were to engage a European bricklayer. But the snag comes when he wants other craftsmen, such as plumbers or electricians, skills that the Africans have not yet been trained to perform. It will subsequently prove very difficult, even impossible, to get a European electrician to wire his house if the bricks have been laid by an African. It is therefore possible for Southern Rhodesia to boast that they have no discriminatory industrial legislation. They do not need it as things are . . .' (Gussman, 1962: 101).

Job reservation has been made even more crucial to the maintenance of white supremacy by restrictions upon the economic determination of wage levels. The differential between African and European wages was not wholly based on differences in the value of the services provided, but was affected by the disparity in bargaining power of the two groups and by conventional ideas as to what was appropriate for an African. European industrialists were often willing to raise African wage levels and appreciated that the increase in African purchasing power would have a generally beneficial effect, but they were effectively restrained by the white farmers (Gray, 1960: 225–9). The belief that the African's place was in the reserves and that he was not entitled to a standard of living better than that which he had enjoyed prior to the European conquest, coupled with European power and the structure of European politics, depressed urban living standards. An impartial examination of this question relating to the middle 1950s necessarily concluded: 'There is really no room to doubt that from one-fifth to two-fifths of urban Africans in the Rhodesias are not earning enough to keep their families and that of those with two children or more the majority are undernourished and underclothed' (Mason, 1960: 150).

African labour in Southern Rhodesia in the early 1950s tended, from the standpoint of the European employer, to be inefficient; productivity was low; the workers, having no security in urban society and no prospect of building up a long-term career there, did not respond to the usual industrial incentives. Town life was ill-disciplined, overcrowded, insanitary, and subject to the pass laws, and a man who was not gainfully employed could be expelled from an urban area even though he was born there and knew no other home. At work, Africans were subject to supervisors 'whose chief qualifications for the post are a harsh manner and a ready flow of invective in the native tongue' (Gussman, 1953: 139). African trade unions were not recognized in law and strikes were illegal. Thus suspicion and conflict between employer and employee were much greater than is characteristic of Western industrialism, and work suffered accordingly. It was in the employers' interest to promote the stabilization of the labour force so that an urban African community might develop which would produce more efficient workers, but other interests opposed this: the European farmers have been mentioned in this connection; the European workers' trade unions feared that their interests might be threatened; the government also was apprehensive. One summary runs:

'Settled labour is more efficient because, if it is really settled, it has something to work for beyond immediate needs and because the danger of unemployment provides an incentive. European employers welcome the greater productivity but they fear the social and political consequences. A settled African community would expect to enjoy the right of self-determination within the community as the corner-stone of its security and this might impinge in many ways on European sovereignty in the towns. It is, therefore, a demand which no Euro-pean municipality is prepared to grant' (Gussman, 1953: 143).

Since then, Rhodesian policy has changed. The central government has established home-ownership schemes which have had some effect, but up to the end of 1965 the municipalities had not followed suit. Little progress has been made towards the stabilization of the urban population (Mitchell, 1966b).

In Northern Rhodesia the recession of 1931 hit the Copperbelt very hard: African employment fell from 30,000 to under 7,000 (Gann, 1964: 252) and the redundant workers had to retire, with their depen-dants, to the reserves. The fear of another recession and the danger that there might be no secure industrial base for an urban African society, with the necessary social services, led the government there to reject proposals for labour stabilization. Though the colonial administrators often defended the African against the settler, they were less liberal in anything affecting the maintenance of law and order, for this bore upon their own interests and convenience (Franck, 1960: 90). The settler outlook gradually spread among the colonial administrators (Leys & Pratt, 1960: 16; cf. Gann & Duignan, 1962: 64n). Thus European policies towards the Africans were in part the outcome of a conflict of interests within the European group.

Urbanization in Rhodesia did not, therefore, provide conditions under which the upper members of the lower category could climb to positions superior to the lowest Europeans, nor did it permit them to create a separate social realm relatively free from European surveillance. Contacts across the colour line became less personal and communication was impaired; Blacks and Whites had less and less understanding of one another and the repression of sexual temptations added its contribution to the other forces making for separation (cf. Gray, 1960: 324–5; McEwan, 1963: 279n). One inquiry shows that whereas the African 'boss boy' might look for social companionship to the lower-middle group of white workers more readily than to any others in the white community – for members of this group most nearly approximated him in educational, social, and economic background and interests – in fact, it was these lower groups among the Europeans who were most opposed to contact with Africans (Franck, 1960: 242, but cf. Rogers & Frantz, 1962: 124–8). A recent study in Rhodesia of urban African attitudes towards Europeans found African men more hostile than their wives towards Europeans, and their wives more hostile than unmarried women; it showed that the more an African was in touch with the sentiments of his or her fellows, the more hostile he was inclined to be. When asked in what ways Europeans were different from them, Rhodesian Africans listed differences of wealth more frequently than Africans in Ghana had done in a similar investigation. The author of the Rhodesian study concluded that the Africans were 'almost universally hostile' to the Europeans; 'this hostility was based not on political doctrine or persuasion, nor on any sense of group cohesiveness in the face of discrimination by the white minority, rather was it intensely personal, and being rooted in individual grievance and observation many times repeated. . . .' By contrast with the situation in Ghana, 'no regret was expressed at the passing of the traditional culture; the problem of how to achieve self-government and remove the yoke of the white man was too pressing to indulge in regrets for the vanishing past' (McEwan, 1963: 289, 290).

In 1965, as this is written, the confrontation between Africans and Europeans in Rhodesia is sharper than ever before, and a resolution of the power conflict cannot long be delayed. Urbanization instead of easing racial subordination has intensified it. In the Deep South the pattern of social relations in the rural districts constituted a highly integrated social order; Whites and Negroes belonged to a single social system; roles of all kinds were tightly interrelated, and deviant interracial behaviour quickly caused repercussions over a wider area of relations. Urbanization brought a loosening of the network, permitting greater flexibility. In Southern Rhodesia the rural network of social relations was not tightly integrated in that Europeans and Africans belonged to partially independent social subsystems. Urbanization brought them closer together and strengthened European domination. The pattern of racial subordination bore directly upon a wider range of the everyday situations in which Africans were involved. For them to reject subordination in any context threatened the whole system; the consequences of any such deviation were therefore more serious and more immediate. The effects of industrialization, channelled by white political interests, have been to make the colour line more distinct and inclusive without moving it from the horizontal; consequently, African opposition to the racial order has unified. There are no effective interest groups of a composition that crosses the colour line and the system holds out no rewards for political compromise. The only long-term solution is for the whole society to be drawn into the ambit of some wider political unit which would stimulate a regrouping of forces and introduce greater flexibility.

INDUSTRIALIZATION AS A SOURCE OF CHANGE

In a reasoned critique of the tendency to regard industrialism as a solvent of racial discrimination, one sociologist concludes: 'available evidence everywhere sustains the thesis that when introduced into a racially ordered society industrialization conforms to the alignment and code of the racial order' (Blumer, 1965a: 245). Industry can (and does) tolerate a wide latitude of inefficient operation and still achieve acceptable production and profit. Discriminatory policies may represent a departure from the economic optimum but in an imperfect market the loss may not be enough to stimulate any change of policy. Enterprises are dependent upon staff who belong to the local community and share its values, so that the freedom of action of those who would introduce changes is limited. Yet in much of Africa it is unreal to think of industrialization as introduced into an ongoing society. More often, industrialization has created a society which did not previously exist. It has drawn together people from different social groups and given them new interests in common. The study of race relations in the industrial centres of colonial Africa therefore entails examination not only of relations between Blacks and Whites but also of relations between the groups that go to make up each of these categories. In the case of the Africans it is necessary to study the processes by which people from different regions and cultures come to make common cause and the way in which divisions among them affect the total pattern of relations.

Particularly instructive studies of group formation and alignment among newly urbanized Africans were conducted in the early 1950s by social scientists working in the mining towns of the Copperbelt in what was then Northern Rhodesia and is now Zambia. They took special note of the way in which the urban social pattern was determined by the exigencies of copper-mining as a productive process introduced from outside, dependent upon the world market for the product, and organized on the basis of capital raised outside Africa. Being trained in social anthropology, these scholars were also impressed by the great contrasts between rural and urban living in this part of the continent. From these features sprang the two most distinctive contributions of the group: the application to urban social structure of the model of structural opposition developed in political anthropology, and the analysis of the consequences of rural-urban migration in terms of the alternation between separate social systems instead of seeing them in psychological terms as the products of a process of detribalization. For a proper appreciation of these contributions it is necessary to consult the work of the writers themselves: Max Gluckman (esp. 1958), J. Clyde Mitchell (1956), and A. L. Epstein (1958), though the line of thought has since been further developed in the South African research of Philip Mayer (1961, 1962).

The model of structural opposition can best be understood with the aid of a simple diagram (*Figure 12*). This diagram illustrates how, in

Figure 12　Structural opposition on the Copperbelt

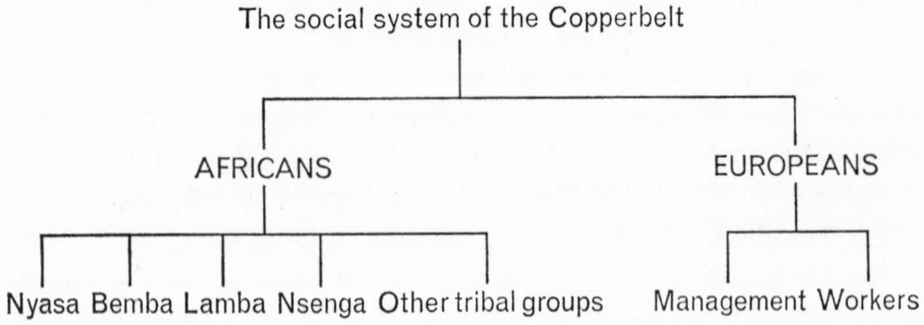

certain respects, e.g. with regard to fluctuations in the marketability of copper, the entire population of these towns formed a single community with a common interest. In other respects, the population divided into smaller groups with opposed interests. When an issue was defined in racial terms, all Africans united to form a solidary group opposed to all Europeans. Within each of these groups other conflicts might arise which put Africans of one tribe or of one economic class in opposition to those of another, or divided mine managements from their European employees. The groups formed in response to stimuli within a continuing system of relations. Initially, both the managements and the European colonial administrators regarded the Africans as falling naturally into tribal groups. The Africans came from villages where they were subject to the authority of chiefs on the tribal pattern. It was thought, therefore, that they should be governed along tribal lines in the cities also, and tribal headmen or elders were appointed to represent each group. When industrial disputes developed, however, the Africans circumvented the system cf tribal representation, forming a trade union which represented their shared interests as African workers irrespective of tribe (Epstein, 1958).

The European thinks of tribalism as a feature of African rural life, but the contrary position can equally well be urged. People may grow up in a group and not know what is distinctive of it until they come into contact with members of other groups. What does he know of England who only England knows? Many pre-industrial peoples have no names for themselves other than words which mean 'people' – implying that others are not really human. African students find a common African identity when they are studying overseas; tribal Africans find a tribal identity when they meet men from other tribes, and in this sense tribalism is a phenomenon of the city and the labour camp. Mitchell separates these two uses of the term by speaking of 'tribal structure' for the traditional pattern, and of 'tribalism' for the mode of categorizing people in the contact situation, though 'ethnicity' has been suggested as a better label for the second of these (Mitchell, 1956: 30; Wallerstein, 1960). Given that differences between tribes were suppressed when the situation was interpreted as calling for African solidarity, it is appropriate to ask why tribal distinctions should have been more important, or in what sense they were more important, than distinctions of class. The answer must be that most of the Copperbelt workers were then of similar socio-economic status so that class criteria did not differentiate them much, whereas a constant flow of newcomers of different tribes was pouring into the towns. The new men were not immediately absorbed into the prestige system but their tribal distinctiveness was thrown into relief by their new contacts. Tribal categories therefore constituted a preliminary basis for the formation of new ties and groupings. Consequently, divisions between persons of different tribes were interpreted by some Africans as grounded in tribal sentiments even though the real points of conflict were of a different order. A struggle for power within the African Mine Workers' Union was interpreted as a struggle between tribal groups. The attempt of the more skilled workers from Nyasaland to form a separate union catering to their distinctive interests as salaried staff was resisted by the others and regarded as tribal separatism; the emergent class grouping was not recognized (Epstein, 1958: 235–6). Therefore Mitchell concludes:

'. . . in their opposition to the Europeans, Africans ignore both their "class" and tribal differences. Inside a tribal association such as those found in Southern Rhodesia I would expect opposition to be phrased in terms of "class" differences. I would expect the dissension within a teachers' or clerks' association to be phrased in terms of tribalism. The same people who stand together in one situation may be bitterly opposed in another' (1956: 43).

Within the European population, divisions of interest were most apparent in connection with the policy of African advancement advocated by the managements and resisted by the European trade unions. The cleavage never opened very wide because the two groups felt dependent on one another in the face of African pressure. The European workers evinced an underlying insecurity (Powdermaker, 1962: 83–84), and hankered after a clear status gap with a horizontal colour line; they used their bargaining position to gain valuable concessions from the managements.

This focus on the political and industrial aspects of intergroup relations on the Copperbelt has been complemented by work providing additional detail on the domestic and leisure-time aspects. The Copperbelt provided many avenues of employment for African men but relatively few for women. Most of the African domestic servants in European households were men. Because of the employment situation, European influence upon African culture was mediated through the men; the women had an easier life in the towns than in the countryside, but they were more dependent upon the men both economically and in respect of participation in the social changes. Listening to the men's complaints about European supervisors instead of knowing Europeans personally, the women were more hostile to Europeans than were their menfolk. In essays written by teenage boys and girls, 40 per cent of the boys displayed a favourable attitude towards Europeans, compared with only 9 per cent of the girls. In this respect the Copperbelt differs from Rhodesia and presents a marked contrast with the Deep South, where Negro women were in closer touch with Whites than were Negro males, and were the chief agents for transmitting the Whites' culture in the Negro community (Powdermaker, 1962: 202–6). The racial pattern on the Copperbelt had not destroyed the domestic authority of the male, as in South Africa, and gave the women relatively little opportunity to exploit the advantages of their new roles.

A second feature of the Copperbelt studies was mentioned earlier: the conception of rural-urban migration as a movement between different social systems on the part of people who might not change much as individuals (by adopting new values, etc.) but who were obliged to modify their behaviour to meet the requirements of each system. Those who viewed this movement in terms of 'detribalization' thought of the African townsman as an African first and a townsman second. Max Gluckman has argued to the contrary that the new urbanite is to be seen as a townsman first and an African second: 'The starting point for analysis of urbanization must be an urban system of relations, in which the tribal origins of the population may even be regarded as of secondary interest.' An African townsman is a townsman. An African miner is a miner, and as such he needs not a chief, but a trade union, not the social relationships his parents knew, but ones appropriate to his new situation. Gluckman emphasizes the discontinuity between the two systems by claiming: 'the moment an African crosses his tribal boundary to go to the town, he is "detribalized", out of the political control of his tribe' (1961: 69). This statement can be viewed either as a methodological principle instructing research workers to examine the interconnections of urban institutions, or as an empirical proposition asserting that rural and urban social systems are completely different. The former implication is excellent advice, but the latter requires closer examination. There was a striking contrast between the two systems in Northern Rhodesia, but elsewhere the difference has been less marked. Thus, in comparison with Northern Rhodesia, in West Africa the countryside has been permeated by urban values to a greater extent, migrants have shorter distances to travel, and there is a denser pattern of settlement along the lines of communication. In the towns, the smaller-scale, more differentiated pattern of employment, and the private ownership of housing, permit the perpetuation of many rural patterns in urban surroundings. As a result, the urban system does not impose roles upon those who live within it to the same extent as does the society of the Copperbelt. In colonial West Africa there were fewer Europeans and their interests were not so extensive, so there was less of a cleavage between Black and White. Intermediary groups –

Lebanese, Indians, and Creoles – were more important. Class distinctions within the African population were greater, and tribal groups were divided from one another to a larger extent by variations in prestige. Consequently, the differences between rural and urban systems in much of West Africa were not as great as they were in Northern Rhodesia, and it may therefore be more appropriate to regard the African townsman there as being, for some purposes, a tribesman first and a townsman second (the highly urbanized country of Senegal is an exception – cf. Crowder, 1962: 81–82).

CULTURAL DIFFERENCES AND SOCIAL RELATIONS

Reference has already been made, in the chapter on South Africa, to the fact that cultural differences may distort one group's understanding of what members of another group are trying to communicate. The main sources of conflict between inherited values have been identified as underlying ideas about the ownership of land, the significance of cattle ownership, and values attaching to marriage, sex, and the family. Europeans have assumed that economic rationality and material worth are universally valid concepts and have been unwilling to accord any respect to African values concerning the use of time, leisure, etc. (van den Berghe, 1965: 218–27). White settlers have been inclined to take signs of cultural difference as showing that Africans did not think as they did, and, further, as indicating African backwardness. For West Africa, one study compared, first, the post-Reformation European notion of work as a moral obligation and the central significance of a man's vocation to his self and his status, with the African conception of the 'big man' as someone with dependants to work for him; second, the European assumption that progress is possible and desirable with the traditional African pattern in which a man takes his ancestors as models without seeking to surpass them; third, the European reliance upon complex impersonal modes of social organization with the African's expectation of standing in personal relation to all the people with whom he regularly comes into contact (Banton, 1957: 111–15). An example of the kind of friction that can arise from discrepant mutual expectations can be seen in the story from the former Belgian Congo of the departmental head who did not tell his African office staff that his father had just died; they learned the news from another source and commented, 'You see, he regards us as workers, not as people' (Slade, 1960: 38).

A Belgian missionary pointed out how cultural differences might be significant for relations between employers and employees (Charles,

1952). He held that an examination of tribal law in the Congo revealed differences from European law in respect of the conception of contracts. In tribal law, an employer and a worker who accepted his offer entered into partnership; the employer was regarded as a somewhat special kind of clan chief and therefore had the chiefly functions of benefactor, guardian, and protector. Thus the African worker at first regarded the European employer as bound by obligations which the latter did not recognize; when he failed to observe them the African was embittered. The European, on the other hand, regarded the African's expectations as evidence of his allegedly childlike nature. Such a cultural difference is evident in the report that at one East African concern a group of African workers were resentful because the company refused their request for two cattle at Christmas to which they felt entitled 'because they were a long way from home'. The company held that the workers had contracted to work for definite sums and that there had been no agreement that they should receive more than other workers on special occasions (Sofer, 1954: 75).

A series of examples of how persons brought up in different cultures may misinterpret one another's signals has been listed by two American writers (Hall & Whyte, 1960) who consider variations in the significance of voice tone, touch, time, and distance. Their observations are not based on evidence from colonial Africa, but they have sufficient general relevance to demand quotation.

'The Saudi Arab shows respect to his superior – to a sheik, say – by lowering his voice and mumbling. The affluent American may also be addressed in this fashion, making almost impossible an already difficult situation. Since in the American culture one unconsciously "asks" another to raise his voice by raising one's own, the American speaks louder. This lowers the Arab's tone more and increases the mumble. This triggers a shouting response in the American – which cues the Arab into a frightened "I'm not being respectful enough" tone well below audibility.'

In Indonesia physical contact has a significance quite different from that in Europe, just as some European nations consider it appropriate for men to embrace each other whereas other nations disapprove of anything more demonstrative than a handshake. In Java, for a stranger even momentarily to place his hand on someone's shoulder in public can be the occasion of acute humiliation.

In the Middle Eastern countries, to require someone to complete a task by a deadline may appear only offensive. The standard Arab method for getting a task completed quickly is what the authors call 'needling' – something considered bad manners in the United States. An Arab businessman whose car broke down explained it this way:

'First, I go to the garage and tell the mechanic what is wrong with my car. I wouldn't want to give him the idea that I didn't know. After that, I leave the car and walk around the block. When I come back to the garage, I ask him if he has started to work yet. On my way home from lunch I stop in and ask him how things are going. When I go back to the office I stop by again. In the evening, I return and peer over his shoulder for a while. If I didn't keep this up, he'd be off working on someone else's car.'

To which the authors add, 'If you haven't been needled by an Arab, you just haven't been needled.'

In North America, they say, the 'proper' distance at which to stand when talking to another adult male you do not know well is about two feet, at least in a formal business conversation. (Naturally, at a cocktail party the distance shrinks, but anything under eight to ten inches is likely to provoke an apology or an attempt to back up.)

'To a Latin American, with his cultural traditions and habits, a distance of two feet seems approximately what five feet would be to us. To him, we seem distant and cold. To us, he gives an impression of pushiness. As soon as a Latin American moves close enough for him to feel comfortable, we feel uncomfortable and edge back. We once observed a conversation between a Latin and a North American which began at one end of a forty-foot hall. At intervals we noticed them again, finally at the other end of the hall' (Hall & Whyte, 1960).

Misunderstandings deriving from cultural differences may influence the conduct of personal relations, but their analysis contributes little to the explanation of group conflicts. Discrepancies in the value accorded to different activities and possessions may affect group perceptions from the outset but the contact situation is certain either to reduce or to exacerbate these discrepancies. It is inadequate, therefore, to consider the significance of cultural differences for intergroup relations without looking fairly closely at the structure of relationships in which members of the two groups meet or perceive one another.

The structure of work relations is particularly instructive in this respect. A good analysis of the way in which values within an industrial plant and within the wider community interact upon one another has been carried out for the town of Jinja in Uganda (Sofer, 1954). This town was built up by Asians as a trading centre. From 1949 it enjoyed a construction boom when work began on a dam across the Nile to generate hydro-electric power. Two years later, the town's population was 14,900 Africans, 5,100 Asians, and 800 Europeans. Senior government posts were open only to Europeans and it was imperial policy to place long-term African interests before the interests of Asians, who concentrated on commercial activity. This pattern was repeated in most spheres of social life. For many years there was a tacit prohibition on the importation of Europeans to do work incompatible with the political position and social rank of their group. As Europeans were not attracted to settle there, they did not themselves acquire extensive interests in the country, and placed restrictions upon the Asians' doing so.

Industrial relations conformed to the general social hierarchy: Europeans were recruited to fill the managerial posts, Asians as supervisors, and Africans as unskilled workers. People of these three categories brought to the employment situation their distinctive cultural expectations of work behaviour and different degrees of industrial skill. To each group, the expectations of members of other groups appeared unreasonable. Asked whether they preferred to work under a European or an Asian, Africans indicated a clear preference for the European who seemed to be more interested in keeping Africans at a distance than in keeping them subordinate. The European owed his racial community an obligation to behave in a dignified and restrained manner, and had a prestige which induced the African to respond more easily to his orders. An African was bound by an elaborately deferential etiquette in his interaction with a European; the latter did not make a reciprocal deference return, but had implicit obligations towards the African to afford him leadership, protection, and behavioural models. These obligations provided the justification for his presence in the country and were surrounded by a complex set of official and unofficial sanctions within the European community. The Africans believed that the Europeans did not have African interests at heart, and they were most suspicious of any change proposed by them. Greatest friction arose between Africans and Asians. As the Asian had less prestige than the European, the African was slower to respond to his orders and it was therefore necessary for the Asian to be more vehement to achieve the same result. Squeezed between temporarily immigrant Europeans and the rising African mass, the Asian was anxious to show the European that he was superior to Africans and to dissociate himself from them. The African, on the other hand, knew that the power of an Asian supervisor was closely circumscribed by that of the European. He could challenge any order of an Asian's in the security that the European would arbitrate between them. Furthermore, the Asian group readily became a scapegoat for African discontents.

In the course of his analysis, Cyril Sofer argues that instances of friction in the case under study do not arise only or mainly from cultural differences between the racial groups, but that 'they stem also, and perhaps more importantly, from the structure of characteristic social relationships which exist between the groups' (1954: 72). Men are recruited to perform particular roles which bring them into defined relationships with members of other groups, so that they see only certain aspects of these other groups' cultures. Thus their roles and relationships influence the attitudes they develop. Closer examination showed that each group's position in the social system was reflected in, and supported by, its view of the society as a whole, of the other groups, and of itself. The European viewed the system as harnessing European leadership to help Africans to attain higher living standards and a greater measure of political autonomy. He thought of the Asian as hard-working and clever at business, but crafty and devoted exclusively to the pursuit of material wealth. The African he perceived as ignorant, childlike, suspicious, and unco-operative. The Asian considered the chief purposes of the prevailing policy to be the preservation of the power of the British and the defence of British and African interests against economic development under Asian leadership. Asians saw Europeans as hypocritical but shared their view of the African. To the African it seemed that the whole organization of the society was based upon foreign exploitation of himself and his country. He perceived the European as rich, powerful, and clever, but haughty and insincere in his protestations of benevolence. The Asian appeared to the African as dishonest, unscrupulous, and resentful of African progress because it spelled his eventual expulsion from the country. This influence of roles upon attitudes provided reinforcement for a social system that might otherwise have been too unstable.

The same study also shows that changes initiated within an industrial concern can influence roles and relations in the community outside. In the Jinja instance, a number of European artisans were introduced for construction work. Being in a low rank compared with other Europeans, they tended at first to behave in the same way as the Asians in trying to demonstrate their superiority to those below them. As their numbers grew, however, these Europeans felt a greater security within their own group and began to behave in a more relaxed and tolerant way in their relations with others (cf. also Sofer & Ross, 1951; Sofer & Sofer, 1955:

52–55). Thus industrial changes created a European subcategory inferior in many respects to a considerable number of Asians and to a growing elite of Africans educated in Europe. The pattern of colour differentiation became less distinct. Events in the wider community had effects in industry and developments in industry had repercussions in the community because both plant and community relations were involved in a wider system. The consequences of changes had cumulative effects. As African political power increased, so the overall system became more coherent and the cumulative tendencies became stronger.

Some roles offer people an opportunity to obtain a favourable impression of members of another group and to build up more harmonious relations with them. In general, such harmony is more easily obtained when members of different groups are brought together in pursuit of common goals rather than in a way that draws attention to the differences between them. A point to note is that some social systems make available, even to those people who want to get to know members of the other group, very few opportunities for meeting the others on a basis that can lead to greater mutual understanding. A European on the Copperbelt who took an interest in African sport might find this such an opportunity, and one that seemed acceptable to his fellow Europeans, but most relationships would serve only to recapitulate the pattern of European dominance. In Uganda by the late 1950s there were no laws preventing, or even hindering, informal social relations; the exclusion of non-Europeans from the more expensive hotels, and similar discriminatory practices, had all been abandoned. Yet informal interracial social life was severely restricted by the lack of common interests. Some Europeans – such as people of evangelical inclination and college teachers – were exceptions, but 'Whatever do you find to talk to Africans about when you have them to tea?' was a question often put to one lecturer (Goldthorpe, 1958: 268–9). Africans, being used to different housing, income level, and style of life, entertained Europeans even less frequently. Such direct contacts as there were took place chiefly at one or the other party's place of work, which explains the Sofers' aphorism about Uganda at this time: 'race relations stop at half past four'.

The policies of employers or governments sometimes affect the structure of characteristic social relations by bringing members of different groups together in one kind of relationship and minimizing contact in others. Often these policies are not deliberately framed to this end, but sometimes the implications of such decisions are anticipated. When land was allocated to European farmers in Kenya, separate zones were established for them. In Tanganyika, however, the entire country was regarded as native land. For Europeans, farm blocks of reasonable size were selected within the tribal areas in consultation with the chiefs. This interpenetration of racial settlement lessened the opposition between the racial groups and may have contributed in some measure to the relative absence of racial friction in Tanganyika (Goldthorpe, 1958: 259–60).

RACIAL STRATIFICATION IN A PATERNALIST ORDER

The distinction between white settler colonies and other colonies is clearly of consequence for patterns of race relations, even though many variations between territories are left out of account by any twofold classification. In Southern Africa the status gap between the rough, self-reliant pioneers and the Africans, organized into powerful chiefdoms, was often fairly small. Pioneers, traders, and missionaries might all be concerned to win the favour of a powerful chief and they often pushed out into districts where the imperial government could give them little protection. In the course of time the settlers mobilized their political power to put the colour line on an institutional basis. In the non-settler colonies or tropical dependencies there was, by definition, little or no European settlement. Ultimate political power resided in the metropolitan country. The European population consisted in large part of skilled persons called in to perform duties which could not be discharged by locally born people, so that there was little cause to take active measures in support of a status gap. There was systematic racial discrimination in non-settler colonies, and European behaviour towards Africans could be as repressive as in any settler colony (for a striking interpretation of African reactions to Belgian colonial rule in the Congo, see Turnbull, 1963). Nevertheless, it would be misleading to speak of the existence of a colour line in these territories if the same term is to be used for the position in colonies like Southern Rhodesia. A colour line is a line held against pressure, which determines the transmission of status from one generation to another. In West Africa and in Uganda there were times when it could be claimed that the colonial administration had developed its own material interest in the countries in question (as sources of relatively well-paid employment and of personal power, etc.) and that colonial officials defended this interest against anyone who threatened it, especially the rising elite of African professional people. It can also be argued that at times the West African administration used its political power to assist European commercial interests. In Nigeria up to 1927, legislation specifically required that the agent in charge of a mining lease be a European. A small number of European firms were allowed to acquire a privileged position in the import and export trade. In the allocation of trading licences, the administration of trade controls, and the formulation of tax policies, the government dealt mostly with this select group of companies. This policy was strengthened by the need for trade controls during World War II. It may have stemmed in part from a bureaucratic preference for dealing with large established organizations (Coleman, 1958: 80–89). But, despite any contrary instances, the general tendency in the tropical dependencies was against the administrations' developing any important material interests in the countries they governed or becoming the agents of those who had such interests. Their numbers, relative to the densely settled African populations of the more humid coastal region, were very small, so that the discrimination bore mainly upon the African elite. Spatial segregation was less evident; a colour bar operated in connection with admission to social clubs and in patterns of sociability in general, but it was sometimes tempered by personal acquaintance.

Some territories vacillated between the settler and the non-settler patterns. Kenya provides an instructive case, for there the Indian community was strong enough to constitute a third category in the social system. Mary Parker has argued that in the early days the greatest threat to the European settler came from possible Indian competition. How did the British settlers react? When mobilizing support they appealed neither to British nationality (for this would have included a group of the Indians) nor to British descent (for this would have excluded a group of settlers from South Africa who were potential allies). They utilized racist conceptions to try to unite the entire white community, drawing in the Kenya government and its officials when possible. Specifically, they maintained: (a) that the 'White Highlands' were the only area suitable for white colonization and that Indians could live equally well at lower altitudes; (b) that European culture, morality, and methods of production were superior to those of both Indians and Africans. By the successful pressing of such arguments as principles for government policy, competition was narrowly restricted; the largest area of possible support was consolidated by the easily recognized sign of race (Parker, 1951: 42). One division within the European community was between the government employees and the taxpayers who, ultimately, had to pay them. Might not the European large taxpayer line up with the Indian taxpayer in demanding economies? He could not, because he himself had propounded the racist theory and in some measure had come to believe it. In industrial relations he sought to divide the total employee opposition by giving European employees generally a vested interest in the prevailing order. In such a situation the racist thesis had a self-fulfilling quality for, by restricting competition, it made the other groups seem more inferior than they might otherwise have appeared. Nevertheless, some Indian merchants did overcome the handicaps and, in the years after World War II, European and Indian employers recognized common interests and collaborated with one another. In elections for such offices as that of mayor, Europeans feared the alliance of Indian and African councillors. At times, Europeans and Indians were uncertain whether they should combine with one another or each seek African support against the other. The Indians could at one stage have utilized the racist theory against the Africans, but the need to defend themselves against European criticism had obliged them to deny racist ideas, appealing for equality of opportunity and the disavowal of discrimination. Thus the Indian employer was left vulnerable to pressure from his own labour force; he met this by joining with European employers and manipulating divisive religious associations within the Indian community (Parker, 1951: 41–52). It can therefore be seen that in a three-category system opportunities for alliances across racial lines are many times greater than in a two-category system.

In West Africa there were very few occasions on which the governments were drawn towards the policies of the settler colonies. Moreover, urbanization provided a niche in which the elite of upwardly mobile Africans could establish themselves as a group. This position of theirs was not important for the tilting of a distinct colour line so much as for changing, by political action, the whole basis of race relations. Urbanization did not mean the founding of new towns, European in conception, but the extension and development of African settlements in which Europeans were always a minority. By bringing Africans – especially the younger ones, with less demanding kinship responsibilities – together in a denser mass under new leadership, urbanization greatly aided the development of African political strength.

The first step in the creation of modern West African nationalism was the formation of groups representing and developing the viewpoint of the African elite, such as the Gold Coast Aborigines' Rights Protection Society of 1897 and the National Congress of British West Africa of 1920. Through such bodies the African intelligentsia was able to work out alternatives to the pattern of colonial rule. The groups were strongest where they could be based on the leadership of educated Africans who were members of the liberal professions – lawyers, doctors in private practice, etc. – and therefore not dependent upon the colonial administration for their livelihood. These men could build up a professional clientele only in the towns; they could hammer out their political ideas only where there were numbers of them living in close association; when, prior to independence, they were elected or appointed to represent 'native interests' on national or local councils, it was for urban constituencies, for in the country districts it was the chief who was regarded as the political representative of the people.

The colonial governments were often reluctant to recognize elite groups as representative of anyone except themselves. Thus in 1920 Sir Hugh Clifford expostulated:

'There has during the last few months been a great deal of loose and gaseous talk . . . which has for the most part emanated from a self-selected and self-appointed congregation of educated African gentlemen who collectively style themselves the "West African National Conference". . . . It can only be described as farcical to suppose that . . . continental Nigeria can be represented by a handful of gentlemen drawn from a half-dozen Coast tribes – men born and bred in British administered towns situated on the sea-shore, who in the safety of British protection have peacefully pursued their studies under British teachers' (quoted Coleman, 1958: 156).

Colonial administrators often sought to strengthen their hold by dividing the potential opposition. In the Gold Coast after World War I, for example, some paramount chiefs were actively engaged in the work of the central government and were made the allies of the administration against the Cape Coast lawyers who led the Aborigines' Rights Protection Society. In Sierra Leone the colonial government was content to use individual Creoles for its own purposes while identifying itself as trustee of the interests of the hinterland peoples, and in this capacity blocking Creole advance. The political history of such groupings needs to be studied in detail for each of the territories, the relevant point for the present being only that, because there was no inclusive colour line, the colonial governments could find allies outside the European population.

In the development of the colonial order, the position of the native elite was critical. Either the colonial government succeeded in winning the elite's support for its own policies (and the price of this support rose appreciably as the years went by) or members of the elite mobilized native opposition to the government. A recognition of the alternatives became almost explicit in Governor-General Carde's description of French educational policy: *instruire la masse et dégager l'élite*. The policy of assimilation attempted to put into effect such recommendations by offering *évolués* the privileges of the ruling group. In Senegal there was at one stage a numerically significant elite, based upon the liberal professions, which supported French colonial policy. As in the case of the Sierra Leone Creoles, its energies were for long directed to obtaining from the imperial power those rights and dignities which it had been promised (Crowder, 1962: 15). After World War II its numbers rose further, competition with Europeans intensified, and the group came to express an intense reaction against colonialism, drawing heavily upon Marxist theories and attracted to a mystique of *négritude*. The Portuguese likewise offered a more privileged status to *assimilados*, but with the increased emigration of unskilled Portuguese workers and their families to Angola and Mozambique this policy seems to have been restrained. When the native elite was numerically small, its members were exposed to the contradictory expectations of the colonial masters and of their own people. It was often difficult for colonial governments in Africa to satisfy the elite. For example, as Africans obtained professional and higher educational qualifications and secured positions in the senior division of the colonial civil services, the question arose of their salary scale. Europeans were paid at rates high enough to attract personnel from overseas, who were involved in additional expenses. If the government paid African staff at the same rates, this would magnify inequalities of income within the African population and impose a tax burden that was certain to increase. If, on the other hand, it fixed their salaries at a lower point, this was to open the way for charges of racial discrimination. Where, as in the then Belgian Congo, it was relatively easy to keep the African population isolated from developments in the wider world, the support of the elite could, for a time, be obtained in return for relatively small privileges.

In the evolution of Africans' and Europeans' attitudes towards each other, World War II was of the greatest significance. The war had a tremendous impact throughout the colonies, quite apart from the stimulus it gave to economic development. African soldiers were taught to have no regard for the racial status of enemy Europeans and Asians; many saw Europeans defeated in battle and subordinated as prisoners-of-war; they visited other lands, sometimes lay with white prostitutes, and acquired a new image of the white man. Large contingents of British and American troops were stationed in some places; their behaviour, like that of European seamen, often contrasted with the pukkah-sahib conventions of the colonial civil servant. After the war, the political situation within African colonies changed more rapidly. European attitudes may also have modified. In the new international situation the colonial powers were less confident and more sensitive to pressure from other nations. The first challenge to the basis of their position came from Ghana, then the Gold Coast, where the leaders of the Convention People's Party persuaded many of their fellow countrymen that they had remediable grievances, and built the first effective independence movement. The British response to this challenge was decided not in Accra (as it would have been in a settler colony) but in Westminster. Colonial officials in the Gold Coast took their orders from above. Ghana's progress to independence (legislative council with African elected majority in 1946, partial self-government 1951, complete independence 1957) greatly accelerated the pace of change elsewhere. In 1958 a referendum on the Constitution of the Fifth French Republic gave Africans in French colonies the choice between total independence and internal autonomy within 'the (French) Community'. The new Constitution permitted the territories to opt for independence later should they wish, but Guinea was unwilling to wait. In the mid-1950s also, influenced by the doctrines of African intellectuals in Paris associated with the review *Présence Africaine*, members of the Congolese elite began to react against the European assumption that Africans were in a process of development from an inferior to a superior stage, and to think in terms of the contact between two civilizations (Slade, 1960: 14). The Belgians had not built up any tradition of struggle and negotiation with African representatives, and so, faced by mounting demands from Congolese leaders for a share in government and impressed by French and British progress in decolonization, they capitulated – with results that everyone now knows.

African attitudes towards Europeans in the early stages of the liberation movements were not as straightforward as readers in Europe and North America might perhaps expect (cf. Sithole, 1959: 146–64). Some of the force behind nationalist sentiment came from the attempt to resolve conflicting feelings such as respect for European puissance and resentment over minor humiliations of everyday contact (the parallel with the motivation of 'cargo' movements may prove closer than any analyses have hitherto suggested). Young Africans' admiration of Western-style norms and achievement was confounded with the experience of particular Whites to generate a fundamental ambivalence (Rogers, 1959: 62–63; Jahoda, 1961: 42–43). West Africans sometimes affirmed that they had nothing against Europeans as people, but everything against them as rulers of their country. This development of a strictly political attitude to questions of race relations was reflected in an investigation in Uganda which showed that the more educated young people were, the more they were opposed to non-African participation in the government of their country (Gutkind, 1957).

In the paternalist order of the non-settler colonies, European behaviour and attitudes towards Africans were not patterned by any such
simple opposition as that engendered by a colour line. They varied
more, and the critical factors often derived from occupational and other
roles. Demands for racial solidarity were less extensive than in the
settler colonies. From a psychological standpoint, any European was in
an exposed position. All the social scaffolding which in his or her home
society was built round the values taught to children, and many of the
social controls which supported the cultural norms, had been removed.
Where Whites were few in number, considerable determination was
required to maintain at all times the norms and thereby the prestige of
the imperial culture. To help him in this task a man might institutionalize his own behaviour, creating personal customs and routines which
reminded him of the expectations of absent others: the idea of the
explorer or administrator dressing for dinner in the African bush is not
really as foolish as it may seem to the stay-at-home. A club or clique of
friends may provide the individual with a similar kind of support, and
with a means of supervising the behaviour of people who are identified
with him and whose misconduct might therefore rebound upon himself.
The social exclusiveness of minorities needs to be seen in this light. The
European official in Africa thought it only natural that he should keep
his club for himself and his fellows, as a place where he could relax
without any of the awkwardness that would arise if he admitted people
who did not share his assumptions. A senior European official who had
had too much to drink in the club on a Saturday evening would not have
been perturbed had this happened in the presence of a low-ranking
European who, because of his ethnic background, counted as one of the
group. Nor would he have minded if an African servant had been there.
But in the company of an African professional man he would have felt
unable to behave with the same freedom; he might have shared more
specialized interests with the educated African than he could share
with the low-ranking European, but for ordinary leisure purposes these
were of little account. Such self-segregation on the part of Europeans
was bitterly resented because their circle had a wider significance in
representing the social apex of the entire society. The successful African
professional or business man thought that he had made the grade and
felt affronted over his exclusion in a way that he would never have done
over rejection by Indian or Lebanese circles. Thus in colonies with a
growing African elite the question of racial discrimination in club
membership acquired a significance out of all proportion to the real

desires of the parties to obtain or avoid one another's company.

Many of these European clubs in the British colonies were, in theory at least, for members of the 'senior service' or some category that was not defined in racial terms. In practice, Africans were not elected to membership. When, in the years before independence, more and more Africans were promoted to higher posts, the element of discrimination became increasingly obtrusive. Most of the men belonging to such clubs met Africans regularly in the course of their work and had no difficulty in relating to them on an individual-to-individual basis; the acceptance of African members was a problem only to the group. As E. M. Forster wrote of Chandrapore, 'individually it knew better; as a club it declined to change'. Two authors show how it was the character of relations between Europeans that decided how long resistance to African membership could be maintained. The protocol-minded club for higher government officials, being the most affected by outside influences and the least determined by its own inner development, was the first to capitulate (Proudfoot & Wilson, 1961: 319). In the case they studied, as in others, the title to the land on which the European club stood was vested in the government. Once the Africans captured the government, they could threaten the club members with eviction. The centralized character of European colonial power meant that the social transformation at independence was extraordinarily rapid.

Another major factor determining the structure of relations within the European group was the presence of white women. In the early years of many colonies the Europeans were an all-male group and, on the West Coast at least, they mixed fairly freely in African social life. When, with the improvement of communication and medical services, they brought their wives out, they withdrew into their own community. The women met Africans in very few roles other than those of servants and obtained a narrower view of them than did their menfolk. The relationship between domestic employer and servant has in most times and countries been productive of tension, especially when there was a cultural gap between the parties. African servants might not comprehend European ideas about hygiene, and the slowness and alleged unreliability of houseboys became one of the very few topics on which all European housewives had something to say. For them, the adjective 'African' came to symbolize lower material and moral standards, and an encircling majority with whom they themselves had no direct relationships such as to give a sense of purpose to their presence in the country. This situation, together with the influence of sexual jealousy, may be responsible for the very general observation that European women expressed stronger prejudice towards Africans than the men did. They, after all, had to compete with Africans for their menfolk's attention. The stronger their influence, the more exclusive Europeans were likely to be (Banton, 1957: 115–17). A study of small isolated European communities in East Africa shows how the pressures within these groups hindered adaptation to the changing political environment. European wives were involved in their husbands' work without being able to participate in it. As they were continually meeting the same group of neighbours, the women paid less attention to their appearance than they might otherwise have done. In-group gossip became the substance of their lives. Officials low in the government hierarchy were, with their wives, usually in the majority. They tended to be sceptical of imperial policy, hostile to African advancement, and influential with regard to the tone of community affairs. When senior African civil servants were appointed to these stations they saw no advantage in establishing social contacts with the Europeans. Attempts to promote such contacts often only increased tension. As independence approached, Europeans became more negative about their roles in the transfer of power and their morale deteriorated (Tanner, 1966). Once again, the source of trouble lay less in individual attitudes than in the structure of group relations (cf. also Hamnett, 1966).

It has been said that in West Africa antipathy towards Africans was strongest among the lowest-ranking classes of Europeans who resented the university-trained African's claim to a higher status (Little, 1955: 276). Similar inferences have been drawn elsewhere. Class factors of this kind sometimes combine with the frictions of the domestic employer-servant relationship: Hortense Powdermaker specifically comments upon the wives who had never previously employed servants and never used any terms of normal politeness (1962: 813; cf. Gray, 1960: 231–2). Africans often treat domestic servants harshly, but without regarding them as an inferior race or generating the same sort of resentment. American social scientists concerned with training Peace Corps volunteers for service in Africa have noted that such personnel easily err in the opposite direction, embarrassing African domestic servants by being too familiar with them. Most of these volunteers have not been accustomed to having servants and need to be instructed in the properties of this relationship before being advised about the complications that arise if the parties belong to different groups defined by race.

This view of the determinants of race relations in colonial territories could probably draw confirmation from a detailed study of the social pressures upon white missionaries in their relations with Africans.

Though missionaries do not need to maintain political control and are not obliged to keep themselves apart from the members of their congregation, most of them have – understandably – remained oriented to European values and social ties. Some Catholic and Anglo-Catholic missionaries have minimized such bonds, renouncing racial privileges and living at a material level near that of the Africans; but a greater number, especially those who have had their families with them, have felt a need for the social and psychological support of other Whites in the district (cf. Cairns, 1966: 218–22; Rotberg, 1965: 53–54, 60–66, 140–2). A Protestant missionary, reporting on a study of mission practices in Africa, emphasized the economic gulf between the European or American missionary and the African minister. Because of this, missionaries have carried segregation into the church:

> 'In a few areas the social segregation of the Africans seemed to be conditioned largely by the social segregation and discrimination of government officials of the country. Settlers in some areas had passed on their colour-bar relations to the missionary groups and the two white groups reinforced one another by their acts of discrimination. Some of the missionaries seemed to have brought their prejudices with them to Africa. Their self-appointed superior roles were supported by a paternalism which had been established by their missionary predecessors' (Parsons, 1953: 507).

All along, there had been certain divisions of interest between governments and missions. The former often acted through the traditional tribal authorities, whereas the missions sought converts from all sections of the population and then supported them against the pressure to which they were frequently subjected. Such divisions could be managed, but when African nationalists upset the paternalism of the colonial governments they upset the paternalism of the missions too, and the latter had to change their policies in many ways. For example, though Nyasaland was not then independent, the Church of Scotland missions were obliged to oppose the proposals for the Central African Federation in the early 1950s because their congregations held such strong views on the subject.

With a change in the structure of political power, there can be very rapid changes in the pattern of race relations. Herbert Blumer, recapitulating an argument outlined by Everett Hughes (Hughes & Hughes, 1952: 64–65), has underlined how changes in managerial practices in the American South followed upon new policies instituted by the federal government, pressures from the national labour unions, and threats of economic boycotts organized by Negro groups. There have been similar changes in the policies of European firms operating in former colonies once they have been obliged to increase the nationals' participation in management. In South Africa, industrialization has brought an intensification of racial distinctions, not because this is required by industrial circumstance, but because of governmental legislation and policy (Blumer, 1965a: 247–9). Such evidence conflicts with the Marxist argument that economic interest groups will seek to control political policy; it suggests that often they wish only to be left undisturbed and react to political changes in whatever way seems most likely to minimize interference from outside.

The transition from colonial status to independence in Africa seems generally to have reduced any feelings of hostility towards Europeans on the part of Africans. After independence, the number of Europeans in these territories has usually increased owing to the greater employment of specialists and technicians in connection with development programmes. An experimental study in India showed that attitudes towards the British became more favourable after independence (Adinarayan, 1953). A New Zealand psychologist who conducted an inquiry in Nigeria just prior to independence concluded that, in acceding to the popular demand for political change, 'the British have fostered a climate of good will towards Europeans which has few parallels in Africa' (Rogers, 1959: 63). In another recent investigation in Sierra Leone it was found that, in a test situation, Africans expressed less social distance towards Europeans and Americans than towards Africans of other tribes (Dawson, 1965: 224–5). Independence has also changed the relations between indigenous groups. In Zambia, for example, the Coloureds previously had an anomalous political identity; but a representative of this community became an active member of President Kaunda's cabinet and under the new régime the coloured community has become an accepted element in the African population.

These findings suggest that Lloyd Warner's discussion of changes in the colour line was seriously incomplete. He maintained that the line might swing round and become diagonal. This chapter has supported the earlier conclusion that a colour line of the kind in question is found only in two-category systems and that tilting is possible only if institutional changes permit the compartmentalization of social relations so that upper members of the lower group may enjoy a superior position in class terms and still be denied political power. But the evidence from Southern and Western Africa shows that urbanization does not necessarily entail such changes. Warner assumed that the major change possible in race relations in the Deep South was dependent upon changes in the relation between the two groups without any change in their distinctiveness, and he did not consider the possibility that members of the lower category might find allies outside the local social system represented by his diagram. He indicated that the colour line might swing further round, but did not consider the possibility of its being dissolved. Although much of the African evidence does not come from two-category systems, it suggests that where members of a subordinate category can mobilize effective political pressure it is easier to eradicate a colour line than to tilt it.

CHAPTER ELEVEN

Integration and Pluralism

In the comparative study of race relations one country which has rightly attracted particular attention is Brazil. The history of race relations in Brazil is of special relevance because it begins almost contemporaneously with that of the United States, but, despite certain points of resemblance, develops differently, along a course which is the more interesting because it is uneven. Brazil is a huge country – considerably larger than the whole of Europe if Russia is excluded – and its diversity comprehends both rural poverty in economically stationary regions near the Equator and the competitive society of São Paulo, the industrial city on the southern coast with a population of over 4 million that is reputedly growing faster than any other in the world. Consequently, Brazilian experience at some time or in some place reflects many of the major problems of race relations. Historically, one of the more striking features is that Brazilian society moved away from a threatened two-category system towards an integrated order, in which dark-skinned people were concentrated at the bottom of the social scale but the sign value of racial appearance could be outweighed by wealth or other claims to status. In more recent times it has seemed that industrialization is strengthening racial distinctions, but the trend in race relations cannot be considered independently of changes in the politico-economic structure.

RACIAL STATUS IN BRAZIL

The most noted interpreter of Brazilian history to the outside world has been Gilberto Freyre. He has shown how the colony's social and economic system (rural patriarchy, latifundia, and single-crop agriculture) brought about the dispersal of the Whites over extensive stretches of territory and, by obliging them to live among slaves, tended to reinforce the patriarchial order of the *casa grande* or 'big house', involving the master and his family, his coloured mistresses, mulatto children, and Negro nurses and servants. This pattern was strengthened by the initial tendency for Portuguese immigration to include no white women, and by the religious and legal influences discussed earlier. At a very early stage of colonization miscegenation led to the appearance of persons intermediary to the Portuguese, the Indian, and the Negro categories. Freyre attached importance to the ethos of the Portuguese colonists as members of a society which had known much intermingling with the Moors and in which the Coloureds had been the match of the Whites militarily and politically (the last of the Moorish kingdoms in the Iberian peninsula fell to the Spanish crown only eight months before Colombus sailed for America). But it is also proper to emphasize the structure of power. The Portuguese state and the Catholic Church exercised considerable influence from the home country and were not under pressure to mollify their supporters in the colony. Poor communications dampened economic competition and encouraged planters to set a high value on the psychological rewards of a dominant status in a local community; they spent on their dependants much of what they earned from their crops and were little attracted to the possible material rewards of a more systematic exploitation of the resources. These circumstances made it more difficult for a settler ideology or political organization to develop.

Freyre's interest in domestic slavery has encouraged a rosier impression of race relations in early Brazilian history than would be given by a comparable study of industrial slavery. The average life of a Negro slave on the Brazilian plantations or in the mines during the eighteenth century has been estimated at from seven to ten years. Such a slave was also subjected to very considerable exploitation and prejudice. C. R. Boxer sums up the position by observing that the household slaves were usually, though not invariably, a good deal better off than the field-hands or the miners. Those Negro women who were favoured with their master's attention might aspire to lead an enviable life – unless there was a white mistress to wreak a jealous and sadistic vengeance upon them. Freed slaves and their descendants were better off than slaves but they were still subject to discrimination in law. They enjoyed fewer rights than their white fellow citizens, and the punishments inflicted upon them were more severe (Boxer, 1963: 101). It is pertinent to recall that many of the liberal Portuguese who, like Padre Antonio Viera, S.J., championed the cause of the South American Indians at this time, did not regard the enslavement of Negroes as wrongful or protest so strongly about their ill treatment. Montesquieu seems to have been touching upon some contemporary assumption that racial variation was proportionate to differences in pigmentation when he listed his surely satirical arguments in vindication of Negro slavery and included among them the statement: 'These creatures are all over black and with such a flat nose that they can scarcely be pitied' (1748, 1949 edn. I: 238).

Colonial Brazil (i.e. from about 1534 to 1815) was sometimes characterized as 'a hell for Blacks, a purgatory for Whites, a paradise for Mulattoes', but the last statement is a decided exaggeration. Mulatto women were often favoured for sexual entertainment. 'It is the *Mulata* who is the *real* woman', a Brazilian saying declares, and another distinguishes 'White women for marriage, mulatto woman for bed, Negro woman for work'. Negro men might receive similar testimonials. It was said that Indian women gave themselves to men of their own race out of a sense of duty, to white men for gain, and to Negroes for pleasure (Boxer, 1963: 115; Freyre, 1946: 13; 1963: 245). But such evidence should not distract attention from the subordination of Negroes in most other spheres. Boxer writes that prejudice against African connections was so strong that in 1771 the Viceroy ordered the degradation of an Amerindian chief who, 'disregarding the signal honours which he had received from the Crown, had sunk so low as to marry a Negress, staining his blood with this alliance'. If in colonial Brazil mulattoes in some respects found a paradise, in others they were kept strictly to the servants' quarters (1963: 121).

Maranhão, Minas Gerais, and São Paulo were, from the early part of the nineteenth century, regions of precocious industrialization based even more than the agrarian regions upon slave labour. Personal ties between masters and slaves were broken and the worker became only a substitute for a machine. The diet of the slaves in these regions changed for the worse, for the objective of these early industrialists was to utilize to the fullest the youthful energy of the slave, rather than to prolong his life by providing sufficient food and adequate housing. Nevertheless, several observers considered that even here the slaves were better fed and housed than free European workers and peasants of the same period (Freyre, 1963: 184–6). Portuguese economic policy from the eighteenth century onwards had been to favour the cities and the merchant classes instead of agriculture. Brazilian society became consolidated around a stronger government, the law courts were freer from the pressures of powerful individuals, and the Church grew more independent of the regional oligarchies. Urbanization also entailed an attenuation of patriarchal bonds. Settlements of shanties and slums sprang up alongside the great city houses, but there was little communication between the two. Sharper antagonisms arose between the rulers and the ruled, between white children brought up in the house and coloured children brought up in the street unaffected by the fraternization that had been common on the plantations (Freyre, 1963: xxiv).

Yet the looser texture of urban society permitted a variety of social changes. Freyre underlined the importance in the nineteenth century of the university graduate, the sons or sons-in-law of the big families who concentrated power in an intellectual bourgeoisie instead of the rural gentry. Their political sentiments were more liberal and their rise was also the rise of many pale-skinned mulattoes; by this time there were families with members of varying complexion, and many a pure White might have a mulatto relation (1963: 366–8, 411–12). The growing power of these groups must explain Freyre's remark that 'there is a basis of truth in the rather far-fetched allegation that the first Emperor lost his throne because he was not a native-born Brazilian, and the second, because he was not a mulatto' (1963: 420–1) (the Empire lasted from 1815 to the establishment of the Republic in 1889). City life was not divided into the categories 'slave' and 'free' as was life in the rural areas. The cities provided a social environment in which wage-earning coloured workers could establish themselves. Their group was, in the second half of the nineteenth century, a decisive element in the transformation of the social order (Ianni, 1962: 181).

In the United States, Negro descent and the status of slave had become identified with each other so that emancipation could be achieved only by violence and a revolutionary change in the political structure of the states where slaveholding was extensive. In Brazil, emancipation was a gradual process. The Emperor advocated this reform in 1866. In 1871 a statute provided for the registration of all slaves (some 1,700,000 in number) and the emancipation of certain categories. In 1885 those aged over sixty years were brought within these provisions; by this time it was impossible to maintain a slave code that had been morally condemned and in 1888 the remainder were emancipated without any compensation for their owners. It has been said that in Brazil abolition was an affair of the Whites, not of the Blacks. Though liberal abolitionist agitation played a part in accelerating legislation, the underlying drives were, first, the recognition that slave labour was much less remunerative than free labour, and that a régime founded on slavery was out of keeping with the new forms of production; and, second, the desires to free the capital frozen in the buying and administration of slaves and to increase the geographical mobility of agricultural labour. The Whites had become used to having two types of behaviour, one towards slaves, mostly pure Negroes, and the other towards free coloured people, mostly mulattoes. After abolition, there was a flight of slaves to the towns, where many of the men lapsed into vagabondage and drunkenness. Thus the stereotyped condemnations of the slave were transferred to the new concept of 'the black man' and the heritage of slavery was maintained. As a political movement, abolition did not transform the slave into a citizen, but the slave worker into a free worker. Suffering from a background of deprivation, he entered the new labour market in a position of weakness (Bastide, 1965: 9–14; Ianni, 1962: 235; Fernandes, 1964, I: 12–38).

World War I, by discouraging external trade and migration, gave a great stimulus to the industrialization of Brazil. World War II had a similar effect; by this time the Negro was being integrated into the urban proletariat and a new class consciousness could be observed in the trade unions. Prior to this development the Negroes remained virtually where they had earlier been in the social order, and presented no threat to the lighter-skinned people. Therefore the Whites did not feel fear, resentment, or frustration towards coloured people, and personal ties, usually of a paternalist character, could easily be formed. Relatively small numbers of Negroes and mulattoes climbed higher in the social scale. A public ideology of racial equality could coexist with the private practice of discrimination because colour was compounded with other forms of differentiation which, in Latin America generally, are more stable than in modern Europe and occasion greater social distance. People readily asserted, 'We are one people, we are all Brazilians', or 'There is no colour problem in Brazil', or 'The prejudices in Brazil are not race prejudices but class prejudices'. Discrimination was not based on clear-cut racial categories as in the United States, but entailed varying degrees of social distance related to the outward appearance of any particular individual, so that it is questionable whether *preto* (the Brazilian term for a dark-skinned man) is properly translated as 'Negro' when that word has acquired so many additional associations.

RURAL-URBAN CONTRASTS

It was argued in Chapter Four that physical differences are easily vested with social significance as signs of group membership or rank. The degree of significance ascribed to any given physical distinction depends upon the structure of the society in question and how it brings particular categories of people into opposition or competition. It was suggested, and now needs to be substantiated, that Brazil furnishes examples of a generalization: that in certain kinds of society differences of skin colour acquire little salience because there are few stimuli pressing people to

form groups on a basis of such differences. This proposition is illustrated most clearly by studies of small rural communities, but smallness
of scale and the occupational basis of the way of life do not adequately
explain the variations, for some towns show less racial tension than do
smaller communities. Consciousness of colour seems to derive from the
social structure, which can itself be seen as the product of stimuli among
which scale and occupation are prominent. First among the determinants of the social structure it is perhaps best to place the nature of
the economic order. Over most of rural Brazil this is agricultural production, with a relatively low rate of technological change. Production is
on a fairly small scale and does not bring large numbers of workers
together or force them into any undifferentiated economic category.
Second, population density is relatively low: the chief centres are rather
isolated small towns in which many of the residents are personally
acquainted with a high proportion of the men and women with whom
they are likely to come into contact. In these communities the patterns
of political dispute, of economic and social tensions, and of rural-urban
relations are not such as to divide the population along the same lines
repeatedly or to exacerbate the customary social distinctions. Third, as
in economically backward regions elsewhere, there are the psychological
elements of such a culture: the inhabitants show a low need for achievement, relatively little capacity for empathy (or ability to envisage themselves in others' roles), and little concern with or understanding of
possible alternative forms of political organization, but they place a high
value upon the short-term gains to the individual of a marginal improvement in social status by comparison with other possible rewards.

In 1950, over 70 per cent of a total of more than 52 million Brazilians
lived in small towns of fewer than 5,000 people, or out in the countryside. Studies directed by Charles Wagley of four settlements provide
evidence of the structural features mentioned above. The smallest was
Itá, a settlement of fewer than 600 people, and the centre for a rural
community of about 1,500 or more, located in the Amazon valley
(Wagley, 1952: 116–41; 1953). The economic life of the people was
based on slash-and-burn subsistence agriculture and on the collection of
rubber and other forest products. All three racial stocks, and all possible
mixtures of the Caucasoid, the Amerind, and the Negro, were present in
the population. Though – perhaps because – the physical types shaded
imperceptibly into each other – the people were very conscious of
physical traits and used them readily when classifying their fellows.
There were many unfavourable stereotypes of the dark man of Negro
descent, of the Indian and the *caboclo* (or man of mixed Indian and

Caucasoid extraction). These distinctions, and the values that went with them, were not used as the basis for group formation but in order to compare and rank individuals. At a reception for a visiting notable, those attending would be lighter in pigmentation and more Caucasoid in appearance than the general population, but they would include nevertheless a number of officials, the owner of the largest commercial house, and several other people of dark complexion or mixed descent. It is interesting to note that among Wagley's informants there was less agreement concerning the racial classification of high-status people of dark colour, for 'money whitens the skin'; a high status might inhibit others from accurately perceiving a person's complexion. The principal obstacle to upward social movement was not physical appearance but social position at birth and the stagnant character of the economy. Educational facilities were meagre. Antiquated methods limited rubber production. There was no market that offered economic opportunity to the lower-class town-dwellers.

Some idea of what happens when this kind of community enters the transitional phase to greater economic productivity can be gathered from Ben Zimmerman's study of Monte Serrat in the arid backlands of north-eastern Brazil (Wagley, 1952: 82–115). The city (population about 1,600) was surrounded by a zone of food-crop cultivation, but farther out people were occupied in cattle-ranching and subsistence farming. The rural districts had a population about three times that of the city though the population density was very low and farms were widely separated. Most of the people were of mixed Indian and Caucasian extraction; about 10 per cent were definitely Caucasoid and a smaller proportion Negro or mulatto. City people considered themselves superior to those from the country, and the rural-urban division was more important than race in determining social rank; but still the contrast in living styles was much less than that between country and town in Zambia (as discussed in the previous chapter). Differences in living standards within the city were also relatively small. As in Itá, racial distinctions were used in evaluating the social claims of individuals, but they were not all-important. At the previous *prefeitural* election there was no mention of the fact that one of the contenders (the successful one) was a dark brunet with Indian traits, whose opponent was white. But, says the author, the position might be changing. In neighbouring cities there were a number of clubs to which Negroes were not admitted *because* they were Negroes. In Monte Serrat the successful introduction of a new cash crop (sisal) was making it possible for individuals to purchase status and was loosening their dependence

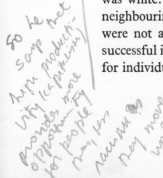

upon the network of kinsfolk and patrons. Economic change was beginning to divide people more clearly into categories and there were indications that class conflict might become defined in racial terms.

Minas Velhas is an old mining town of some 1,500 people (of varying
degrees of Negro-Caucasian mixture), situated in the mountain region
of the state of Bahia (Wagley, 1952: 47–81; Harris, 1956). Gold-mining
had suffered a sharp decline, but the town remained the centre of a
homecraft industry producing jewellery, harnesses, saddles, and leather
goods, including footwear. In Minas Velhas, says Harris, the superiority
of the white man over the Negro was considered to be a scientific fact as
well as the incontrovertible lesson of daily experience. Stereotypes of
the Negro as subhuman were well developed. Nevertheless, the behaviour of the townspeople was not in close accord with such ideas. A
poor white man might insist that any Negro, even a doctor, was his
inferior, but when he addressed a Negro of high social status, or a Negro
storekeeper, he used the same forms of deference in his speech as he
would when addressing a white person who was his social superior. Race
was but one of several status criteria and could be offset by wealth,
education, or a prestigeful occupation. Because social status was the sum
of scores on partly independent criteria, there were no socially important
groups defined by purely physical characteristics. Three or four social
status groups could be discerned: the bottom group (including one-
quarter of the households) consisted predominantly of dark-skinned
people living on the margins of society; with rags for clothes, they could
not go to church and their children could not attend school. The top
group was entirely white. In between came over half the population,
forming, from the economic standpoint, one class, but, from the social
standpoint, two groups differentiated by colour. There was no collective
sense of oppression. The number of institutions that seemed to express
interclass tension was limited precisely because the bone of contention
was not the principle of rank, but how that principle should be interpreted on a particular level of the hierarchy. The point of tension was
the competition between the two middle groups. The development of
homecrafts had meant that an unusually heavy concentration of Negro
and mulatto artisans was to be found in the same economic bracket as
that enclosing most Whites. The artisans' tools were the same, their
skills equal, and they made the same products; yet only the Whites were
admitted to the social club. The Negroes, whose competition was
stronger than in most parts of Brazil, sought not to destroy the group
above them, but to join it. The Whites were under pressure to limit the
number of Negroes who moved up the scale, and the extent to which

they did so (indeed, the town's two satellite villages were racially segregated). But if Negroes were to improve their economic position and social acceptance was still to be withheld from them, then they would probably form their own parallel institutions and the community would split into a caste-like society. Any substantial rise in the general standard of living would increase the danger. Marvin Harris concluded that 'serious attention should be devoted to the possibility that the future may bring more militant and widespread racial tension to Minas Velhas'.

At the time these comparative studies were conducted there seemed to be least class and racial tension in Vila Recôncavo, a small coastal town just north of Salvador, with a population of 1,462 (Wagley, 1952: 16–46, 151–2). Only a small proportion of five thousand or so people in the locality counted as pure Whites, and these all belonged to families owning sugar plantations, or, if they lived in the town, were officials or professional people, or their dependants. The plantation workers, and the poor people generally, were Negroes or mulattoes. The plantations were run on paternalistic lines, the owners being well acquainted with the workers and their families, and the relationship being highly personal, intimate, gentle, and frank. A small cane mill in the locality was administered in a similar fashion by the owners, in contrast to the position in other parts of the Recôncavo where the personal element was lacking and industrial tension easily developed. Unfavourable stereotypes of the Negro were widespread, but were not the basis for group formation, a successful Negro being able to improve his social status to some extent. Harry W. Hutchinson concluded his study by observing: 'As modern attitudes and ideology penetrate Vila Recôncavo, there are more and more problems of class relationships; the population is becoming extremely class-conscious, and there is an increasing desire to rise in the social hierarchy.' Later he reported that the cane mill had come under new, non-paternalist management and that there had been a strike in the sugar industry, with violence and with Communist involvement. Class lines, and oppositions, were becoming clearer and this meant greater racial tension (Hutchinson, 1957: 179–92).

An understanding of how it is that in such communities people do not readily line up in the sort of way their verbal statements about race might suggest is further assisted by Bertram Hutchinson's analysis of the patron-dependant relationship. When the many parts of Brazil were initially occupied by Europeans, the landowner needed to recruit, and retain, his labour force. In such circumstances a paternalistic pattern easily developed, in which the patron was under considerable obligation to his dependants; it led to 'the Brazilians' belief that the privileges of the few constitute a resource in which all, at times of difficulty, may hope to share—a belief which goes far to explain the relative absence of inter-class envy and resentment in the country' (Hutchinson, 1966: 8). For the mass of the population the possibility of real independence, of needing no patron, has never been a realistic aspiration, and this circumstance underlies their present readiness to be dependants of the state. Popular Catholicism (as opposed to Catholic theology) has encouraged such tendencies, by stressing the role of the saint as an intermediary in the search for material advantage. One author, in fact, has argued that the rural workers' unease stems not from a growing class consciousness in the Marxist sense, but from the failure of the traditional rural patrons to meet their dependants' expectations under changed conditions (Galjart, 1964). Only in the cattle regions of the south and north-east can traces be found of co-operation between neighbours in pursuit of shared interests. In the agricultural areas, the reciprocal exchange of services, useful at certain points in the farming cycle, seems never to have been developed as has been common in other parts of the world. The author infers that 'it is perhaps because of the essentially vertical relationship which the patron-client habit produces, at the expense of horizontal associations between equals, that despite widespread insecurity there has been little resort to formal co-operation among the people, who, in contrast to the Portuguese, display comparatively little neighbourly feeling' (Hutchinson, 1966: 18). The individual's dependence upon his extended family, and upon his family's patron, weakens any tendency for him to organize with those who share a common class interest; it dampens any opposition between colour groups, keeping racial tension to the claims of individuals and families – especially evident when there is any question of a daughter or son marrying someone of dark colour and poor connections.

Some much larger Brazilian towns show a pattern of race relations in some respects similar to that described for the rural communities. The town of Salvador (at that time more often called Bahia, after the state of which it was the capital) was studied in the 1930s, at which period it was a culturally passive area with a largely pre-industrial order (Pierson, 1942). The relatively stable population of 294,000 was, in considerable part, of mixed origin, individuals of either pure European or pure African descent being in a minority. It was found that few marriages of any kind crossed class lines. Dark colour was not an absolute barrier to marriage into the upper classes, if it was compensated by wealth, intelligence, or personal charm. The greater importance of the social status

aspect was exemplified in the common expression, 'a rich Negro is a
white man, and a poor white man is a Negro'. Such prejudice as existed
was primarily class prejudice. The race problem, in so far as there was
one, tended to be identified with the resistance a group offered, or was
thought to offer, to absorption and assimilation into the dominant white
group. The public philosophy was 'We Brazilians are becoming one
people'. Pierson's study, drawing comparisons with the United States,
gave overseas readers an unduly favourable impression of race relations
in Brazil as a whole. In the early 1950s a second study was undertaken in
the same town, with reference to the social ascension of coloured people
(Azevedo, 1953). The author showed that each group had its own conception of race relations: according to the Whites there was no colour or
race prejudice, whereas the Negroes seemed convinced that the Whites
had a concealed but intense desire for segregation and wished to keep
darker people at the bottom of the social scale. A commentator has
observed: 'The difficulty which many of the persons questioned found,
despite their high intellectual standard, in expressing their views on the
race problem, shows a wish to repress unpleasant memories and is
evidence of subjective tensions in "successful" Negroes and mulattoes'
(Bastide, 1957: 500–2 – in the course of a most useful review of the
Brazilian studies). Generally speaking, however, this research confirmed
the findings of the earlier inquiry in revealing a pattern of covert and
marginal discrimination which restrained the movement of coloured
people up the social scale.

Similar circumstances have been found in the coastal city of Recife,
with a mixed population of 765,000 (1959) in which individuals of
relatively pure European ancestry are clearly in a minority. The influence of religion in the development of Recife's inter-ethnic culture was
surveyed historically by René Ribeiro, who found it impossible to
isolate the element of belief from the other influences involved in the
provenance and organization of religious institutions at particular historical periods. The Christian principle of respect for the human person
was an important element in the functioning of the patriarchal régime
and had continued to contribute to the general pattern of tolerance. The
racial problem was not, in Recife, a focus of interest and a constant preoccupation for individuals of diverse background; indeed, when some
persons of mixed Negro and Indian descent were asked about this in the
course of the inquiry, they stated that they had never been aware of any
such problem until they encountered discrimination when overseas
(Ribeiro, 1956: 145–6). The author explains how considerations of
social status, religious affiliation, and political belief may generate

contrary influences upon interpersonal behaviour, and this point is illustrated by the results of social-distance tests administered to persons of different religious affiliation drawn from the churches, the universities, and the schools (and therefore with middle- or upper-class backgrounds). It is also evident in some of the personal explanations obtained from the respondents; thus one wrote:

'You know that, as a Catholic intellectual, schooled in the doctrines of the Church, I neither have, nor can have, nor ought to have any racial prejudices. . . . My evidence, however, will not be that of the intellectual . . . but that of the man, the grandson of a *senhor de engenho* who is full of prejudices. . . . I have never reacted violently when a coloured man has sat down in the same omnibus, at the same table, or in the same cinema as myself. What irritates me is . . . the mulatto's wanting to take the place of a white man, dressing like a white man, wanting to marry a white woman, driving around in his own car. . . . Negroes and mulattoes neither can nor should give orders to white people . . . inferior people. Good for work. They have souls and must be baptized. They must seek salvation and go to Heaven. But be equal with the white men, no. . . . I think that it is the Catholic intellectual who is right, but it is the man who actually lives and feels' (1956: 215–16).

Some results of the social distance tests can be noted from *Figures 13* and *14*. The inquiry showed, among other things, that the distance displayed towards dark-skinned Brazilians as possible relatives by marriage was nearly as marked as that shown to orientals and other national groups seen as culturally foreign or politically antagonistic, such as Armenians, Jews, Russians, and Indians. Similarly, less distance was displayed towards stranger groups of European or Latin American extraction than towards mulatto Brazilians. Women, independently of age, economic and educational status, and religion, showed more distance than men towards all the ethnic and national groups included in the test – though when interpreting this finding it is necessary to consider the social constraints upon the woman's role in the society in question. It is difficult to compare the results of social-distance tests administered to groups in different places because the interpretation of the questions may easily vary. Some of these difficulties are explored in Chapter Thirteen. Yet, despite the technical pitfalls, the results of such tests can usefully illuminate certain aspects of race relations in different localities.

Figure 13 The social acceptability of Negroes reported by university
students in Recife and São Paulo compared with results for the
U.S.A. recorded by Bogardus

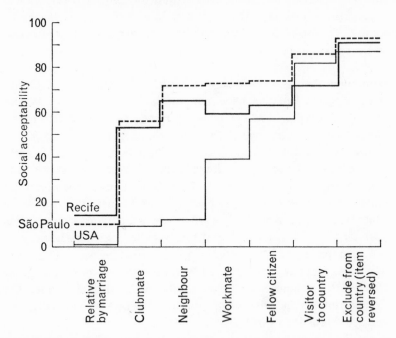

This figure is based on Ribeiro (1956:129); the totals for the U.S.A. are drawn
from Bogardus (1928).

Slavery in southern Brazil did not follow the north-eastern pattern
described by Freyre. In the state of São Paulo agriculture remained at
subsistence level for two centuries, the big plantations appearing only in
the nineteenth century and developing in an era of abolitionist propaganda. In Curitiba the slave régime was a rigorous and drastic system for
the control of the captive labourer, bearing comparison with the plantation slavery of the United States. The slave had no civil rights (Ianni,
1962: 134–5, 148–9). From the latter part of this century the immigration of European workers was encouraged as an alternative to the
employment of Negroes. Thus the emancipated Negro was not accepted
into the national community as the white man's equal but was absorbed
as a dependant into a hierarchically ordered society. As, later, the Negro
became a competitor (especially with the interruption of European
immigration during World War II), the old stereotypes were moulded
into a prejudice oriented to 'keeping the black man in his place'.
The proportion of dark-skinned people in the population is much

Figure 14 The social acceptability of mulattoes reported by university students in Recife and São Paulo compared with results for the U.S.A. recorded by Bogardus

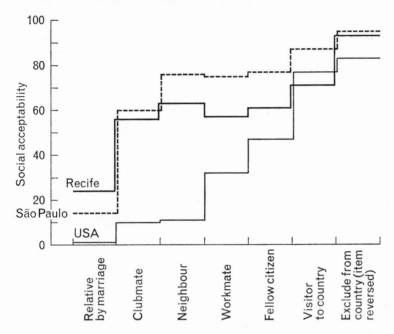

This figure is based on Ribeiro (1956:129); the totals for the U.S.A. are drawn from Bogardus (1928).

lower in southern Brazil than in other parts of the country; consequently, Negro traits can be regarded as signs of an out-group in a way that would not be possible in localities where more than half the population have such traits. An analysis of colour and social mobility in the coastal city of Florianopolis (south of São Paulo) brings this out clearly (Cardoso & Ianni, 1960). Florianopolis has been a city with a poor and relatively little-differentiated economy. The population in 1950 numbered 67,000 persons, less than a tenth of whom counted as coloured. The coloured men tended to be employed chiefly in manufacturing industry and the women in domestic service. Nevertheless, the authors discerned the presence of a colour line. Prejudice was strong and skin colour was used as a sign of different patterns of expected social behaviour (1960: 229). One indication of this was that little distinction was made between Negroes and mulattoes. Racial traits had been selected as the best way of expressing the belief that Negroes were naturally rather than socially inferior to Whites, and of permitting the latter to exploit them. The limited economic opportunities had not allowed a seignorial life-style to develop on any large scale but relations between Whites (even though poor) and Negroes (even though free) had been shaped as relations between dominators and dominated, masters and slaves. It was possible, however, that the legacy of slavery was weakening and that, in place of the treatment of coloured people as a category, there would emerge a sequence of social strata related to pigmentation (1960: 144–52). The degrees of social distance expressed by white students aged fifteen to twenty-five years (see *Figure 15*) led

Figure 15 The social acceptability of Negroes and mulattoes reported by students in Florianopolis

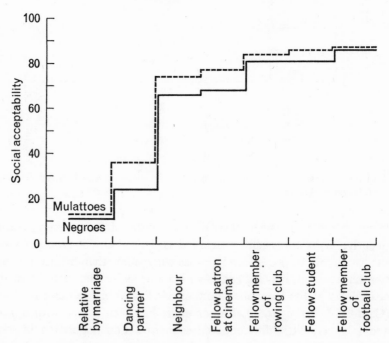

Source: Cardoso & Ianni (1960: 243)

the authors to the view that discrimination was openly displayed when there was any question of the Whites' admitting coloured people to social relations on the primary group level, whereas in respect of secondary groups it was concealed by a pattern of etiquette that absolved them from openly expressing prejudice (1960: 187). A comparable case-study is that of Itapetininga, a town of 34,437 people (Negroes 5 per cent, mulattoes 4 per cent of the total) in São Paulo state (Nogueira,

1955). There, too, belief in white superiority was dominant. The older coloured people had kept their attitudes of timidity and deference towards Whites; the young were more conscious of their rights but were still bound by the old patterns and sought to improve their position as individuals. Miscegenation, significantly, was decreasing.

Thus it is apparent that variations in population balance, and the degree of urbanization, are major influences upon interracial social patterns. When the tensions of an industrial economy are added, the range and incidence of discrimination are likely to increase further. During the 1950s, some 6,300,000 Brazilians are believed to have moved from the countryside to the towns, so that urbanization and industrialization represent tendencies of considerable quantitative significance. Some of their consequences can be seen in a study of Rio de Janeiro in the early 1950s, at that time the federal capital. Large numbers of coloured people were being concentrated in the urban industrial proletariat, which was leading to the internal differentiation of the coloured population on a class basis. Infant mortality in the coloured population was almost twice as high as in the white. Coloured people tended to have very little educational background in comparison with Whites. There was no residential segregation, but coloured residence was much denser in the poorer districts, especially the *favelas* or shanty towns. Many coloured people were improving their social position, but the darker they were the more resistance they met. Coloured women tended to avoid entering into domestic service with its traditional associations of dependency, preferring a more contractual relationship with an employer (Costa Pinto, 1953: 63, 144, 157, 324). It is interesting to note that while white responses in a social-distance test indicated a greater willingness to accept contact with mulattoes than with *pretos*, on another test the preference tipped slightly in the other direction. Analysis also showed that hostile stereotypes were more frequently held of mulattoes than of Negroes (68 per cent as opposed to 53 per cent agreement) and that feelings of sympathy were less frequently expressed towards mulattoes than towards Negroes (30 per cent compared with 47 per cent). Because Negroes were not then competing very effectively with Whites, hostile feelings were less frequently activated, but mulattoes could be disliked because Whites thought them socially anomalous, or projected onto them feelings of sexual guilt (1953: 191–4, 205–23). The author maintained that 'the most definite and characteristic rationalization of racial tension in Brazil is the old affirmation a thousand times refuted by the facts but a thousand times repeated by men, both Whites and Negroes (though more by the former), according to which "there is no racial prejudice in Brazil". This idea is found throughout the world and for this reason has become part of our national pride' (1953: 325). He argued that the changes brought by industrialization were increasing the tensions associated with racial differences.

A questionnaire administered to 580 white students in São Paulo teacher training colleges revealed the prevalence of the unfavourable stereotypes mentioned already so many times. Its findings indicate that the results of Ribeiro's inquiry (*Figures 13* and *14*) need to be interpreted with caution. Of the respondents, 91 per cent accepted the stereotype of Negro lack of hygiene, 87 per cent that of physical unattractiveness, 80 per cent that of superstition, 77 per cent that of lack of financial foresight, 76 per cent that of amorality, 73 per cent that of aggressiveness, etc. There seemed to be one school of thought that preferred mulattoes to Negroes because the former were nearer to Whites, and another that was more hostile to mulattoes because of opposition to miscegenation, suggesting the presence of an ideology of 'pure' races. With the stereotyping went an insistence upon excluding coloured people from intimate personal relations, and almost complete endogamy. Yet at the same time the subjects professed an adherence to democratic norms: 92 per cent believed that Negroes and Whites should have equal opportunities. This investigation suggests that, even after allowance has been made for the way in which class prejudice operates to the disadvantage of coloured people, there remains a basic residue of racial prejudice proper (Bastide & van den Berghe, 1957; cf. Bastide & Fernandes, 1959: 364–5). Though there have been some public manifestations of racial hostility in São Paulo, such as the petitions of traders that particular streets be closed to Negroes, discrimination is usually of a private character: a Negro is not refused a post because he is a Negro – he is told that unfortunately it has already been filled; he is not refused promotion – he fails to pass the medical examination (Bastide, 1965: 21). In a work published in 1951, a dark-complexioned São Paulo physician reported that though coloured people met with no discrimination in respect of public facilities, discrimination could be expected in some of the more exclusive barber shops and restaurants. Few dark-skinned people were employed in offices or at sales counters in the business district. There were not many dark professional people or businessmen, and no dark-coloured priest had ever celebrated Mass in the cathedral (cf. Pierson, 1955: 457–8). The paradox of private discrimination coupled with public protestation of equality is, of course, not limited to Brazil.

The economic crisis of the early 1930s led to the formation in São

Paulo of the 'Black Front', a movement which later spread through the industrialized regions of Brazil, attempting to achieve a popular front of all coloured people in the face of discrimination. The movement's ideology was not clearly defined and there seem to have been conflicting elements. On the one hand was the call to Negroes to take up the values of the Whites if they wanted to succeed; on the other was the argument that coloured people should not imitate Whites by competing for positions as teachers and civil servants – where resistance was strong—but should try to rise through the progressive proletarianization of the Negro masses (Fernandes, 1964, II: 34–95). More recently, the idea of *négritude* has won some favour among coloured intellectuals. Reviewing the position at the end of 1962, Roger Bastide discounted 'the myth of *négritude*' and stressed the consequences of the economic changes. Negroes were being assimilated into the industrial proletariat. More fair-skinned peasants were moving from the arid zones into the big cities, seeking unskilled employment at a lower level than that of the Negro workers, and thus breaking the equation of colour with industrial status. Industrial concentration and the development of the trade union movement were having a similar effect (Bastide, 1965).

Events may prove this interpretation correct, but it should be regarded with caution for the present. Race relations in big cities are conducted on a basis different from that underlying the life of small rural towns. Instead of low population density, relations based on personal acquaintance, and a low level of aspiration, urban life brings a greater variety of social contacts of an impersonal and competitive kind. As cities grow in size, so persons of different social class are in important respects divided more from one another. At work men are stimulated to combine with others against categories of people with whom they have little personal acquaintance. Claims to rights in the industrial sphere can be identified with distinctions of colour. Opportunities for social mobility can make men more conscious of social distinctions and more inclined to use them as weapons for their own advancement. There is reason to believe that industrial influences in the rural towns have led to increased emphasis on racial characteristics as criteria of social status (Wagley, 1952: 155). In the big cities this tendency is subject to fewer restraints. In Brazil, as elsewhere, identifiable features of urban living can be expected to exacerbate racial tensions.

RACE RELATIONS WITHOUT RACIAL CATEGORIES

Concern with variations in racial patterns within Brazil should not conceal the contrast between the position in Brazil as a whole and that

in the two-category systems described earlier. Brazil presents the case
of a social system without racial categories; one in which colour values
have been integrated into the general status order. The individual
nature of Brazilian racial placement is illustrated by the finding that
brothers and sisters may be regarded as representing quite different
racial types (Harris, 1964: 57). The contrast is most apparent with
reference to persons of mixed descent who are anomalous with respect
to the criteria of a two-category system and are forced into the lower
category. In the United States special terms for intermediary persons,
such as mulatto, quadroon, octoroon, etc., have fallen out of use with
the polarization of the system and the attempt to prevent the term
'Negro' being considered derogatory. In Brazil there is a great variety of
terms, differing somewhat from one locality to another. In Vila Recôncavo, for example, the term *preto* is applied to dark people with Negro
physical features, but the *pretos* rank themselves according to five distinctions of shade and feature. Then, in gradual transition, come the
following descriptive terms: *cabra, cabo verde, escuro, mulato escuro,
mulato claro, pardo, sarará, moreno, louro, branco da terra* (someone
who is completely white to outward appearance but may have some
other ancestry). This scale covers the consequences of White-Negro
crossing and takes no account of Indian mixture, which is classified in a
further battery of terms. Another study in the state of Bahia found that
forty different racial types were mentioned by a sample of a hundred
persons, but they did not always agree about whether one type was used
to classify persons lighter or darker than those of another type, and a
given informant was found to be quite capable of employing different
racial terms for the same person after a short lapse of time (Harris, 1964:
58).

The Brazilian situation contrasts with that in two-category systems in
another respect: that of the kinds of pressure operating for the maintenance of social distance. In two-category systems, the upper members
of the upper category need the support of the 'lower uppers', so they
have to defend their interests against pressure from the rising 'upper
lowers'. In Brazil there are no collective pressures of this kind. The
struggle centres on the ascent of particular individuals and especially
on the consequences of peoples' being identified with dark-skinned
associates; therefore the tension is greater in spheres of sociability such
as club membership and, above all, family connections. The differences
between the kinds of discrimination found in Brazil and in the United
States have been perceptively discussed by a Brazilian scholar, Oracy
Nogueira, who describes the kind based on an individual's appearance

as 'prejudice of mark' and the kind deriving from his ascription to a particular birth-determined category as 'prejudice of origin' (1959: 170–5). As labels, these expressions are not very satisfactory, but it is important to specify the differences between the two systems as precisely as possible. Nogueira's contrasts between the two forms (which are made largely from the standpoint of the socially superior party) may be formulated as follows:

(i) In the integrated order, prejudice entails avoidance and the maintenance of social distance, whereas the two-category system leads to the unconditional exclusion of members of the lower category in situations of possible competition, irrespective of the merits of particular individuals.

(ii) In the integrated order, prejudice tends to be intellectual and aesthetic; whereas in the two-category system it tends to be more emotional and to be directed, in an unreasoning way, towards all members of the lower category.

(iii) In the integrated order, the prevailing ideology is pro assimilation and amalgamation, culture being thought more important than race; in a two-category system, the ideology approves the preservation of distinctions and stresses the importance of race rather than culture.

(iv) In the integrated order, the etiquette of interracial relations emphasizes the control of the behaviour of social superiors to prevent their hurting or discomforting their inferiors; whereas in a two-category system the etiquette exercises more control over the behaviour of persons in the inferior category so as to check the aggressiveness of certain members of the upper category (note that this proposition relates only to selected features of interracial etiquette).

(v) In the integrated order, consciousness of discrimination is intermittent and individuals try to compensate for their demerits by copying the behaviour of their social superiors; in the two-category system, consciousness of discrimination is continuous and obsessive, the lower category reacting collectively.

(vi) If, in an integrated order, the proportion of persons with disfavoured traits is high, less prejudice is shown; whereas in a two-category system prejudice increases as the proportion of members of the discriminated group grows.

(vii) In the integrated order, an individual's chances of upward mobility are lower the more disfavoured traits he has; class prejudice therefore supplements race prejudice; a two-category system offers no approved modes for crossing the colour line.

(viii) In the integrated order, people's reaction against racial prejudice tends to be fused with the class struggle; whereas in a two-category system the lower category tries to organize as a national minority.

These propositions help to classify the more salient differences between the patterns characteristic of Brazil and of the Southern United States but leave two kinds of question outstanding. First, is it right to describe the Brazilian racial order as integrated? If the position in Brazil does not illustrate the main element in integration, what substitute should be found for the expression 'prejudice of mark' and how should integration be defined? Second, why should tension in such a society be strongest in the areas of sociability and marriage? An examination of the latter problem may help towards a solution of the former.

The earlier discussion of two-category systems has shown – while trying not to labour so obvious a point – that they cannot countenance any movement across the colour line. People must stay in the category into which they are born. No intermediary categories can be recognized. Marriage, in such a system, will be important to class structure, for in any stratified society the members of the same household must share the same social status in the locality in which they live and in any sphere of relations in which they participate collectively. Though a husband may have greater personal status claims than his wife, or vice versa, for many purposes they must be treated as a pair. For similar reasons, members of the wider kinship network are identified with one another, though to a lesser extent in an industrial society than in pre-industrial societies, where the extended family frequently exerts political influence. In countries like Brazil, upper-class Whites need to guard against their daughters' associating too familiarly with coloured youths lest they should wish to marry them. Expectations of status identification lead more directly to a fear of coloured men than of coloured women. In any stratified society, people at different points on the status scale learn different norms about household management and social behaviour. To be closely involved with someone who observes different customs, especially those thought socially inferior, can be embarrassing. As the family is also an institution for the socialization of children, a person may seek a spouse who will encourage his or her children to learn the 'correct' style of behaviour. Such interrelations show why differences of social status may be considered impediments to marriage. They show, too, why acceptance in a relationship of marriage is the most convincing sign of social acceptance, and, perhaps, sets the seal upon successful social mobility.

In a two-category system, marriage has this social significance within categories but does not reflect inter-category mobility. In an integrated social order, it reflects all kinds of status distinction and mobility. The stronger these are, the more tension will centre upon marriage, for quite apart from notions of romantic love there are sound sociological arguments for expecting marriage between persons of unequal status. Men at the top of the scale, possessed of considerable power, know that any woman they marry will enjoy the same social precedence as themselves (no one dare treat these wives as their husbands' inferiors). The men will use their power to increase their area of bride selection beyond the narrow range of women of similar status, preferring women of greater intelligence or charm to those of impressive ancestry. Families farther down the scale may be happy to have their daughters make such marriages because of the value to them of alliances with the powerful. In this way a surplus of upper-class spinsters is created, whom men of lower position may regard as desirable brides because of their position and connections. A case in which a woman marries up the scale is known as hypergamy, and when the man marries up it is known as hypogamy (Merton, 1941). But this is to emphasize the formal hierarchy at the expense of other qualities, so that 'the phrase "marrying up" is apt to be confusing . . . when the rich Jewish merchant of late Medieval Europe married his daughter to a poor but talented scholar from the Yeshiva, each of the parties was marrying "up" in one sense, "down" in another' (Davis, 1941: 386). The model mentioned earlier (Chapter Four, p. 67) of social relations as a transaction fits such patterns of intermarriage fairly closely. There are social incentives to hypogamous unions when the man seeks connection with persons of high social rank but needs no economic assistance, and the woman has the family links but lacks financial resources. The incentive to hypergamous unions is usually the gain in status to the woman and her kinsfolk unaccompanied by any loss on the man's part. Thus Davis states: 'culturally defined patterns of selection always involve a trade, a reciprocity which ensures a certain kind of equality by balancing between the two mates all the qualities which enter into the calculation of marital advantage' (1941: 386). When there is a free market in status criteria, even though some attributes may attract strong disapproval, they can always in theory be offset by others.

This transactional approach is not limited in its utility to the analysis of marriage patterns alone, for similar considerations enter into patterns of extramarital union. One author, who stresses the point that the socially inferior party seeks to maximize social status, notes that initially in the Southern States of America and in South Africa a coloured woman might find advantage in being the concubine of a white man. But, as feeling against miscegenation increased, such relations could invoke sanctions. For the Negro woman, marriage to a Negro man of equal status became more rewarding than an unlegalized relationship with a white man of high status (van den Berghe, 1960: 88).

The integration of colour values into a society's conventions for calculating social precedence and rank opens up to members of disadvantaged minorities the possibility of social mobility; but to make use of the opportunity they have to accept in some measure the very valuations (or prejudices) which put them, and their friends and relations, at the initial disadvantage. Some dark people who climb the social scale try to forget or to conceal their origins, and purchase elevation at the price of self-respect; but the effect of limited mobility upon the mass of persons who do not climb may be far more insidious than its pressures – strong though they are – upon this smaller minority. The Brazilian outlook assumes that everyone would like to be white and that the whiter a person is the higher he is likely to be in the social status scale. Therefore, when a dark man climbs by acquiring wealth he is said to whiten himself. For individuals, whitening or *branqueamento* represents an intelligible response to the situation. But for dark people as a category, a policy of *branqueamento* is self-defeating. If everyone tries to follow it, it will be more difficult for anyone to succeed. As Marvin Harris observes, the greater the number of dark people who are whitened by wealth, the more the money that will be required for whitening to occur (in Wagley, 1952: 82). Blackness comes to be seen as even more of a disadvantage and the rate of conversion in the transaction moves so as to put a further premium upon whiteness. The psychological effects upon dark-skinned people of a wholesale desire for whitening are also unfavourable. They entail acceptance by dark people of the belief that Whites are justified in discriminating against them. Thus there has been among dark Brazilians, from the days of slavery, a belief in 'purging one's blood' – that is to say, a justification for dark women to sleep with Whites in order to have children of lighter skin, and a preference for fair-skinned persons as sons-in-law or daughters-in-law.

The union of persons of different complexion, which is sometimes regarded as proof of tolerance, in fact presents more complex aspects.

Where marriage across a colour line is prohibited or penalized, persons of the opposite sex on the other side of the line appear the more exciting sexual partners because they are forbidden. The white man in such circumstances may use his social power to gain access to coloured women, and, partly perhaps as a justification of his actions, he elaborates what has been called the cult of the Dusky Venus. Coloured men and white women may be drawn to each other but white men are more successful than coloured in making it difficult for their womenfolk to enter such illicit relationships. Roger Bastide maintains: 'The Dusky Venus hides the debasement of the black woman as a prostitute; and the Black Apollo is seeking revenge on the white man. It is not so much that love breaks down barriers and unites human beings as that racial ideologies extend their conflicts even into love's embraces' (1961: 18). He sees that motives other than those of 'status maximization' may enter into interracial marriages and that they may testify, not to tolerance, but to the persistence of racial thinking.

So long as physical differences are vested with social significance as signs of group membership or rank, they cannot but influence the social status of individuals and of everyone identified with these individuals. The furthest extreme from a two-category slave order must therefore be one in which racial differences are either not perceived or not seen as having any social relevance. It seems improbable that such a state of affairs has ever existed in other than a small community. The nearest approximation to it must be a society in which racial differences are given the same significance as cultural preferences for particular hair and eye colours, body size and form, grace of manner, etc. Racial traits would not then identify categories of people, though they would be used in ranking individuals. The pattern of relations which above has been labelled 'integrated' is an example of such an order; in the communities discussed, the negative value attributed to a dark complexion is much greater than that attaching to a small stature, but the kind of social reckoning is the same. For these reasons, it seems justified and helpful to regard Brazil and similar countries as exemplifying an integrated racial order – despite the tension centring upon racial discrimination. The definition of 'integration' arouses difficulties because the term can refer to both a process and a state. A minority may become integrated into a society over time, but the nature of the process will depend upon the structure of the society. Integration into an agricultural society makes different demands from integration into pastoral, military, theocratic, and industrial societies. Much may depend, too, upon the structure of the minority and whether it seeks or resists integration. But as an end-state or a kind of social order, 'integration' should denote a pattern of relations attainable in societies with different systems of production. It must also be distinct from a state of amalgamation, in which the minority has become biologically indistinguishable, and from one of assimilation, in which it has become socially indistinguishable. These considerations suggest that a social order in which a minority is distinguished only by cultural values similar to those used in ranking individual members of the majority should be considered integrated.

The actual patterns of relations in particular countries often do not fit neatly into conceptual classifications. The difficulties in deciding whether racial distinctions in Brazil resemble the sorts of distinction made in groups of the same skin colour will be apparent from the descriptive material that has been presented. What may not be apparent is that the pattern of class relations there is more complex than the scale of social status to which reference has been made in interpreting the material. Classes in Brazil are not the open social categories of the kind made familiar by studies of some North American communities. They are more distinctive groups whose members share similar interests in the economic order. The politico-economic aspects of social stratification in Brazil are of great importance to an understanding of the current social position of the darker inhabitants. It is because they stress these aspects that many Brazilian sociologists believe that racial tension can be alleviated only by the proletarianization of the Negro and then by the resolution of the class struggle.

PLURAL SOCIETIES IN SOUTH-EAST ASIA

The expression 'plural society' came into currency through the writings of J. S. Furnivall. He used it to denote a social order different from those so far discussed. This was a stable order, and therefore unlike contact or acculturation; it was an order containing within itself strong group antagonisms, but, in contrast to both integrated and dominative orders, instead of one group controlling another group, particular groups controlled separate sectors of the economy. Thus, in Burma as in Java, there was a medley of peoples – European, Chinese, Indian, and various native groups:

'They mix but do not combine. Each group holds by its own religion, its own culture and language, its own ideas and ways. As individuals they meet, but only in the market place, in buying and selling. There is a plural society with different sections of the community living side by side, but separately, within the same political unit. Even in the economic sphere there is a division of labour along racial lines' (Furnivall, 1948: 304).

Each racial group was self-centred or oriented to its homeland rather than to the country from which it was making a living:

'The European works in the tropics, but he does not live there . . . many . . . spend twenty years or more . . . and, on retiring, . . . know no more of the country than on the day they landed. . . . Foreign orientals, likewise, are transient . . . Europeans often deplore the isolation of the individual in their own section. Men are continually on the move . . . the club and not the home is the centre of social life. . . . Each section in the plural society is a crowd and not a community' (Furnivall, 1948: 306–7).

A Dutch authority observed that in the older Indonesian towns 'the town-dwellers did not form an organic whole. The traders and artisans were grouped in wards according to their national origin each under its own chieftain. . . . The inhabitants developed no common will which could find its realization in civic autonomy.' Most Europeans felt their stay in an Indonesian town to be only temporary, and such a segregated pattern of living never required them to develop local connections. In contrast to the intimate atmosphere of the bourgeois parlour in Holland, the Dutch in Indonesia led a life of display staged in open galleries. No particular attention was paid to furnishing and decorating. When a man was transferred, returned home on leave, or retired, his furniture was simply auctioned (Wertheim, 1956: 170–4). This pattern of living on the part of the Europeans scarcely recommended to other groups that they should put national interests before communal ones.

The Indian minority is important in Burma, Malaya, and Singapore, though since World War II Indian communities have declined in numbers and economic standing. They are prominent in agricultural life (the plantation rubber industry in Malaya, for example, has depended largely upon their labour); they are urban workers, traders, financiers, and professional men. In some respects their position resembles that of the Chinese, but with one crucial difference. In the postwar years India has not appeared to threaten the South-East Asian nations; her government has encouraged overseas Indians to become good citizens of the countries in which they live, and Pandit Nehru was long regarded as a respected Asian leader. In contrast, the Chinese in this region have frequently suffered from the political strain between China and other countries (Freedman & Willmott, 1961: 245–6).

In the Federation of Malaya the Malays, who think of themselves as the indigenous race, constitute 50 per cent of the population and received in 1947 just over 20 per cent of personal incomes; the Chinese make up 37 per cent, and received nearly 60 per cent; the Indians and Pakistanis are 11 per cent of the population and received rather more than 10 per cent; the Europeans and others – about 2 per cent – received somewhat less than 10 per cent of personal incomes (Silcock, 1965: 178–9). Differences of language, custom, and religion ran parallel with distinctions of race, but within the major racial groups other divisions were important. There are at least five mutually unintelligible main Chinese languages and three main Indian languages spoken in Malaya. There has been little intermarriage, and very few Chinese have ever joined the Malay community, though for them to do so required only that they should be converted to Islam. Under colonial rule, the different races were more concerned about their relations with the British, who co-ordinated the whole system, than about their relations with one another. The employers accepted a situation in which different types of labour had different functions and were bought in different markets. On the rubber estates at one period, Indian, Chinese, and Malay labour groups were employed separately, paid in different ways, and provided with different living conditions. Whether this was a conscious policy of 'divide and rule' is debatable. The separate policies were adapted to the different preferences of the groups in question who, in the absence of self-government, saw no need to co-operate. The Malays now constitute the great bulk of the peasantry (rice cultivators, smallholders, and fishermen) though they also contribute an elite of 'middle-class' officials. The Chinese show a wide range of occupations and income – from millionaires to unskilled labourers. Many of the merchants, estate-owners, and professional men are Chinese. Some Chinese have direct relations with Malay peasants in buying their produce, selling them goods, and furnishing them with credit. Such relations easily foster economic jealousy (Freedman & Willmott, 1961: 247).

Since independence, the Malays have used their political power to prevent the Chinese getting a stronger hold over the country. The Chinese firmly believe that their wealth is a natural consequence of their own industry, thrift, and adaptability, whereas Malay poverty is seen as the product of indolence, thriftlessness, and conservatism. The Malays believe that, as the sons of the soil, they should control the country's political life. The Chinese were allowed to infiltrate during foreign rule and they are seen as having collaborated with the foreigners to their own advantage and to the disadvantage of the Malays, until the latter achieved independence. Much of Malaya's policy for economic development since World War II has been directed to the improvement of the economic condition of the rural Malays so that it will be easier for the political balance to be maintained. It seems, therefore, that in Malaya the pattern of race relations has had rather more effect upon the course of industrialization than industrialization has had upon race relations. A recent economic study concludes that present linguistic and cultural policies are neither bringing the two communities together nor training a sufficient proportion of Malays to enable them to take advantage of such opportunities for social advance as might be created by a programme of economic development. An increasing tendency for industry to become an enclave of Western or Chinese culture within a predominantly Malay society may well preserve cultural heterogeneity (Silcock, 1965: 197). The plural society would then rest completely upon the economic reinforcement of cultural distinctions instead of drawing some of its support from colonial overrule.

There are no reliable census data for contemporary Indonesia but it seems likely that the Chinese number between 2 and 3 million in a total population of some 80 million. The Chinese population of Java is the longest-established, some 80 per cent having been recorded as locally born in the census of 1930. Most of them were engaged in trade and commerce, both in the cities and in the countryside where they played an important part in the provision of agricultural credit. Under the Dutch, the Indonesian Chinese were regarded by the Chinese government as citizens of China, and, if born in Indonesia, they were also recognized as Dutch subjects as long as they were in the Indies. Though many of the Chinese in Java do not speak Chinese and follow a way of life that appears very Indonesian, they have still counted socially as Chinese. Their identity as a community has been founded upon a network of associations and a Chinese school system. Less than one-fifth of their children attend government schools. The remainder follow a curriculum that is basically Chinese in content and orientation. Japanese policy, during the occupation, was to assist Indonesian traders against the Chinese, who were squeezed out of the small-scale trade in the villages (Wertheim, 1956: 163). In 1955 the Indonesian government drew up a treaty with the People's Republic of China whereby Indonesian Chinese would be able to choose the citizenship they wanted, but the treaty was never ratified and, since then, pressure upon the Indonesian Chinese has mounted. In 1959 Chinese traders were excluded altogether from rural areas in West Java and neither of the Chinese governments could do anything to help. Their 'homeland' is now more of an embarrassment to them than a source of support

(Freedman & Willmott, 1961: 249–51). President Soekarno followed a policy of bringing the various ethnic communities together by stage-managing opposition between Indonesia as a nation and other powers; nationalist sentiment has demanded that minorities give up any ties that might weaken their loyalties to the nation.

In the pre-independence period – upon which Furnivall's analysis was based – the plural society consisted of a collection of communities which shared no common loyalties or feelings of solidarity. During the war they offered little resistance to the invading Japanese. People co-operated because, within the sphere of public order maintained by the colonialists, it was in their economic interest to do so. 'The typical plural society is a business partnership in which, to many partners, bankruptcy signifies release rather than disaster' (Furnivall, 1948: 308). In illustration of his thesis, Furnivall observed that many villages had preserved some of the scrub jungle close at hand as an amenity. No one cut timber there because the collective will overshadowed individual interest. But when a community lost its homogeneity, concern for the common good was enfeebled and immigrants cleared the scrub to sell it as fuel in the market. European economists once assumed that if every man pursued his private interest this would serve the common good better than any other policy, but there was no such harmony between different kinds of ends in the plural society. As Furnivall observed of the doctrine of economic man, 'when cast out of Europe he found refuge in the tropics, and now we see him returning with seven devils worse than himself' (1948: 312).

This social order can well be compared with the structure of group relations in South Africa. Chapter Eight has shown that whereas there are several distinct ethnic groups in South Africa, a variety of forces tend to bring together people of different groups who have like interests. The government has sought to prevent any such realignment by hindering the formation of 'cross-cutting' social bonds and by emphasizing ethnic distinctions. Government policy has required the cultivation of white solidarity and it has therefore, in spite of itself, brought the non-white groups closer together with the result that, having started with many different groups, the country is moving towards a two-category system of relations. The plural society also starts with several distinct ethnic groups, but the bonds of common religion, political ideals, economic interest, etc., do not cross the racial lines very frequently or constitute firm alternative patterns of grouping. The differences between groups are generally more important than similarities between sub-groups within them. Hardly any stimuli (in the colonial period) effectively drew together the bulk of the population and gave them a sense of common identity. Consequently, the plural society was not only a truly multi-category social order; it was also a relatively stable one. It maintained itself at a higher level of economic development than that of the Brazilian villages described earlier. The population density of South-East Asia is high. The people's motivation to economic advance is relatively high. The economic order frequently stimulates people into forming groups, but chiefly along ethnic lines, and thus the existing divisions are reinforced.

Some light is thrown on the stability of the plural society as a multi-category system by a consideration of the position of Eurasians, or persons of partially European descent. In a two-category system they would have been anomalies, forced into the lower category, but in Indonesia they maintained a separate identity for over a century. By 1848, in Java, the children of European males and non-European females, if recognized by their fathers, counted with the European group whether they were of legitimate or illegitimate birth. The entire social life of the country, however, was so imbued with colour consciousness that these people did not rank equal with Whites and, indeed, social standing within their own community was heavily influenced by the relative darkness of their complexion. Originally, the privileges accorded this group must have been a consequence of the paucity of European women and of the utility, to their employers, of a loyal clerical class independent of the local groups. Later, they became another community within the plural society, but they were caught between the nationalists and the colonial power. Indo-Europeans (or 'Indoes') founded the first Indonesian political party shortly before World War I and it put national independence on its programme, but the bulk of the Indo-European community was regarded by the nationalists as hostile to their interests, and after independence its members suffered from the disfavour of the indigenous peoples (cf. Wertheim, 1956: 137–9). The existence and vicissitudes of an intermediary group of this kind illuminate important features of the society of which it forms part. They draw attention to the part played by the colonial power in protecting the independent existence of a small and vulnerable, but politically useful, group. They emphasize, too, how the withdrawal of the colonialists and the demand for national solidarity against national enemies revolutionized relations between the different communities within the nation. The stability of a plural society, it would seem, is readily upset by external changes, whereas pressure applied upon a two-category society in order to reduce segregation often has the reverse effect.

DIVERSITY AND COERCION

The idea of the plural society as a distinct type seems acceptable with regard to the circumstances of South-East Asia in the colonial period but its applicability in other regions and periods is open to question. Elsewhere the impact of European groups upon indigenous cultures has usually been far greater, and sequences of change have been set in motion which preclude any stable pattern of pluralism. One consequence of this has been that stable patterns of structural opposition cannot develop. In a plural society the different ethnic groups can afford to divide internally because the overriding opposition between groups will bring members back into solidarity in any conflict touching their collective interests. In a fluid situation an ethnic group may divide internally and then some of these subgroups may enter into alliances with people possessing similar interests in other ethnic groups so that the system as a whole never reverts to the *status quo ante*. A study of the Indian minority in East Africa in the early 1950s bears upon this aspect (Morris, 1956).

From the point of view of the Africans, the Arabs, and the Europeans, it was convenient to use the label 'the Indians' and to regard the people so designated as one category. But to the Indians themselves even the categories 'Hindu' and 'Muslim' were of little practical value, and what mattered most was being an Ismaili, a Patidar, a Sikh, a Goan, or a member of one of a dozen such caste or sectarian groups. As the Indian minority grew, so these smaller units became more significant and started to compete with one another. The Aga Khan's Ismaili followers were the most energetic and effective in organization and they began to negotiate independently with various governmental bodies. If at any time they could have discerned a real advantage in forming an alliance with an African or European group they would probably have done so. When the Aga Khan ordered his followers to cut themselves free from their Indian background in order to identify themselves with East Africa (even to the extent of adopting English as their mother-tongue), he only accelerated the process of weakening Indian solidarity to the advantage of a subgroup in what had earlier appeared to be a single ethnic community. Moreover, by pursuing such a course the Ismailis acted as a 'pace-making' group for other subgroups and hastened tendencies to realignment.

In a developing society, subgroups or individuals may move up the social scale and acquire interests or loyalties at variance with the earlier pattern of communal allegiance. In Uganda, an Indian could become rich by acting as a middleman in the production of cotton or coffee. He would display zeal in the affairs of his own community and, as its representative, would meet officials and leading members of other communities. At a certain point in his climb to power, he entered what the Indians themselves called 'the upper class', an interracial social world in which all the ethnic communities were represented; membership in this world carried considerable rewards to individuals, in terms of influence and prestige, and to their communities. Consideration of stratification in a plural order suggested, therefore, that the most significant relations between ethnic groups took place in the upper reaches of the social system and that the low level of mutual appreciation among people at the bottom might not be so important in the long run (Morris, 1956: 207–11). These considerations concerning divisions within the Indian community must apply in many such communities in divided societies.

More difficult issues are raised by the attempt of M. G. Smith to apply to the West Indies 'the work of J. S. Furnivall, especially his concept of the plural society as a unit of disparate parts which owes its existence to external factors, and lacks a common social will' (Smith, 1965: vii). It will be noted that Smith sees the plural society both as combining different groups and as lacking consensus; he is interested in the concept not just for the purpose of classifying societies but as an analytic construct suggesting alternatives to the consensus model of conventional sociological theory. The societies of the West Indies bring together in varying proportions members of many ethnic categories: Europeans, Chinese, East Indians, Amerindians, people of African descent, and many of mixed European and African ancestry. There are significant social and cultural differences between ethnic groups and between social groups of mixed descent. Because of such divisions the West Indian societies, like other plural societies, are units only in a political sense. For lack of consensus, one section must dominate the political structure and enable the society to function as a unit with respect to other societies.

To challenge the theorists of normative consensus and provide a theory of the kind of society that depends for its order upon regulation by force, Smith relies upon the characterization of a group's institutions. When discussing cultural variation he states: 'I prefer . . . to reserve the term pluralism for that condition in which there is a formal diversity in the basic system of compulsory institutions. This basic institutional system embraces kinship, education, religion, property and economy, recreation, and certain sodalities' (1965: 82). Cultural pluralism and social stratification vary independently, each section having its own criteria of rank: 'the plurality is a discontinuous status order, lacking any foundation in a system of common interests and values, while its component sections are genuine status continua . . . it is a serious error to equate pluralism with "class stratification" ' (1965: 83). Where stratification tends to be integrative in locating all members of a society on a single scale, the tensions between the sections of a plural society are disintegrative. The withdrawal of the colonial power has frequently released these forces and imperilled the social order.

Because Smith sees the plural society as characterized by diversity *and* coercion, he fails to explore the relations between the two. Writers who disagree with Smith on other matters might accept the view that social patterns in the West Indies can more readily be understood as the outcome of a situation in which the individual can see no better alternative, than as the expression of a moral acceptance of customary patterns. Thus one concluded that the total picture presented by Jamaican society is one of disnomia: 'Bounded by the framework of poverty the majority of Jamaicans has few channels of expression open to them. . . . The black lower class individual is not only bound by his poverty but is frustrated by the knowledge that if he does overcome the barriers of poverty social frustration is inevitable as a result of his colour' (Henriques, 1953: 160, 167). Poverty creates frustrations independently of pluralism. Other authors maintain that there is a wide acceptance of the values underlying the scale of social differentiation based upon colour (cf. Rubin, 1960). Referring to Jamaica, Henriques speaks of 'the almost complete acceptance by *each* group of the superiority of the white, and the inferiority of the black' (1953: 41). He describes a system of differentiation in some ways similar to that already outlined for Brazil: a continuous scale, with white or fair-coloured people in the upper class and a gradual darkening of colour as social status decreases. A successful dark-skinned man would attempt to 'marry light'. Dark people might use bleaching creams and have their hair straightened because the culture embodied the norm of whitening. A black peasant proprietor observed that the old feeling about unlegalized miscegenation persisted. The black girl who cohabited with a white man had 'Gone lift de colour'. Some mothers would sooner their daughters lived extramaritally with a brown or white man than married a black man. Fair-coloured mothers would prevent their children playing with black or dark children. Hotels might refuse accommodation to dark people. Banks and public institutions were staffed by fair girls. In many stores the counter staff were fair but those not in direct contact with the public were darker (Henriques, 1953: 42–60). Thus it would seem that, though different communities may have their private criteria of rank, there is a common sector which, in countries like Jamaica, is of importance, and that many children are brought up to accept the rightness of this form of differentiation even though it may be used against them more than they can use it against others. Individuals who revolt (and the lower-class cult movements such as the Ras Tafarians may be of special interest in this respect) do not necessarily revolt as a plural section: they may reject the social order as individuals. If this is the case, then Dahrendorf's discussion of the coercion theory of society (see Chapter Four, pp. 63–64) may be more relevant than a theory that presupposes normative consensus, and it may not be necessary to introduce the notion of pluralism.

Another possible source of weakness in Smith's attempt to develop a theory of the plural society lies in the need to treat societies as separate units ('only territorially distinct units having their own governmental institutions can be regarded as societies' – 1965: 79). Consideration of the Indonesian case has suggested that the strength of divisions between the sections comprising the society is in inverse relation to the extent to which members of the entire society feel in opposition to some other society. The plural society, more than most kinds of society, has to be seen as part of a wider system of relations. Even within the society alignments change as the stimuli to group formation change. It is un helpful to describe members of a particular subgroup as showing, for example, a particularistic or a universalistic orientation, unless the structure of group oppositions is specified. That this raises some very difficult issues will be apparent from Smith's contention that 'The United States and Brazil are heterogeneous societies that contain plural communities and evince pluralism without themselves being plural societies. Neither color-caste nor class stratification implies basic institutional differences and, in my view, the term ethnic minorities should be reserved for those national groups that share the same basic institutions as the host society, but preserve distinctive styles.' Therefore, 'American Negroes do not form a separate cultural section. They are a subordinate social segment of a culturally heterogeneous society.' Though 'certain Negro communities in the South differ sharply in their social, religious, and economic organization from those of the adjoining whites . . . we must regard such Negro-white populations as plural communities but not as societies' (1965: 84–85). It does not seem helpful to put the emphasis upon the character of a community's institutions at the expense of the structure of relations in which the various communities are involved, for it is this structure that brings them into particular forms of conflict and co-operation.

It seems best to separate the elements of diversity and coercion in the concept of the plural society and to use the concept solely in a classificatory sense. It can then denote societies in which there is a common realm of political rights and social valuations together with separate spheres of community living, so that individuals have additional social identities in certain spheres of their lives. The earlier discussion emphasized that an integrated system of values may still be discriminatory; in the increasingly competitive urban society of the future, ethnic minorities may cease to seek social acceptance from the majority, preferring, on the one hand, to demand equality in civil rights but, on the other, to cultivate their own style of life. Ethnic pluralism may prove well adapted to the circumstances of an automated technology and a highly industrialized system of production. The various forms of pluralism therefore merit further analysis in the context of social change in North America as well as in South-East Asia.

CHAPTER TWELVE

Prejudice and Conformity

It is well to remember that the modern use of the word prejudice in discussions of racial friction is a very recent one. For centuries it was used in the sense of 'prejudgement', in accordance with its linguistic origin in the Latin *praejudicium*, a term employed in Roman law to denote a pre-trial judicial examination to determine the legal status of certain would-be litigants. In all the diatribes and jeremiads about racial conflict inspired by social Darwinism there was (to the best of the author's recollection) no mention of prejudice in its present meaning. Jean Finot's *Le Préjugé des Races* (English translation entitled *Race Prejudice*, 1906) is exclusively concerned with rebutting arguments asserting the superiority of European races. J. H. Oldham in *Christianity and the Race Problem* (1924), while rejecting the doctrine of inborn racial aversions, uses the term to denote sentiments of racial antagonism without respect to their character or psychological source. Though the causes of antagonism are analysed with care, there is no suggestion that prejudice is anything but a rational response to the circumstances in which people find themselves. Only later was it appreciated that prejudice is not necessarily dissolved by the demolition of arguments upholding racial inequality and that people of prejudiced disposition are left untouched by intellectual harangues. How recently the idea of prejudice in its modern meaning has been added to our intellectual armoury can also be seen from the perusal of encyclopaedias and works of reference. Neither the *Encyclopaedia Britannica* nor *Chambers's Encyclopaedia* – though they include numerous articles on petty kinglets and so on – has yet found room for an article on prejudice. *The International Encyclopaedia of the Social Sciences* (1967) will remedy this, of course, but it is nevertheless interesting to reflect upon how the absence of the concept of prejudice as an irrational attitude must have affected people's perceptions of racial friction in previous generations, and indeed how our own contemporary views are likely to seem crude to students of future generations.

THE FRUSTRATION – AGGRESSION THEORY

The writer who, more than anyone else, deployed the Freudian understanding of unconscious sources of behaviour in the analysis of interracial friction was John Dollard, with his book *Caste and Class in a Southern Town* (1937). This book paid particular attention to the irrational elements in behaviour. The criticism of other social scientists subsequently forced the author to pay closer attention to intergroup antagonisms as a rational response in situations of rivalry and to attempt to find a more adequate place for this aspect in his theory. The result is to be found in an essay entitled 'Hostility and Fear in Social Life' (Dollard, 1938). Criticism of Dollard's view is sometimes directed at the book alone, but it is necessary to consider the article also if justice is to be done either to the author or to the potentialities of the Freudian approach. Dollard introduced his second thoughts by saying: 'Close analysis of the word [race prejudice] reveals at least two distinct situations in which it is used: one where irrational antagonism is vented against other people, and the other where rational, that is intelligible, hostility is aroused in defence of a given status or economic order.' The latter situation gave rise to a form of behaviour he termed *direct aggression*, as opposed to the former which evoked *displaced aggression*. In situations of direct aggression the individual identified his opponent and attacked him. The competition in towns of the American South for 'white man's jobs' was a case in point, for, according to Dollard, bitter animosity was manifested against the rival Negro workers, and political measures were adopted to limit their ability to compete. In situations of displaced aggression, on the other hand, the individual did not attack the frustrating agent but displaced his resentment onto a scapegoat. This change of direction might come about because the frustrating agent was too powerful, or because the frustration came from within the individual's own social group and he valued his membership too much to risk losing it. The assumption of displacement then enabled the psychologist to explain situations where groups showed animosity without having any immediate reason for doing so. According to writers of the Freudian persuasion, all members of societies have to repress some of their individualistic impulses; all are frustrated by the very process of childhood socialization, but cannot vent their displeasure upon their parents both because they are subordinated to them and because they have incorporated ideas about their parents into their own personalities, so that they cannot reject their parents without damaging their own selves. The internal conflict is externalized as an opposition between the 'in-group' and the 'out-group'; this is the psychological structure underlying the phenomenon of 'ethnocentrism' – found when an individual's commitment to the values of his own group prevents him understanding the behaviour of people belonging to other groups. Because of the internal tension in individuals, there is always a fund of free-floating aggression waiting for a target to present itself. This target may be a rival or a scapegoat. If it is a rival, direct aggression will be evoked, but it will be accompanied by a certain amount of displaced aggression adding extra force to the rational attack. This part of the theory can help to explain how disturbances rooted in straightforward grievances may provoke frenzied behaviour out of proportion to the actual stimulus.

In its simplest form, the frustration-aggression theory holds that when an individual's attempts to achieve satisfaction are interfered with, aggression is generated; if this cannot be released in an attack upon the individual or group responsible for the interference, it is displaced onto a scapegoat. Why one particular group rather than another should be chosen is explained in terms of its visibility, its vulnerability (a scapegoat must also be a safe goat), and its tendency to symbolize the true source of frustration. Quite apart from scapegoating, more conventional forms of social inequality seem to have psychological functions. Freudian thought suggests that, unconsciously, members of one stratum use their social superiors in order to keep one another under control – and for this purpose inequality based upon a clear-cut if unfair attribute (like colour) is more effective than a differentiated behavioural attribute, such as ability (Holmes, 1965: 53). Where members of a society can work out their own patterns of social relations there will be less internal hostile tension. But where people are subjected to autocratic rule the impulses of group members will be thwarted. The best safeguard against internal disruptive antagonisms seems, then, to be the presence of an external enemy, which gives the hostile forces an approved target (incisive, if fictitious, illustrations of this principle can be seen in George Orwell's delineation of the parts played by Snowball in *Animal Farm* and by Goldstein in *1984*). Societies that regulate strictly the lives of their members need scapegoats. The silliest thing for them to do is to drive a scapegoat into the wilderness, for they will then have to find another.

In this fashion the Freudian mode of analysis shifted the focus of attention away from the question 'Why is Robertson prejudiced?' to the question 'Why does Robertson *need* prejudice?' What is the deficiency in his emotional make-up that obliges him to use this psychic crutch? Similarly, in the study of social relations it prompted social scientists to look at the social patterns that might stimulate scapegoating.

A series of experiments which bore out this theory in a dramatic manner was conducted by Muzafer Sherif (Sherif & Sherif, 1953). With some assistants, he organized summer camps for boys of eleven to twelve years of age, in which the development of group relations could be studied under carefully controlled conditions. Normal healthy boys of a homogeneous background were selected. At the first camp the boys were allowed to associate freely with one another for a while so that spontaneous friendships could develop. They were then divided into two teams using separate bunkhouses and so arranged that each boy found himself in the opposite team from the boy he considered his best friend. This was done to enable the observers to study the consequences of group relations as something independent of personal likes and dislikes. The teams were then kept employed on separate activities for several days. Each team chose a name for itself, and developed its own secrets, jokes, and characteristic ways of performing tasks. Wayward members who failed to follow these norms or to do their share were cold-shouldered or otherwise forced into line. At a second camp the process of forming group identities was the object of particular study. Hierarchies of esteem appeared. The most desirable and important tasks were reserved for the high-ranking boys and a clever experiment demonstrated that the youngsters overestimated the performances of their most highly regarded team-mates and underestimated those of the boys towards the bottom of the hierarchy.

One hypothesis to be tested was that when two groups have conflicting aims – i.e. when one can achieve its ends only at the expense of the other – their members will become hostile to each other even though the groups are composed of normal well-adjusted individuals. Competitive games were held: baseball, touch football, a tug-of-war, a treasure hunt, and so on. Good sportsmanship declined rapidly. The boys began to call their rivals 'stinkers', 'sneaks', and 'cheaters'. They refused to have anything more to do with them, turning against even the buddies they had initially chosen as their best friends. The rival groups made threatening posters and planned raids, collecting secret hoards of green apples for ammunition. At the first camp it transpired that hostility was so easily generated and could rise to such alarming heights that the organizers were obliged to call off the experiment and to devote their skills and energies to restoring harmony in order to send the boys home in a more suitable frame of mind. How could this best be done? Theories on this subject were also subjected to test. It is sometimes held that pleasant social contacts between members of conflicting groups will reduce friction between them. So, in the second camp, the hostile teams were brought together for social events: going to the movies, eating in the same dining room, and so on. Far from reducing conflict, these situations served only as opportunities for the rival groups to berate and attack each other, at times in a quite virulent manner. That hypothesis was scarcely supported by the results, so the organizers turned to another.

If competition generates friction, then the best chance for promoting harmony may be to have both groups working together in a common endeavour. To test what happened when hostile groups found themselves in a common predicament, the experimenters created a series of natural-seeming situations. There was a breakdown in the water supply. Both groups promptly volunteered to search the water line for the trouble. They worked together harmoniously, and before the end of the afternoon they had located and corrected the fault. One day the two groups went on an outing. A large truck was to go to town for food. But when everyone was hungry it was discovered that the truck would not start. The boys fetched a rope – the same one that they had been using in an acrimonious tug-of-war – and pulled together with a will. These joint efforts did not immediately dispel hostility. At first the groups returned to the old bickering and name-calling as soon as the job in hand was finished. But, gradually, the co-operative acts in pursuit of 'super-ordinate goals' broke down the conflict. New friendships developed between individuals in the two groups (Sherif, 1958). Effective social leaders have often been aware of the principles uncovered by these experiments even if they would not have expressed them in the same language. What the experiments did was to systematize knowledge on these matters and to facilitate its improvement and application. They reinforced Dollard's theory with respect to the psychological significance of group ties and the apparently excessive hostility often displayed towards antagonists. Other studies have supported the same view at a number of points. For example, it has been shown that aggressive responses are more frequent when the frustration appears to be of an arbitrary character (Williams, 1964: 84–88).

The frustration-aggression theory has been subjected to criticism. It has been objected that the terms are used loosely: if anyone behaves aggressively it is all too easy to postulate frustration as a cause, and when experimental tests have been set up it has proved difficult to define aggression (Himmelweit, 1950). If no response to frustration is apparent, the defender of the theory may insist that the aggression has been turned inwards; this makes it impossible ever to falsify the theory (cf. Popper, 1963: 33–65). Moreover, it has proved impossible to demonstrate that those individuals who have marked prejudices have endured greater frustrations than others. Furthermore, if there is so much free-floating aggression, it is strange that in wartime propaganda devices should have to be used to *make* soldiers hate their enemies. Sometimes the theory is criticized rather unfairly for failing to solve problems which it does not claim to solve (e.g. Allport, 1958 edn.: 331–2). If it is to be utilized as a working tool it needs the support of additional theories that will account for special circumstances. For example, Jews as a group are subject to special frustrations and might therefore be expected to show more hostility towards other minorities, whereas in fact many tend to identify themselves with members of such groups. The millenarian religious movements of extremely deprived social groups sometimes seem to serve a similar 'safety-valve' function. High levels of frustration can exist without, apparently, making people compensate for this by scapegoating; institutional factors may prove a more powerful determinant of behaviour. Nevertheless, in the study of any single situation it seems probable that the degree of manifestation of prejudice may be related, among other things, to the incidence of frustration (Sherif & Sherif, 1953: 125).

The chief contribution of psychological studies of racial friction before World War II was a change of emphasis – away from the view that the cause of prejudice was something in the object of prejudice towards the idea that the cause existed in the subject, in the person who displayed such an attitude. Prejudice was pictured as an irrational, pathological phenomenon arising from an individual's own inadequacies. But if the word is used in this way, another one is needed to denote the milder manifestations of hostility. A suitable word is 'antipathy', used in a sense opposite to that of 'sympathy'. Antipathy may be motivated by ignorance, by economic interest, by a desire to maintain group exclusiveness, and so on. As an attitude it is arrived at in a rational way, and the cause lies in the subject's relation to the object of aggression or in his image of the object. Attitudes of this kind are culturally and socially transmitted, whereas prejudice is something additional. Antipathy underlies direct aggression and can be modified by rational processes, such as education, whereas prejudice cannot be dispelled unless the individual's psychic imbalance is treated. The difference between prejudice and antipathy is important if only for its significance in the reduction of racial tensions, for a measure that might result in greater harmony if introduced in a situation characterized by antipathy might have quite other effects in one of prejudice. In the former situation people's objective discontents can be relieved, or their ignorance removed; but where, as in the latter case, feelings of hostility are strongly rooted in the unconscious, an educational programme designed to show the scapegoat group in a more favourable light might result either in an increase of hostility or in its transference onto another minority.

The Freudian approach to the study of prejudice received an enthusiastic and insufficiently critical reception from many social scientists in the United States. It was comforting to picture prejudice as an individual disorder, for it was then unnecessary to examine the organization of society in search of any factors that might manufacture or stimulate intergroup hostility. To use the image employed at the end of the first chapter of this book, friction was seen as the product of a psychological force – the flow along the pipe. The task of sociology was pictured as that of explaining when the flow would be turned on or off. As was said earlier, Dollard's is a most useful way of conceiving the interrelations of various factors, but it is not the only way. Trouble arises when one element, singled out for research purposes, is represented as if it were singled out in the real world and were more important than any other. The early advocates of the Freudian view fell into this error.

STEREOTYPES

In the early 1920s an American educational research worker gave some classes of schoolchildren the following silent reading test:

> Aladdin was the son of a poor tailor. He lived in Peking, the capital city of China. He was always lazy and liked to play better than to work. What kind of boy was he: Indian, Negro, Chinese, French or Dutch?

To his bewilderment, he found that many children in the border states were so impressed by the statement that the boy was lazy that they answered that he must be a Negro (Lasker, 1929: 237). From his, and others', observations, grew a series of inquiries into the formation and function of such set ideas. They are called stereotypes, but it is advisable to notice that this word is used in two senses: to refer to a tendency for a given belief to be widespread in a society (perhaps better called an image or a received idea); and to denote a tendency for a belief to be oversimplified in content and unresponsive to the objective facts (the true stereotype) (cf. Krech & Crutchfield, 1948: 171–2).

One of the most influential of the early investigations into stereotyping was conducted with students at Princeton in 1932 (Katz & Braly, 1933). The subjects were presented with eighty-four adjectives and asked to pick out those characteristic of various nationalities. Considerable agreement was found among the answers – Germans are scientifically minded, methodical; Italians are artistic, musical; Negroes are superstitious, lazy; Americans are industrious, sophisticated; Turks are cruel, sensual. Eysenck doubted the interpretation of this experiment, so he and a collaborator repeated it in Britain. The results were almost identical. However, they introduced a new element, requesting the subjects to write reports about their own reactions to the task they had been set. This showed the material in a very different light: 19 per cent of the subjects had in the first place refused to do the test, declaring it to be 'meaningless' and 'impossible'. Of those who agreed to do it, 59 per cent considered the task meaningless because they did not know any representatives of these various nationalities; they pointed out that only long residence in a country could enable one to say anything worth while about the people there, and that even then 'people everywhere differ among themselves'. But, if the experimenter insisted on setting them such a task, they had to fall back upon what they had seen at the pictures, read in the newspapers, or heard vaguely in conversation; they were fully conscious that the qualities thus attributed to the various nations probably portrayed nothing but bias and preconceived notions (Eysenck, 1953). At about the same time another research worker repeated the Katz and Braly experiment with a similar group of Princeton students. He found that the stereotypes were by that time very much weaker. Moreover, many of the 1950 students were reluctant to participate in such a task, regarding it as a 'childish game' (Gilbert, 1951). There had been no comparable resistance eighteen years earlier. Recent research has demonstrated that any study of stereotyping that is based on responses to a check-list of attributes is likely to overestimate the extent of prejudice (Ehrlich & Rhinehart, 1965).

Some stereotypes serve economic ends, as is suggested by the remark, 'An Indian can live off the smell of an oily rag' (once widespread in English-speaking Africa). If one believes that 'Orientals can live on a bowl of rice a day' this is a justification for keeping wages low. But in certain circumstances stereotypes involve much more. They have critical emotional significance for those who hold them and they fit together in a twisted but ordered pattern of social relations. The most deeply impressive and intellectually illuminating study of the social pathology of stereotyping is that made by Bruno Bettelheim, who was a prisoner in the German concentration camps at Dachau and Buchenwald for one year. He described the queue of Jewish prisoners outside the clinic, admission to which depended upon permission from the Gestapo guard – a private – which was rarely given.

'The main topic of discussion was one's chances of being admitted to the clinic. The conversation indicated that the prisoners had planned their stories in great detail. Some, for instance, thought it best to stress their meritorious service in the German Army during World War I: the wounds received or the decorations won. Others planned to impress the Gestapo guard by the severity of their suffering. A few decided it would be preferable to tell some "tall story", for example, that a Gestapo officer has ordered them to report at the clinic. The prisoners seemed convinced that the Gestapoman on duty could not see through their schemes. Moreover, they neglected to take into account the fact that he might be an individual with personal biases and that it might be advantageous to appeal to these . . . I said that it was undesirable to follow a preconceived plan because it was difficult to anticipate the reactions of an unknown person. . . . The prisoners asserted that one Gestapoman was like another and accused me of not wanting to share my plan with them.

Jewish prisoners waiting in front of me were not admitted to the clinic. The more a prisoner pleaded with the Gestapoman, the more annoyed and violent he became. Expressions of pain amused him; stories of previous services rendered to Germany outraged him. He chided the prisoners for trying to lie their way into the clinic. He proudly remarked that *he* could not be taken in by Jews and that fortunately the time had passed when Jews could gain their goal by lamentations. When my turn came the Gestapoman asked me whether I knew that work accidents were the only reason for admitting Jews to the clinic, and whether I came because of such an accident. I replied that I knew the rules, but that I could not work unless my hands were freed of dead flesh arising from frostbite. Since prisoners were not allowed to possess knives I asked to have the dead flesh cut away. I made these statements in a matter of fact way, avoiding pleading, deference, or arrogance. The Gestapoman replied: "If this is really all you want, I am going to tear the flesh off." He started to pull with force at the festering skin. Because it did not come off as easily as he might have expected, or for some other reason, the

Gestapo soldier ordered me to enter the clinic. Once I was inside he gave me a malevolent look and ordered me to enter the treatment room. There he told the orderly to attend to the wound. While this was being done the Gestapoman again watched me closely. I succeeded in suppressing signs of pain. As soon as the cutting was accomplished, I started to leave. The Gestapoman seemed surprised and questioned me as to why I did not ask for further treatment. I replied that I had received the service which I had requested. At this he told the orderly to make an exception and to treat my hand. After I had left the room the Gestapoman called me back and gave me a card entitling me to further treatment and to admittance to the clinic without inspection at its entrance' (Bettelheim, 1947).

Using this incident for illustration, Bettelheim then proceeds to show the two opposing stereotypes that characterize this situation. The stereotype is originally a defence mechanism, but as time goes on it is introjected and influences behaviour independently of external pressures. The Jews realized that the guards had formed a nonsensical stereotype and wrongly believed that all Jews were alike, but nevertheless they themselves created a similar stereotype of the Gestapoman. Their schemes for approaching the guard depended upon this assumption of uniformity; to question it would have been to discard the plans which were their only protection against their feeling of helplessness. The stereotype created by the Jews included the ideas that the antisemite was of low intelligence, had little education, and was of low social and cultural status. In this way the disturbing accusations made by such people against Jews were invalidated, and the prisoners' self-esteem was preserved. To safeguard their inner status further, it was necessary to obviate the idea of Jews submitting to their inferiors, and so Gestapomen acquired the characteristics of all-powerful adversaries who were no longer human. Stereotypes often contain self-contradictory propositions; in this case, although the Jews thought the guards all-powerful, they explained their anti-semitism as the result of fear. Further, each group projected upon the other group its own most undesirable motives and accused its members of sexual perversion, sadism, etc., so that the opponent became a sort of evil *alter ego*. *The* Gestapoman was more cruel and bloodthirsty than any individual Gestapoman could possibly be, but in this situation reality-testing was out of the question and it must be remembered that the prisoners were living in conditions quite unlike anything they had been trained for or had previously experienced.

Bettelheim then argues that the anti-semites' – especially the Nazis' – stereotype of the Jew was determined primarily by displacing onto him those attitudes that National Socialism forced them to suppress. The Jews represented their own desires for peace, international co-operation, and an unheroic family life; thus the more pressing their own dis-satisfactions became with the continuance of the war, the more violently had they to treat the Jews. It would be incompatible with the anti-semite's self-esteem to regard the Jews as a defenceless minority group, and so their alleged 'clannishness' comes to represent a powerful, evil, and secret world organization. The more violent the anti-semite is, the more he must justify his actions by regarding the Jews as dangerous, and thus does he provoke more anxiety. By taking on themselves the displacement of purely individual uneasiness about personal qualities, the Jews perform a service to the anti-semites which is recompensed to the 'exceptional Jews' – it has been said that every German had his 'favourite Jew' and that every American in the Southern states has his 'favourite nigger'. If in actual life a Jew acts in accordance with the semi-delusional picture of *the* Jew that the anti-semite has developed, then the latter believes that his hatred of *all* Jews is justified. In the prison camp, whenever Jews approached the guard on the basis of their stereotyped picture of *the* Gestapoman, he dealt with them on the basis of his stereotyped picture of *the* Jew; if a Jew came up with a story claiming particularly 'German virtues' or with an emotional appeal, the guard put him in the category of 'the cunning Jew' who was trying to get round him – which effectively invalidated everything the man might say or do. The guard had little choice: 'In order to conform to the Gestapo ego-ideal he had to suppress all humanitarian feelings. Only those who have observed the violence of the reaction in a person who is suddenly asked to act in accordance with suppressed desires can fully understand the anxiety which such a demand would create in the Gestapoman.' The guard would permit a prisoner to get what he wanted rather than admit that he possessed 'German' virtues. Bettelheim was successful because he did not conform to the delusional image of the Jew as a dangerous opponent and was able to confront the Gestapoman with an interpersonal situation that he could master without the use of self-justifying delusions (Bettelheim, 1947).

CONFORMITY AND SOCIAL PROCESSES

Before the Freudian approach gained its ascendancy, the one theory that had most influence upon ideas about race relations was that of social Darwinism. This saw the individual as a representative of a biological species whose activities were very largely determined by the character of that species. The individual conformed to the social pattern. Freudian thought swung the pendulum back, emphasizing the psychic sources of social behaviour, but the swing went too far. Much of the reaction to Freudian theorizing has consisted therefore, not surprisingly, in the reiteration or rediscovery of the importance of the element of conformity to group patterns in the explanation of individual behaviour.

It would be misleading to present the study of conformity as if it belonged exclusively within the field of psychology. Many writers have followed J. S. Mill in believing that sociology is concerned with the study of social collectivities and have formulated theories about social trends which assume that, for one reason or another, the individual will conform to the more general pattern. Societies have been pictured as organisms, systems, mechanisms, and so on, but most generally as units obeying their own laws, independent of those governing the behaviour of 'individual man'. It is interesting in this light to examine the ideas of the first writer to develop what a modern reader would recognize as theoretical guidelines to the sociological study of race relations: Robert E. Park, an American who took up a permanent academic post only in 1914 at the late age of fifty years. The first systematic expression of Park's system of sociology is contained in the *Introduction to the Science of Sociology*, written jointly with Ernest W. Burgess and published in 1921. Park shows his acquaintance with contemporary European writers, and particularly with those who sought to base the study of society upon a biological foundation, but he goes on to maintain that the social organization of human beings is determined not merely by instincts and by competition but by customs, tradition, public opinion, and contract.

Park wrote of sociology as one of the 'natural sciences': like them, he said, it aimed at prediction and control based on an investigation of the nature of man and society. This meant the study of those aspects of life that are determined and predictable, by reducing the complexity and richness of life to the simplest terms. The most fundamental of these was the conception of society as a system of interaction. Communication was regarded as the medium of social interaction, with imitation and suggestion as its mechanisms. According to Park there were 'four great types of interaction – competition, conflict, accommodation and assimilation'. The chief among these was competition, a 'process through which the distributive and ecological organization of society is created. . . . The division of labor and all the vast organized economic interdependence of individuals and groups of individuals characteristic of modern life are a product of competition' (the Darwinist influence is evident here, not least in Park's failure to state clearly what he means by competition). However, he continues: 'On the other hand, the moral and political order, which imposes itself upon this competitive organization, is a product of conflict, accommodation and assimilation.' Conflict was to be identified with the political order and the political process by which any society consciously dealt with its crises. Accommodation was the process by which individuals and groups made the necessary internal adjustments to social situations which had been created by competition and conflict. It was associated with the social order, which is fixed and established in custom. Whereas accommodation is a characteristic of outward behaviour, assimilation implies a thoroughgoing transformation of the personality, 'a process of inter-penetration and fusion in which persons and groups acquire the memories, sentiments, and attitudes of other persons and groups, and, by sharing their experience and history, are incorporated with them in a common cultural life'.

One virtue of this theoretical framework is its refusal to treat race relations as different in any sociologically essential respect from relations between other sorts of groups. Park thought that patterns of race relations exemplified conflict, and to a lesser extent assimilation, but it is clear that many features can be counted as illustrations of accommodation and competition. The total racial situation in any particular region will present many features and cannot be classed as an example of just one general social process. Another virtue of Park's scheme, particularly notable in a sociologist of his generation, was that, while its principal categories related to features of collective life, indisputably distinct from individual psychology, it was based upon the study of interaction, which was something observable in the day-to-day behaviour of particular people. Thus Park's formulations avoided the high-level abstractions of his European contemporaries and served as a stimulus to empirical investigation. This movement towards better concepts for observational research can be seen in his successive definitions of prejudice. Step by step Park moves from conceptions of social groups and processes in which the individual is but a pawn, towards a more individual understanding of prejudice and a specification of the conditions under which individuals are likely to conform to particular social patterns. In 1917 he wrote: 'Race prejudice is a mechanism of the group mind which acts reflexly and automatically in response to its proper stimulus. That stimulus seems to be, in the cases where I have met it, unrestricted competition of peoples with different standards of living' (1950: 229). In 1921: 'Race prejudice, as we call the sentiments

that support the racial taboos . . .' (1921: 578). In 1924: 'What we
ordinarily call prejudice seems then to be [a] more or less instinctive and
spontaneous disposition to maintain social distances . . . [it] seems to
arise when, not our economic interests, but our social status is menaced.
. . . Prejudice is on the whole not an aggressive but a conservative force;
a sort of spontaneous conservatism which tends to preserve the social
order and the social distances upon which that order rests' (1950: 259–
60). In 1928 he wrote an essay entitled 'The Bases of Race Prejudice',
in which he first accepted the view of prejudice in a general sense as the
sort of prejudgement that is natural and inevitable in social life – 'a man
without prejudice is a man without conviction, and ultimately without
character'. He then went on to develop his idea of race prejudice as 'a
phenomenon of status . . . in its more naive and innocent manifestations,
merely the resistance of the social order to change'. Because the Negro
was rapidly improving his position in American life, Park concluded:
'There is probably less racial prejudice in America than elsewhere, but
there is more racial conflict and more racial antagonism' (1950: 230–7).

Park's ideas were never set out systematically in a single treatise but
appeared in occasional articles and in introductions to books by his
students; often these were introductions to the books he had hoped they
would write, rather than to the ones they actually did write (Hughes,
1964: 19). One of the most influential of his ideas was that of 'social
distance'. Park conceived of social distance between people as a measure
of their influence over one another as expressed in the relative intimacy
of their relations. He wrote:

> 'Not only is it true that we have this sense of distance with reference
> to whole groups of persons but it is also true that "race" and "class"
> consciousness frequently interferes with, modifies and qualifies per-
> sonal relations; relations which, under other circumstances, it seems,
> might become of the most intimate and understanding sort. For
> example, the lady of the house may be on the most intimate personal
> relations with her cook, but these intimate relations will be maintained
> only so long as the cook retains her "proper distance". There is
> always some sort of social ritual that keeps the cook in her place,
> particularly when there are guests' (Park, 1950: 257).

The idea of social ritual as an important factor regulating social distance
in the mistress-cook relationship and supporting a process of accommodation was developed in Park's later writings and teachings. At one
place he points out: 'while etiquette and ceremonial are at once a
convenience and necessary in facilitating human intercourse, they serve

even more effectively to maintain social distance and to preserve the rank and order of individuals and classes' (1950: 241). The etiquette of race relations in the South became the topic for a book by one of Park's students (Doyle, 1937), and the theme received more extensive treatment from a Negro scholar (Johnson, 1943). Another seminal idea linking the study of individual behaviour to social processes was his notion of the 'marginal man'. In describing perhaps the most general process of all, Park maintained: 'the race relations cycle which takes the form, to state it abstractly, of contact, competition, accommodation and eventual assimilation, is apparently progressive and irreversible' (1950: 150). Peoples may for a time live side by side, preserving their distinctive cultures, but in the long run intermarriage will increase and the movement to assimilation will grow. The burden of adjustment falls most heavily upon the individual who, like the child of a mixed marriage, belongs to two communities:

> 'The fate which condemns him to live, at the same time, in two worlds is the same which compels him to assume, in relation to the worlds in which he lives, the role of a cosmopolitan and stranger. Inevitably he becomes, relatively to his cultural milieu, the individual with the wider horizon, the keener intelligence, the more detached and rational viewpoint. The marginal man is always relatively the more civilized human being. . . . The emancipated Jew was, and is, historically and typically the marginal man, the first cosmopolite and citizen of the world. He is, par excellence, the "stranger" ' (1950: 376, 354).

It was by means of such imaginative insights that Park brought the study of social processes down to everyday level. But Park's students were virtually the first generation of empirical sociological research workers in the modern style and it takes time to hammer even penetrating ideas into firm scientific concepts. Sociological writing at this time dealt with individual variations in prejudice only in common-sense terms. Ideas about the mechanisms inducing people to conform to social norms were still comparatively unsophisticated. Consequently, the Freudian approach, with its new interpretation of the personality factor, possessed a special intellectual excitement and had a greater impact.

THE PREJUDICED PERSONALITY

Psychological research carried out in the late 1930s and early 1940s revealed that people who were prejudiced towards one minority group tended to be prejudiced towards others, and, indeed, were apt to express antagonism towards fictitious groups whose names they had never previously heard. This finding gave a new impetus to attempts to identify the kind of personality associated most strongly with the expression of prejudice. While this work was in progress, Jean-Paul Sartre, in his essay *Portrait of the Anti-Semite*, displayed an impressive insight into the problem and sketched a portrait which was later confirmed by more painstaking methods. At one point Sartre refers to a friend who had an elderly cousin who used to come to dinner and of whom everyone used to remark significantly, 'Jules cannot bear the English'. He continues:

> 'My friend cannot remember anything else ever having been said about cousin Jules. But that was enough: there was a tacit understanding between Jules and the family, everyone ostentatiously avoided talking about the English when he was there, and this precautionary measure gave him a semblance of existing in the eyes of his relatives, while they in turn were rewarded by the agreeable feeling of taking part in a consecrated ceremony. Then, at a propitious moment, someone, after careful prethought, and as if accidentally, would make some observation on Great Britain or its dominions, and cousin Jules would pretend to fly into a great rage, and feel for the space of a second that he really did exist: which gave rise to much satisfaction all round.'

Many people, says Sartre, are anti-semitic in the same way that cousin Jules was an anglophobe, and, naturally enough, they have not the slightest idea what their attitude really implies (1948: 43). He might almost have summed up his argument by saying that the prejudiced personality is based on the axiom 'I hate, therefore I am'.

Writers inclined towards psycho-analytic interpretations of behaviour have suggested that strongly prejudiced individuals are, in the main, those who have suffered from a bad home background during childhood years, their parents having been on bad terms with one another, and they themselves, as children, rejected by one or other parent and deprived of affection. The prejudice they develop later in life represents an attempt to 'restore a crippled self', something used as a defence mechanism in an endeavour to allay their own anxieties (Ackerman & Jahoda, 1950). At the same time, prejudiced individuals try to gain strength by associating or identifying themselves with groups that are seen as powerful and dominant.

This question of why some people develop prejudice rather than others has been illuminated by the results of an intensive inquiry showing how certain personality characteristics tend to be associated with the expression of anti-semitic opinions. The authors of *The Authoritarian Personality* (Adorno *et al.*, 1950) found that individuals' tendencies to anti-semitism could be measured fairly accurately by the 'F scale', which was constructed to yield an estimate of receptivity to fascist ideology. Nine features of the characteristic fascist personality are listed (1950:228):

> '*conventionalism:* rigid adherence to conventional middle-class values
> *authoritarian submission:* submissive, uncritical attitude towards idealized moral authorities of the in-group
> *authoritarian aggression:* tendency to be on the look-out for, and to condemn, reject, and punish people who violate conventional values
> *anti-intraception:* opposition to the subjective, the imaginative, the tender-minded
> *superstition and stereotype:* belief in mystical determinants of the individual's fate; the disposition to think in rigid categories
> *power and "toughness":* preoccupation with the dominance-submission, strong-weak, leader-follower dimension; identification with power figures; overemphasis upon the conventionalized attributes of the ego; exaggerated assertion of strength and toughness
> *destructiveness and cynicism:* generalized hostility; vilification of the human
> *projectivity:* the disposition to believe that wild and dangerous things go on in the world; the projection outwards of unconscious emotional impulses
> *sex:* exaggerated concern with sexual "goings on".'

This work provoked considerable criticism, some of it very damaging (e.g. Christie & Jahoda, 1954), but it also set on foot a great volume of research which has helped powerfully to elucidate the psychology of prejudice.

Eysenck (1953) has held that on some issues the opinions of the authoritarian anti-fascist are very similar to those of the fascist and that there are, in fact, two dimensions on which attitudes are to be measured: Radical-Conservative, and Toughminded-Tenderminded. On the first axis it is found that adherence to the radical view in politics is associated with less strict views about sexual morality. Towards the Tenderminded end of the second axis it is noted that people who consider the death penalty barbaric are also apt to favour compulsory religious instruction. Those who hold that coloured people are inferior and who are inclined to prejudice are better classified as Conservative-Toughminded than as fascist, because the former term brings out both dimensions. The data and deductions on which these conclusions are based have, however, been subject to severe criticism (cf. *Psychological Bulletin*, Vol. 53, 1956: 169–86, 411–51).

The application of the Freudian approach to the special features of the colonial situation has been pioneered by a French writer who made a special study of Madagascar (Mannoni, 1956). He maintained that the traditional tribal society conditioned its members to a feeling of dependence upon one another; when they were confronted with psychologically more independent people, like adult Europeans, they had difficulty in adapting to the relationship. At first they were apt to see in the European the master, the protector, and the scapegoat. The Europeans who went out to the colonies tended to be people who had inferiority feelings disposing them to aggressiveness and the domination of others, and when the institutional supports of social life in Europe were removed these tendencies became sharper. The European did not understand the native people's expectations of their relationship, or was inclined to distort what he did know in order to preserve the image of the native as someone onto whom he could project his own repressions. Thus their own predicament prevented the Europeans from weaning the native group from its dependence and, consequently, there came a time when the latter felt harshly rejected; the dependence then nourished a sharp animosity and might result in armed uprising. The desire for mastery on the part of the colonizer (which, from the psycho-analytic standpoint, is an infantile characteristic) has been called the 'Prospero complex' because of the striking resemblances between the relations found in the colonial situation and those so skilfully sketched in Shakespeare's *Tempest*. Prospero maintains his rule over the island by magic. At the beginning of the play he lays aside his magic garment and tries to tell his daughter Miranda the story of his life. He tries to treat Miranda as an equal but cannot do so. Similarly with Ariel, the spirit he found in the island and rescued; Ariel represents the 'good native'; Prospero has promised him his liberty, but up to the very end fails to give it to him. To Caliban, who represents the 'bad native', Prospero is consistently harsh, justifying his severity by accusing Caliban of having tried to violate his daughter. There is no logical connection between the punishment and the offence, which seems, indeed, to be in part a projection of Prospero's own incestuous desires. On which Mannoni comments: 'It is easy to see why it is always his daughter or his sister or his neighbour's wife (never his own) whom a man imagines to have been violated by a negro; he wants to rid himself of guilt by putting the blame for his bad thoughts on someone else' (1956: 106). At the end of the play Prospero returns, without his magic, like some pensioned colonial potentate retiring to political impotence in Bournemouth or Burgundy.

'What the colonial in common with Prospero lacks, is awareness of the world of Others, a world in which Others have to be respected. This is the world from which the colonial has fled because he cannot accept men as they are. Rejection of that world is combined with an urge to dominate, an urge which is infantile in origin and which social adaptation has failed to discipline. The reason the colonial gives for his flight is of no consequence ...' (1956: 108).

Psycho-analytic interpretations tend to pass a severe judgement upon the vagaries of the social world; those who write, and those who read, books upon questions of race relations might fare no better under this searchlight than those who have worked in the colonial services of European nations.

THE INTERPRETATION OF F-SCALE SCORES

The generalizations about the 'authoritarian personality' discussed above were derived from subjects' responses to questions forming the so-called F scale. This, it will be remembered, was constructed to measure receptivity to fascist ideology. The scale has been criticized because it measures deviations from a mid-point towards the authoritarian extreme, but does not cover deviations in the opposite direction. Two particular lines of criticism will be considered here: first, the argument that the high association between authoritarianism and prejudice is not caused by any necessary relation between the two features, but arises because both are the products of a single, more fundamental, cause; and, second, the argument that the use of the expression 'authoritarianism' distracts attention from some of the critical elements.

It has been argued that the expression of fascistic opinions may reflect an accurate judgement of social and psychological reality in the lower social strata or in low-status subcultures. Responses to the F scale indicate that one of the characteristics of prejudiced persons is a deep mistrust of other people. But, for many poor people, American society does in fact resemble a merciless jungle. There are many areas in the great cities in which too much trust can easily get someone killed. A number of studies show a systematic association between socio-economic position and psychological conditions likely to be associated with authoritarianism. An extensive study of mental health in New York City, for example, found that rigidity, suspiciousness, depression, hypochondriasis, alcoholism, immaturity, neurasthenia, withdrawal, and passive dependency were all most prevalent in the lower classes and least prevalent in the upper class. There is consistent evidence from several studies that low education tends to be associated with authoritarian responses. Negative correlations have been obtained between authoritarianism and social status, and between ethnocentrism and social status. There are therefore good grounds for believing that both authoritarianism and prejudice may be characteristic of persons in economically and socially deprived positions in the social structure (for a review of these studies, see Williams, 1964: 88–96).

What is it that the F scale measures? It is widely believed that anti-Negro prejudice is more frequent in the South than in other regions of the United States, yet recent investigations have reported F-scale means in the Southern states that fall well within the range of means of comparable non-Southern groups. In both North and South there is a generalized anti-minority prejudice associated with authoritarianism, but many non-authoritarians conform to the discriminatory norm in the South in a way that – to judge from verbal tests – they could not in the North. The more tolerant Southerners tend to be social deviants – non-churchgoers, independent voters, downwardly mobile in occupational status, veterans, and relatively well educated. Thus, in evaluating the significance of ethnocentrism, the research worker stressed principally the 'socio-cultural and social adjustment factors' (Pettigrew, 1959). The same investigator studied the attitudes expressed, in 1956, by white students at the University of Natal, South Africa, and compared them with similar expressions from the American South. He concluded that there was no higher psychological potential for prejudice in these areas than in more tolerant parts of the globe. The cultures in which white persons in both regions participated incorporated norms of intolerance towards Blacks: people were taught these norms and were under pressure to comply with them. The writer added: 'Data from the South African students hint that susceptibility to conform may be an unusually important psychological component of prejudice in regions where the cultural norms positively sanction intolerance.' He argued further that the available evidence would support the hypothesis that: 'In areas with historically imbedded traditions of racial intolerance, externalizing personality factors underlying prejudice remain important, but socio-cultural factors are unusually crucial and account for the heightened racial hostility' (Pettigrew, 1958: 40).

The influence of conformity has also been underlined by American studies which draw attention both to the considerable conformity component already in the scale (the first characteristic listed is, after all, 'conventionalism: rigid adherence to conventional middle-class values') and to the technical questions of the construction and administration of the scale. It provides no adequate opportunity for persons who are actively opposed to fascist ideology to express their adherence to contrary values. Any subject with a tendency to assent to the statements offered to him by an interviewer (and conformist persons will show such a tendency) will consequently be likely to obtain a higher authoritarian score. Thus it can be agreed that a significant element in authoritarianism as measured in the earlier investigation was acquiescence or conformity in this other respect. Further studies have demonstrated that the F scale reflects the placing of subjects on a scale of psychological anomie (or 'normlessness'). Measures of authoritarianism overlap with measures of anomie and ethnocentrism. Each tends to decrease with higher levels of education and income, but at every level of income or education the anomic individuals are more likely to be ethnocentric (Roberts & Rokeach, 1956; cf. McDill, 1961). It has also been argued that, whereas in the middle class (towards which *The Authoritarian Personality* samples were biased) prejudiced individuals are conformists, in the working class the prejudiced tend to be people who reject their society; and therefore the emphasis should be placed on the way in which social structures influence personal controls over behaviour (Bettelheim & Janowitz, 1950 (1964 edn.: 74–7)). Thus the great volume of recent research shows that, even as a psychological phenomenon, prejudice is not something homogeneous and simple, but a compound of different forces which need to be measured separately.

THE DETERMINANTS OF CONFORMITY

Why should people conform to group or cultural norms? Investigations in the last few years have thrown new light upon the psychological rewards that people receive from conformity. To the observer, these rewards may seem too small to be of much account, but the people in question place a high value on them and it is their perceptions that determine their behaviour. Experimental studies have shown that people will modify their opinions to conform to the group's even when these are in flagrant contradiction with their initial opinions. Let us say that an experimenter puts five people in a darkened room and then projects onto one of the walls for two seconds a picture of Brigitte Bardot. Next, he asks the subjects to identify the figure. Four of them are in league with the research worker and they assert that the picture was one of Elvis Presley. In a significant, at times quite surprising, proportion of cases, the fifth man would also say it was of Elvis Presley. Some people seem to conform to group norms just for the sake of the approval it brings them from their fellows; others conform because they are thereby protected from attack by outsiders; both kinds of conformers, however, are likely to say that they conform because the practice in question is simply the custom of the group. More sensitive research techniques are needed to differentiate the various types of conformity.

George C. Homans has advanced some ideas suggesting ways in which these investigations might be developed. He draws attention to the paradoxical position of the high-status member of the group: such a person tends to observe the more important norms more strictly than other people in order to maintain his standing, but he also can afford to disregard minor norms more airily than other people can. A newcomer to a group, by contrast, tends to be of low status; he must win approval and respect by demonstrating his willingness to conform. This is why previously tolerant people, on settling in a racially segregated community, may quite rapidly come to express opinions more intolerant than those voiced by well-established members of the community. However, if the low-status person finds that the demands for conformity are too exacting relative to the rewards that may be expected, he will be more inclined than other people to disregard group norms: he can afford to. With respect to many norms, the upper-status man has little to gain by conformity; the lower-status man has little to lose by its opposite (Homans, 1961: 354). But this is not the case when really cardinal norms are in question: the upper-class White in a situation of racial segregation may find his interracial behaviour under closer surveillance than that of the lower-class white man.

Conformity may as well be induced by the fear of punishment as by the prospect of reward. Whereas experimental studies of conformity often centre upon rewards that seem trivial because they represent just small increments in something already possessed to some degree, the punishments for non-conformity are often severe. If a white shopkeeper in rural Georgia allows Negro clients to be too familiar, many white customers may suddenly withdraw their custom and the man may be forced out of business. If a Negro was accused of making advances to a white woman, his punishment was often not a reduction in group approval but the loss of his life. The fear of such consequences establishes a sort of floor to structures of conformity; above it, people may accord approval and respect to those who observe various norms and there is an area of tolerance in which each individual may make his choice.

CHAPTER THIRTEEN

Social Distance

To study the determinants of conduct it is necessary to find some suitable procedure for classifying particular items of behaviour. Analyses of intergroup relations, for instance, often depend upon a distinction between discriminatory and non-discriminatory behaviour. Yet such 'either-or' distinctions are of relatively little utility. The value of the concept of social distance, by contrast, lies in the way in which it enables the research worker to evaluate the extent of discrimination and to conceptualize it as a continuum. It compels him to analyse intergroup relations in a manner equally applicable to intragroup relations, fastening upon a general characteristic of social life instead of upon the circumstantial and at times distracting features of group conflict. This use of the concept, which was implicit in R. E. Park's remark, 'Everyone, it seems, is capable of getting on with everyone else, provided each preserves his proper distance' (1950: 257), has, however, been overlaid in the course of time by certain other connotations which need to be distinguished from it.

THE BOGARDUS SCALE

In 1925 Emory S. Bogardus published a first account of a social-distance scale he had devised, at the suggestion of Park, for measuring and comparing attitudes towards national and racial groups. The procedure for the test was to present subjects with a list of statements indicating varying degrees of social intimacy, together with a set of names of social groups. The subjects were asked to reply in the following terms:

> According to my first feeling reaction, I would willingly admit members of each race (as a class and not the best I have known, nor the worst members) to the classifications which I have marked.

As part of the 1932 revision, a panel of judges rated sixty statements about degrees of distance, and seven emerged as representing roughly equidistant points along a scale of increasing distance. They were:

1. Would marry
2. Would have as regular friends
3. Would work beside in an office
4. Would have several families in my neighbourhood
5. Would have merely as speaking acquaintances
6. Would have live outside my neighbourhood
7. Would have live outside my country

It was contended that these seven statements represented a scale of social distance against which attitudes towards different stranger groups could be compared. Bogardus himself was interested in calculating racial-distance quotients for comparing the mean distance expressed towards different minorities. Having administered the test to a large panel of American subjects in 1926, he repeated it in 1946 and 1956, finding a basic stability in attitudes towards the stranger groups coupled with a number of readily comprehensible variations associated with international changes and the steady process of assimilation (Bogardus, 1959).

In the early studies, subjects were presented with a chart divided into columns for ticking off degrees of distance. This procedure was criticized by later investigators who noted that some subjects would accept certain strangers as, say, workmates, while rejecting them as neighbours. They therefore posed the entire range of questions separately in random order, so that if there were ten stranger groups and seven alternatives, seventy questions had to be asked. This technique improves the reliability of the test and makes it possible to check the subjects' consistency or inconsistency. However, the Bogardus scale has been criticized on graver issues. In a brief but penetrating discussion Krech and Crutchfield maintain that the test is influenced by factors other than attitudes: 'Social distance is a complex quality, related in the most intimate way to the ego standards of the individual, his conceptions of prestige in the eyes of the group, etc. Even though a man may hate the English and place them in an extreme negative position on an attitude scale of the Thurstone or Likert type, he might not reject them as residents in his own street.' They conclude: 'the scale as it now stands seems to include two different types of reactions of the individual: (1) his relative willingness or unwillingness to be exposed to the object, (2) his relative willingness or unwillingness to be identified with the object' (1948: 222–4). If subjects' responses reflect more than one kind of reaction then the scale is not unidimensional. In another review Mozell Hill drew attention to Park's original conception of social distance as a means whereby a group maintains its identity. He pointed also to results he and others had obtained which suggested that 'the technique is not a true scale at all', because in some circumstances people will accept strangers in what, according to the Bogardus scale, are near distances while rejecting them in more distant ones (Hill, 1953).

Responses to the Bogardus test indicate how people think they would behave in certain circumstances. When the test was first formulated, many social scientists believed that it was possible to account for behaviour in terms of the attitudes of individuals and that social distance was governed by their image of the stranger group. Thus Bogardus has defined social distance as 'the degree of sympathetic understanding that functions between person and person, between person and group, and between group and group. Sympathy refers to feeling reactions of a favorably responsive type, and understanding involves that knowledge of a person which also leads to favorably responsive behavior' (1959: 7). This definition takes no account of non-psychological sources of social distance. A study of the data cited in Bogardus's recent review demonstrates that distance may spring from a variety of sources, three of which merit mention in the present context:

(i) Social distance may be the outcome of people's negative attitudes, deriving from unfavourable ideas about members of another group. This has been the dominant view in studies on this topic.

(ii) Social distance may equally well, however, be a characteristic of certain types of social relation, notably those between a superordinate and a subordinate, a senior and a junior, and between people of comparable social standing but potentially conflicting obligations. People are unwilling to enter into a relationship with someone they consider unqualified to assume the reciprocal role. Unwillingness to be identified with a stranger is one variety of this form of distance, for the unwillingness exists with reference to particular relationships; few people mind being associated with a stranger in the relationship of superordinate to subordinate, provided that others will not misinterpret the relationship.

(iii) Distance may reflect a relative lack of common interests or experiences. Many occupations have their technical language, and small communities their special pursuits. Such groups have, in effect, their distinctive cultures; there may be no adequate place in them for people who cannot participate in the group activities, even though they are of comparable social standing and the group members are not unfavourably disposed towards them. This form of distance might more properly be described as cultural; it can also arise within cultures, as in schools in which middle-class teachers have charge of working-class children and do not share the same values.

Not all distance is social. If a man avoids his colleague because of temperamental incompatibility, this is a purely individual variation. Similarly, some seniors behave with greater familiarity than others towards their juniors. In so far as this reflects differences in people's interpretations of the same role, within permitted limits, it is not a form of social distance. However, if, for example, it should transpire that those seniors who are most vulnerable to criticism from their peers are constrained to observe greater or lesser distance towards their juniors, then a social influence can be discerned.

The different causes of social distance may supplement each other. Strongly unfavourable attitudes towards a minority are often found in a situation in which members of the minority are confined to inferior positions. The association between membership of the minority and low rank is such as to give rise to distinctively racial status as in the situations regarded as exemplifying colour-caste. Not infrequently, however, two factors pull in opposite directions. Charles S. Johnson stated: 'There are situations within the legal and institutional structure separating the races in the South which permit a considerable degree of personal intimacy between whites and Negroes; but that intimacy is permissible only when both parties know what can and cannot be done and the appropriate social distances prescribed by racial etiquette are maintained.' Difficulty often arises over what he terms the taboo against interracial dining and drinking: 'A Negro school-teacher was entertaining a group of white school visitors when mealtime arrived. No other facilities being available he offered them dinner. They ate willingly enough and to prove their friendship insisted that he get a small table and eat in the same room' (1943: 118, 143). Friendship and custom pulled in opposite directions and the degree of distance actually observed was a compromise between the two.

As the distance observed in particular cases is a compound of different and perhaps conflicting components, it is unprofitable to employ an inclusive definition. Each form of distance must be defined in its own terms, for it is an analytical construct which does not have to reflect the full variety of interpersonal distance as an empirical phenomenon. It would seem more fruitful to analyse the various factors independently and to try to devise scales for each of them.

ATTITUDES AND RELATIONSHIPS

Bogardus's line of interest has been continued and developed by Henry C. Triandis, who noted that differences of race, religion, nationality, occupation, or political ideology might underlie the distance people in one culture expressed towards strangers, but that no one had examined variations in the significance attached to these attributes from one culture to another. Whereas race seemed to be most important for Americans, other studies suggested that elsewhere nationality might be stressed more (as by the Lebanese) or that differences of religion might take priority (as in the Philippines). The usual technique confounded these factors for it did not reveal the extent to which, for example, rejection of Irishmen was the outcome of their religion or of their nationality. Triandis therefore asked subjects to indicate whether they would accept, in fifteen relationships, a Swedish truckdriver, white, of different religion from themselves; a French physician, Negro, of the same religion; a Portuguese civil engineer, Negro, of different religion, etc., permitting all the feasible combinations (in subsequent investigations he has added age and sex classifications). A comparative study of the distance expressed by students in Athens and in Illinois concluded that about 77 per cent of the distance expressed by the Greek students could be attributed to the nationality factor, 22 per cent to religion, 1 per cent to occupation, and 0·7 per cent to race; of the distance expressed by the American students, about 86 per cent could be ascribed to race, 7 per cent to religion, 2·9 per cent to occupation (an earlier Illinois study utilizing different specimen occupations had, however, found that 17 per cent of the variance in distance scores was accounted for by occupation), and, finally, 0·4 per cent to nationality (Triandis & Triandis, 1960, 1962). A further study along similar lines found that male high-school students in Germany placed weight primarily on occupation as a factor evoking distance (the variance rose to 82 per cent among Catholic students); second, upon religion (rising to 12 per cent among Protestant students); and third, upon race and nationality (rising to 6 per cent, but with a different rank order of rejection on the part of non-religious students). University students in Japan, who completed questionnaires of the same basic structure as that used for the German sample, also placed most weight upon occupation (though much less than in Germany); the Japanese emphasized race more than the Germans did, and attributed very little significance to the religion of the stimulus person. The weights given to the different factors depend very much upon the composition, with respect to class, religion, ethnic background, and sex, of the sample completing the questionnaire (Triandis, Davis & Tazekawa, 1965).

With social-distance data of this type, it is also possible to examine the personal characteristics of those subjects who express most and least distance, and to use semantic tests to discover what it is about the 'stimulus objects' that evokes distance. In this way, psychological research provides evidence for what a sociological view would antici- pate, namely, that the expression of social distance is determined by a combination of individual sentiment and shared norms about what constitutes proper behaviour in a particular society. Triandis attempts to interpret his data by using three basic constructs: conformity, cogni- tive dissonance, and insecurity. That the ascription of a stranger to a particular minority with a defined place in the social universe is a principal determinant of expressed distance suggests that conformity to group norms is the most important of all. Economic interest and per- sonal prejudice often motivate people to behaviour they realize to be in conflict with the professed values of their society: this is an element of dissonance. The insecure person is less capable of tolerating dissonance and tries to obliterate it by adopting uncritically some supportive ideo- logy. The Greek-American comparative study concludes: 'Conformity to group norms accounts for about one-third of the variance in social distance, while personality characteristics account for less than one- third of their variance. About one-third of the variance is due to error and characteristics of the subjects that were not measured in the present research' (Triandis & Triandis, 1962: 20).

But, even so, the Triandis' mode of approach does not explain why the statements about distance fall into a particular order in a given society – why, for example, 'I would accept this person as a neighbour' expresses appreciably more intimacy than 'I would live in the same apartment house with this person'. To explore what a relationship entails, irrespective of the characteristics of the other person called upon to be a party to it, requires an analysis not of sentiments but of roles, not of conformity but of social structure. The sociologist therefore has as great a professional interest in the study of social distance as has the psychologist. The relation between the concerns of the two discip- lines may be exemplified by considering the way in which the results of social-distance tests have usually been presented. The normal method (at least in the earlier studies) was to isolate the attitudinal element; the seven degrees of distance were used only to enable the investigator to assess the potency of subjects' attitudes (see *Figure 16*). These degrees of distance each embody a relationship in which the subject might

Figure 16 The social distance reported by Americans as a reflection of attitudes towards strangers

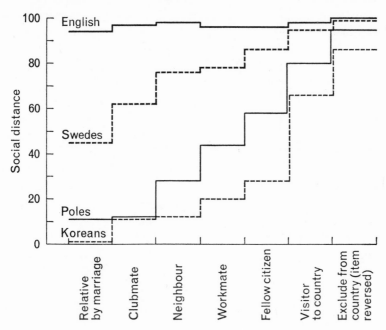

Source: Bogardus (1928)

conceivably associate with members of the groups in question, but this procedure took no account of the social implications of the relationships. It was chiefly directed to the calculation of distance quotients for different groups. Thus, in reporting the results of his 1946 and 1956 inquiries, Bogardus listed only the quotients and gave no data on the various relationships (1947: 55–62; 1959: 30–40). As the scale is not unidimensional, the results are appropriately represented by histograms rather than by graphs.

Yet it is equally legitimate to isolate the relationship element in social distance as the one of principal interest and to treat the stranger groups as varying only in their relevance to the way in which subjects prefer to avoid contact with them in certain kinds of relationship (see *Figure 17*). This approach brings out explicitly the implications of the different relationships in respect of varied stranger groups.

New statistical techniques such as scale analysis expose this duality but, at an introductory level, comparison of the two figures shows more simply the relation between the two chief constituents of social distance. The procedure used for *Figure 16* gives a relatively accurate representation

Figure 17 The social distance reported by Americans as a reflection of
the implications of relationships with strangers

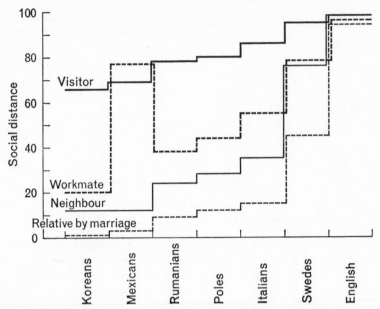

Source: Bogardus (1928)

of social distance when the attitude component is dominant, and
that for *Figure 17* when the relationship component is in the ascendant.
Both have complementary weaknesses but both are equally legitimate.

This re-examination of the relationship component reveals a number
of points that previous practice has tended to obscure. In the first place,
the extent to which distance is observed is determined not only by the
group being tested but also by the characteristics of the stranger groups.
Bogardus's panel of judges assessed the degrees of distance implicit in a
number of possible relationships without reference to any particular
group. But relationships that are equidistant in respect of the general
and abstract category 'stranger' may not hold for any particular group
whatsoever, since behaviour towards someone regarded as belonging to
a stranger category is in part a response to the peculiar characteristics
assumed to define his particular category. This is evident from variations
in the intervals between responses for different groups in *Figure 16*, but
it is emphasized by some of the responses given in *Table 3*. This table is
based upon Bogardus's first inquiry, because the book that describes it
is one of the very few publications on social distance that present data
in a manner that permits re-analysis. From this table it will be seen, for

Table 3   The social acceptability in America of fifteen nationalities

Percentage acceptance

Stranger category	Relative by marriage	Clubmate	Neighbour	Workmate	Fellow citizen	Visitor	Exclude (reversed)
English	94	97	98	96	96	98	100
Americans	90	93	93	92	91	99	100
Swedes	45	62	76	78	86	95	99
Russians	16	28	31	45	56	78	92
Italians	15	26	35	55	71	86	95
Poles	11	12	28	44	58	80	95
Hungarians	10	18	26	43	71	80	93
Rumanians	9	19	24	38	52	78	95
Armenians	9	15	28	46	58	82	95
Jews, German	8	2	26	40	53	75	86
Bulgarians	7	15	16	20	43	78	93
Mexicans	3	12	12	77	46	69	85
Japanese	2	12	13	27	29	39	98
Filipinos	2	15	20	37	52	72	95
Koreans	1	11	12	20	28	66	86

Adapted from Bogardus (1928, p. 25). Note that the acceptance of German Jews by other Jews (Bogardus's Table IV) is sufficient to produce acceptance levels of 9·7 and 10·0 in the first two columns. In a personal communication, Professor Bogardus has confirmed that these latter are the correct figures.

example, that the distance between relationships 6 and 7 for Japanese is roughly equal to that between 4 and 7 for Koreans. The nationalities included in this table have been selected in order to call attention to variations of this kind, so they are not properly representative of the results Bogardus has obtained. But among these variations two anomalies are of particular interest: the relatively great acceptance of Mexicans as fellow workers and the rejection of German Jews as clubmates. Bogardus describes the Mexican as a labourer who does not compete with Americans or displace them from anything they value highly; his docile manner excites no antagonism (1928: 20). This, however, is not an altogether satisfactory explanation of his acceptance on this item, because the statement indicates acceptance 'to employment in my occupation'. The entries for German Jews in columns 1 and 2 are erroneous (see footnote to *Table 3*), but dips in the curves may be noted for English and Americans on columns 4 and 5 and for Mexicans on columns 5 and 6 (for a recent criticism along similar lines, see Holzkamp, 1965).

The phenomenon is, in any case, within the range of everyday experience. Some people may object to their kinsfolk marrying a Catholic on the grounds that the children will be exposed to Catholic doctrines at an impressionable age, but have no objection to association with a Catholic in any other relationship. Someone else may accept a Negro as a close friend but not wish to have him as a neighbour because of the fear – justified or not – that property values might be affected. The same group of people when indicating the distance they would severally observe in respect of two stranger groups might list the relationships in different orders of avoidance.

In the second place, a re-examination underlines the influence of group variations within the sample. Bogardus gives tables showing that the social-distance preferences of Negroes and Jews are radically different from those of the bulk of the sample. It is therefore meaningless to add together these contradictory preferences to arrive at a national pattern. In *Table 3*, for example, the high place accorded to Englishmen is clearly associated with the fact that, of 1,725 subjects, 772 were of English descent and a further 508 of Scots, Irish, or Welsh descent.

The question of the order of the statements representing degrees of distance is brought out in an interesting fashion by a study of inter-tribal relations in Zambia. With the aid of African research assistants, J. Clyde Mitchell drew up seven statements which it was thought would correspond most closely to those of Bogardus. They were:

1. Would admit him to near kinship by marriage
2. Would share a meal with him
3. Would work together with him
4. Would allow to live nearby in my village
5. Would allow to settle in my tribal area
6. Would allow as a visitor only in my tribal area
7. Would exclude from my tribal area

Twenty-one tribal groups were selected. Each of the statements was formulated as a question for each group, giving 147 questions in all. The test was then administered to 329 African scholars at a local secondary school. Only a preliminary account of the results of this study is available as yet, but according to Mitchell they show that the order of the statements employed needs revision. For Zambia in the mid 1950s, the correct order of the statements listed above was 1, 5, 4, 2, 3, 6, 7.

The most striking feature of this finding is the original misplacing of statement 5. There is a parallel here with one of Hill's results. He found, when administering the test to adolescents in all-Negro communities in Oklahoma, that affirmative responses to the statements that they would (i) be willing to marry a white person, (ii) have no objection to inviting a white person into one of their social clubs, (iii) be willing to attend school with white children, (iv) be willing to have a white person living in their town, ran as follows: 8 per cent, 61 per cent, 78 per cent, 38 per cent. Admission of Whites to residence in their town had, for adolescents in an all-Negro community, much the same significance as admission of stranger tribesmen to settlement in their territory had for Rhodesian Africans. Mitchell's results suggest that the Africans regarded the extension of hospitality to a stranger as a customary duty of relatively little significance compared with the major step of allowing a stranger to occupy their tribal land permanently and to introduce a possibly disharmonious note into local affairs. (One can only assume that statement 5 suggested this possibility more strongly than statement 4, which logically should imply it even more definitely.) Hill's data indicate a similar reaction. This kind of result is of the utmost value because it draws attention to the inaccuracy of the sort of assumption every investigator makes and rarely questions. Often, investigators unconsciously tailor their interpretations to preserve their assumptions; techniques that expose them as clearly as this are invaluable.

Mitchell shows in his paper that the responses to different peoples fall into a clear pattern. To the extent that two peoples come from the same region and have similar forms of social organization, they observe less distance in respect of each other. A third factor is that of prestige. Less distance is shown towards the former warrior peoples of high renown; more is shown towards peoples whose menfolk will accept employment as night soil men, or other occupations of low prestige. The ranking of peoples in this way suggests new questions to the anthropological field-worker.

SITUATIONAL VARIATIONS IN RESPONSE

Individuals' responses when asked whether they would accept or reject members of another group may have little value as predictors of how the same individuals would behave in real situations. There is a famous study by an American sociologist who went on a trip in the Western United States with his wife and a Chinese couple (Lapière, 1934: 230–7; for a modern replication of this study, see Kutner, Wilkins & Yarrow, 1952). Together they stopped at 184 restaurants and sixty-six hotels, and were refused service only once. After returning to his university the sociologist sent out questionnaires to a large number of restaurants and hotels, including all the ones they had visited. In the questionnaires he asked, among other things, if the proprietors would accept someone of the Chinese race as a guest in their establishment. Ninety-two per cent of the replies from the places they had visited were in the negative, and the response from the control group was very similar. This clearly suggests that when a restaurateur is faced with a situation in which just two respectable Chinese appear with two respectable American sponsors he defines it in a very different way from a situation in which he is faced with a piece of paper asking him to commit himself to a principle which, if uniformly applied, might cause him embarrassment. In the former case the restaurateur can deny the Chinese service only by making a personal objection and by presenting himself in an illiberal guise; it is quite possible, moreover, that such a situation may have to be handled by a waiter who does not know quite what to do, or that the party may be seated at a table before it is noticed that two are Chinese. In the case of the questionnaire, however, the restaurateur can say 'no' without involving himself in any unpleasantness, and it is this course that seems the safer. The discrepancy between actual behaviour and behaviour predicted on the basis of questionnaire responses shows that responses to distance tests must be interpreted with caution. Opinion polls about voting intentions are not subject to the same degree of error because, when asked how he will vote, a person defines the situation in much the same way as he defines the actual voting situation; the verbal answers given in such polls are therefore relatively good predictors of behaviour. When a person is asked if he would exclude a Chinese from his restaurant, his response reflects primarily his personal attitudes and his apprehensions about the possibly unfavourable consequences of so doing; he does not take into account the pressures inherent in any actual situation. For this reason verbal responses are poor predictors of behaviour in these sorts of situation.

Lapière's study brings out the way in which interracial behaviour may be determined by the roles the parties are playing rather than by their sentiments as individuals. Therefore it is appropriate to ask what sort of people enter into roles in which they will have to meet members of other groups. Describing an inquiry in New York State, conducted from Cornell University, Robin M. Williams wrote:

'Community wide sample surveys showed that members of various ethnic categories in Hometown tended to follow beaten social paths that did not often intersect with paths of other groups. These observations were confirmed by project observers . . . most people seemed to develop an "Indian path" – a well-beaten, often trod, social trail from home to work, back to home, to lodge meeting, back to home, on Sundays to church and back, and then perhaps to visit relatives and friends. Once the pathways had developed, persons tended to stay on them; only once in a while did they go into parts of the forest frequented by other tribes' (Williams, 1964: 141–2).

The factors that chiefly determine which Americans will meet members of other minorities are the social variables of sex, age, education, and economic status. An independent investigation in Chicago similarly found that a disposition to avoid contact with Negroes in certain relationships was related to status differences among the respondents and to the extent to which Negroes had moved into the neighbourhood (Winder, 1956). But behaviour within a contact situation is more likely to be determined by the psychological variables of attitude and personality (Williams, 1964: 163).

Men and women tend to have rather different social networks (or, in Williams's terminology, to tread different social trails). The values professed in racially divided societies are frequently enunciated and enforced by power networks among the men. Women, because many of them are dependent upon men for social status, may be particularly vulnerable to sanctions upon nonconformity and they sometimes therefore tend to express greater social distance towards strangers (cf. Pettigrew, 1960: 252). Williams found that, though men have more opportunity than women to make interracial contacts, when allowance is made for the factor of opportunity it appears that American women are as likely as men to form friendships across ethnic lines (1964: 144, 200). His inquiry also showed that the distance people express towards particular minorities may be the product of local circumstances. For example, in two cities studied there was a close association between occupational status and the social distance expressed towards Jews and Negroes, but the associations ran in reverse directions. The low-status people displayed much more distance towards Negroes whereas distance expressed towards Jews increased uniformly with occupational status. Presumably each category was responding to the group which represented the most actual threat to its own privileges (1964: 54, 179).

This line of argument leads to what at first sight seems a reversal of the Freudian view of prejudice, though the difference really stems from using the word in another way. Much of the rejection of out-group members is patterned; it is related to the roles the parties are playing and it serves to maintain an existing system of discrimination. Thus Williams asserts that prejudice 'is primarily a response to interaction with *ingroup* members . . . ethnic prejudices do not really refer to *personal* likings (or preferences for association) at all, but rather to the acceptance of *shared (cultural) definitions and evaluations of social categories as such* . . . Interpersonal likings and associational preferences . . . could never form the *structural* alignments represented by the classification of some 18,000,000 varied human beings as "Negroes" in our society today' (1964: 77, 113-14). Williams is here referring not to prejudice as it has been conceived in the previous chapter, but to social distance, which, if psychologically motivated, is often the product of what has been distinguished as antipathy. Moreover, any implication that the structural pattern can be explained in terms of shared cultural definitions and evaluations needs qualification because the definitions and evaluations in question are not *uniformly* shared throughout American society. Probably they are held strongly by the parties to particularly influential networks and are either forced upon others or transmitted to them along the lines of other networks. Sociological research might profitably be directed to locating points at which racial exclusion is not functionally necessary to the maintenance of selected networks. The Cornell research in fact shows that people are more likely to change their attitudes about racial contacts when they experience a major change in their social networks – as by taking a new job, entering military service, moving to a different community, going to college, or getting married. The key people in informal social networks may well be those who have least personal difficulty in managing varied social situations and who tend to participate in a high proportion of social activities (Williams, 1964: 144, 191-200).

Some people are more exposed to interracial contact than others are. Research of the kind just discussed shows what sort of people tend to be more involved in such relations, but the question needs to be pursued further. These people, after all, are not exposed to contact to a uniform extent all day long; they meet members of other groups when they play particular roles only. Some of them shuttle between institutional structures in which there is much contact and spheres in which there is very little, just as migrant workers in Africa may move backwards and forwards between town and country or between interracial work enterprises and native locations. One of the best studies describing proximate spheres of racial contact and segregation relates to the Panama Canal Zone (Biesanz & Smith, 1951). In the same urban area, one side of a street might be in the Zone, under United States control, and the other side in the Republic of Panama. Some people lived and worked on the same side of a dividing line, but many lived in the Republic and worked in the Zone. Panamanian Negroes tended to conform to discriminatory practices when they went to the Zone, and white Americans tended to accept racial equality when they came into the Republic.

The *raison d'être* of the Canal Zone was the operation of the Canal with all the various ancillary tasks which this entailed, such as the control of yellow fever and malarial mosquitoes. Such work required a complex system of formal or bureaucratic organization, and high levels of skill and discipline. There had to be a division of labour based on technical competence and responsive to a system of incentives that would attract both specialists from the United States and local employees with less scarce skills. This had earlier resulted in the division of employees into 'gold-roll' and 'silver-roll' categories, separating not only skilled from unskilled labour but the United States and Panamanian standards of living. 'Gold-roll' people received better housing in segregated districts; were permitted to trade in commissariats carrying a higher prestige line of goods, and to send their children to schools offering better teaching, equipment, and curricula; had separate waiting-rooms at the medical dispensaries, and different churches, clubs, places of recreation, and cemeteries. Whole towns were known as gold or silver towns. This pattern of non-monetary remuneration tended to make an independent role into a basic role (the authors say 'a specialized status into a generalized status') and anything that has this effect tends to increase racial discrimination. In the Zone, recruitment to the more important jobs was restricted to United States citizens on grounds of military security. The authors maintained that though there were reasonable functional grounds for the employment of Negro West Indians and Panamanians on the silver roll only, there was no such explanation of why very few Negro United States citizens were employed in the Zone and why those few who did have gold-roll jobs and salaries were nevertheless required to accept silver-roll housing and non-monetary remuneration. Race had come to be used as a role sign and it often overrode other ways of categorizing people.

Panamanian society, by contrast to that of the Zone, displayed lower technological rationality; less differentiation of occupational roles; a low evaluation of the ethics of 'earning one's way'; unstable government with a personalized style of administration, in which less distinction was made between a man and his office; unstable families with a loose but extended kinship structure; strong, informal, male friendship groups; and no clear division of racial categories. In Panamanian life the chief reward a man sought had been the esteem of his peers, but the industrial influence was introducing a more competitive outlook. A technically trained, middle-class Panamanian with a gold-roll job might be given only silver-roll privileges; often he got only a silver-roll job regardless of his abilities. He was apt to conclude that because he had a darker complexion the Yankees had ascribed him to the Negro category. At times, complaints about racial discrimination became a focus of agitation against 'Yankee imperialism'; at other times, though, the lighter-skinned Panamanian reacted against his low placement by emphasizing his relative whiteness and expressing prejudice against his darker-skinned countryman.

For some people in Panama, movement between social spheres of high and low discrimination was movement between spheres of work and leisure. Such a pattern is found in industrial cities also (cf. Banton, 1965: 191–2). A study in the United States mid-West compared the willingness of the same group of workers to accept Negroes in two contexts. As members of an all-white civic club the men refused to admit Negroes to the neighbourhood in which they lived, but as members of a union strongly opposed to racial discrimination they supported non-segregation and racial equality in the work situation. A series of interviews demonstrated that the more the people were involved in the collective life of the neighbourhood, the more they resisted the idea of Negroes as residents there; the same interviews showed that the more deeply the men were involved in union activities, the more strongly did they accept Negroes at work, so that the people who were the most committed to discrimination in one context were the most opposed to it in another. The contrast was traced to the way in which organized bodies provided their members with norms indicating how they should define the situations in which they were involved (Reitzes, 1953; cf. Minard, 1952).

Interaction in leisure-time situations tends to be particularly influenced by considerations of status, but there are other factors that seem to be of general relevance. One writer selected four intergroup situations occurring in Puerto Rico, and by analysis deduced that little racial distance was to be expected (a) in situations perceived as secular and impersonal or (b) in leisure-time situations among the lower classes. On the other hand, the exclusion of Negroes was to be expected (c) in upper-class leisure-time situations and (d) in the top levels of secular achievement, since in such circumstances a dark colour had connotations of low prestige (Rogler, 1948).

The analysis of case studies in this fashion leads to generalizations holding within the culture in question, but some more abstract mode of conceptualization is necessary to take account of variations within institutions. For example, in 1951, two departments at the same railway depot near London reported quite different experiences in respect of the employment of coloured immigrant workers (Banton, 1955: 145–6). In the locomotive workshops, coloured workers had been successfully employed in a number of jobs; but the department responsible for the maintenance of the permanent way had experienced very considerable trouble, and, though desperately short of staff, would not engage any

more coloured workers. The critical difference between the two departments appeared to be in the ability of management in the former to
exercise relatively close control over work relations because most operations were carried out on the spot in a group of buildings. Work roles
were defined by the formal organization, with management seeing not
only that the work was done but that it was done in the way it wanted.
In the permanent way department, close supervision was impossible;
work was organized informally according to the workers' ideas of how to
arrange matters. The men worked in gangs out on the permanent way
under a chargehand, and many of these gangs victimized any coloured
man allocated to them, forcing him to give up the job. The inability of
management to define work roles closely, and to enforce its definitions,
meant that the workers imported into the work situation the discriminatory norms of the surrounding community. Other evidence also suggests
that when situations are defined impersonally, in formal terms, discrimination can more easily be prevented.

Sometimes there is no organization like a trade union or a club to
indicate which of several possible sets of norms is the most appropriate
in a particular sort of situation. To explore this aspect, some members of
the Cornell research team located establishments (such as restaurants
and taverns) known to discriminate, and patronized them regularly.
Then, while the observers were present, Negro research workers
entered and demanded service. The observers noted what happened,
afterwards returning to check on the consequences of the incident and
to interview as many of the key participants as possible. The situations
studied were considered unpatterned because most majority-group
persons in small Northern cities had very few contacts with members of
minority groups and racial discrimination was officially disapproved. It
was unusual for Negroes to go into establishments where they believed
themselves unwanted, so that waitresses and bartenders could not be
sure what kind of behaviour different parties would expect from them.
Analysis of what happened in forty-three such situations led to the
conclusion that, in public places of business, the manager or person in
charge frequently could not say in advance whether he would discriminate. He waited until an occasion arose and then sought cues from his
white patrons to see whether they would object to his serving Negro
customers. The first Whites to provide such cues had proportionately
greater influence. Inquisitive Whites who asked whether Negroes
would be served were more likely to receive a negative reply, partly
because, when the inquirer was white, such a reply was less likely to
occasion any withdrawal of patronage, and partly to be on the safe side.

But in real situations the chances were that, rather than refuse service, the manager would serve the Negro in such a way as to discourage his staying or returning. In some cases – such as these in New York State – the manager also had to beware of retaliation from Negroes who could invoke anti-discrimination legislation against him. Therefore his re-action to the intruders depended upon whether he categorized them as 'two out-of-towners who did not realize they were not welcome here' or 'a couple of troublemakers who were trying to provoke an incident'. When a manager looked around for cues and received evidence of con-tradictory expectations from different participants, he tended to resolve the conflict by exempting the situation from one of the two definitions offered him: either (a) a type of event could be exempted, as when a liberal-minded restaurant-owner justified discrimination against Negroes by arguing that the prosperity of his business took precedence over other values; or (b) a particular individual could be exempted, as when a bartender would serve a former classmate of his, though he discriminated against other Negroes (Williams, 1964: 318–31).

At present, the most promising avenue for any attempt to formulate general propositions concerning the observance of distance seems to be that of role analysis. It is possible to consider very many situations in terms of the relationship between three parties: *ego*, the actor whose position is taken as the starting-point; *alter*, the person towards whom his behaviour is directed; and the *onlooker*, a member of ego's group who appraises his conduct and may cause ego to be rewarded or punished for it (as by the conferring or withdrawing of esteem). Ego's apprehensions about what may be entailed by entering into relations with alter correspond to Krech and Crutchfield's formulation of dis-tance as caused by unwillingness to be exposed to an object, while ego's apprehensions about the onlooker's judgements correspond to peer-group pressures, or unwillingness to be identified with the object in question. Within a formal organization, an individual is less likely to be worried about identification because his role is well defined; he is more likely to be concerned about exposure, that is, the result anticipated from admitting to a relationship someone who may not know the rele-vant rules of conduct or whose participation may have untoward consequences. Much will depend upon ego's ability to control any deviation on alter's part, either by conveying expectations or by punish-ing infractions. Another important variable is the role alter is called upon to fill and the relationships he will have to enter. A businessman might not mind employing a stranger in a position defined by relatively simple regulations, but be reluctant to take him on in one that required an understanding of the customers' domestic background or an ability to make judgements of their trustworthiness – for which greater awareness of the significance of minor traits of behaviour is needed. Regarding distance, then, as a generalized concept covering degrees of avoidance and discrimination, it may be suggested that ego will maintain greater distance:

(i) the more alter is thought to be unaware of the norms governing social relations in ego's group;

(ii) the more the relationship in question is regulated by implicit modes of communication;

(iii) the weaker the sanctions are for bringing the stranger into line if he behaves inappropriately.

Outside the work sphere, the relationships in which people may meet strangers tend to be rather different, and ego is likely to be more concerned about the implications for his social standing if he is identified with members of stranger groups. A man's social standing is heavily influenced by the sort of person he is known to associate with, therefore people do not like to be seen too frequently in the company of their social inferiors or of persons regarded as socially deviant. But a man's reputation is not necessarily damaged if he is seen walking down the road with a tramp or a prostitute; his behaviour might well be regarded as unorthodox and as calling for some explanation; however, if the man were wearing a policeman's uniform or a clergyman's collar, this might well be held to legitimize the relationship. In such cases the man's occupational role is understood to involve him with such people in the course of his duties and his action is not regarded as reflecting upon his private claims to status. Someone who is new to a district or who has recently assumed a role may be more vulnerable to criticism or challenge than someone who is well established; also, individuals vary in their tendency to worry about peer-group censure. But the chief factors in the avoidance of identification seem to be covered by the further propositions that ego will maintain greater distance:

(iv) the more alter's group is of low prestige;

(v) the less public justification ego's role gives him for associating with persons ascribed to the category in question.

The fourth proposition has been formulated to cover the more typical situations of discrimination; where socially inferior persons maintain distance from superiors because of peer-group pressures their behaviour is in line with proposition five. The relevance of these propositions will become more apparent in the examination of evidence adduced in the final chapter.

CHAPTER FOURTEEN

Urbanization and Separation in the United States

THEORETICAL RECAPITULATION AND STATEMENT

Race relations, as the expression is normally understood, arise because individuals are classed as belonging to particular categories. The customary categories influence, and are rooted in, the feelings and behaviour of the members of the society. But everyone belongs in other categories as well. The racial groupings are relevant only in certain circumstances. In Chapter Four it was contended that groups form because, when responding to stimuli, people choose to align themselves in association with certain persons and in opposition to others. It was said that these stimuli to alignment are not randomly generated, but are influenced in their strength and direction by factors in the substratum of social life, in which are to be included the political and economic basis upon which societies come into contact and the material interests of particular groups. It was further maintained that the high level of consensus about fundamental values which is postulated by some kinds of sociological theory is, in practice, characteristic only of the small community which, because of its members' personal acquaintance with one another and the variety of interlocking groups, reveals a high social density. In small communities of this kind there are many divisions and occasions for dispute, but there are no deep cleavages or abiding group antagonisms. Such communities present different aspects to the outsider and the insider. They can tolerate without undue difficulty what appear gross inequalities of privilege, as in connection with class differentials in Europe or racial distinctions in the Brazilian towns mentioned in Chapter Eleven. As that chapter maintained, these inequalities do not stimulate people strongly to align themselves in constantly opposed groups because the conflicts are contained within face-to-face relations; the mode of production is relatively continuous and therefore there are fewer economic struggles; psychologically, people show low empathy, low need for achievement, and a high valuation of relatively small status gains.

With a higher level of productive activity and a greater scale of social relations, a dense texture of social relations cannot be maintained. When large ethnic sections are brought into contact – as in South-East Asia – a pluralist order may emerge at a pre-industrial stage. Even without ethnic division, economic development, if it continues, brings so much larger aggregations of people together that cleavages begin to appear along the lines of social distinction. Different social sections, frequently based on class differences, acquire distinctive viewpoints and values, and con-sensus is to that extent reduced. Inequality then presents a different and more difficult political problem. Simultaneously, economic inter-dependence is intensified and yet forms of social conflict become more threatening because this interdependence is so easily upset. The legal inequalities of pre-industrial times and the customary inequalities of the village community cannot be openly tolerated. If they persist (as, indeed, they usually do to some extent) they are no longer legitimate. The demand for political equality requires that everyone submit to the law, acknowledging that each person shares certain common obligations to the state and to his fellow citizens. Self-respect comes to be regarded as a human right, and, because people cannot feel self-respect unless they are accorded respect by others, citizens of different rank are expected to treat one another with consideration, recognizing their human similarities as well as their social dissimilarities. In an industrial democracy, the inheritance of status or social advantage easily becomes a source of political tension. Though the kind of inequality implied in the image of the farm labourer touching his cap to the squire is strongly disliked, other forms of inequality are accepted. Willingness to accept social distinctions must always be viewed within the framework of a people's beliefs and expectations about social relations. In an industrial democracy, people may believe that the rich deserve their privileges because they think they got to the top in fair competition or because their economic activity has created gainful employment for a host of others; or they may be less resentful of distinction because uncon-sciously they identify themselves with someone from their own minority or stratum who has got to the top (the 'log cabin to White House' saga is one aspect of this, and the demagogic political style another); such identifications enter into the adulation of movie stars and may even depend upon an imagined future participation in the rewards of rank, as with the man who expects one day to win the football pools or the national lottery. Such attitudes – and they are both varied and wide-spread – serve to make social distinctions supportable; they enable urban industrial society to hold together in spite of the fissures that appear in different places.

Some of the most notable forms of social separation in urban living are those deriving from the increasing independence of the spheres of work and leisure. In pre-industrial societies, even manufacturing is frequently carried out within the household. But in the industrial cities of today people live at a distance from their place of work. If they wish, they can exclude all their work associates from their leisure-time relations and join with others to whom, because of their income, hobbies, sports, or personal attributes, they are acceptable almost irrespective of the way in which they make their money (Banton, 1965: 187-9). The separation of work and leisure enables people to make decisions in the work sphere with reference to the demands of that sphere and to pay less attention to their social implications for the parties concerned. If a man is promoted he can move to another residential district and change his leisure-time associations. One consequence is the growth of large housing estates and districts full of people from the same socio-economic status who have little personal acquaintance with the life-styles of those who live in other districts. As cities grow in size, so persons of different social class are segregated more and more in respect of residence and therefore of schooling and the use of many public facilities. The city is a great divider as well as a mixer. The social and cultural distance between managerial and production employees in many industries adds to this social separation. Consequently, relations between persons of different social class are more frequently categorical relations in which each regards the other as a representative of a type and does not know him or her as an individual. Relations between persons of different social rank are more often of an impersonal kind. This means that if something happens to suggest that one section of the population is receiving unfair privileges, it serves as a stimulus mobilizing an opposed section to protest. Though the separation of social classes in industrial societies has not developed in the way that Marx predicted, it is a source of some of the major tensions of the present time. When to class differences is added racial difference, the likelihood of fundamental cleavage is increased.

The rhythm of industrial production is subjected to many interruptions because of changes in the demand for products, in the cost of labour and materials, in technological processes, etc. Any of these interruptions may serve as an occasion for conflict, ranging two groups against one another. There are far more stimuli to group alignment in a modern urban area than in a pre-industrial society. The United States has benefited because the divisions exacerbated by economic growth have to some extent been counterbalanced by other divisions, particularly the ethnic differences within the white population. People have been less inclined to align themselves on a class basis because in many circumstances they have been more ready to identify themselves with ethnic or religious groups. Immigrant minorities have entered American society in succession and have moved up the spiral of assimilation as they learned American ways and were lifted by the pressure of other groups coming in underneath them. Consequently, some writers have been led to regard Negro Americans as just another minority comparable with Italian-Americans, Irish-Americans, Jewish-Americans, etc., and to assume that when Negroes show comparable success in adapting themselves, they will achieve a comparable acceptance. This view of the matter seems strange to the European observer impressed by the difference often associated with race and accustomed to meeting Europeans of other nations and finding them much like himself. In the United States the arguments for regarding the Negro as another minority seem stronger than they do to the European. The differences between European ethnic groups have often appeared very great, especially in the first generation, when immigrants have associated closely with their fellows, speaking the same tongue and following similar religious observances. At one stage everyone was a Polish-American, a Greek-American, or a something else-American. There were no un-hyphenated Americans. Everett C. Hughes told the writer that when, as a student, he went to work in Chicago during a university vacation, his fellow workers asked, 'What are you?' He replied that he was an American, like his parents and grandparents before him; but this answer was not acceptable. 'American' was not an ethnic identity and everyone had to fit into some ethnic category. Eventually they decided that he was an Englishman! In such circumstances it is more reasonable to regard Negroes as one minority like all the others. Yet ethnic distinctions among the Whites have not retained their strength in successive generations, and these divisions have tended to close up more rapidly than the racial gap. Other objections to the conception of Negroes as an ordinary ethnic minority in American society can be advanced. They will be considered later. The present argument is that, where ethnic alignments run counter to class alignments, they hinder one kind of social fissure from opening up; where they run in the same direction, they make the cleavage deeper. It is further asserted that class differences acquire a different character and significance in the city in comparison with the smaller rural community, and that they may easily exacerbate problems of race relations.

FROM SOUTH TO NORTH

In Chapter Seven it was held that the colour line had been able to swing round in the South only because urbanization and economic change permitted a Negro upper class to establish itself in a superior position without making any Whites directly subordinate to it. Part of the price the Negro upper class pays for its position is social isolation. Myrdal recorded his impression: 'this tiny upper group of the Negro community often lives in a seclusion from white society which is simply extraordinary and seldom realized by white people. Measured in terms of the number of personal contacts with white people, there are Negro doctors, dentists, teachers, preachers, morticians and druggists in the South who might as well be living in a foreign country.' He quoted another author who thought a new type of Negro had appeared; such people 'own their own homes, so the white landlord does not see them; they carry insurance with a Negro insurance company, so no white collector comes to the door; their groceryman is a coloured man; they travel by auto rather than by street car or train; as a rule they live in the segregated residence districts; their physician, lawyer, dentist, and often their banker is a Negro' (Myrdal, 1944: 645, 1370). This isolation of the Negro professional class in the South suggests a qualification of some of the customary views about the distinctive pattern of race relations there. It is said, for example, that in the North the Negro may get 'higher, but no closer', whereas in the South he may get as close as he likes provided he gets no higher. The Negro upper class does 'get higher', so intimacy is intolerable. It is said that the Northerners love the Negro race, but hate the individual, whereas the Southerners hate the race but love the individual. Yet Southerners feel no affection for the Negro upper-class individual. Even more notable, though, is the evidence that the paternalist pattern of intimacy no longer obtains even for lower-class Negroes in the South (and may never have obtained for more than a few servants). A series of sympathetic interviews with Negro youth in the South was notable for the almost complete lack of reference to intimate, personal, and friendly relations with white persons or families. Myrdal concluded: 'for the Negro youth growing up today in the Black Belt, both in cities and in the country, this old protective master-servant pattern seems to have almost entirely disappeared . . . in planning for future race relations in the South the factor of personal intimacy and friendliness between individual whites and Negroes upon the old patriarchal principle should be left out entirely as lacking in practical importance' (1944: 649).

Urban living entails an increase in the number and variety of casual contacts across the colour line for people of all classes, but it tends to reduce the number of personal contacts in which an understanding of other individuals can be acquired and developed. Casual contacts can easily reinforce a stereotype or highlight the more unattractive of a group's characteristics. Myrdal observed that the Northern white man, who formerly felt little prejudice against the few Northern Negroes and was inclined to idealize Negroes as part of his Civil War heritage, reacted unfavourably when the 'great migration' that started in 1915 brought thousands of illiterate, dirty, and poor Negroes from the Deep South. In three years, about half a million Negroes migrated to Northern industrial cities. The proportion of Negroes in the North who had come from the cotton-growing states (as opposed to the border states) shot up (Myrdal, 1944: 652; Walker, 1957: 456). In Chicago in 1910, a few Negroes had been scattered all over the city and they had been invited to many white houses as neighbours. The increasing number of Negroes flowing into the urban mould of social relations placed Negro-White relations on a categorical basis, in which personal attributes rarely overrode racial classification; Negroes were isolated in separate residential districts and there were few personal ties across the colour line.

Wartime conditions enabled Negro migrants from the South more easily to establish themselves in the Northern cities. Could they retain their position in harder times? Conflicting views as to the Negro's rights seem to have underlain the series of riots which broke out in 1919, though the incidents that set off the fighting may have been trivial. In Chicago, for example, one hot July day in 1919 a Negro boy swam across the imaginary line that was supposed to separate Negroes from Whites at a bathing beach. He was stoned. The incident led to a five-day riot which took at least thirty-eight lives, destroyed $250,000 worth of property, and left over a thousand persons homeless (Drake & Cayton, 1945: 65–69). Myrdal represents riots as the Northern and urban counterpart of the Southern and rural phenomenon of lynching, though there have been riots in Southern cities. Riots differ from lynchings in that they are not a one-way punishment but a two-way battle. Housing segregation, by concentrating Negroes in a few compact areas, makes it easier for them to fight back (Myrdal, 1944: 566–9). Comparative study of interracial disorders in the urban centres of the North suggests that violence is to be seen as a white response when Negroes have been applying pressure upon the traditional pattern of subordination (Grim-shaw, 1963: 288). In more recent riots it has been sections of the Negro community that have taken the initiative.

Between 1930 and 1936, about half the skilled Negro workers in the United States were displaced from their usual occupations. A third of them found unskilled work. In 1936, 36 per cent of the Negro males and 28 per cent of the Negro females in the urban labour force were un-employed – compared with figures of 21 per cent and 19 per cent for Whites. In Detroit, 60 per cent of the Negro male workers were un-employed. World War II brought about an increased use of Negro labour for skilled work in industry. The changes may be attributed to: (i) the continuing northward migration and urbanization of the Negro population; (ii) an increased demand for labour in the expanding defence programme; (iii) the influence of the federal government in penalizing discriminatory employment policies; (iv) the relaxation of discriminatory policies by organized labour (Walker, 1957: 458–9).

During the period when the United States was recovering from the Depression, and just prior to the country's entry into the war, a major study of the Negro in Chicago was carried through (Drake & Cayton, 1945). This research, published under the title *Black Metropolis*, is of additional interest because it was directed (in association with H. R. Cayton) by W. Lloyd Warner, who had been supervising the study of Natchez, Mississippi, discussed in Chapter Seven. Warner states that once the Mississippi research had developed the class-caste interpreta-tion, the question arose whether it applied in other parts of the country. Were there analytically separable systems of social class and colour-caste in the Northern cities? Was the pattern present in some modified form perhaps? What happened to the Negro community and to the social classes of the Negro in industrial and urban surroundings? When the Chicago study had been completed, Warner concluded that, while Chicago represented a great improvement in the status of the Negro, the type of status relations controlling Negroes and Whites remained the same as in Natchez and continued to keep the Negro in an inferior and restricted position:

'He cannot climb into the higher group although he can climb higher in his own group. Legally, he is permitted to marry across the colour line but there is very little intermarriage. The children of such mar-riages are always Negro and suffer, as do their parents, the restrictions and deprivations of the Negro caste. The rewards and punishments, the rights and duties, knowledges and advantages are unequally

distributed. In short, there is still a status system of the caste type'
(Drake & Cayton, 1945: 781).

Comparing Chicago with Mississippi, there had been a reduction in the
Negro's disadvantages with respect to public relations, but, on balance,
little change or even an increase in his disadvantages in private relations.
In the public sphere, the Negro enjoyed greater electoral power, more
freedom of association, greater equality in pay, easier access to
public education, less segregation in transport, parks, and public
facilities. Against this had to be set the greater segregation of dwelling
areas in Chicago and the continuing racial division of labour, so that in
respect of significant social contacts Negroes were more isolated. In
his later Munro lectures Warner placed slightly more emphasis upon
the 'encouraging signs of betterment', deducing that 'the position of
the Negro in Chicago is much better and far more like that of a white
than it is in Deep South . . .' (1952: 25).

Subsequent developments have shown that the changes caused by
urbanization on the Northern industrial pattern were more complex
than at first appeared: in some respects Negroes enjoyed greater advantages, in others less; it is not possible to put both material and moral
changes into the same balance-sheet and derive a simple calculation of
the overall gain or loss. It has already been suggested (Chapter Seven,
p. 161 above) that racial subordination in the Deep South has damaged
Negro personality structure to a lesser extent than has the Northern
urban way of life. Studies of the selection of dolls of different colour
by Negro children aged three to seven years reveal that, while the
children generally prefer the white doll, think the brown doll 'looks
bad', consider the white doll 'a nice colour', and in some cases identify
themselves with the white doll, these tendencies are stronger among
those attending Northern integrated schools than among those attending
segregated Southern schools (Clark & Clark, 1947: 169–78). As such
findings probably reflect the incidence of self-hatred, they are of wide
significance.

In the comparison of South and North, two aspects were given
insufficient attention in Warner's analysis: changes in the Negroes'
reference groups, and the multiplier effect of segregation in a complex
industrial social system when there is little foreign immigration. In
the first place, Negroes from the South may initially have found the
lack of 'Jim Crow' in public facilities to be exhilarating, but soon they
stopped comparing their position with that they had previously occupied
in the South. They contrasted their disadvantages with the privileges

enjoyed by Whites and experienced what has come to be called 'relative deprivation'. In the study of the American soldier it was found, for example, that soldiers in units with few promotions were *more* satisfied with promotion opportunities than were those in units with more promotions (Stouffer *et al.*, 1949, I: 250–3). People may overlook improvements in their own position if they become conscious of greater improvements from which others are benefiting. In 1954 the Supreme Court decision against segregated schooling suggested that the American Dream might, perhaps, be for Negroes as well; but changes in school segregation came only slowly. When, in the years following, Negro Americans became aware of the progress to independence of African nations, and of the respect and international attention paid to African leaders, the comparison they drew with their own almost stationary position became increasingly bitter (Isaacs, 1963: 288–93, 332–42). There was a marked rise in the price that had to be paid if the loyalty of many Negroes to the American social order was to be ensured.

In the second place, in a small-scale social unit in which a high proportion of people are acquainted with one another personally, there are factors that temper the harshness of categoric discrimination and maintain a certain, though limited, sense of equity. In a large-scale social unit the operation of discrimination is more inflexible and extensive. The proportion of superficial contacts is higher, and in such contacts racial placement is more significant. If new immigrant groups are coming in beneath the group that has previously been the chief sufferer from discrimination, the criteria evoking discrimination may change and the situation stay flexible; but when large-scale immigration ceases – as it virtually ceased in the United States from the time of World War I – and one racial distinction becomes of major importance, then rigidities develop similar to some of those of two-category systems. Myrdal emphasized:

'While Swedes, Italians, and Jews could become Americanized in a generation or two, and disperse themselves into the more anonymous parts of the city, Negroes were caught in their "quarters" because of their inescapable social visibility; and the real estate interest kept watch to enforce residential segregation. With residential segregation naturally comes a certain amount of segregation in schools, in hospitals, and in other public places even when it is not intended as part of policy. Personal contacts become, as a matter of course, more or less restricted to Negro neighborhoods. . . . Even the poor classes of whites in the North come to mistrust and despise the Negroes. The European immigrant groups are the ones thrown into most direct contact and competition with Negroes . . . the development of prejudice against Negroes is usually one of the first lessons in Americanization. Because they are of low status, they like to have a group like the Negroes to which they can be superior' (Myrdal, 1944: 601, 603).

The circle of segregation can be as vicious in the North as in the South. Perhaps its chief cause has been the Negro's marginal position with respect to employment. He has been 'last hired and first fired'. Although they comprise only 10 per cent of the labour force, Negroes recently accounted for 20 per cent of total unemployment and nearly 30 per cent of long-term unemployment. In 1961 only 50 per cent of Negro men (compared with two-thirds of white men) worked steadily at full-time jobs. From 1951 to 1963, the level of Negro male unemployment was on a long-run rising trend.

The psychological and social effects of this situation on working-class Negro family structure have been perhaps even more far-reaching than the economic effects. It has been harder for the Negro man to obtain continuous employment than for the Negro woman, but, when neither has a job, the failure of the male to serve as a family provider is underlined even further by welfare policies which (for good reasons) are implemented by social workers (normally women) who deal with the housewife. When the men are prevented by circumstances from assuming the responsibilities society ascribes to the role of household head, it is not surprising if they give up trying. In 1960 one-quarter of Negro households in the New York metropolitan area had a female head, in comparison with one in ten of white households. The illegitimacy rate among Negroes was fourteen or fifteen times that among Whites. There were not enough foster homes for Negro children in need of care; more children lived apart from parents and relatives; more lived in institutions. More Negroes lived in crowded houses; more had lodgers and other related and unrelated persons living with them (Glazer & Moynihan, 1963: 50–51). The infant mortality rate – often considered the best single measure of a community's health – was nearly twice as high for Harlem as for New York City as a whole. Similar – though less glaring – differences can be found on a national scale between Negroes and Whites and between urban and rural Negro populations. Moynihan concludes: 'In every index of family pathology – divorce, separation and desertion, female family head, children in broken homes, and illegitimacy – the contrast between the urban and rural environment for Negro families is unmistakable' (1965: 19).

One important qualification must be noted. While the family structure of working-class Negroes is highly unstable and becoming even more disorganized, that of middle-class Negroes seems to be growing steadily stronger and more successful. Middle-class families have fewer children than working-class families have, but middle-class Negroes have even fewer children than do middle-class Whites, suggesting a desire to conserve the advances they have made and to ensure that their children will do as well as or better than themselves (Moynihan, 1965: 29).

The breakdown of the working-class Negro family has led to a startling increase in dependency upon welfare relief. The proportion of families receiving assistance in which the fathers are absent because of desertion has risen from one-third to two-thirds since the end of World War II. The position of Negroes in Northern cities is getting not better, but worse. Only 4 per cent of Harlem's population are recent migrants from the South, yet the juvenile delinquency rate there is nearly two and a half times the city average. In Chicago in 1960, 44 per cent of the Negro residents were locally born and perhaps two-thirds of those over forty-five had lived in cities for over twenty years or more. Yet fully one-quarter of the Negro families were receiving public welfare assistance; Negroes accounted for 25 per cent of the city's population, but for over 80 per cent of the relief recipients. In Detroit, Negroes made up 30 per cent of the population but 80 per cent of the people on relief. Negro crime rates are also disproportionately high (Silberman, 1964: 33, 45–46). The Negro's position is deteriorating because long-term unemployment disrupts the family and deprives the young child of the sort of environment he needs if he is to develop his potentialities. Negro children drop out of school or fail to make progress. Negro youth in Harlem have, at the eighth grade, a median IQ of 87·7, which means that perhaps a third are returning scores perilously near to those of retardation. The IQ scores of both male and female children with fathers in the home are, at the lowest social-class level, higher than those of children who have no father in the home. Young people who grow up in these circumstances become incapable of holding a steady job. They have no self-confidence and cannot absorb setbacks. Minor irritants and rebuffs are magnified and instability increases. Narcotic addiction in central Harlem rose from 22·1 per 10,000 in 1955 to 40·4 in 1961. The absence or inadequacy of a father probably has a more disturbing effect upon boys than upon girls. Negro women seem to give their daughters more help and encouragement (perhaps to get their own back for the way they have been treated by men). Though almost twice as many white males as females attend college, until very recently there were more Negro women in college than men and there is much evidence that the women are the better students (Moynihan, 1965: 31, 35–44).

A recent national survey found that non-Whites suffered far more from the criminal offences of others than Whites did. Twenty times more non-Whites than Whites reported that they had been the victims of robbery; nine times more non-Whites than Whites had been the victims of burglary. A study in Chicago showed that crime tended to keep within racial boundaries. Although two-thirds of those guilty of assault were Negro males, if a white person was assaulted, the assailant was more likely to be white than Negro (United States, 1967: 39–40).

The weakness in family life, in community self-help, and in morale combines with both the expectation and the reality of discrimination to reinforce the social and economic vulnerability of Negro Americans. In most localities Negroes inherit the racial status of their parents as a matter of law or custom. In many places they inherit their economic status because the dominant group will not let them have any other. In the industrial cities there is no conscious enforcement of a colour line in this connection, but Negroes tend to inherit the economic status of their parents because their whole social background puts so many of them at a disadvantage in a highly competitive society. A new kind of colour line appears, though hardly anyone actively desires it. The danger of such inherited disadvantage in a competitive society is one of the lessons taught by the 1965 riots in Los Angeles. Unskilled Negroes are being increasingly set apart economically as an almost unemployable lower category within the urban proletariat. This tendency for the lines of ethnic group and social class membership to merge is likely to strengthen even further in the immediate future, for technological and market changes are reducing the demand for unskilled and semi-skilled labour and expanding employment in professional, managerial, clerical, and sales jobs, many of which require considerable education and training. These white-collar occupations account for no less than 97 per cent of the total increase in employment that occurred between 1947 and 1963. The professionalization of the labour force is proceeding apace, but Negro male workers are concentrated in the unskilled, poorly educated section of the labour market, where the squeeze will be strongest. (Negro women, on the other hand, have been holding their own in clerical, technical, and professional employment.) When the Armour Company closed its Oklahoma City meat-packing plant it provided a retraining programme for workers made idle by automation, but, of the 170 who applied, 110 could be given no retraining because they lacked the minimum skills in reading and mathematics. The Negroes' economic level relative to that of Whites has been falling. They made great advances during World War II and the boom years that followed, so that the median income of Negro families rose from being 37 per cent of that of white families in 1939 to 57 per cent in 1952. But by 1961 it had fallen back to 53 per cent and remained at the same level in 1962 and 1963 (Silberman, 1964: 40–42, 237; Moynihan, 1965: 25). Employment is coming to depend upon technical skills and paper qualifications to a much greater extent than it did at the time when the European immigrants entered the country. The fire under the assimilationist melting-pot was a belief in the benefits of unrestricted competition in which every individual had a fair chance. The European unskilled immigrant could compete on a basis of his willingness to work and to learn; he was not damned by the limitations of his schooling.

In the American cities of the nineteenth and twentieth centuries – or so Glazer and Moynihan convincingly argue – the ethnic group was not a mere survival of immigration but a new social form. Ethnic groups were interest groups, and the political organization of cities and states adapted to them (1963: 16–20). Sometimes the interests they represented overlapped greatly with class interests, and were therefore the more powerful, though the ethnic label often distracted attention from the class grouping. Class divisions were supposed to be foreign to America, but ethnic organization was expected and respectable. The Negroes were unable to utilize the ethnic framework as the other groups did, because the events of the past had prevented their acquiring the same sense of group belonging. In the South it had been to the advantage of the upper category of Negroes to keep the lower one divided. Negroes were sufficiently Americanized (e.g. in language) and at home in the country for this to hinder their developing any group organization. Successful Negroes were offered a prospect of a certain social acceptance provided they dissociated themselves from the unsuccessful. Consequently, Negroes did not develop the patterns of community leadership and philanthropy which were characteristic of other ethnic groups (on the ineffectiveness of Negro community organization in Chicago, cf. Wilson, 1960: 5). The middle class was confronted by a range of Negro social problems too oppressive to constitute a collective challenge. Not that the upwardly mobile group has been very successful in developing its own strength: in 1950 there were 4,026 Negro doctors in the United States – only 600 more than in 1910, when most Negroes lived in the rural South; in 1950 also, but 1,450 lawyers and 1,800 dentists were Negro (Silberman, 1964: 69).

The failure of the Negro middle class to make the same progress as the entrepreneurial and professional people in the European immigrant groups to some extent reflects the Negro group's more exposed psychological position. Social advancement has required that members of this group dissociate themselves from the black masses and subscribe to the values of the groups with whom they have to deal or whose acceptance they seek. This has led many to identify themselves with the white propertied class and to acknowledge its criticisms of the Negro, yet they are never able to make this identification complete for in too many situations they are liable to suffer discrimination on account of their racial status. The late E. Franklin Frazier presented a sharp criticism of certain features of the beliefs and social life of the new Negro middle class. He represented the often exaggerated stories about the extent and importance of Negro business activity as a social myth kept alive because it suited people's interests. It was 'one of the main elements in the world of "make believe" which the black bourgeoisie has created to compensate for its feelings of inferiority in a white world dominated by business enterprise'. Whites had encouraged the myth because it distracted Negroes from their grievances; its acceptance by Negro leaders reassured the Whites that these men were enemies to radical political doctrines (Frazier, 1957: 129–45). The black bourgeoisie, he said, had neither linked itself to the genteel tradition of the small Negro upper class deriving from the free Negroes of pre-Civil War days, nor developed elements from the folk culture of the Negro masses. Its historical forbears were the Negro slaves and servants in white households, who saw the white man in the home but never when engaged in the serious matter of business. As a consequence they devoted much time and their meagre resources to trying to carry on a form of 'social life' similar to the Whites'. The new middle-class's feelings of inferiority and insecurity gave rise to a pathological struggle for status within the isolated Negro world, much of which revolved round balls, clubs, and social occasions. 'Playing, then, has become the one activity which the Negro may take seriously.' The preoccupation with present social display is the greater because many middle-class Negroes have good cause to fear competition from Whites when many patterns of segregation are weakened. They oppose segregation in respect of accommodation and public facilities but benefit from it in that a Negro professional man may be able more easily to build up a Negro clientele and a Negro teacher may be able to obtain a post with lower educational qualifications than would be required in a white school (1957: 162–91). The chief weakness of this study is its failure to make clear that the behaviour

Frazier holds up in contempt is not characteristic of the whole Negro middle class and that many men and women who, by occupation or income, could be ascribed to the class – like the author himself – did not make their peace with the social order or seek the transitory compensations of conspicuous consumption. More recently, Negro urban communities have been replacing the old pattern of a few omnicompetent representative leaders with a new middle-class cadre of professional leaders serving agencies with specific objectives, but their power is weakened by the apathy of working-class Negroes and by the defensiveness springing from the desire not to reveal or widen the divisions within the Negro population (Wilson, 1960: 295–310).

URBAN TRENDS

Negro Americans of the twentieth century have been caught up in two migrations: from South to North and from country to city. In 1910 eight Negroes out of ten lived in the eleven states of the Confederacy (see Table 1, col. 3, p. 132 above). Only 1,900,000 lived in other states. But the minority grew more rapidly – to nearly 4 million in 1940 and over 9 million in 1960 – roughly half the Negro population of the United States. At the same time, the Negro population growth within the old Confederate states was only 12 per cent to 1940 and 9 per cent to 1960. In the same Southern states, in 1910, 7 per cent of Negroes lived in cities; in 1940, 21 per cent; in 1960, 41 per cent. In the other states the urban move was equally massive: by 1960 Negroes constituted 14 per cent of the population of New York, 23 per cent of Chicago, 26 per cent of Philadelphia, 29 per cent of Detroit, 35 per cent of Baltimore, 34 per cent of Newark, N.J. (since risen to over 50 per cent), 54 per cent of Washington, D.C., 37 per cent of New Orleans, 38 per cent of Atlanta, and 37 per cent of Memphis. In Los Angeles County the Negro population over the period 1940–60 rose from 75,000 to 464,000. The proportion of the Negro population living in cities is now higher than the proportion of Whites who are urbanized. These twin movements have been stimulated and guided, on the one hand, by the mechanization of Southern agriculture and the reduced economic attractions of farm work relative to industrial employment, and, on the other, by the desire of urban white people to move out to the suburbs when they have the income to make this possible. Thus the twelve largest cities between 1950 and 1960 lost over two million relatively successful white residents and received, in return, almost as many Negro immigrants (Silberman, 1964: 7, 29–32).

The spatial expansion of the Negro population in the larger cities

Table 4   U.S.A.: Negro population by region, 1910–1960

Region	Negro population			Percentage Negro		
	1910	1940	1960	1910	1940	1960
NORTH	1,027,674	2,790,193	6,474,536	1·8	3·7	6·7
New England	66,306	101,509	243,363	1·0	1·2	2·3
Middle Atlantic	417,870	1,268,366	2,785,136	2·2	4·6	8·2
East North Central	300,836	1,069,326	2,884,969	1·6	4·0	8·0
West North Central	242,662	350,992	561,068	2·1	2·6	3·6
SOUTH	8,749,427	9,904,619	11,311,607	29·8	23·8	20·6
South Atlantic	4,112,488	4,698,863	5,844,565	33·7	264	22·5
East South Central	2,652,513	2,780,635	2,698,839	31·5	25·8	22·4
West South Central	1,984,426	2,425,121	2,768,203	22·6	18·6	16·3
WEST	50,662	170,706	1,085,688	0·7	1·2	3·9
Mountain	21,467	36,411	123,242	0·8	0·9	1·8
Pacific	29,195	134,295	962,446	0·7	1·4	4·5
U.S. TOTAL	9,827,763	12,865,518	18,871,831	10·7	9·8	10·5

Sources:

Figures for 1910 are from U.S. Bureau of the Census, *Negroes in the United States 1920–32*; for 1940, from U.S. Bureau of the Census, *Sixteenth Census Reports, Population*, Vol. II; for 1960, from U.S. Bureau of the Census, *U.S. Census of Population: 1960, General Population Characteristics*, *U.S. Summary* (Washington, D.C.: Government Printing Office, 1935, 1950, and 1961).

KEY MAP SHOWING THE
REGIONS AND GEOGRAPHIC DIVISIONS OF THE UNITED STATES

NYC — NEW YORK CITY
DC — DISTRICT OF COLUMBIA

THE WEST REGION STATES OF ALASKA AND HAWAII ARE NOT SHOWN ON THESE MAPS

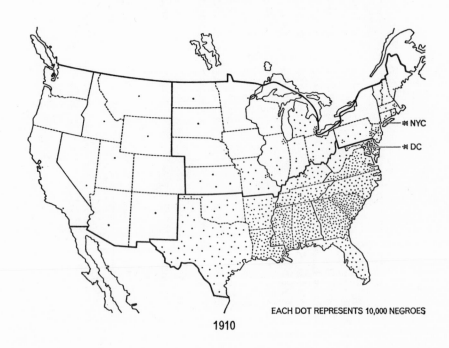

EACH DOT REPRESENTS 10,000 NEGROES

1910

north and from country to city, 1910–1960

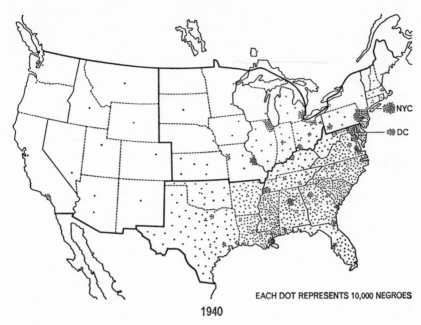

EACH DOT REPRESENTS 10,000 NEGROES

1940

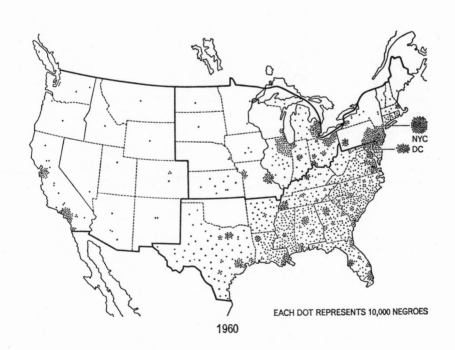

EACH DOT REPRESENTS 10,000 NEGROES

1960

follows roughly similar patterns. One universal rule is that residential concentrations are segregated. A second is that, once an urban district begins to swing from predominantly white to predominantly Negro occupancy, the change will continue. In some Eastern cities it is possible to maintain low-cost housing projects on an interracial basis as long as non-Whites do not exceed 20 per cent of the total residents. Once this point is reached, Whites will not remain in, or move into, the project. Elsewhere the 'tipping-point' may be somewhat higher (for recent analyses suggesting some modification of these tendencies, see Taeuber & Taeuber, 1965). A third generalization is that the pattern of Negro residential movement is from the core of the city outward; it also tends to be one of expansion into areas of high residential mobility, so that the in-migrant Negro and the out-migrant white populations have comparable social characteristics in respect of educational attainment, rate of unemployment, room-crowding, home-ownership, and white-collar employment. The sheer cost of suburban housing excludes Negroes from many suburban areas. When house prices are insufficient to keep them out, there are legal devices and building regulations which can be manipulated to achieve the same effect. One builder told an interviewer that he would very much like to sell suburban houses to Negroes but that to try to do so would ruin him economically: 'If I sold just one suburban home to a Negro, the local building inspector would have me moving pipes three-eighths of an inch every afternoon in every one of the places I was building; and moving a pipe three-eighths of an inch is mighty expensive if you have to do it in concrete.' Such practices can be combined with social and economic pressures upon white owners of older houses and upon real-estate brokers to prevent sales to Negroes (Grodzins, 1958: 5–8).

To understand the strength behind discrimination in housing it is necessary to appreciate that the reasons why a particular community excludes Negroes are not the same as the reasons why particular residents are unwilling to sell to Negroes. One house-owner may wish to sell to a Negro but be restrained because it would seem an act of treachery to his neighbours or because he feared that, were he to do so, other residents might attack him or his interests or his dependants. When Whites about to leave a city have sold their houses to Negroes, 'poison-pen' letters have, on occasion, been sent to their employers in their new workplaces. It is even possible that a majority of residents might wish to see an end to exclusion, and yet no change of overall policy would result. Just as some prophecies are 'self-fulfilling', so if sufficient people believe that their community is opposed to a certain policy then to all intents and purposes their community is so opposed. To explain the stability of the group norm it is necessary to allow for ignorance of others' private feelings, for a tendency to let the most conservative people hold up development favoured individually by many others, for an unwillingness to break with custom on account of an abstract principle with ramifying implications, for the exercise of economic and political power in defence of the *status quo*, and so on. The social norms also vary. In nationwide surveys by the National Opinion Research Center it was found that white Southerners were more willing to accept Negroes as neighbours than to permit Negro youngsters to attend school with their children. The reverse was true in the North. A Southern housewife said: 'I don't mind living beside them, but I don't want the children to go to school with them. I just don't.' A Northern housewife, interviewed on the same question, said: 'I approve of them. They should have the same rights. But I wouldn't want to live with them' (Hyman & Sheatsley, 1956). The frequent use of ethnic labels reinforces the implicit notion that because people look different they are different in other respects; housing segregation adds further reinforcement and a vicious circle is created. When a pattern of residential segregation along class lines has been established, people fear that, if minority members move in, the neighbourhood will go down. If minority members do obtain houses, other residents may take fright, with the result that prices fall and further people are attracted who might otherwise have been excluded. The self-fulfilling prophecy operates and the neighbourhood does lose prestige. In the South, residential segregation has not been customary. Servants have lived on the premises. Association at school, on the other hand, has possessed greater significance than in the Northern cities with bureaucratic school systems and more mobile populations. Nor should it be forgotten that some people profit from the maintenance of segregated housing patterns. Slum properties in an ethnic ghetto can bring in a surprising income. Real-estate speculators may try 'blockbusting' – installing a Negro family in a white block, whipping up anxiety, then buying properties cheap to resell later at a fat profit to incoming Negroes. Important, though, as these rational sources of aggression may be, it is not suggested that they constitute a sufficient explanation of hostility such as that shown to the Negroes who marched in Chicago in 1966 in protest against residential exclusion. Other fears and frustrations (such as have been alluded to in Chapter Twelve) seemed to contribute substantially to the hatred displayed on these and similar occasions.

United States sociologists have hitherto paid more attention to the determinants of individual sentiments about neighbourhood exclusion than to the determinants of social norms. Myrdal noted that when white Southerners were asked to rank, in order of importance, various types of discrimination, they consistently presented a sequence on the following lines:

1. The ban upon intermarriage and sexual relations between Negroes and white women.
2. Customs regulating interpersonal relations, e.g. restrictions upon interracial dancing, bathing, dining, drinking, and the rules requiring deferential behaviour from Negroes.
3. Segregation in the use of public facilities such as schools, churches, and means of conveyance.
4. Restrictions upon Negro voting and political activity.
5. Subordination of Negroes in the courts, by the police, and in other public institutions.
6. Subordination of Negroes with regard to the securing of land, credit, employment, public relief, and other matters related to earning a living.

Whites, he said, would offer least resistance to the weakening of practices towards the bottom of this list; Negroes, on the other hand, were least concerned about removing discrimination in the spheres at the top of the white man's list and most anxious to acquire greater equality in fundamental economic rights (Myrdal, 1944: 60–61). In the early 1950s, a Cornell research team checked upon these patterns in a national sample of 248 cities. It was found that, with very few exceptions, Negroes in Northern cities of all sizes could try on clothes in department stores, sit in the same part of buses as Whites, use the same public rest-rooms, and sit among Whites in cinemas. They were often excluded from swimming pools, restaurants, churches, and hotels, and Negro men found it particularly difficult to get their hair cut in white barber shops. In the South, Negroes' use of most public facilities was clearly unacceptable. But there were puzzling variations. In 76 per cent of cities it was taken for granted that Negroes might use the same public rest-rooms as Whites, whereas in only 39 per cent was there equality of acceptance of Negroes to service in white restaurants. This finding is not consonant with Myrdal's idea that the order of discrimination is related to degrees of 'personal intimacy'. Is seating in the same restaurant so much more intimate than the use of the same toilet facilities? The source of resistance seems in this case to lie in apprehensions about the status implications of identification with Negroes. But the extent to which association with Negroes in a restaurant (as opposed to, say, in a hospital), will be regarded as detracting from people's status is likely to vary considerably. The research workers in fact concluded that the ordering of discrimination derived in large measure from functionally arbitrary historical circumstances (Williams, 1964: 126–8).

The evidence concerning patterns of discrimination underlines two general lessons very strongly: that urban societies are far from being closed systems in which all the parts are interdependent, and that the data on discrimination must be viewed within a framework of urban sociology as well as one of intergroup relations studies. These two lessons will be considered in turn. The first one revolves round the point that a change may take place quite peaceably in one city which would lead to bitter conflict in another. For instance, a recent study from the Boston area comments on the rising number of *self-integrators*, that is, Negro families who install themselves in the midst of white neighbours as Negro families. They do not imitate the 'black bourgeoisie' nor deny their Negro identity. In many cases their establishment in new neighbourhoods has had no effect at all upon property values or the composition of the area. The experiences of nine families are described: they found that some would-be sellers and bankers put difficulties in their way, but in nearly every case their new neighbours proved helpful and congenial (Hughes & Watts, 1964). There are also some notable discontinuities between situations of discrimination in the South. Where separate water fountains are provided it has been found that, if an 'out of order' sign is put on the white fountain, Whites use the other one without hesitation. A North Carolina humorist, Harry Golden, notes that White and Negro stand at the same grocery and supermarket counters; deposit money at the same bank-teller's window; walk through the same stores, and stand at the same drugstores. As long as both parties are upright, all is well; trouble starts when the Negro sits down.

'. . . here is the Golden "Vertical Negro" Plan. All the next session [of the state legislature] needs to do is to pass one small amendment which would provide only *desks* in all the public schools of our state – *no seats*. [Our children] are not learning to read sitting down, anyway; maybe standing up will help. This will save more millions of dollars in the cost of our remedial English course when the kids enter college . . .' (Golden, 1958: 121–3).

The idea is not really very far-fetched. In some towns, when Negroes have forced the desegregation of public libraries, the authorities have removed all seating-places and then carried on as before. Awareness of these inconsistencies has led some sociologists to argue that those concerned to improve racial relations should concentrate upon gaining the support of the leading figures in the community power structure; these people can more easily change the conventional definitions of social situations and manipulate the element of indeterminacy in the system (Dean & Rosen, 1955). Such an approach makes the assumption that the issues presented by intergroup relations are primarily strategic rather than moral; it tends to exclude from consideration the arguments for change that cannot attract support from conservatively inclined community leaders (McKee, 1958-59).

Residential segregation by race increased in the United States from 1940 to 1950 and the trend has almost certainly continued. Why this should be so cannot be explained in terms of individual sentiments; it must be examined within a framework of ideas about how social relations develop in cities. Of central importance is the consideration that, with increasing urbanization, the spheres of work and leisure become separated. As has been seen, Whites who oppose segregation at work may favour it in residence. Negroes may pass for white in their workplaces but return to live among Negroes. In the opening section of this chapter an attempt was made to show how such evidence could be interpreted as part of a more general trend. In line with the criticism of Myrdal's view (Chapter Seven, p. 163 above), it may be argued that urbanization leads to a greater compartmentalization of social life and hence to inconsistency in behaviour in different spheres. People are disturbed by inconsistency; therefore it is not surprising that different courses of action acquire cultural clothing so that they do not appear contradictory. Does Myrdal's thesis about a moral dilemma hold with respect to housing segregation? A study in the New York metropolitan area of white residents' beliefs about 'Christian' or 'fair' behaviour, and their personal sympathy towards practices of neighbourhood exclusion, revealed clear contradictions (Friedrichs, 1959). In everyday life, however, people follow their social trails without worrying much about consistency. Silberman is in no two minds about it:

'The tragedy of race relations in the United States is that there is no American Dilemma. White Americans are not torn and tortured by the conflict between their devotion to the American creed and their actual behaviour. They are upset by the current state of race relations, to be sure. But what troubles them is not that justice is being denied but that their peace is being shattered and their business interrupted' (1964: 10).

The same writer also sees racial and urban problems as intertwined. Once, he says, American cities continually took in newcomers, not only using them, but equipping them to take their places as fully participating members of American society. Bringing people into the mainstream of national life has been the principal business, and the principal glory, of American cities. It is so no longer. Now, instead of serving as the incubators of a new middle class, faithful to the American Dream, the urban slums breed one of the most divisive forces in modern America. Negro leaders can look forward to the day when their people will constitute a majority of the electorate in many of the large cities. City planners try to tempt back the white middle class; programmes of urban renewal have been bitterly described as 'Negro removal' because they have entailed the demolition of previously Negro blocks without the provision of any alternative housing. The biggest racial problems arise within the urban context, and solutions will have to be sought within that context.

THE NEGRO DILEMMA

W. E. B. DuBois, the Negro scholar and protest leader, believed that no thoughtful Negro American had failed at some time to wonder, 'What, after all, am I? Am I an American or am I a Negro? Can I be both? Or is it my duty to cease to be a Negro as soon as possible and be an American?' (quoted Essien-Udom, 1964 edn.: 139). This has been the root of the Negro's dilemma. So thoroughly was his African heritage extirpated and so extensively has he absorbed American ideals that it is difficult for him to reject his Americanness. Yet discrimination makes him feel a Negro and impels him to reject the culture that defines Negro characters as inferior. He is too much of each to be able easily to deny either, but which identity is gaining ascendancy? Which represents the best long-run bet for the man in doubt? This dilemma has been growing more acute during the last thirty years; the tension between the alternatives has increased, but the odds on each of them have not changed very much since DuBois wrote, over sixty years ago. Much of the trouble springs from the way in which, in American life, the Negro identity is defined in negative terms of rejection. The alternative of Americanism seems to imply the denial and, indeed, contempt, of Negro-ness. It is hard for a group to build an organization and a common loyalty on shared misfortune without a counterbalancing faith in its own value. If, instead, the idea of being Negro could be made elevating and positive, then the dilemma could be solved. Being Negro would come first and the imperfections of Americanism would matter less. Moreover, such a transformation might be within the Negro's power, as the redefining of American values is not.

This way of looking at things is the Negro angle onto what Myrdal thought a paradox – that assimilation into the mainstream of American life seemed to demand of the Negro that he disparage almost everything that had been characteristic of Negroes: 'It is the very absorption of modern American culture which is the force driving the Negroes to self-segregation to preserve respect' (1944: 657). The more Negroes learned, the more they resented discrimination and became disposed to withdraw from national society. It has been suggested that, since Myrdal wrote, this conflict has become greater. On the one hand, it seems that Whites will more readily accept Negroes if they respect them as Negroes rather than as people who have assimilated (however illogical this may seem to the rationalistic observer). Thus it has been reported that Negro respondents who manifest a militant group pride 'are significantly more likely to have inter-racial social contact than non-militants and, conversely, those who score high in group self-hatred clearly tend to have less contact than those who are relatively lacking in self-hatred'. In other words, it is the individual who identifies positively with his racial group who is likely to have interracial contact (Williams, 1964: 295–6). On the other hand, it seems that the difficulty of reducing the social and economic gap between Negroes and Whites has adversely affected Negro morale so that self-hatred and negativism among Negroes are more widespread. The Negro clergyman leading a campaign for the two-way bussing of children to achieve an even balance of Negro and white children in New York schools stated, in a radio interview, that if his timetable for integration was not adopted, he 'would rather see the public school system destroyed'. So strong a concern with minority interests is reminiscent of South-East Asian pluralism. Some Negroes seem to have stopped worrying about who or how many people should get hurt, provided only that there is change. When people are desperate – as they seem to have been in the Los Angeles riots – it is more difficult to make ethnic self-segregation a preliminary to the cultivation of self-respect.

The idea of a Negro dilemma can constitute an illuminating perspective from which to study Negro institutions, for it should be remembered that there have been many of these, particularly in the religious sphere. The variety has been great enough for trends of adaptation and selection to be discernible. Churches have been the more important in the Negro community because of the multifunctional character of religious organization. They have been able to provide instruction, recreation, spiritual comfort, and mutual assistance, and to constitute an elementary form of political organization in circumstances which restricted outright political activity. With northward migration and the lessening of overt white pressure, it became possible to establish secular associations explicitly concerned with the political defence of Negro rights. Being more narrowly based, they could not obtain anything like as much support from the Negro masses as the churches could. Both kinds of institution were caught up in the racial dilemma: the churches, because Christianity was identified with the white man; the political movements, because they were fighting white men by appealing to the legal system of white men. In seeking to have segregation laws over-turned, Negro objectors claimed that they were incompatible with the Constitution – a document drawn up by white men acting without thought for Negroes. As long as segregation was legal, the struggle for desegregation was a fight against the political humiliation of the Negro people; but it implied a desire for integration, ignoring any possibility that being Negro could become, for some people, a condition to be desired, or that the Negro community might have distinctive interests requiring recognition and defence. Thus Negro protest 'trapped itself into a rhetoric where it is forced to conjoin its quest for the individual rights of Negroes to the premise that any co-existence among Negroes *qua* Negroes is degrading (because segregated) and hence a deprivation of equal rights' (Brotz, 1964: 72). The fight against segregation com-mitted Negroes more firmly to Americanism; its setbacks stimulated the contrary pulls and the dilemma got worse.

European immigrants to the United States had a choice whether they should struggle with, or against, the forces of assimilation. The Negro American has not had this choice. The circumstances of his importation deprived him of his distinctive culture, making him seem a beggar at the white man's table and thereby strengthening the tendencies to reject and scorn Negroes. The absence of an African heritage, as Brotz argues, makes his assimilation *more* difficult. Only by creating a Negro com-munity which the individual Negro is free either to identify himself with or to reject can Negro leaders build a counterweight to white power (1964: 122–7). Such a community must be spiritually or politi-cally equal to the white community, if not in numbers at least in claim-ing to be a group of the same order. One such solution is to assert that Negroes constitute a distinctive nation; that they should therefore rule themselves, controlling their own social, economic, and political institu-tions. If this is so, what sort of institution might succeed in converting the masses to the doctrine and organizing them so that it might become a reality ? Both political associations and religious cults have moved in this direction, but it seems that success demands some combination of both approaches.

The only Negro political movement to have won mass support was nationalistic. It was the Universal Negro Improvement Association, created by Marcus Garvey, a Jamaican who started organizing in New York in 1917. In two months he won 1,500 followers. Five years later, the Association may well have had a million members or more. Garvey's objective was not the advancement of Negroes in America, but the redemption of Africa for 'Africans at home and abroad'. America he regarded as, in effect, a white man's country. All white men were fundamentally alike. One man might abstain from joining the Ku Klux Klan, but only because he was too cultivated; under the surface he had no more respect for the Negro than any other white man. Garvey assailed the fair-skinned Negro leaders, 'near Whites', he called them, urging upon his followers the desirability of keeping pure their Negro blood. When Europe was inhabited by a race of cannibals, he said, Africa nourished a race of god-like black men, masters of every art.

Garvey's movement developed a religious wing also. Bishop G. A. McGuire told the faithful to 'erase the white gods from your hearts'; by 1924 a picture of a Black Madonna and Child was to be found in many Negro homes and the worship of a Black Christ was openly advocated. But, as is well known, Garvey's Association crashed in ruins. His African schemes were thwarted. The Black Star shipping line which was to transport Negro Americans to Africa foundered in legal and commercial entanglements. Other Negro leaders put pressure on the federal government and Garvey was convicted for using the mails to defraud in the promotion of stock in the Black Star line. After a period in jail he was deported (Cronon, 1955). Recently, his widow claimed: 'after Marcus Garvey had returned millions to Africa spiritually, he had done his work' (Essien-Udom, 1964 edn: 73). He did not persuade the majority of Negro Americans to identify themselves as Africans or to think of Africa with pride, but he did effect a transformation in the conceptions of many thousands and pioneered the way for later movements.

The religious cults have often been bizarre in comparison with the straightforward character of Garveyism. Apparently as early as 1900, Negro preachers were travelling through the Carolinas teaching that Negroes were the lost sheep of the House of Israel. During the period 1919–31 there are records of at least eight Black Jewish cults in Harlem (Brotz, 1964: 1, 10). A 'Moorish Science Temple', teaching that Negro

Americans were really Moors and Muslims, was founded in Newark in 1913. Heretical forms of Christianity have appeared, such as the Father Divine Peace Mission which began to attract substantial numbers in New York towards the end of the 1920s, and the United House of Prayer, led by Bishop C. M. Grace, which has won greater support from Southern Negroes than most of the Northern innovations. Father Divine's followers believed him to be God. He died in 1965. Bishop 'Daddy Grace' claims to be 'co-equal with Jesus' (Fauset, 1944: 26). If the claims other prophetic leaders make for themselves are less extensive, they are still large by mundane standards. The number and variety of such movements have been remarkable. The non-Christian ones have been nationalistic, telling their hearers that the so-called Negroes are really Moors, or Muslims, or Jews, etc., and that only when they understand their real identity and history can they fulfil themselves. They have an answer to DuBois's question, 'What am I?' They offer an explanation of how Negro Americans have come to be what they are, and promise that when Negroes realize their identity they will, as by magic, be rid of their handicaps. They attack the conventional Negro leadership, claiming that, since their people are different from the Whites, they want no integration. The so-called Negro must set himself free. Thus Brotz refers to 'the auto-emancipatory impulse which is the fundamental drive behind all these nationalistic sects – Black Muslim, Black Jewish, Black Coptic' (1964: 59). The deviant Christian cults are not nationalistic, but they too address themselves to the spiritual problems of the Negro masses. The numerical strength of any movement, nationalistic or not, seems to depend upon its power to regenerate its followers, rooting out their feelings of inferiority; upon its ability to harmonize the material benefits that can come from heightened morale and mutual aid with the immaterial uplift of an absorbing faith; and upon its adaptation to the tensions in the class structure of the Negro community. (Garvey, for example, gained favour among the masses by praising blackness and deriding the mulattoes, but the antagonism this attitude evoked probably outweighed the value of the support it brought him.)

Most important of all, it must be remembered that, as Max Weber showed long ago, the worldly success of a religious doctrine may stem, not from the purposes of the teachers, but from quite unintended consequences of their teachings. A good illustration of this is the prohibition of sexual activity to members of the Father Divine Peace Mission. Why, at an early stage of the movement, before he had ever taken the name 'Father Divine', its leader should have made this stipulation, it is

impossible to say. A writer who has attempted to reconstruct the movement's development surmises that, watching the disintegration of a
similar church, Father Divine insisted to his followers not only that he
was their sole god but that they must abandon every loyalty except the
one to himself. Parents and children, husbands and wives, had to give
up any thought of one another. Divine was their father, therefore all
members, of whatever generation or race, were brothers and sisters.
Sexual relations between them would be incestuous, because incompatible with their spiritual family relations. The prohibition on sex also
enabled Father Divine to cope more effectively with the racial division
and its tender spots. He abandoned an earlier doctrine of black superiority in favour of one that declared there 'really is no race'. 'Colour' and
'race' are delusions fostered by bad Americans. There are white as well
as Negro members of the Mission, and Whites as well as Negroes live
in the 'heavens' that are its residences. To permit both racial intermingling and sexual relations would make the movement very vulnerable to
its critics and rivals; it would probably disrupt the movement itself by
distracting members from concentrating upon their god. The ban on
normal sex therefore makes possible interracial equality, which seems
important in offering Negro members an escape from the outside world
(Harris, 1954: 21–22, 92–93).

How is it that Father Divine's followers have been able to accept the
denial of sex? It can be argued very convincingly that the sickness of
life as a Negro in the Northern ghettoes has been most acute in the
sphere of family relations, and that no movement will attract many
followers unless it can offer some remedy for it. The doctrine of absti-
nence is such a remedy, even if a drastic one. Life has been difficult for
Negro women, unable to depend on their menfolk as reliable bread-
winners or husbands. It has been even more difficult for men, so often
denied by circumstance the opportunity to act out their roles in the
manner that not only their wives but they themselves expected. The
women's domestic domination only exacerbated their husbands' sense
of failure, their drunkenness and faithlessness. The men who joined the
Father Divine Peace Mission could stop worrying about being men and
about the obligation to earn money for their wives and children. It was
easier to give up wives and children when they were reminders of an
inferior racial status and an inability to meet the demands of the male
role. It was easier to give up sex when experience had shown that they
could not support their wives or children. Father Divine offered his
male followers a role they could fulfil and their love for him seemed
the greater because it sublimated their sexual drives. These same

circumstances also explained how Negro women could accept the ban on sex. Father Divine, who decreed physical purity for them, became a more satisfying protector-provider than their men had ever been. In the ecstatic 'vibrating' by which the women members displayed their love for Father Divine, they seemed to find a substitute for normal sex (Harris, 1954: 92–107). Thus the consequences of the no-sex ban, whatever its original purpose, greatly assisted the material progress of the movement. How much property and wealth have been accumulated cannot be calculated, but they are certainly considerable. Furthermore, by offering a completely different way of life, the Mission has been able to take in and regenerate social outcasts, giving them a new faith which helps their recovery from bodily ills.

It can similarly be argued that the appeal of the Black Muslims (who call themselves the Nation of Islam or Temple of Islam) is due, to a considerable extent, to the way in which their organization meets needs unmentioned in statements of its objectives. This aspect of its work has been overshadowed in the attention paid to its racial militancy. The aims of the movement have been summed up by a Muslim minister as: 'To get the white man's foot off my neck, his hand out of my pocket and his carcass off my back. To sleep in my own bed without fear, and to look straight into his cold blue eyes and call him a liar every time he parts his lips.' Religious values, concludes one of its students, are not part of the movement's basic appeal and are of secondary importance (Lincoln, 1961: 27). Whether this interpretation can be fully supported by evidence is open to question. Garveyism was a political movement which extended into the religious sphere. The present Black Muslims are representatives of what has been an eccentric religious movement, deriving additional force from its political appeal and its political functions. It marries the political and religious approaches to the Negro's predicament more successfully than any previous movement and balances them more equally.

The political programme of the Muslim movement is kept rather vague, perhaps because the leaders are not clear about it, perhaps in order to preserve flexibility, perhaps for fear they might be charged with sedition. They are definitely opposed to integration, which they regard as a white man's stratagem that the North wants to force on the South to improve America's image abroad. Why integrate with the white man's world when that world is so corrupt that it is heading for disintegration? The Muslims ask instead for 'some good earth, right here in America, where we can go off to ourselves'. Usually the territory envisaged is 'two or three states'. The basis of their argument is that the white man took the land from the Indians and the Negroes have laboured there for four centuries – three under legal slavery – without ever having been given a share in the country (Lincoln, 1961: 87–97). In line with the view that they form no part of the American nation, the followers of Muhammad are enjoined not to vote in local or national elections: 'We do not believe in voting Negroes to go to Washington and serve the white people. We want our own nation and if Negroes are good enough to serve in Washington, they should be good enough to serve in their own nation' (quoted Essien-Udom, 1964 edn.: 291). They criticize the N.A.A.C.P. (National Association for the Advancement of Coloured People) for seeking integration in contradiction to the Negro's true interest. It is described as 'the Big Niggers' organization. It was founded by whites, the bosses are whites and Jews . . .' Its leaders are said to be in love with the white race. Muslims express contempt for the 'sit-ins' in restaurants and stores, maintaining that by such measures Negroes are merely forcing the white man to let them put more money in his pocket.

The Nation of Islam is led by Elijah Muhammad, a small yellow-complexioned Negro who started building up his organization about 1932. It grew slowly at first, but gathered momentum in the 1950s. In 1959 a hostile TV documentary programme attracted publicity, bringing it the condemnation of many Whites but the support of many Negroes. In the early 1960s there were 5,000–15,000 registered followers, at least 50,000 believers, and a much larger number of sympathizers (Essien-Udom, 1964 edn.: 84). At the close of a very sensitive study of the movement, one author states his conviction that:

'Muhammad's ideological pronouncements, which are popularly termed "black supremacy", are aimed at purging lower-class Negroes of their inferiority complex. The "real" rather than the "ostensible" enemy of the Nation of Islam or of the Negro masses in general, is not the white people *per se*, but the Negro himself – his subculture, his image of himself and of his "place" in society, his attitude toward white people, and his idealization of all that is white. From the point of view of all black nationalists, the Negro can never be really free until he has purged from his mind all notions of white superiority and Negro inferiority and then ceases to despise himself and his group' (Essien-Udom, 1964 edn.: 361).

How does Muhammad attack this inferiority complex? He tells his followers that they are not 'Negroes' – that this is only a label the white man has placed upon them to make discrimination more convenient.

Muslims prefer to be called Black Men; the others they refer to as 'so-called Negroes'. Entry into membership is marked by the discarding of a slave-name (i.e. one deriving from the name of the owner of an ancestor of the member) and by rebirth into a new identity with a new name followed by the letter X to denote both the change ('ex') and the mystery of destiny. Often the change in religious status makes possible a change of personality: Muslims have been able to regenerate criminals, alcoholics, and narcotic addicts more effectively than all the welfare agencies (Lincoln, 1961: 82–83, 108–10). It is doubtful whether any purely political movement could have as great an impact in this respect. The Nation of Islam represents the 'chosen'; God is considered to be a black man and Elijah Muhammad is his Messenger. The white race are devils who were created 6,000 years ago by a black scientist, who grafted them from the black people but in so doing bred out their humanity. The white man is said to have a smaller brain and less physical strength than the black man. A Muslim minister teaches: 'Heaven is a condition. That condition the white man now has . . . Negroes have their hell right here in the United States.' This doctrine leads to the view that at judgement day 'the last shall be first'; so Muslims believe that this time of reckoning is imminent. However, on other occasions and for other audiences Muslim speakers reject any suggestion that it is sufficient to wait for compensation in another life. They appeal to those who want to see some action in the here and now, and repudiate the withdrawal characteristic of the lower-class Christian cults. Yet it should always be remembered that Black Muslim doctrines are sufficiently diverse to enable them to be presented in many different guises.

Like the Father Divine Peace Mission, the Nation of Islam offers answers to the problems of family living in the Negro ghettoes. Men are told that they are the heads of their families; that they have authority over their womenfolk, but must respect and protect them – especially from white men. The women are enjoined to address their husbands as 'sir'. The sexes are segregated in the Temple and in the parochial schools. A convert explained: 'Islam makes you appreciate black women. I appreciate my black women by showing them my politeness at its most highest degree [sic]. This applies mostly to Muslim women because a regular Negro woman would not understand such politeness. She would think I was a queer if I tried to treat her nicely and respect-fully.' This pattern of behaviour has a strong attraction to men whose male ego has been subordinated in the customary way of life of the Negro family in the slums. Conversely, the respect paid to feminine virtues gives Muslim women a new sense of self-respect and dignity (Essien-Udom, 1964 edn.: 99–103). The women are especially advised not to imitate 'the silly and often immoral habits of the white woman', which can only wreck their marriages and spoil their children. Modesty, thrift, and service are recommended as their chief concerns (Lincoln, 1961: 83). The nationalist cults all break with the stereotype of the Southern Negro by discouraging emotionalism and enforcing a dignified form of worship. In the Commandment Keepers Congregation of the Living God (the 'Black Jews' of Harlem), independent testimony and various forms of enthusiasm expressed during services are condemned as 'niggeritions' (Brotz, 1964: 35). The Muslims adopt a similar view. But one effect, in varying degree, of all these movements – and of many Protestant churches in European history – is to bring, through their religious beliefs, a seriousness and steadfastness into their followers' lives, which make them better workers from an employer's standpoint. The way of life encouraged by Muhammad enshrines moral values reminiscent of the New England Puritans and commends habits associated with respectable middle-class living. Formality in costume and entertaining, sobriety in taste, composure and restraint in demeanour – these are characteristic of the Muslim style. Even those Negroes who do not approve of other aspects of the movement profess 'great respect' for the conduct and discipline of its adherents' private lives. The Nation assists its members to strive for traditional American middle-class values while maintaining their identity with the Negro community (Essien-Udom, 1964 edn.: 136–9, 230–1, 362). Thus one of the unintended consequences of the religious doctrine is upward social mobility and therefore a deepening commitment to America.

Essien-Udom concluded that there were three discernible groups among those who joined the movement. The first consisted of people who wanted to lead a 'better' life, subtly competing with the Negro middle class. In the second were those who were dissatisfied with the status of 'blackness' in America and disgusted with conventional Negro leadership. The third were people who had consciously searched for a politico-religious solution to their lack of any satisfying identity; the elite of members belonged to this group (1964: 96). The Negro masses, he says, are not clamouring for any return to Africa; they want to improve their conditions in America. They believe their aspirations are comprehended in America's profession of freedom, justice, and equality for all men without regard to colour, race, religion, or creed. They may agree (as Lincoln concludes) that the white man will never of his own accord accept non-Whites as his equals, but they believe that pressure can bring results. As Brotz says, in a way the Muslims have already answered their claim for territorial autonomy: 'It is the Negro section of the city from which they cannot easily escape and which they intend to make livable' (1964: 113). In the Negro ghetto, men feel estranged both from the larger society, which scorns them, and from their own racial group, which they themselves despise. The exhortations of leaders like the Rev. Martin Luther King have had little influence in these neighbourhoods. But the black nationalists, by building up the idea that being black is something to be cherished, are able at least to check the feeling of alienation. The Muslims have been more successful than most in this respect. Their movement responds to the class division within the Negro population. Lower-class Negroes are attracted to the idea of the successful middle-class Negro, but they are also repelled by it because their circumstances make it extremely difficult for them to climb the class ladder. The Muslim movement reflects the increasing status consciousness and conflict in the lower class and questions the conventional Negro leadership. It is an attempt to alter the balance of power within Negro society (Essien-Udom, 1964 edn.: 348, 351–65). Any interpretation of the Black Muslims or other black nationalist movements is unreliable that fails to locate them in the context of Negro urban life or to see how they are oriented to problems within as well as outside the Negro community.

CHAPTER FIFTEEN

Patterns of Social Rejection in Great Britain

The racial situation in Britain presents several features which make it of particular interest for comparative study. The settlement of appreciable numbers of people from Africa, the West Indies, India, and Pakistan is relatively recent. Though British colour values have been heavily influenced by the country's imperial experience, this immigration has occurred in an era of decolonization when people have been much more conscious than before of the international implications of racial issues. Immigration has brought into Britain groups of men and women from very different countries who, because they all had brownish skins, were lumped together by the British as one class of people – 'coloured', although each group initially may have had more in common with the British than with the other groups. This situation draws attention to the significance of psychological and cultural determinants of racial 'visibility': because someone is coloured it is assumed that he is different; indeed, being coloured seems to be more important than whether or not he is really different – for if he is treated as different he will become different. In this respect the white man creates the role 'coloured man', and all those who are forced into it develop common interests. But race relations in Britain present a rather complicated case for comparative analysis because the implications of racial difference cannot be disentangled from the aspects that stem from the newcomers' handicaps and reception as immigrants. Some students of the subject have emphasized the perspective of immigration more than that of race, and others the reverse. Which matters most depends upon the question to be answered, but to a limited extent it can be helpful to review the evidence in terms of these two perspectives.

THE IMMIGRATION PERSPECTIVE

In comparison with most of the countries so far considered, or even with most European countries, English society from at least the latter part of the seventeenth century up to recent times has shown a remarkable homogeneity. The determinants of class, status, and power in different regions have been very similar and have derived from national institutions. Centralization was facilitated by a relatively dense distribution of population over a small territory, and by powerful common socializing agencies for the higher classes (such as boarding schools and the armed services). There was created an almost uniform pattern for social mobility, and a chain of social groups which dictated nationally relevant standards of social acceptance and rejection. Distinctive provincial patterns of speech and behaviour persisted, but a provincial who wished to claim status outside his own region was well advised to study the national norms of civility. The influence of the standard-setting groups gave English society a particular homogeneity in the eyes of outsiders and enabled it to assimilate new groups from within and without its boundaries. The pressure to conform to English conventions was felt by Scots, Welsh, and Irish as well as by people from overseas. In the eighteenth century at least, coloured people do not appear to have been the objects of any severe prejudice. Many of them then were domestic servants and they seem to have been popular with the lower classes, though, from 1764, there are references critical of Negro-white mixture which appears to have been relatively common. A historian of the domestic servant comments on the 'almost complete absence of racial bias', and states: 'the continental servants encountered widespread hostility while the colonial servants were everywhere cordially embraced' (Hecht, 1954: 56). Other evidence does not contradict this estimate of the significance then attributed to skin colour.

Any host society demands certain standards of newcomers before it accepts them. If the standards are set too high, the newcomers do not try to meet them. If they are set too low, the newcomers do not place much value upon the acceptance accorded them. Yet if the standards are set very high, but still within reach, and the rewards of acceptance kept proportionately attractive, then those who win acceptance will take over the values of the social system and its norms concerning mobility will be perpetuated. In England, the standards were set very high. The successful immigrant or social climber could not gain admittance to the upper social reaches in his own lifetime, but, by sending his children or grandchildren through the right socializing agencies, he could ensure that his lineage would have a place inside the magic circle. The power of attraction exerted by this mode of signalizing and reinforcing worldly success can be seen in the Anglicizing of the Irish, Welsh, and Scottish middle classes as reflected in the social bases of their nationalist movements. It can be seen in the relative ease with which leading members of the rising commercial and manufacturing classes of the nineteenth century were absorbed into the middle and upper classes. It can be seen in the acceptance, by many of the working class, of the ideal of the 'gentleman', and in the political strength of the Conservative party in that class. It can be seen, too, in the process by which Jewish families have become established in the most exclusive social circles and in the way in which immigrants – including some coloured men – have become remarkably English in their habits and outlook; the modifications in their behaviour have exceeded any mere defensive colouring and have represented a personal commitment to the values of English social life. The English were not prepared to accept Jewish citizens as constituting a political minority but obliged them to seek political influence through the existing parties, with the result that their Jewishness has been a relatively minor factor in the policies of the many Jewish parliamentarians.

Fundamental to the homogeneity of English society was the inclusiveness and consistency of the class system. The more inflexible estate-like forms of social differentiation characteristic of many continental nations had early been subdued by the demands of economic adaptability and state policy. All the chief ways in which people can be distinguished – wealth, pedigree, education, accent, demeanour, etc. – acquired values on a common scale of class differentiation so that, to a significant extent, a prestige-conferring title could be set off against a lack of 'presence' and so on. No one criterion – like complexion in a racially divided society – took absolute precedence (cf. Banton, 1965: 175–8). It is contended here that, when those social differences that have implications for a person's claims to status can be reduced to a common denominator of social ranking, the society will be more easily able to assimilate immigrants without putting its own social patterns under stress.

That people can climb from one social class to another does not necessarily weaken class differences and may indeed strengthen them, for the socially ambitious person strives to obtain the distinguishing characteristics of people in the higher class, and when he has 'arrived' he is apt to draw the line all the more sharply between those who have those characteristics and those who do not. Thus opportunities for climbing may only increase social selectiveness.

A homogeneous society tends to have a different view of human nature from that found in a more heterogeneous one. Margaret Mead came to the conclusion that 'the English regard culture as something that is very slowly and painfully learned, and while less often critical of foreigners than Americans are, do not expect them to become English'. Enlarging upon this distinction between the two nations, she wrote: 'the Americans see the world as man-controlled, a vast malleable space on which man builds what he wishes, from the blueprints he has drawn, and when dissatisfied simply tears the structure down and starts anew.' On the other hand, 'the British see the world as something to which man adapts, in which he assumes no control over the future, but only the experienced foresight of the husbandman or the gardener, who plants the best seed and watches over the first green blades' (Mead & Métraux, 1953: 19, 404). When the various parts of society are, or seem to be, highly interdependent, the members are more ready to think of society itself as a kind of organism – though, in general, the organic conception is more characteristic of the middle- and upper-class outlook.

The network of relations that constitutes a society is maintained by a series of common understandings as to the rights and obligations of the persons who occupy positions in it. Social life can be seen as a sequence of relationships, each of them being defined by the rights and obligations of the parties to it. Norms of conduct in given situations may be explicitly stated in the law of the land, or they may be implied in the conventions to which people subscribe. The continuance of social life is dependent upon the observance of these norms by the members of the society, and sanctions are applied against those who infringe them. In heterogeneous societies little is left to chance, and a high proportion of the norms by which conduct is to be regulated are made explicit; if not in the constitution of the law, they are explicit in public discussion and are consciously taught to newcomers. Britain, as could be expected of a relatively homogeneous society, seems to rely heavily upon implicit norms and tacit modes of instruction. Britons, naturally, would be the last people to be aware of this, but American sociologists, accustomed to the strenuous efforts made to turn varied groups of immigrants into patriotic American citizens, are frequently impressed by this aspect of British social life. Thus George C. Homans writes: 'Any society rests on a set of unstated assumptions, British society more than most: that is, indeed, its strength' (1962: 115). Similarly, Ruth Landes observed that Americans favour the explicit statement of aims, but 'here in Britain you have an ancient community of populations bound by the wordless understandings that root in long acquaintance . . . in Britain people do not have to be told how to act, for they are as one long habituated organism' (1952: 751).

These implicit notions about the proper way to behave, about the unannounced rights and obligations of people in particular positions, constitute the unspoken language of British social life. The Briton expects those with whom he has dealings to observe an unspoken code. If they deviate from it he will indicate, by his tone of voice, a change of manner, or by silence, that he does not approve the turn events are taking, and if the other party fails to take the hint the relationship may be broken off. Seen from this standpoint, strangers are people whose behaviour cannot be predicted or controlled. Because the codes of behaviour are implicit in conventions, Britons are aware of them more in breach than in observance: a variety of things are 'not done', but there are relatively few positive regulations. Reliance upon the unspoken language is greater in the social strata near the top end of the scale than in those at the bottom. In the higher classes, acceptance of certain tacit standards is such that the minor social neglect of a person of inferior prestige can be a powerful sanction, and the more urgently someone seeks to climb the scale the more sensitive will he or she be to such pressures. In the rougher working-class districts, like those in the neighbourhood of the docks, sanctions of this sort have little effect, and the resort to violence or the support of the police is far more frequent as a means of obtaining conformity, and then to the more elementary obligations rather than to social refinements. Thus it is easier for the stranger to gain social acceptance in the lower social categories.

The extent to which a stranger is accepted by groups higher up the prestige scale will be partly dependent upon the extent to which he has learned their ways. Only then can they interpret his behaviour accurately and convey to him fairly easily their own sentiments. The intuitive understanding of others – which makes mutual control possible – is achieved more rapidly when a person is dealing with people who have a background similar to his own; he knows that they will see matters in much the same light as he does and that there is no great danger of his being misinterpreted. This consideration illuminates the reserve shown in dealings not only with strangers of another nation but also with people of another social class. An Oxbridge girl student showed her understanding of this (even if her assumptions were questionable) when she explained: 'the people who don't speak King's English don't want to mix with us; they stick together. It's natural for us to associate with members of the same class; it's more *comfortable*' (Webster, 1954).

Much the same social pattern, in an American context, can be discerned in the novels of J. P. Marquand.

The structure of social relations in England has naturally influenced people's ideas about policies in the group relations sphere. In the past, English society has been relatively successful in admitting small numbers of newcomers and making Englishmen of them. This philosophy explains why many well-informed people – Jews and coloured men included – have doubted the value of any direct attack on those whose doctrines promote racial hatred or of any positive programme to develop goodwill towards ethnic minorities. For many years, people were inclined to ignore the existence of a coloured minority in Britain or to belittle the significance of the problems arising from its presence. The political and institutional structure was not geared to ethnic divisions and so, when racial tensions became an electoral issue, it was to the acute embarrassment of many politicians. In the 1964 general election, for example, candidates who came out strongly against coloured immigration gained votes in certain constituencies. Some electors were ready to vote against the immigrants. It was largely a negative sentiment. They were not, as they might have been in the United States, voting for their own ethnic group. A homogeneous society can tolerate some kinds of differences, such as the English appreciation of eccentricity and individual idiosyncrasies; others are not so disruptive that it cannot reduce them in the process of assimilation to national and class norms; but some forms of human difference are incompatible with English culture and can be valued only for their own sake. This may explain why Englishmen seem to think it better that non-Englishmen should concentrate upon being good specimens of their own kind. As Santayana said, the Englishman 'is relieved if only natives will remain natives and strangers strangers, and at a comfortable distance from himself' (Santayana, 1922: 32). Such an outlook lends itself easily to the assumption of inbred diversity when it may not be justified. Popular knowledge of human biology in Britain is at a low level, but, even when due allowance is made for simple ignorance, there seems to be an undue proclivity for the explanation of variation in terms of heredity. A recent comparative inquiry concluded that 85 per cent of Britons in a national sample exaggerated the significance of heredity, and that there was a higher propensity to hereditarian thinking in Britain than in France or the German Federal Republic (Tumin, 1967). The metaphors of 'blood' and 'stock' have bitten deep into the English vocabulary and are unthinkingly but daily recapitulated by teachers, dramatists, journalists, and politicians.

The British attitude towards foreigners has been the subject of many mildly disapproving jokes. Even when at its most contemptuous it probably did not quite come up to the idea that 'niggers begin at Calais', nor did it lump together all foreigners as being a single category. There is an appreciable gradation. Thus Ruth Landes referred to the Negro as 'relegated to the far nether end of that great range wherein the Briton strings the places of all the non-Britons of the world' (1952: 751). Whereas some Britons distinguished between the African and the Indian (at the very least), and landladies went by skin colour, being more willing to have the fair-complexioned man than the dark, many English people in the early 1950s were unable to make distinctions between the various groups that made up the category 'coloured'. Thus the writer remembers being told at this time by a Nigerian that he had been called in at his workplace to act as an interpreter. He found that he was expected to explain something to a Pakistani. So he said a few sentences in his mother-tongue, to satisfy the white man, and then tried to do the real explanation by gestures and single words. There were many such incidents to suggest that most Britons found differences of skin colour so striking that they did not notice the ways in which some coloured people differed from others, or the respects in which some Whites and some coloured people shared common characteristics and interests. Only the small proportion of Whites who were in regular contact with the newcomers stopped thinking of coloured people as a homogeneous category.

It seemed reasonable to suppose that, as more English people gained experience of the immigrants, and as the latter differentiated themselves by the kind of response they made to the host society, so the tendency to think of coloured people as fundamentally alike would give way before the other tendency to rank all foreigners according to degrees of strangeness. There were some striking historical parallels between the current reception of coloured people and English reactions to earlier immigrant groups of white skin. Hostility to Flemish and Huguenot immigrants in the sixteenth and seventeenth centuries had at times been virulent. A Frenchman in London in the mid-eighteenth century could be subject to more violent abuse in the streets than any African was likely to encounter two hundred years later. As the similarities between the different immigrations seemed more illuminating than the differences, the writer utilized this perspective when presenting his first study of race relations in Britain. This was an account of social relations in a dockland area in the East End of London, where some three to four hundred Africans and West Indians had settled. It was preceded by a

short review of some of these earlier influxes, including that of the East
European Jewish immigrants towards the end of the nineteenth century
(Banton, 1955). Implicit in this presentation was the belief that the
important differences between the immigrants and the hosts were the
cultural ones; these would be overcome in the course of time; differences of skin colour would take a little longer to become unimportant.
Nevertheless, this interpretation explicitly rejected any conception of
assimilation as a one-way process of absorption, stressing the value of
organization and social control within the immigrant community as
helping the whole group to put itself in a position that would give the
individual members some choice as to the extent to which they wished
to identify with a coloured community or seek acceptance in a white
one. The 'coloured quarter' where the immigrants resided, interspersed
among relatively poor working-class Whites, was pictured not as a ghetto,
but as a transition area for new arrivals and as a social centre for coloured
immigrants living in more isolated circumstances (1955: 93–94, 235–8).

The immigration perspective was also utilized, rather more emphati-
cally, in a later study, based primarily on research during 1956 and
1957, of a London neighbourhood with a high concentration of West
Indian residents. The author initially regarded her work as a study of a
racial situation but, 'very early in the course of field work, it became
clear that this general approach was inadequate and usually inapplicable
or misleading in the British setting . . . the immigrant-host framework,
on the other hand, seemed to offer a far more satisfactory mode of
interpreting the dynamic processes which were clearly taking place on
both sides'. The study concluded with the suggestion that the West
Indian migrants and their children will follow in the assimilationist
path of the Irish immigrants. A minority will push upwards into the
white-collar strata, but the bulk will be absorbed into the working class
and will disperse from the original centres of settlement. 'This adaptation and advancement will lead to close social relationships with the local
population, and probably to increased intermarriage and to an at least
partial biological absorption of the West Indians in the local population'
(Patterson, 1963: 6, 399). Before attempting any evaluation of such an
interpretation, it will be advisable to consider how the white population
responded to the newcomers in the years before colonial immigration
became a significant political issue.

BRITISH BEHAVIOUR TOWARDS COLOURED IMMIGRANTS

In the early 1950s it frequently seemed that British people were uncertain about what constituted the most appropriate mode of behaviour

towards coloured immigrants. Thus, the norms that Britons thought should govern their actions in public relations with coloured people (i.e. as representatives of Britain) differed from their private opinions expressing their more personal sentiments. For example, when interviewed, employers in East London often appeared to believe that immigrants ought to be given a fair chance and that it would be bad for the country – which had special responsibilities towards overseas Commonwealth citizens – if unemployment were to be unduly high among immigrants. On the other hand, they believed also that it was uneconomic to employ immigrant workers if suitable white workers were available, and they felt a greater responsibility towards their 'own folk'. Their roles as employers were geared to private interests and there was a conflict with their public views as citizens. To the employer, a coloured workman appeared as a risk, for he was unlikely to have the background of experience that a white worker had and he might need extra supervision. He was a risk, too, in that if he were taken on other workers more valuable to the concern might be dissatisfied. After all, any departure from the accepted pattern is a risk. But if all the employers drew the same conclusion, a series of private decisions added up to a public policy, and to one that was contrary to the country's national values and interest.

The coexistence of two sets of rather different norms created a situation in which a very small variation might result in the adoption of quite a different course of action. One story that illustrates this very neatly described how a coloured man applied for a vacancy with a London firm, only to be told that it had been filled. He did not believe this and asked his white wife to telephone the firm. She did so. She told them – with notable sagacity – that she had a coloured lodger who was a good workman, and asked if they would consider him. They agreed to do this; so the coloured man put on a different suit of clothes, went back, and was given the job. The writer had sufficient experience of similar incidents to accept the truth of this story. Frequently, the slightest recommendation, a testimonial from an unknown source, or an appealing look, was enough to tip the scales and secure something for one coloured man that would be denied to another. How are such changes of front to be explained ? In the example above, the employer's attitude towards coloured people can scarcely have changed during the hour or so between the two meetings. What presumably changed was his definition of the situation. People respond to situations not as they really are but as they are thought to be. This employer, it would seem, recognized two norms: that he should take no unnecessary risks when recruiting employees, and that the coloured man deserves a fair chance. At first he knew nothing about the applicant and felt the first obligation to be the more weighty. Later, he defined the situation as one in which the risk counted far less than the obligation to help a deserving stranger. Or the question of civic responsibility may not have entered at all: the employer may simply have come to feel that the applicant was as good as any he could expect. In either event, the norms did not change, nor the employer's commitment to them. The additional information, slight though it was, sufficed for him to define the second situation as being sufficiently different from the first for another course of action to be appropriate.

Some coloured men were good at turning this uncertainty to their own advantage. They quickly acquired an understanding of the Englishman's point of view, learned by which signs he guided himself, and found how to win his approval. There were other immigrants who combated the stereotyped conception of the coloured man by demonstrating that they were different. Commonwealth students in London used to wear, almost invariably, their college scarves or other items of university dress in order to distinguish themselves from working-class immigrants and from stowaways who, in the postwar years, were often in the news, their behaviour attracting unfavourable comment. Former seamen in Manchester who wished to be taken for students might sport such scarves, and even illiterates could be seen with folded copies of *The Times* or *Manchester Guardian* under their arms. In the dockland districts, also, some of the older coloured residents dressed carefully in well-brushed dark suits and took a rolled umbrella on their walks so that they would not be mistaken for newcomers who did not know how to behave themselves. But if some immigrants were clever in exploiting the uncertainties of interracial norms, others regularly evoked hostility. They would make demands that were considered unreasonable and thus invited reproof; in their resentment they only repeated their demands the more insistently until they became incapable of sustaining harmonious relations with Whites. When definitions of appropriate behaviour vary, the possibility of stage management arises. Not only may strangers try to present their own case in the best possible light, but others may step in to help them. The term 'sponsorship' has been suggested for this form of support (Collins, 1957: 247). Immigrant groups in some towns – including, in some cases, coloured groups, and, in others, groups such as the Hungarian refugees who came after the uprising of 1956 – have been more favourably regarded because they have been sponsored by prominent citizens. The local people's definition of how the newcomers should be received has been shifted over towards the more sympathetic side of the spectrum of possibilities.

Norms may be changed by strategies of this kind, but a more important influence upon them is the overall change in what groups have to offer one another – in the balance of social transactions. The norm of public behaviour towards coloured people in Britain was greatly influenced by the imperial-colonial relationship. Britons were pictured as a more advanced nation, materially and morally superior to 'the coloured man'. In their capacity as imperial mentors, Britons laid claim to special rights in their dealings with their colonial wards. But there are no rights without obligations, and their superiority – real or illusory – imposed on Britons the responsibility for helping backward people to advance. The assumption of this responsibility justified the claim to special rights. In the early 1950s, relationships that conformed to the old notion of imperial trusteeship were still often regarded as providing the correct setting for dealings with coloured men. Students from the colonies sometimes found that English people who offered hospitality were imbued with what seemed to them a patronizing attitude. In the past, colonials had received tangible benefits in return for the deference they paid to the white man, and the transaction had been for a time advantageous to both parties. After World War II, with the mounting pressure for colonial independence, students from the African territories, at least, no longer accepted the old pattern of relationship. They did not thank Britons for being concerned about their spiritual welfare. They did not accept invitations from people who enjoyed reminiscing about their colonial service and how much the natives had loved them. People who invited them to tea but were shocked at the idea of their guests' inviting their daughter to college dances were apt to be told that they were hypocrites. Rather than be parties to a relationship based on the old norms, the coloured colonials often preferred to withdraw from it altogether (Banton, 1959: 93–94, 144–54). For a relationship to acquire a customary character it must be acceptable – temporarily at least – to people on both sides.

More than one set of norms may appear relevant in a situation, and there may therefore be an area within which definitions can be manipulated, but the individual is not completely free in his choice of which norm to follow. Each choice elicits a measure of social reward or punishment, depending upon whether others consider that the correct course of action has been followed. During the period under consideration, concern was often expressed about the unfriendly reception accorded to colonial students who might, as a result, return home full of bitterness towards the British. In this context, a girl who went dancing with coloured students under approved auspices might be seen by her parents as doing a grand job entertaining the poor lads so that they would not go home disgruntled – and keeping them away from the Communists (who, at one time, were believed to meet every boat bringing new arrivals)! If, however, she failed to persuade others to put this construction upon her activities, she ran the risk of being regarded as a girl of depraved taste, and of suffering consequently in her reputation.

Earlier, the public norms concerning behaviour towards coloured people were suffused with expectations of philanthropy and patronage. These have been much reduced, but the discrepancy persists between the norms governing the public and private spheres. There is scarcely any racial discrimination in respect of civic rights or in the administration of public services. Legislation now makes it an offence to practise such discrimination in places of public resort (including restaurants, public houses, dance halls, swimming pools, and vehicles or vessels used for public transport). Discrimination enters more readily into decisions of a private character. Granted that the Englishman does not accord social acceptance to many other Englishmen of different class, religion, regional origin, etc., what hinders the pattern of relationships with coloured people being assimilated to that obtaining among Whites ? The writer has already argued in Chapter Thirteen that the answer to such questions depends upon the determinants of social distance.

There, a distinction was used between a person's willingness to be exposed to a stranger and his willingness to be identified with a stranger. Avoidance of coloured men because of apprehensions about how they might behave was represented as consisting of fears that, as strangers, they might not know the correct norms of conduct, that English people would have difficulty in communicating to them the conventional expectations, and that the sanctions upon deviant behaviour were inadequate. The Englishman, like anyone else brought up in a relatively homogeneous society, knows that awkward scenes may develop when people do not share the same customs and cannot take one another's hints; he feels the embarrassing scene acutely and avoids getting into a situation in which it might arise. Most people, at one time or another, have had the experience of wishing to help someone, but of being afraid that if they did so the other person might become too demanding and it would be difficult to shake him off. The occasional case illuminates a general principle. People fight shy of entering into the sorts of relationship which they feel are likely to get out of control. Their view of how such relationships should be conducted may be unfair to the other party, but it governs their behaviour nevertheless. The Englishman could not be sure that his intention of extending to the coloured man only a limited acceptance would be recognized or understood by that man. He could not be sure, if he was kind to a stranger, that the man would appreciate the limits of his gesture and not take advantage of his kindness. He did not want to be suddenly confronted with an inordinate demand for help, financial or otherwise, which was all too possible, since so many coloured people experienced difficulty in finding work and housing. Consequently, where the Englishman suspected that the coloured man was unfamiliar with the customary English patterns of conduct, he preferred to keep clear of possible entanglement.

The conventional understandings about behaviour depend in part upon foreknowledge of norms and in part upon people's ability to read the signals that others automatically transmit to them. A person can usually tell from others' responses whether they think he is behaving correctly or going astray. If they indicate disapproval, he modifies his conduct. Newcomers have difficulty in reading the signals. A Nigerian nurse, exasperated by English reliance on tacit understandings, complained:

> 'I was warned by friends about English landladies. The English characteristic of a landlady is not saying what she means and so misleading the lodger into feeling everything is all right until it blows up unexpectedly . . . English people are most difficult to deal with even though at most times they appear quite charming. They say "yes" when they don't mean "yes". They are very polite, and this may mean that there are fewer quarrels, but sometimes in life it is a good thing to speak directly. However, since English people speak the same way to each other, I don't think you can accuse them of hypocrisy; evidently they understand each other.'

In some relationships the implicit norms are of little account and it does not matter if the other man is unfamiliar with the culture. Though it is usual to address the bus conductor in a particular manner, to say 'please' and 'thank you', this is not essential. The rights and obligations of conductor and passenger are explicit in the law and the company's regulations, and, if either party infringes them, well-understood remedies are available. Nor need the landlady be greatly worried for herself about taking in a coloured student; if he offends she can give him notice. The employer need not be greatly concerned lest a coloured workman should prove lazy, for he can always discharge him. In such cases the representative of the host society commands an adequate sanction against an infringement of a norm.

A stranger is someone who does not know the local norms and cannot read the usual signals, or who refuses to conform and cannot be brought into line by the normal sanctions. He is not necessarily a foreigner. The small child, the wealthy eccentric, the tramp, the village idiot – all are strangers to their society in that their behaviour cannot be predicted with any confidence, and the various informal pressures that usually produce conformity make little impression upon them. To a certain extent it does not matter whether a newcomer is ignorant of the norms; if others believe him to be ignorant they will avoid him. In English eyes the coloured man often appeared more of a stranger than he really was. His different complexion and modes of behaviour made him stranger than anyone else. Ruth Landes has suggested that: 'The Englishman's remarkable stress on personal and social discipline is deeply affronted by the Negro's incomprehensible and perhaps theatrical zest and spontaneity. To him this is possibly the most alien element of all, counting as irresponsibility and naked indulgence.' The coloured man represented more than ignorance of the local customs; he exemplified the indiscipline feared by the English. He was the archetypal stranger.

Avoidance of coloured people at this time could therefore be attributed to ideas about their likely behaviour. It could also, in some situations, be interpreted as an unwillingness to be identified with them. In English eyes someone with a dark complexion was given a lower position in the class scale than someone otherwise identical, but with a light complexion. As Kenneth Little – who first formulated this line of analysis – observed, ' "colour" has the same socially inferior connotation as English spoken ungrammatically, or without the "correct" accent, or of wearing a muffler instead of a collar and tie' (Little, 1952: 45). A dark skin colour subtracts a few points from a person's claim to social rank; it can be counterbalanced in some situations by the acquisition of extra points for education or wealth, and in this way colour differences can ultimately be absorbed into a more complex system of rank and differentiation. Some societies of Latin America and the Caribbean have moved far in this direction. The lower prestige accorded to members of a dark-skinned grouping induces social distance because, to a considerable extent, a man's social standing depends upon the sort of people with whom he associates. If he wants to be respected he will be careful in his choice of friends, preferring people higher up the scale to people lower down, or to those whose status might be questioned.

Little's thesis has in this respect been substantiated by a study of the colour discrimination displayed by London landladies. They were principally worried that their peers and neighbours might conclude that they accepted coloured lodgers only because they could not get Whites (not an illogical inference, given the general pattern of preferences). An inability to attract white lodgers implied that the lodgings were of too poor a standard for the price asked and therefore reflected adversely on a landlady's social standing (Carey, 1956: 68–71, 154–6). One research worker disputes that colour values are being generally absorbed into the system of status differentiation, maintaining that dark-skinned people can have 'no recognized place in British society at all' (Richmond, 1958: 368; 1961a: 65). It is true that the 'colour-class' proposition has not yet been tested for a full range of social situations and that important discontinuities may well exist, but a recent study did find that far fewer Indian upper-class than middle-class students in Britain reported experience of racial discrimination (Singh, 1963). Another consideration to be borne in mind is that some fears about identification with coloured people may spring from beliefs about their being sexually uninhibited and from unconscious associations with blackness, and that these fears may be more potent with respect to some relationships than others.

People whose social position is secure relative to those about them will not be so concerned should any unusual associations of theirs become the subject of local tittle-tattle, but social climbers will be sensitive to informal sanctions. Women are, in general, more dependent upon the approval of their neighbours than are men, for, as has been said, the man's status is the status of his job, the woman's the status of her home. The landlady's house is both her job and her home, so she is more exposed than most to the threats of gossip. At their workplaces, many men associate with persons of inferior status while on the job; they do not have to worry about being identified with them, for their role in the organization legitimizes the association. When it is a question of a man's choice of companion at the lunch table in the canteen, or of his partners in leisure-time activities, however, this source of social distance is more potent. The same argument may also explain some of the discrimination against Jews in Britain. Whereas sporadic discrimination occurs in services such as insurance, credit, advertising, and hotel accommodation, the principal sphere of regular discrimination is the exclusion of Jews from suburban golf, tennis, and other social clubs. Many of the members of these clubs will, individually, have harmonious relations with Jewish people; admission or exclusion is a problem of group relations. In the social status scale, a Jewish background usually counts as a slight disadvantage, one that could easily be outweighed by some advantage in another sphere were not Jews thought of as a homogeneous group. It is argued that if one Jew is admitted to membership of a club, it will be difficult to exclude other applicants and the club will be flooded by 'them'. Because it is socially permissible to disparage Jews the club comes to appear less 'exclusive' (note the two senses of the adjective). Such forms of social distance stem from fears of identification with the outsider more than from fears of exposure to him.

Often, people are more afraid than they need be of the likely effects of their associating with coloured people. Excessive caution is more easily understood when it is seen how unusual behaviour can permit uncharitable or malicious interpretations. Ignorance of what other people really feel can also be seen as necessary to some social patterns, in imposing a brake upon over-rapid change. As has already been argued, patterns of social distance do not depend upon individual attitudes in any one-to-one fashion. They are customary practices interrelated with shared beliefs and the operation of varying social institutions. When English people said that others of their acquaintance would dislike working with a coloured man, or having one as a neighbour or visitor, they were saying that they believed this to be contrary to the group's norms of conduct, *not* that each one of them, individually, was opposed to such relationships. Many of them would have been willing, in certain circumstances, to risk infringing what they believed to be the group norm, but there were few incentives encouraging them to try.

Ignorance about others' sentiments may evoke the self-fulfilling prophecy: the belief that people disapprove may discourage experiment as much as actual disapproval does. There is a system of interrelations such that the consequences of someone's action may be quite contrary to his or her intentions. In the sphere of intergroup relations the sociologist may be able to make a better prediction than most people of what the consequences of a particular action will really be. For example, in the 1950s many female students at British universities felt strongly opposed to racial discrimination. They wished to demonstrate to coloured students that not all white people were hostile or prejudiced. So at a university dance a girl might wish to give evidence of her convictions by showing that she was not unwilling to dance with a coloured student. Other coloured students would notice this and conclude that here was one girl who was not prejudiced. Some of them who had asked English girls to dance would have been turned down and might well have found the experience a little humiliating. They would therefore be more inclined to seek dances from a girl whom they defined as un-prejudiced in this connection. Therefore, the girl who initially wished to show only goodwill might find she was receiving a whole series of invitations to dance from coloured students. She might well find it more difficult to say no to them than to white boys. If the white students saw her dancing with one coloured student after another they might infer that she did so from choice, and refrain from asking her to dance with them. In this way she could become typed as a 'coloured man's girl' and find it more difficult to get attention from white students. Nor might that be the full extent of her troubles, for, since many of the coloured students came from countries where women were allowed less freedom, they might interpret her behaviour as a desire for greater intimacy than she actually wished. The difficulties associated with knowing the norms and reading the signals, and the effectiveness of the available sanctions, would then come into play. Thus a whole series of predictable consequences which were no part of the girl's original intention might flow from her initial willingness to dance with a coloured man.

THE RACIAL PERSPECTIVE

Some writers have implied that the position and prospects of coloured immigrants in Britain depend more on their being coloured than on their being immigrants. They do not find it helpful to picture Jamaicans and Pakistanis as caught up in a process of assimilation, and argue that contra-assimilative tendencies can be discerned. Some people may be led by their interests and preconceptions to prefer one or the other approach in principle, but others will judge them by their appropriate-ness to particular situations. In general, there are grounds for thinking that, since the middle of the 1950s, the immigration perspective has become less appropriate to studies of the British scene and the racial one more so. Experience in the industrial cities of the United States has become more relevant to British problems. The changes that prompt such a conclusion have been brought about by the increase in the coloured population, by the political significance that questions of im-migration and race relations have acquired, and by the further develop-ment of tendencies within the British economic and social structure.

West Indian migration to Britain attracted attention first. From a negligible annual total at the beginning of the 1950s it rose to 24,500 in 1955. Later in the decade it fell back in response to rising unemploy-ment in Britain, only to rise again more steeply as arguments for restrict-ing immigration gained wider support in Britain. At the same period, immigration from India and Pakistan increased, to a proportionately greater extent. Though immigrants from these countries were less obtrusive socially, they presented greater long-term problems of health and assimilation; the number of potential emigrants in their home countries was also much greater (Desai, 1963). Attention had been focused on problems associated with West Indian settlement by the disturbances that occurred in Nottingham and in North Kensington, London, in September 1958. They were widely described as 'race riots', an expression that may cause readers to overlook the fact that no one was killed, and no one – apparently – seriously disabled. Later it transpired that some of the antagonism towards coloured people in North Kensington could be ascribed to the actions of unscrupulous landlords in utilizing coloured tenants to force out white tenants who, because they were protected by rent restriction legislation, were paying rents greatly below the free market level. The government of the day took no active steps to assist with problems in industrial cities which, in an era of very full employment, attracted the coloured job-seekers. Local pressures for the restriction of immigration therefore mounted, and the Commonwealth Immigrants Act was introduced; it came into effect in 1962. Thereafter, coloured immigration continued at a level rather higher than it had been in the mid-1950s, though with Indian and Pakistani immigrants outnumbering West Indians. The Labour party came into power in 1964 and used the Act to reduce coloured immigration to a very much lower level. At the end of that year it was estimated that there were about one million coloured people in Britain: 430,000 from the West Indies, 165,000 from India, 100,000 from Pakistan, 125,000 from other countries, e.g. Ceylon, Hong Kong, Malaya, Aden, Nigeria. The number of children born in the United Kingdom to coloured immigrants could not be calculated with any accuracy but must have taken the total near the million mark (Hooper, 1965).

In the 1964 election, coloured immigration became for the first time an issue of national political significance. For years, leaders of the principal parties had believed that the best way to deal with racial differences was to refuse to recognize them. They did not want to differentiate on a basis of colour but found that this was now what an increasing proportion of the electorate wanted. They feared that if one party became identified with a tough line on immigration the other might be forced to outbid it. Much depended upon what their opponents might do and, since the salience of the issue varied from one constituency to another, it was difficult for the head office to enforce adherence to a national line. As a result, a few candidates broke ranks. At least one contender won a seat because of his exploitation of racial feeling. These events seemed to bring to a head tendencies that had been gathering strength for several years. Previously, the domestic racial problem had seemed of little account. As it received more attention and came to be seen in a domestic rather than a Commonwealth context, so the colour issue attracted more displaced aggression. Groups hostile to coloured settlers became better organized (Glass, 1960: 147-92; Foot, 1965: 195-200). Colour prejudice became a little more respectable. Emphasis upon colour as distinguishing a category of people increased. At the 1966 election these tendencies were checked, and perhaps even to some extent reversed, but the position remained delicate.

At the same time it began to appear that the urban trends characteristic of the United States might be repeated in Britain to some extent. The immigrants went to the areas where the jobs were, and this meant going to the areas of housing shortage. They could find accommodation only in the 'twilight zones' of urban decline, consisting often of large late-Victorian middle-class houses that the British working class did not want and could not afford. To finance the purchase of such houses (especially when mortgages were hard to obtain) was far from easy. Those who managed to buy houses had to fill them with tenants in order to raise an adequate income from the property. Because larger families of any colour have difficulty in finding accommodation when the wage-earner has only a moderate income, they tend to be forced into such neighbourhoods. Immigrant families of all kinds are concentrated there—English, Irish, and coloured families often sharing the same house. These are not ghettoes by any means, and it is very unusual for as many as half the houses in a street to be occupied by coloured people. Nevertheless, these tend to be identified as coloured neighbourhoods' and, because of the magnitude of the rehousing problem, it has been the policy of at least one major municipality to contain the neighbourhood rather than develop it (Rex & Moore, 1967). Such conditions intensify the problem in the schools, and parents in some localities have complained vehemently that their children's educational progress is being retarded because many immigrant children in the classrooms do not speak English properly and require extra attention. With the growing awareness of the significance of schooling for subsequent careers, this aspect of the matter has become more relevant to race relations studies. The identification of coloured people with these areas of urban decay, and with the various problems of schooling and health that centre upon them, is probably affecting the general image of the coloured man in Britain. Earlier, the things English people associated with him were of a negative character; he was rejected because of beliefs about what he was not, rather than because of beliefs about what he was. The coloured man did not belong at any particular point on the social scale, for there were quite a lot of coloured doctors, students, and persons of standing, relative to the total coloured population. Nor was the coloured man identified with the local scene, because the students were returning to their homelands and the domestic situation was not in the forefront of people's minds. Attitudes seem to have been changing. There is now more of a tendency to associate positive features with the coloured man, to see him as a permanent resident with dependants, and as someone at the bottom of the social hierarchy whose presence is linked with a variety of social problems.

Changes within the English social structure also suggest that the immigration perspective may be of diminishing utility. World War II now seems to mark a period in which a cumulative series of changes began. In the 1950s there was an upsurge of literary and cultural inspiration in the provinces, which has retained its momentum. The social and political elite were identified and pilloried as the 'Establishment'. As new individuals rose to positions of power and influence, they seemed less inclined to seek a place in the traditional social elite. National distinctiveness is now being reduced by the uniform technological requirements of industrial production and the ease of travel. American ideas of competitiveness and diversity have evoked stronger echoes in Britain. Thus it is certain that British society is no longer as homogeneous as it was when the earlier wave of Jewish immigrants arrived. Probably it is invalid to think of integration as a single process operating across the whole society, and preferable to assume that there are different processes of integration in separate spheres (politics, work, leisure, etc.) of a partially independent character.

Recent sociological studies in the United States seem to have a bearing on this problem although their precise relevance is still far from clear. Earlier in this century some Americans envisaged intergroup contacts from the standpoint of assimilation: the newcomers would increasingly conform to the norms of the white Anglo-Saxon Protestant minority. This outlook was challenged by the ideology of the 'melting-pot', which looked forward to the emergence of a new America formed by the blending of disparate elements. Both these views have had to be rejected (Gordon, 1964: 84–131). It has been found that though the descendants of Irish immigrants marry non-Irish more frequently than they used to, their spouses are from Polish, Italian, or other Catholic communities; in inter-faith marriages there is a growing tendency for one partner to adopt the other's religious adherence. Four socio-religious communities have emerged: white Protestant, white Catholic, Jewish, and Negro Protestant. In respect of marriage these communities have become more separate, so there are at least three melting-pots (Herberg, 1955; Lenski, 1961: 362–6). This evidence suggests that many parts of the United States are moving towards a kind of cultural pluralism in which members of the different groups mix easily in some circumstances, keep separate in others, and rival one another in yet others. On this reasoning, the controversies surrounding John F. Kennedy's candidacy for the presidency in 1960 mark not the end of discrimination against Catholics but the beginning of a group rivalry that will be taken up by Negroes and Jews. Such pluralism differs from that described for South-East Asia in that the cultural differences (e.g. in language) are smaller and the area of political consensus greater. Quite what will prove the best terminology for describing these various varieties of pluralism remains to be seen. The American case shows how the idea of assimilation can be an oversimplification; it suggests the advantage of the notion of integration as permitting finer differentiations, but the boundary between integration and pluralism (if there is one) remains obscure.

In Britain one or more melting-pots may develop as the result of marriage between the descendants of coloured immigrants, but it is difficult to make any reasoned prediction. Religion does not divide the white population into distinct communities. By comparison with the United States, rates of church attendance are low and are declining. Yet it is possible that even were discrimination in employment and housing successfully combated, the minority communities might prefer to remain separate in certain spheres of social life. The prospect of ultimate social acceptance may not appear so desirable that they are willing to earn it by muting their protest about present inequalities. Members of the majority and the minority often value particular kinds of equality differently. Notably, they view incidents of racial friction from con-trasting standpoints. Majoritarians are relativists: they judge their society (with which, of course, they are identified) by comparison with what other societies have, or have not, achieved. In societies known for racial friction there may be long periods of comparative calm, and it is these that are considered, by majoritarians, to be the normal state of affairs. On the other hand, minoritarians are absolutists: they emphasize that civil rights cannot be qualified and criticize the national society by reference to the preferred ideals that it never quite attains. When they contemplate intergroup tensions they are naturally greatly concerned with what can happen when events get out of control; the violence and frenzy of 'abnormal' times may matter more to them than the intervals of quiet.

THE INHERITANCE OF STATUS

The racial situation in Britain could develop in any of several different ways. Whether events will approximate more closely to an interpretation in terms of immigration and assimilation, or to one which envisages

Figure 18   The social acceptability in Britain, in three relationships, of Americans, Germans, Jews, and West Indians

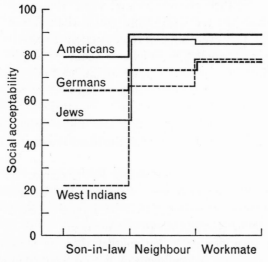

Source: National survey reported in Tumin (1967)

movement towards a pluralistic pattern of racial communities preserving their distinctiveness in respect of marriage and leisure-time associations, will be decided by the reception accorded to the present second generation of immigrant children when they leave school. This is not a long time to wait for an answer, for it has been estimated that by 1978 one in six of the school-leavers in Birmingham will be a young coloured person. When the second generation leaves the schools it will no longer be possible to represent race relations in Britain as a matter of immigration, or to see coloured people as strangers who could be sent back to their own countries. Thus the image of the coloured man will be modified. Will the pattern of social distance be modified?

In the early 1960s it seemed that there was a three-step pattern of social acceptability (see *Figure 18*). On the first step, two Britons out of ten were inclined to reject West Indians as fellow workers, by comparison with two out of ten who would reject Germans, three out of twenty Jews, and one out of ten Americans. Such rejections seemed to stem from ideas about coloured people as strangers, and the rejection of the second generation might be expected to fall to a level comparable to that displayed towards Jews. On the second step, between three and four Britons out of every ten were inclined to reject West Indians as neighbours or friends, compared with under three for Germans and rather more than one out of ten for Jews and Americans. These rejections were presumably attributable primarily to fears of identification, and, since the second generation of immigrants would be almost as visibly different as their parents, the rate might remain near that shown towards Germans in the study from which these figures are drawn (Tumin, 1967). However, some of the objections to coloured people as neighbours were grounded in complaints about the way in which they maintained their properties; in so far as the level of such complaints and of erroneous beliefs generally may be reduced, so the tendency to maintain distance could well fall more substantially.

The last step in social distance is that represented by marriage. Almost eight out of ten Britons reject the idea of being related to West Indians by marriage, compared with less than five for Jews and Germans, and two out of ten for Americans. In this connection fears about exposure and identification are combined. In no relationship can differences of habit and custom have more immediate implications than in marriage. By no relationship are the members of two family groups more closely identified with one another than by marriage. Earlier observations about the determinants of distance hold good in respect of marriage, for it requires the sharing of behavioural norms and facility in communicating expectations, and it is a relationship in which the sanctions upon deviant behaviour are weak. If either party loses patience with the other, the imposition of sanctions hurts the would-be punisher as well as the punished. Indian novelists, and social scientists who have studied India, have shown the importance in that country of making the right match, for the family as a whole and for the marriage prospects of the brothers and sisters of the bride and groom. Marriage patterns in Britain do not have to conform to rules of caste, but there is plenty of evidence that the question of comparability in class terms is one to which many people are sensitized. In marriage, identification is almost complete, and a person's occupational role cannot neutralize the connotations of marriage ties with people ascribed to lower prestige categories. It seems unlikely that these factors will operate with very much less force for the second generation of immigrants. British people, when asked for their feelings about racial intermarriage, most frequently explain their rejection of the idea not in terms of class or cultural differences but as a response to simple differences of colour, irrespective of birthplace; it seems that major changes in the structure and outlook of the nation would be needed before these perceptions would change.

For many years now, some observers of race relations in Britain have placed their faith in the younger generation, believing that when White and Coloured grew up together there would be little intergroup hostility. Opposed to such optimism has been the observation that young people very often take over the attitudes of their elders when they succeed to their roles. Industrial society becomes increasingly competitive and this can easily cancel out the effect of any moralistic lessons at school about interracial brotherhood. While it is necessary to consider the influence of mass media and of long-term cultural tendencies, it is important to appreciate that they do not operate uniformly upon all members of a society and that there may be critical periods in which people's attitudes fall into patterns from which it is subsequently difficult to move them. Adolescence is often such a period.

The tendency for adolescents to wear similar clothes and behave in uniform stylized fashions is sometimes attributed to a need for conformity, as if there were factors in the individuals' physical or psychic development that made this need stronger at this stage. Comparative study indicates that adolescence has different features in different cultures, and that the behaviour of adolescents has to be seen in terms of the social transition from adolescence to adulthood. In industrial societies a young person's roles prior to adolescence are heavily influenced by the home and the school. They are standardized, and permit little variation to suit individual preferences and abilities. In the post-adolescence period an individual has to compete with others for success at work and in leisure; most of his principal roles he must achieve for himself. The 'youth culture' of adolescence can be seen as facilitating a transition from the one stage to the other. The adolescent insistence on independence from adult control accustoms the individual to take more and more responsibility on his own. In the youth culture phase he becomes dependent upon the peer group instead of his parents, taking from his age-mates his ideas about human values and social precedence, but gradually he emancipates himself even from this dependency (Parsons, 1951: 305). Thus, in the adolescent phase young people are under pressure to form gangs or cliques, to group themselves by sex or any other easily recognized principle of division. Racial distinction can therefore suddenly acquire much greater significance in adolescence, particularly since young people at this time start thinking about marriage and exploring its preliminaries. Adolescent dating is usually selective and often highly competitive; so mixed groups in which there is familiarity between boys and girls tend to be exclusive. Sometimes parents, too, are anxious to discourage interracial mixing at a time when their children are considered impressionable and irresponsible. These factors must in part explain the difficulty experienced by youth clubs in or near the urban neighbourhoods where coloured people have found housing. The clubs are often unable to retain white members if they admit coloured ones, for some parents refuse to let their daughters attend clubs visited by coloured youths. Clubs with white and coloured members may be much more of a problem to run, and second-generation immigrant children tend to be under-represented in such organizations.

It is possible that these tendencies may strengthen and that the second-generation West Indian, Indian, or Pakistani child in Britain may find himself in a position comparable to that of the child of a Negro who migrated to New York City in World War I. The path to assimilation via social acceptance may be blocked, with the result that a coloured man's dilemma will arise in Britain: whether to accept an inferior status or to try to mould a new identity. For Indian or Pakistani children the pattern might follow the well-known one in which the parents try to raise their children in the culture of their homeland, whereas the children are attracted to the values of the country in which they have grown up. For such children the major conflict is often the domestic one and this could, in Britain, dampen down second-generation demands for acceptance, giving the British a little longer in which to come to terms with their new fellow citizens. There is some evidence to suggest that where an immigrant community is cohesive and well organized – as with the Sikhs in Southall – it may excite more antagonism from the local people (Deakin, 1965: 163); but as long as there is discrimination against people in a particular category, they may benefit from links with a group of similar people who can provide material and moral support. For children of Indian and Pakistani parents such a community is to hand. For children of West Indian parents the position is less straightforward. The parental generation of West Indian immigrants often displays a deep ambivalence towards English social patterns: on the one hand, there is a powerful desire for acceptance; on the other, a reaction against discrimination and dissatisfaction with the restrained outlook of the English. The West Indian community in Britain does not readily form associations to advance its interests. People who come from one island may not co-operate readily with those from another. Their individualism in this respect can be understood against the background of their history, but it is reinforced in the present by the absence of any felt sense of a shared identity that needs to be defended. Some do not wish to see their group organize itself politically for fear of alienating the English. West Indians cannot therefore support one another in the face of adversity to the extent that the Asian groups can. If the level of unemployment in Britain were to fall, or some other development cause an increase in interracial tension, morale in the West Indian group might become precarious. The children who grow up in West Indian homes may be exposed to greater stress for similar reasons. On present evidence, however, it seems unlikely that any Negro immigrant nationalism will assume a religious form as it has in the United States. A study of West Indian pentecostal sects in England concluded that they did not at the time represent any rejection of white society but served rather as a buffer between the West Indian heritage and the conventional expectations of the English (Calley, 1965).

Another contrast may be drawn between Britain and the United States: in the way in which the majority perceives problems of race relations. In Britain, as might be expected from a relatively homogeneous society, there is a strong emphasis upon equal justice to all persons. People are concerned that the immigrants should get their deserts – not less, for that would be wrong; not more, for that would mean giving less than their share to the local people who also need social services and other facilities. In the United States there is a greater willingness either to argue that justice requires extra assistance to the disadvantaged to help them to catch up, or to take a non-moralistic view of the costs of different policies. If a section of society becomes alienated from the remainder so that its members take to crime and vandalism, it may be cheaper to buy their loyalty by implementing a programme that brings them back into the mainstream without humiliation. To try to calculate their deserts and then base a policy upon this calculation is probably impossible; could it be done, it would probably prove the more expensive proceeding. The sanctions of the homogeneous society, of the small community based upon personal acquaintance, are not effective in industrial societies. If the second generation of immigrant children are not enabled to compete fairly with their age-mates for work and housing they may prove a rebellious and expensive minority. In an industrial society the costs of disaffection are heavy, whether it be on a basis of class, religion, region, or race, but if it be race there is the added complication that intergroup friction has international significance.

References

ACKERMAN, NATHAN W. & JAHODA, MARIE (1950). *Anti-Semitism and Emotional Disorder: a psychoanalytic interpretation.* New York: Harper.

ADINARAYAN, S. P. (1953). Before and after Independence: a study of racial and communal attitudes in India. *British Journal of Psychology* **44**: 108–15.

ADORNO, T. W., FRENKEL-BRUNSWICK, ELSE, LEVINSON, DANIEL J. & SANFORD, R. NEVITT (1950). *The Authoritarian Personality.* New York: Harper. American Jewish Committee, Studies in Prejudice.

AGASSI, JOSEPH (1963). Towards an Historiography of Science. *History and Theory, Studies in the Philosophy of History*, Beiheft 2. 'S-Gravenhage: Mouton.

ALEXANDER, CHARLES C. (1962). Prophet of American Racism: Madison Grant and the Nordic Myth. *Phylon* **23**: 73–90.

ALLISON, A. C. (1954). Protection afforded by Sickle-Cell Trait against Subtertian Malarial Infection. *British Medical Journal* Pt. I: 290–4.

ALLPORT, GORDON W. (1954). *The Nature of Prejudice.* Cambridge, Mass.: Addison–Wesley. Reissued New York: Doubleday (Anchor), 1958.

ANDERSSON, EFRAIM (1958). *Messianic Popular Movements in the Lower Congo.* Uppsala: Studia Ethnographica Upsaliensia **14**.

ARDENER, E. W. (1954). Some Ibo Attitudes towards Skin Pigmentation. *Man*, article 101: 71–73.

ARENDT, HANNAH (1958). *The Origins of Totalitarianism.* 2nd edition. London: Allen & Unwin.

AZEVEDO, THALES DE (1953). Les Élites de couleur dans une ville brésilienne. Paris: UNESCO. Also, *As elites de côr um estudo de ascenção social.* Biblioteca Pedagogica Brasileira, Vol. 282. São Paulo: Companhia Editora Nacional, 1955.

BAILEY, F. G. (1963). Closed Social Stratification in India. *Archives Européennes de Sociologie* **4**: 107–24.

BAKER, RAY STANNARD (1908). *Following the Color Line: American Negro citizenship in the progressive era.* New York: Doubleday. Reprinted New York: Harper, 1964.

BALANDIER, GEORGES (1955). *Sociologie actuelle de l'Afrique Noir.* Paris: Presses Universitaires de France.

BALANDIER, GEORGES (1958). Brèves remarques sur le 'Messianisme' de l'Afrique Congolaise. *Archives de Sociologie des Religions* **5**: 92.

BANTON, MICHAEL (1955). *The Coloured Quarter: Negro immigrants in an English city.* London: Jonathan Cape.

BANTON, MICHAEL (1956). An Independent African Church in Sierra Leone. *The Hibbert Journal* **216**: 57–63.

BANTON, MICHAEL (1957). *West African City: a study of tribal life in Freetown.* London: Oxford University Press.

BANTON, MICHAEL (1959). *White and Coloured: the behaviour of British people towards coloured immigrants.* London: Jonathan Cape.

BANTON, MICHAEL (ed.) (1961). *Darwinism and the Study of Society.* London: Tavistock Publications.

BANTON, MICHAEL (1964). *The Policeman in the Community.* London: Tavistock Publications; New York: Basic Books.

BANTON, MICHAEL (1965). *Roles: an introduction to the study of social relations.* London: Tavistock Publications; New York: Basic Books.

BANTON, MICHAEL (1966). Race as a Social Category. *Race* **8**(1): 1–16.

BARZUN, JACQUES (1965). *Race: a study in superstition.* New York: Harper.

BASTIDE, ROGER (1957). Race Relations in Brazil. *International Social Science Bulletin* **9**: 495–512.

BASTIDE, ROGER (1959). Calvinisme et Racisme. Unpublished paper presented to the 4th World Congress of Sociology, Stresa, Italy.

BASTIDE, ROGER (1961). Dusky Venus, Black Apollo. *Race* **3**(1): 10–18.

BASTIDE, ROGER (1965). The Development of Race Relations in Brazil. In Guy Hunter (ed.), *Industrialisation and Race Relations: a symposium.* London: Oxford University Press, pp. 9–22.

BASTIDE, ROGER & FERNANDES, FLORESTAN (1959). *Brancos e negros em São Paulo.* Serie Brasiliana No. 305. São Paulo: Companhia Editora Nacional.

BASTIDE, ROGER & VAN DEN BERGHE, P. (1957). Stereotypes, Norms and Inter-racial Behaviour in São Paulo, Brazil. *American Sociological Review* **22**: 689–94.

BEDDOE, JOHN (1870). President's Address. *Anthropological Review* **8**, lxxix–lxxxiii.

BEDDOE, JOHN (1885). *The Races of Britain.* Bristol: Arrowsmith.

BENDYSHE, T. (1865). The History of Anthropology. *Memoirs read before the Anthropological Society of London* **1**: 335–458.

BENEDICT, RUTH (1942). *Race and Racism.* London: Labour Book Service. Published under the title *Race: Science and Politics*, New York: Modern Age Books, 1940.

BERREMAN, GERALD D. (1960). Caste in India and the United States. *American Journal of Sociology* **66**: 120–7.

BERRY, BREWTON (1965). *Race and Ethnic Relations.* 3rd edition. Boston: Houghton Mifflin.

BETTELHEIM, BRUNO (1947). The Dynamism of Anti-Semitism in Gentile and Jew. *Journal of Abnormal and Social Psychology* **32**: 153–68.

BETTELHEIM, BRUNO & JANOWITZ, MORRIS (1950). *Dynamics of Prejudice: a psychological and sociological study of veterans.* New York: Harper. Reprinted in the same authors' *Social Change and Prejudice*, New York: Free Press, 1964.

BIDDISS, MICHAEL D. (1966). Gobineau and the Origins of European Racism. *Race* 7(3): 255–70.

BIESANZ, JOHN & SMITH, LUKE (1951). Race Relations in Panama and the Canal Zone: a comparative analysis. *American Journal of Sociology* 57(1): 7–14.

BLAU, PETER M. (1964). *Exchange and Power in Social Life*. New York: Wiley.

BLUMENBACH, J. F. (1865). *The Anthropological Treatises of Johann Friedrich Blumenbach . . . and the inaugural dissertation of John Hunter, M.D. . . .* London: Publications of the Anthropological Society of London.

BLUMER, HERBERT (1965a). Industrialisation and Race Relations. In Guy Hunter (ed.), *Industrialisation and Race Relations: a symposium*. London: Oxford University Press, pp. 220–53.

BLUMER, HERBERT (1965b). The Future of the Color Line. In John C. McKinney and Edgar T. Thompson (eds.), *The South in Continuity and Change*. Durham, N.C.: Duke University Press, pp. 322–36.

BOGARDUS, EMORY (1925). Measuring Social Distance. *Sociology and Social Research* 9: 299–308.

BOGARDUS, EMORY S. (1928). *Immigration and Race Attitudes*. Boston: D. C. Heath.

BOGARDUS, EMORY S. (1947). Changes in Racial Distance. *International Journal of Opinion and Attitude Research* 1(4): 55–62.

BOGARDUS, EMORY S. (1959). *Social Distance*. Los Angeles (privately published).

BOSANQUET, NICHOLAS (1965). Civil Rights Work in Mississippi. *Race* 7(2): 167–76.

BOXER, C. R. (1963). *Race Relations in the Portuguese Colonial Empire 1415–1825*. Oxford: Clarendon Press.

BOXER, C. R. (1964). Negro Slavery in Brazil: a Portuguese pamphlet (1764), translated and annotated. *Race* 5(3): 38–47.

BRANDEL-SYRIER, MIA (1962). *Black Woman in Search of God*. London: Lutterworth.

BRAUSCH, G. E. J. B. (1956). The Problem of Elites in the Belgian Congo. *International Social Science Bulletin* 8: 452–7.

BROCA, PAUL (1864). *On the Phenomenon of Hybridity in the Genus Homo*. London: Publications of the Anthropological Society of London.

BRONOWSKI, J. (1961). Introduction, in Michael Banton (ed.), *Darwinism and the Study of Society*. London: Tavistock Publications, pp. ix–xx.

BROTZ, HOWARD (1964). *The Black Jews of Harlem: Negro nationalism and the dilemmas of Negro leadership*. Glencoe, Ill.: The Free Press; London: Collier–Macmillan.

BRYSON, GLADYS (1945). *Man and Society: the Scottish inquiry of the eighteenth century*. Princeton: Princeton University Press.

BUNTING, BRIAN (1964). *The Rise of the South African Reich*. Harmondsworth: Penguin Books.

BURRIDGE, KENELM O. L. (1960). *Mambu: a Melanesian millennium*. London: Methuen.

BURROW, J. W. (1966). *Evolution and Society: a study in Victorian social theory*. Cambridge: Cambridge University Press.

BURTON, RICHARD F. (1865). Notes on certain Matters connected with the Dahoman. *Memoirs read before the Anthropological Society of London* 1: 308–21.

CAILLOIS, ROGER (1954–55). Illusions à Rebours. *Nouvelle Nouvelle Revue Française*, Dec. 1954: 1010–24; Jan. 1955: 58–70. Partially translated in 'Illusions in Reverse', *Encounter* 31, April 1956: 40–46.

CAIRNS, H. A. C. (1966). *Prelude to Imperialism: British reactions to Central African society, 1840–90*. London: Routledge & Kegan Paul.

CALLEY, MALCOLM J. C. (1965). *God's People: West Indian pentecostal sects in England*. London: Oxford University Press.

CAMPBELL, ERNEST Q. (1961). Moral Discomfort and Racial Segregation – an examination of the Myrdal hypothesis. *Social Forces* 39: 228–34.

CARDOSO, FERNANDO HENRIQUE & IANNI, OCTAVIO (1960). *Cor e mobilidade social em Florianopolis. Aspectos das relações entre negros e brancos numa comunidade do Brasil meridional*. Serie Brasiliana No. 307. São Paulo: Companhia Editora Nacional.

CAREY, A. T. (1956). *Colonial Students*. London: Secker & Warburg.

CASH, W. J. (1941). *The Mind of the South*. New York: Knopf. Reprinted New York: Doubleday (Anchor), 1954.

CASSON, STANLEY (1939). *The Discovery of Man: the story of the inquiry into human origins*. New York: Harper; London: Hamish Hamilton, 1940.

CATTERALL, HELEN TUNNICLIFF (1926–37). *Judicial Cases concerning American Slavery and the Negro* (with additions by James J. Hayden). 5 vols. Washington D.C.: Carnegie Institution of Washington.

CHARLES, REV. P. PIERRE (1952). Tribal Society and Labour Legislation. *International Labour Review* 65: 426–41.

CHESTERTON, CECIL (1919). *A History of the United States*. London: Dent (Everyman's Library).

CHOMÉ, JULES (1959). *La Passion de Simon Kimbangu*. Brussels: Présence Africaine.

CHRISTIE, RICHARD & JAHODA, MARIE (eds.) (1954). *Studies in the Scope and Method of 'The Authoritarian Personality'*. Glencoe, Ill.: The Free Press.

CLARK, K. B. & CLARK, M. P. (1947). Racial Identification and Preference in Negro Children. In T. M. Newcomb & E. L. Hartley (eds.), *Readings in Social Psychology*. New York: Holt, pp. 169–78; also in the 3rd edition of the same work, edited by E. E. Maccoby, T. M. Newcomb & E. L. Hartley, New York: Holt, 1958, pp. 602–11.

COHEN, HAROLD (1948). An Appraisal of the Legal Tests used to Determine who is a Negro. *Cornell Law Quarterly* 34(2): 246–55.

COLEMAN, JAMES S. (1958). *Nigeria: background to nationalism*. Berkeley, Calif.: California University Press.

COLLINS, SYDNEY (1957). *Coloured Minorities in Britain*. London: Lutterworth.

COLSON, ELIZABETH (1953). *The Makah Indians: a study of an Indian tribe in modern society.* Manchester: Manchester University Press.

COSTA PINTO, L. A. (1953). *O negro no Rio de Janeiro. Relações de raças numa sociedade em mudança.* Biblioteca Pedagogica Brasileira, Vol. 276. São Paulo: Companhia Editora Nacional.

COX, OLIVER CROMWELL (1948). *Caste, Class and Race: a study in social dynamics.* New York: Doubleday.

COX, OLIVER C. (1961). Berreman's Caste in India and the United States. *American Journal of Sociology* **66**: 510–11.

CRAMB, J. A. (1915). *The Origins and Destiny of Imperial Britain.* London: John Murray.

CRONON, E. D. (1955). *Black Moses: the story of Marcus Garvey and the Universal Negro Improvement Association.* Madison: University of Wisconsin Press.

CROWDER, MICHAEL (1962). *Senegal: a study in French assimilation policy.* London: Oxford University Press.

CUNNINGHAM, D. J. (1908). Anthropology in the Eighteenth Century. *Journal of Royal Anthropological Institute* **38**: 10–35.

CURTIN, PHILIP D. (1964). *The Image of Africa: British ideas and action, 1780–1850.* Madison: University of Wisconsin Press; London: Macmillan.

DAHRENDORF, RALF (1959). *Class and Class Conflict in Industrial Society.* London: Routledge & Kegan Paul; Stanford, Calif.: Stanford University Press.

DAVIS, ALLISON & DOLLARD, JOHN (1940). *Children of Bondage: the personality development of Negro youth in the urban South.* Washington: American Council on Education.

DAVIS, ALLISON, GARDNER, BURLEIGH B. & GARDNER, MARY (1941). *Deep South: a social anthropological study of caste and class.* Chicago: University of Chicago Press.

DAVIS, KINGSLEY (1941). Intermarriage in Caste Society. *American Anthropologist* **43**: 376–95.

DAWSON, JOHN (1964–65). Race and Inter-group Relations in Sierra Leone. *Race* **6**: 83–99, 217–31.

DEAKIN, NICHOLAS (ed.) (1965). *Colour and the British Electorate: six case studies.* London: Pall Mall; New York: Praeger.

DEAN, JOHN P. & ROSEN, ALEX (1955). *A Manual of Intergroup Relations.* Chicago: University of Chicago Press.

DEIGHTON, H. S. (1959). History and the Study of Race Relations. *Race* **1**(1): 15–25.

DESAI, RASHMI (1963). *Indian Immigrants in Britain.* London: Oxford University Press.

DINGWALL, ERIC JOHN (1946). *Racial Pride and Prejudice.* London: Watts.

DOBZHANSKY, TH. & MONTAGU, M. F. ASHLEY (1962). Natural Selection and the Mental Capacities of Mankind. Reprinted from *Science*, 1947, **105** (2736): 587–90 at pp. 148–54 of M. F. Ashley Montagu (ed.), *Culture and the Evolution of Man*, New York: Oxford University Press (Galaxy Books).

DOLLARD, JOHN (1937). *Caste and Class in a Southern Town*. New York: Harper; 3rd edition, New York: Doubleday (Anchor), 1957.

DOLLARD, JOHN (1938). Hostility and Fear in Social Life. *Social Forces* 17: 15–26.

DOLLARD, JOHN et al. (1939). *Frustration and Aggression*. New Haven: Yale University Press.

DOVER, CEDRIC (1952a). The Racial Philosophy of Ibn Khaldun. *Phylon* 13: 107–19.

DOVER, CEDRIC (1952b). The Racial Philosophy of Jehuda Halevi. *Phylon* 13: 312–22.

DOVER, CEDRIC (1952c). The Racial Philosophy of Johann Herder. *British Journal of Sociology* 3(2): 124–33.

DOVER, CEDRIC (1954). The Black Knight. *Phylon* 15: 41–57, 177–89.

DOYLE, B. W. (1937). *The Etiquette of Race Relations in the South*. Chicago: University of Chicago Press.

DRAKE, ST. CLAIR & CAYTON, HORACE R. (1945). *Black Metropolis*. New York: Harcourt Brace; London: Jonathan Cape, 1946 (the London edition was published with the authors' names in reverse order).

DUBOIS, W. E. B. (1903). *The Souls of Black Folk*. Chicago: McClurg; Greenwich, Conn: Fawcett, 1964; London: Longmans, 1965.

DUMONT, L. (1961). Caste, Racism and 'Stratification': reflections of a social anthropologist. *Contributions to Indian Sociology* 5: 20–43; also, in French, *Cahiers Internationaux de Sociologie*, 1960, 29: 91–112.

DYKES, EVA BEATRICE (1942). *The Negro in English Romantic Thought, or a Study of Sympathy for the Oppressed*. Washington D.C.: Associated Publishers.

EHRLICH, HOWARD J. & RHINEHART, JAMES W. (1965). A brief report on the Methodology of Stereotype Research. *Social Forces* 43(4): 564–75.

ELKINS, STANLEY M. (1959). *Slavery: a problem in American institutional and intellectual life*. Chicago: University of Chicago Press.

EPSTEIN, A. L. (1958). *Politics in an Urban African Community*. Manchester: Manchester University Press.

ESSIEN-UDOM, E. U. (1962). *Black Nationalism: a search for identity in America*. Chicago: University of Chicago Press; also New York: Dell, 1964. Abridged edition, Harmondsworth: Penguin Books, 1966.

EVANS-PRITCHARD, E. E. (1937). *Witchcraft, Oracles and Magic among the Azande*. Oxford: Clarendon Press.

EVANS-PRITCHARD, E. E. (1940). *The Nuer: a description of the modes of livelihood and political institutions of a Nilotic people*. Oxford: Clarendon Press.

EWART, J. C. (1911). *Telegony. Encyclopaedia Britannica*. 11th edition, 26: 509–10.

EYSENCK, H. J. (1953). *The Structure of Human Personality*. London: Methuen.

FAUSET, A. H. (1944). *Black Gods of the Metropolis.* Philadelphia: University of Pennsylvania Press.

FERNANDES, FLORESTAN (1964). *A integração do negro a sociedade de classes.* São Paulo: Universidade de São Paulo, Faculdade de Filosofia, Ciências e Letras.

FIDDES, EDWARD (1934). Lord Mansfield and the Somersett Case. *Law Quarterly Review* 50: 499–511.

FINOT, JEAN (1906). *Race Prejudice.* London: Constable. (Eng. trans. of *Le Préjugé des Races.*)

FITZHUGH, GEORGE (1854). *Sociology for the South, or The Failure of Free Society.* Richmond.

FITZHUGH, GEORGE (1857). *Cannibals All! or, Slaves without Masters.* Richmond. Edited by C. Vann Woodward, Cambridge, Mass: The Belknap Press of Harvard University Press, 1960.

FOOT, PAUL (1965). *Immigration and Race in British Politics.* Harmondsworth: Penguin Books.

FRANCK, THOMAS M. (1960). *Race and Nationalism: the struggle for power in Rhodesia–Nyasaland.* London: Allen & Unwin.

FRAZIER, E. FRANKLIN (1949). *The Negro in the United States.* New York: Macmillan.

FRAZIER, E. FRANKLIN (1957). *Black Bourgeoisie.* Glencoe, Ill.: The Free Press.

FRAZIER, E. FRANKLIN (1964). *The Negro Church in America.* Liverpool: Liverpool University Press.

FREEDMAN, MAURICE & WILLMOTT, WILLIAM E. (1961). Recent Research on Race Relations: South-East Asia, with special reference to the Chinese. *International Social Science Journal* 13(2): 245–70.

FREYRE, GILBERTO (1946). *The Master and the Slaves: a study in the development of Brazilian civilization.* New York: Knopf.

FREYRE, GILBERTO (1963). *The Mansions and the Shanties: the making of modern Brazil.* New York: Knopf.

FRIEDRICHS, ROBERT W. (1959). Christians and Residential Exclusion: an empirical study of a northern dilemma. *Journal of Social Issues* 15(4): 14–23.

FURNIVALL, J. S. (1948). *Colonial Policy and Practice: a comparative study of Burma and Netherlands India.* Cambridge: Cambridge University Press.

FYFE, CHRISTOPHER (1962). *A History of Sierra Leone.* London: Oxford University Press.

GALJART, BENNO (1964). Class and 'Following' in Rural Brazil. *América Latina* 7(3): 3–23.

GANN, L. H. (1958). *The Birth of a Plural Society.* Manchester: Manchester University Press.

GANN, L. H. (1964) *A History of Northern Rhodesia.* London: Chatto & Windus.

GANN, L. H. (1965). *A History of Southern Rhodesia.* London: Chatto & Windus.

GANN, LEWIS H. & DUIGNAN, PETER (1962). *White Settlers in Tropical Africa*. Harmondsworth: Penguin Books.

GELLNER, ERNEST (1963). Nature and Society in Social Anthropology. *Philosophy of Science* **30**: 236–51.

GEORGE, K. (1958). The Civilized West looks at Primitive Africa, 1400–1800. *Isis* **49**: 62–72.

GILBERT, G. M. (1951). Stereotype Persistence and Change among College Students. *Journal of Abnormal and Social Psychology* **46**: 245–54.

GILIS, CHARLES-ANDRÉ (1960). *Kimbangu, fondateur d'Église*. Brussels: Éditions de la Libraire Encyclopédique.

GILLIN, JOHN (1948). Race Relations without Conflict: a Guatemalan town. *American Journal of Sociology* **53**: 337–43.

GLASS, RUTH (1960). *Newcomers: the West Indians in London*. London: Centre for Urban Studies and George Allen & Unwin.

GLAZER, NATHAN & MOYNIHAN, DANIEL PATRICK (1963). *Beyond the Melting Pot: the Negroes, Puerto Ricans, Jews, Italians, and Irish of New York City*. Cambridge, Mass: The MIT Press & Harvard University Press.

GLUCKMAN, MAX (1955). *Custom and Conflict in Africa*. Oxford: Blackwell.

GLUCKMAN, MAX (1958). *Analysis of a Social Situation in Modern Zululand*. Rhodes–Livingstone Papers No. 28. Manchester: Manchester University Press. (A reprint of an article in *Bantu Studies*, 1940, **14**: 1–30, 147–74.)

GLUCKMAN, MAX (1961). Anthropological Problems arising from the African Industrial Revolution. In Aidan Southall (ed.), *Social Change in Modern Africa*. London: Oxford University Press, pp. 67–82.

GOBINEAU, J. A. DE (1915). *The Inequality of Human Races*. London: Heinemann. (Eng. trans. of part of *Essai sur l'inégalité des Races Humaines*, Paris, 1853–54.)

GOLDEN, HARRY (1958). *Only in America*. New York & Cleveland: World Publishing Co.

GOLDTHORPE, J. E. (1955). An African Elite. *British Journal of Sociology* **6**: 31–47.

GOLDTHORPE, J. E. (1958). *Outlines of East African Society*. Kampala.

GOODMAN, MARY ELLEN (1964). *Race Awareness in Young Children*. Revised edition. New York: Collier Books.

GORDON, MILTON M. (1964). *Assimilation in American Life: the role of race, religion and national origins*. New York: Oxford University Press.

GOSSETT, THOMAS F. (1963). *Race: the history of an idea in America*. Dallas: Southern Methodist University Press.

GRAY, RICHARD (1960). *The Two Nations: aspects of the development of race relations in the Rhodesias and Nyasaland*. London: Oxford University Press.

GREENE, J. C. (1954a). Some Early Speculations on the Origins of the Human Races. *American Anthropologist* **56**: 31–41.

GREENE, J. C. (1954b). The American Debate on the Negro's Place in Nature, 1780–1815. *Journal of the History of Ideas* **15**: 384–96.

GRIFFIN, JOHN HOWARD (1961). *Black Like Me*. Boston: Houghton Mifflin; London: Collins, 1962.

GRIERSON, P. J. HAMILTON (1903). *The Silent Trade*. Edinburgh: Green.

GRIMSHAW, ALLEN D. (1963). Actions of Police and the Military in American Race Riots. *Phylon* **24**(3): 271–89.

GRODZINS, MORTON (1958). *The Metropolitan Area as a Racial Problem*. Pittsburgh: University of Pittsburgh Press.

GUSSMAN, BORIS (1953). Industrial Efficiency and the Urban African. *Africa* **23**: 135–44.

GUSSMAN, BORIS (1962). *Out in the Mid-day Sun*. London: Allen & Unwin.

GUTKIND, PETER C. W. (1957). Some African Attitudes to Multi-racialism from Uganda, British East Africa. *Pluralisme Ethnique et Cultural dans les Sociétés Intertropicales*, pp. 338–55. Bruxelles: Institut International des Civilisations Différentes.

HADDON, ALFRED C. (1934). *History of Anthropology*. London: Watts (The Thinker's Library).

HAGBERG, KNUT (1952). *Carl Linnæus*. London: Jonathan Cape.

HAILEY, LORD (1938). *An African Survey*. London: Oxford University Press.

HALL, EDWARD T. & WHYTE, WILLIAM FOOTE (1960). Intercultural Communication: a guide to men of action. *Human Organization* **19**(1): 5–12.

HAMNETT, IAN (1966). The Maseru Stockfell Club: a multi-racial experiment in Southern Africa. *Race* **8**: 175–84.

HANKE, LEWIS (1959). *Aristotle and the American Indians: a study in race prejudice in the modern world*. London: Hollis & Carter.

HANKINS, FRANK H. (1931). *The Racial Basis of Civilization: a critique of the Nordic Doctrine*. Revised edition, New York: Knopf.

HARRIS, MARVIN (1956). *Town and Country in Brazil*. New York: Columbia University Press.

HARRIS, MARVIN (1964). *Patterns of Race in the Americas*. New York: Walker.

HARRIS, SARA (1954). *The Incredible Father Divine*. London: W. H. Allen.

HECHT, J. JEAN (1954). *Continental and Colonial Servants in Eighteenth Century England*. Northampton, Mass.: Smith College Studies in History, **40**.

HELPER, HINTON ROWAN (1857). *The Impending Crisis of the South: how to meet it*. New York: Collier, 1963.

HENRIQUES, F. (1953). *Family and Colour in Jamaica*. London: Eyre & Spottiswoode.

HERBERG, WILL (1955). *Protestant-Catholic-Jew: an essay in American religious sociology*. New York: Doubleday (Anchor).

HILL, MOZELL (1953). Some Problems of Social Distance in Intergroup Relations. In Muzafer Sherif & M. O. Wilson (eds.), *Group Relations at the Cross Roads*. New York: Harper.

HIMMELWEIT, HILDE (1950). Frustration and Aggression: a review of recent experimental work. In T. H. Pear (ed.), *Psychological Factors of Peace and War*. London: Hutchinson, pp. 161–91.

HIRN, YRJö (1941). *Goda Vildar och Ädla Rovare*. Helsingfors.

HOBSBAWM, E. J. (1959). *Primitive Rebels*. Manchester: Manchester University Press.

HOBSON, J. A. (1902). *Imperialism*. London: Allen & Unwin.

HODGEN, MARGARET T. (1964). *Early Anthropology in the Sixteenth and Seventeenth Centuries*. Philadelphia: University of Pennsylvania Press; London: Oxford University Press.

HODGKIN, THOMAS (1956). *Nationalism in Colonial Africa*. London: Muller.

HOFSTADTER, RICHARD (1944). *Social Darwinism in American Thought*. Philadelphia: University of Pennsylvania Press. Revised editions, Boston: Beacon Press, 1955; New York: Braziller, 1959.

HOGBIN, H. IAN (1958). *Social Change*. London: Watts.

HOLMES, ROGER (1965). Freud and Social Class. *British Journal of Sociology* 16(1): 48–67.

HOLZKAMP, KLAUS (1965). Zur Messung der sozialen Distanz: Die Objektabhängigkeit von Bogardus-Skalen. *Sociologus* 15(2): 93–110.

HOMANS, GEORGE C. (1961). *Social Behavior: its elementary forms*. London: Routledge & Kegan Paul; New York: Harcourt, Brace.

HOMANS, GEORGE C. (1962). *Sentiments and Activities*. New York: Free Press of Glencoe; London: Routledge & Kegan Paul.

HOOPER, RICHARD (ed.) (1965). *Colour in Britain*. London: BBC.

HUGHES, EVERETT CHERRINGTON (1964). Founders of Social Science: Robert Park. *New Society* No. 118 (31 December): 18–19.

HUGHES, EVERETT CHERRINGTON & HUGHES, HELEN MCGILL (1952). *Where Peoples Meet: racial and ethnic frontiers*. Glencoe: The Free Press.

HUGHES, HELEN MCGILL & WATTS, LEWIS G. (1964). Portrait of the Self-Integrator. *Journal of Social Issues* 20(2): 103–15.

HUNT, JAMES (1865). On the Negro's Place in Nature. *Memoirs read before the Anthropological Society of London* 1: 1–64.

HUNT, JAMES (1866). Address delivered at the Third Anniversary Meeting of the Anthropological Society of London. *Anthropological Review* 4: lix–lxxxi.

HUTCHINSON, BERTRAM (1966). The Patron-Dependent Relationship in Brazil: a preliminary examination. *Sociologia Ruralis* 6(1): 3–29.

HUTCHINSON, HARRY W. (1957). *Village and Plantation Life in North-eastern Brazil*. Seattle: University of Washington Press.

HUTT, W. H. (1964). *The Economics of the Colour Bar: a study of the economic origins and consequences of racial segregation in South Africa*. London: Deutsch.

HUTTON, J. H. (1946). *Caste in India: its nature, functions and origins*. Cambridge: Cambridge University Press.

HUXLEY, JULIAN S. & HADDON, A. C. (1935). *We Europeans: a survey of 'racial' problems.* London: Cape; New York: Harper, 1936.

HYMAN, H. H. & SHEATSLEY, P. B. (1956). Attitudes towards Desegregation. *Scientific American* **195**: 35–39.

IANNI, OCTAVIO (1962). *As metamorfoses do escravo: apogeu e crise da escravatura no Brasil meridional.* São Paulo: Diffusao Européia do Livro.

INTERNATIONAL COMMISSION OF JURISTS (1960). *South Africa and the Rule of Law.* Geneva: International Commission of Jurists.

ISAACS, HAROLD R. (1963). *The New World of Negro Americans.* New York: John Day.

JAHODA, GUSTAV (1961). *White Man: a study of the attitudes of Africans to Europeans in Ghana before independence.* London: Oxford University Press.

JAHODA, GUSTAV, VENESS, THELMA & PUSHKIN, I. (1966). Awareness of Ethnic Differences in Young Children: proposals for a British study. *Race* **8**(1): 63–74.

JAMES, H. E. O. & TENEN, CORA (1951). How Adolescents think of People. *British Journal of Psychology* **41**: 145–72.

JAMES, H. E. O. & TENEN, C. (1953). *The Teacher was Black.* London: Heinemann.

JARVIE, I. C. (1963). Theories of Cargo Cults: a critical analysis. *Oceania* **34**(1 & 2): 1–31, 108–36.

JOHNSON, CHARLES S. (1943). *Patterns of Negro Segregation.* New York: Harper; London: Gollancz, 1944.

JOHNSON, JAMES WELDON (1933). *Along this Way.* Harmondsworth: Penguin Books.

KAHL, JOSEPH A. (1957). *The American Class Structure.* New York: Rinehart.

KATZ, DAVID & BRALY, KENNETH (1933). Racial Stereotypes of One Hundred College Students. *Journal of Abnormal and Social Psychology* **28**: 280–90.

KAUFMANN, ROBERT (1964). *Millénarisme et acculturation.* Institut de Sociologie de l'Université Libre de Bruxelles.

KEATLEY, PATRICK (1963). *The Politics of Partnership.* Harmondsworth: Penguin Books.

KEITH, SIR ARTHUR (1917). How can the Institute best serve the needs of Anthropology? *Journal of Royal Anthropological Institute* **47**: 12–30.

KEITH, SIR ARTHUR (1931a). *Ethnos, or the Problem of Race considered from a new point of view.* London: Kegan Paul, Trench, Trubner & Co.

KEITH, SIR ARTHUR (1931b). *The Place of Prejudice in Modern Civilization.* London: Williams & Norgate.

KEITH, SIR ARTHUR (1948). *A New Theory of Human Evolution.* London: Watts.

KLOOSTERBOER, W. (1960). *Involuntary Labour since the Abolition of Slavery: a survey of compulsory labour throughout the world.* Leiden: E. J. Brill.

KNOX, ROBERT (1850). *The Races of Men: a fragment.* London: Renshaw.

KÖBBEN, A. J. F. (1960). Prophetic Movements as an Expression of Social Protest. *International Archives of Ethnography* 49: 117–64.

KOSTER, HENRY (1816). *Travels in Brazil.* London.

KRECH, DAVID & CRUTCHFIELD, RICHARD S. (1948). *Theory and Problems of Social Psychology.* New York: McGraw–Hill.

KUPER, HILDA (1947). *The Uniform of Colour: a study of white-black relationships in Swaziland.* Johannesburg: Witwatersrand University Press.

KUPER, LEO (1965). *An African Bourgeoisie: race, class, and politics in South Africa.* New Haven & London: Yale University Press.

KUTNER, B., WILKINS, CAROL & YARROW, PENNY R. (1952). Verbal Attitudes and Overt Behaviour involving Racial Prejudice. *Journal of Abnormal & Social Psychology* 47: 649–52.

LANDES, RUTH (1952). Race and Recognition. *The Listener* 48 (6 November): 751 & 763.

LANGER, WILLIAM L. (1951). *The Diplomacy of Imperialism.* 2nd edition. New York: Knopf.

LANTENARI, VITTORIO (1963). *The Religions of the Oppressed: a study of modern messianic cults.* New York: Knopf; Mentor Books edition, 1965. (*Note:* the English translation of this work is not altogether reliable – cf. *Current Anthropology*, 1965, 6(4): 460–1.)

LAPIÈRE, R. T. (1934). Attitudes vs. Actions. *Social Forces* 13: 230–7.

LASCELLES, E. C. P. (1928). *Granville Sharp and the Freedom of Slaves in England.* London: Oxford University Press.

LASKER, BRUNO (1929). *Race Attitudes in Children.* New York: Henry Holt.

LAWRENCE, PETER (1964). *Road belong Cargo.* Manchester: Manchester University Press.

LEAKEY, L. S. B. (1954). *Defeating Mau Mau.* London: Methuen.

LENIN, V. I. (1916). *Imperialism, the Highest Stage of Capitalism.* Selected Works, Vol. 5. London: Lawrence & Wishart.

LENSKI, GERHARD (1961). *The Religious Factor: a sociological study of religion's impact on politics, economics, and family life.* Revised edition. New York: Anchor Books.

LÉVI-STRAUSS, CLAUDE (1952). *Race and History.* The Race Question in Modern Science Series. Paris: UNESCO.

LEWIN, JULIUS (1963). *Politics and Law in South Africa: essays on race relations.* London: Merlin Press.

LEYS, COLIN (1959). *European Politics in Southern Rhodesia.* Oxford: Clarendon Press.

LEYS, COLIN & PRATT, CRANFORD (1960). *A New Deal in Central Africa.* London: Heinemann.

LINCOLN, C. ERIC (1961). *The Black Muslims in America.* Boston: Beacon Press.

LIND, ANDREW W. (ed.) (1955). *Race Relations in World Perspective.* Honolulu: University of Hawaii Press.

LINDGREN, ETHEL JOHN (1938). An Example of Culture Contact without Conflict: Reindeer Tungus and Cossacks of Northwestern Manchuria. *American Anthropologist* **40**(4): 605–21.

LISTOWEL, JUDITH (1966). Journey's End at Johannesburg. *The Listener* **75** (26 May): 745–6.

LITTLE, K. L. (1947). *Negroes in Britain: a study of racial relations in English society.* London: Kegan Paul.

LITTLE, KENNETH (1952). *Race and Society.* The Race Question in Modern Science Series. Paris: UNESCO.

LITTLE, KENNETH (1955). The African Elite in British West Africa. In A. W. Lind (ed.), *Race Relations in World Perspective.* Honolulu: University of Hawaii Press, pp. 263–88.

LIVINGSTONE, FRANK B. (1958). Anthropological Implications of Sickle Cell Gene Distribution in West Africa. *American Anthropologist* **60**: 533–62.

LIVINGSTONE, FRANK B. (1964a). Human Populations. In Sol Tax (ed.), *Horizons of Anthropology.* Chicago: Aldine; London: Allen & Unwin, 1965.

LIVINGSTONE, FRANK (1964b). On the Non-existence of Human Races. In Ashley Montagu (ed.), *The Concept of Race.* New York & London: Collier–Macmillan, pp. 46–60.

LOCKWOOD, DAVID (1956). Some remarks on "The Social System". *British Journal of Sociology* **7** (2): 134–46.

LOHMAN, JOSEPH D. & REITZES, DIETRICH C. (1952). Note on Race Relations in Mass Society. *American Journal of Sociology* **58**: 241–6.

LOHMAN, JOSEPH D. & REITZES, DIETRICH C. (1954). Deliberately Organized Groups and Racial Behavior. *American Sociological Review* **19**: 342–4.

LONG, EDWARD (1774). *History of Jamaica.* 3 vols. London.

LONSDALE, HENRY (1870). *A Sketch of the Life and Writings of Robert Knox.* London: Macmillan.

LOVEJOY, A. O. (1936). *The Great Chain of Being.* Cambridge, Mass.: Harvard University Press; New York: Harper Torchbooks, 1960.

LUTTRELL, ANTHONY (1965). Slavery and Slaving in the Portuguese Atlantic (to about 1500), in *The Transatlantic Slave Trade from West Africa.* Mimeo, Centre of African Studies, University of Edinburgh, pp. 61–79.

MCCLELLAND, DAVID C. (1961). *The Achieving Society.* Princeton: Van Nostrand.

MCCOLLEY, ROBERT (1964). *Slavery and Jeffersonian Virginia.* Urbana: University of Illinois Press.

MACCRONE, I. D. (1957). *Race Attitudes in South Africa.* London: Oxford University Press.

MCDILL, EDWARD L. (1961). Anomie, Authoritarianism, Prejudice and Socio-Economic Status: an attempt at clarification. *Social Forces* **39**(3): 239–45.

MCEWAN, PETER J. M. (1963). The Urban African Population of Southern Rhodesia. *Civilisations* **13**(3): 267–90.

MCKEE, JAMES B. (1958–59). Community Power and Strategies in Race Relations: some critical observations. *Social Problems* **6**(3): 195–203.

MACMILLAN, W. M. (1949). *Africa Emergent: a survey of social, political and economic trends in British Africa.* Harmondsworth: Penguin Books.

MANNONI, O. (1956). *Prospero and Caliban.* London: Methuen. (Eng. trans. of *Psychologie de la colonisation,* Paris, 1950.)

MARAIS, BEN J. (1952). *Colour: unsolved problem of the West.* Cape Town: H. B. Timmins, for Allen & Unwin. (English trans. n.d.; Afrikaans edition, Johannesburg: Golie Hoop, 1952.)

MASON, PHILIP (1958). *The Birth of a Dilemma: the conquest and settlement of Rhodesia.* London: Oxford University Press.

MASON, PHILIP (1960). *Year of Decision: Rhodesia and Nyasaland in 1960.* London: Oxford University Press.

MAYER, PHILIP (1961). *Townsmen or Tribesmen: conservatism and the process of urbanization in a South African city.* Cape Town: Oxford University Press.

MAYER, PHILIP (1962). Migrancy and the Study of Africans in Towns. *American Anthropologist* **64**(3): 576–92.

MEAD, MARGARET & MÉTRAUX, RHODA (eds.) (1953). *The Study of Culture at a Distance.* Chicago: University of Chicago Press.

MEDALIA, NAHUM Z. (1962). Myrdal's Assumptions on Race Relations: a conceptual commentary. *Social Forces* **40**(3): 223–7.

MERTON, ROBERT K. (1941). Intermarriage and the Social Structure: fact and theory. *Psychiatry* **4**: 361–74.

MILLER, NEAL E. & DOLLARD, JOHN (1941). *Social Learning and Imitation.* New Haven: Yale University Press; London: Routledge, 1945.

MINARD, RALPH D. (1952). Race Relationships in the Pocahontas Coal Field. *Journal of Social Issues* **8**: 29–44.

MINTZ, SIDNEY W. (1961). Review of *Slavery* by Stanley M. Elkins. *American Anthropologist* **63**: 579–87.

MITCHELL, J. CLYDE (1956). *The Kalela Dance.* Manchester: Manchester University Press. Rhodes–Livingstone Paper No. 27.

MITCHELL, J. CLYDE (1961a). Wage Labour and African Population Movements in Central Africa. In K. M. Barbour & R. M. Prothero (eds.), *Essays on African Population.* London: Routledge & Kegan Paul, pp. 193–248.

MITCHELL, J. CLYDE (1961b). *An Outline of the Sociological Background to African Labour.* Salisbury, Rhodesia: Ensign Publishers.

MITCHELL, J. CLYDE (1966a). Theoretical Orientations in African Urban Studies. In Michael Banton (ed.), *The Social Anthropology of Complex Societies.* ASA Monograph 4. London: Tavistock Publications; New York: Praeger, pp. 37–68.

MITCHELL, J. CLYDE (1966b). Urbanization in Rhodesia. (Unpub. MS.)

MITCHELL, ROBERT C. (1963). Christian Healing. *African Independent Church Movements,* edited Victor E. W. Hayward, Research Pamphlets No. 11. London: Edinburgh House Press.

MONTESQUIEU, BARON DE (1748). *The Spirit of the Laws*. New York: Hafner Publishing Co., 1949.

MOORE, WILBERT E. (1941). Slave Law and the Social Structure. *The Journal of Negro History*, **26**: 171–202.

MOORE, W. E. & WILLIAMS, R. M. (1942). Stratification in the Ante-Bellum South. *American Sociological Review* **7**: 343–51.

MORRIS, STEPHEN (1956). Indians in East Africa: a study in a plural society. *British Journal of Sociology* **7**(3): 194–211.

MOYNIHAN, DANIEL P. (1965). See under UNITED STATES (1965).

MYRDAL, GUNNAR, with the assistance of STERNER, RICHARD & ROSE, ARNOLD (1944). *An American Dilemma: the Negro problem and modern democracy*. New York: Harper.

NIGERIA MAGAZINE (1957). Cherubim and Seraphim. *Nigeria Magazine* **53**: 119–34.

NOGUEIRA, ORACY (1955). Relações raciais no municipio de Itapetininga. In Roger Bastide and Florestan Fernandes (eds.), *Relações raciais entre negros e brancos em São Paulo*. São Paulo: Editora Anhembi, pp. 362–554.

NOGUEIRA, ORACY (1959). Skin Color and Social Class. In *Plantation Systems of the New World*. Papers and Discussion Summaries of the Seminar held in San Juan, Puerto Rico, pp. 164–78. With comments by James G. Leyburn, pp. 179–82, and Lloyd Braithwaite, pp. 182–3. Washington: Pan American Union.

NOTT, J. C. & GLIDDON, G. R. (1854). *Types of Mankind*. London.

OLDHAM, J. H. (1924). *Christianity and the Race Problem*. London: Student Christian Movement.

OLIVER, ROLAND (1952). *The Missionary Factor in East Africa*. London: Longmans.

PARK, ROBERT EZRA (1950). *Race and Culture*. Glencoe, Ill.: The Free Press.

PARK, ROBERT E. & BURGESS, E. W. (1921). *Introduction to the Science of Sociology*. Chicago: University of Chicago Press.

PARKER, MARY (1951). Race Relations and Political Development in Kenya. *African Affairs* **50**: 41–52, 133.

PARRINDER, E. G. (1952). *Religion in an African City*. London: Oxford University Press.

PARSONS, ROBERT T. (1953). Missionary–African Relations. *Civilisations* **3**: 505–16.

PARSONS, TALCOTT (1951). *The Social System*. Glencoe, Ill.: The Free Press; London: Routledge.

PATTERSON, SHEILA (1963). *Dark Strangers*. London: Tavistock Publications.

PAUW, B. A. (1960). *Religion in a Tswana Chiefdom*. London: Oxford University Press.

PAUW, B. A. (1963). *The Second Generation: a study of the family among urbanized Bantu in East London.* Cape Town: Oxford University Press.

PEARSON. CHARLES H. (1893). *National Life and Character: a forecast.* London: Macmillan.

PEARSON, KARL (1901). *National Life from the Standpoint of Science.* London: A. & C. Black.

PEHRSON, ROBERT NIEL (1950). Culture Contact without Conflict in Lapland. *Man* 50: article 256.

PETTIGREW, THOMAS F. (1958). Personality and Sociocultural Factors in Intergroup Attitudes: a cross-national comparison. *Journal of Conflict Resolution* 2: 29–42.

PETTIGREW, THOMAS F. (1959). Regional Differences in Anti-Negro Prejudice. *Journal of Abnormal and Social Psychology* 59: 28–36.

PETTIGREW, THOMAS F. (1960). Social Distance Attitudes of South African Students. *Social Forces* 38: 246–53.

PIENAAR, S. & SAMPSON, ANTHONY (1960). *South Africa: two views of separate development.* London: Oxford University Press.

PIERSON, DONALD (1942). *Negroes in Brazil.* Chicago: University of Chicago Press.

PIERSON, DONALD (1955). Race Relations in Portuguese America. In Andrew W. Lind (ed.), *Race Relations in World Perspective.* Honolulu: University of Hawaii Press, pp. 433–62.

POLACK, A. I. (1965). Education: children and adults. In Richard Hooper (ed.), *Colour in Britain.* London: BBC.

POLIAKOV, L. (1967). Racism in Europe. In Anthony de Reuck and Julie Knight (eds.), *Caste and Race: comparative approaches.* London: Churchill, pp. 223–34.

POPPER, SIR KARL RAIMUND (1963). *Conjectures and Refutations: the growth of scientific knowledge.* London: Routledge.

POWDERMAKER, HORTENSE (1939). *After Freedom.* New York: The Viking Press.

POWDERMAKER, HORTENSE (1962). *Coppertown: changing Africa.* New York: Harper.

PRICE, A. GRENFELL (1950). *White Settlers and Native Peoples: an historical study of racial contacts between Whites and Aboriginal peoples in the United States, Australia and New Zealand.* Melbourne: Georgian House.

PROUDFOOT, L. & WILSON, H. S. (1961). The Clubs in Crisis: race relations in the new West Africa. *American Journal of Sociology* 66: 317–24.

RAE, ISOBEL (1964). *Knox the Anatomist.* Edinburgh: Oliver & Boyd.

RAYMAECKERS, PAUL (1959). L'Église de Jésus Christ sur terre par le prophète Simon Kimbangu. *Zaire* 13(7): 675–56.

REDFIELD, ROBERT (1939). Culture Contact without Conflict. *American Anthropologist* 41(3): 514–17.

REDFIELD, ROBERT (1962). *Human Nature and the Study of Society: the papers of Robert Redfield.* Chicago: University of Chicago Press.

REIMERS, DAVID M. (1965). *White Protestantism and the Negro*. New York: Oxford University Press.

REINING, CONRAD C. (1962). A Lost Period of Applied Anthropology. *American Anthropologist* **64**: 593–600.

REITZES, D. C. (1953). The Role of Organizational Structures. *Journal of Social Issues* **9**(1): 45–48.

REX, JOHN & MOORE, ROBERT (1967). *Race, Community and Conflict: a study of Sparkbrook*. London: Oxford University Press.

RIBEIRO, RENÉ (1956). *Religião e relações raciais*. Rio de Janeiro: Ministerio da Educaçao e Cultura.

RICHMOND, ANTHONY (1958). Recent Research on Race Relations in Britain. *International Social Science Bulletin* **10**(3): 344–72.

RICHMOND, ANTHONY H. (1961a). Sociological and Psychological Explanations of Racial Prejudice: some light on the controversy from recent researches in Britain. *Pacific Sociological Review* **4**(2): 63–68.

RICHMOND, ANTHONY H. (1961b). *The Colour Problem: a study of racial relations*. Revised edition. Harmondsworth: Penguin Books.

ROBERTS, ALAN H. & ROKEACH, MILTON (1956). Anomie, Authoritarianism, and Prejudice: a replication. *American Journal of Sociology* **51**(4): 355–8.

ROGERS, CYRIL A. (1959). A Study of Race Attitudes in Nigeria. *Rhodes–Livingstone Journal* **26**: 51–64.

ROGERS, C. A. & FRANTZ, CHARLES (1962). *Racial Themes in Southern Rhodesia: the attitudes and behavior of the white population*. New Haven: Yale University Press.

ROGLER, CHARLES (1948). Some Situational Aspects of Race Relations in Puerto Rico. *Social Forces* **27**: 72–77.

ROSEN, B. C. (1962). Socialization and Achievement Motivation in Brazil. *American Sociological Review* **27**(5): 612–24.

ROTBERG, ROBERT (1961). The Lenshina Movement of Northern Rhodesia. *Rhodes–Livingstone Journal* **29**: 63–78.

ROTBERG, ROBERT I. (1965). *Christian Missionaries and the Creation of Northern Rhodesia, 1880–1924*. Princeton: Princeton University Press.

ROUX, EDWARD (1948). *Time Longer than Rope: a history of the black man's struggle for freedom in South Africa*. London: Gollancz. 2nd edition, Madison: University of Wisconsin Press, 1964.

RUBIN, VERA (ed.) (1960). Social and Cultural Pluralism in the Caribbean. *Annals of the New York Academy of Sciences*, **83**.

SAENGER, C. & GILBERT, E. (1950). Customer Reactions to the Integration of Negro Sales Personnel. *International Journal of Opinion and Attitude Research* **4**: 57–76.

SANTAYANA, GEORGE (1922). *Soliloquies in England, and later soliloquies*. New York: Scribner; London: Constable.

SARTRE, JEAN-PAUL (1948). *Portrait of the Anti-Semite*. London: Secker & Warburg with Lindsay Drummond.

SEELEY, J. R. (1883). *The Expansion of England*. London: Macmillan.

SHEPPERSON, GEORGE & PRICE, GEORGE (1958). *Independent African: John Chilembwe and the Nyasaland Rising of 1915.* Edinburgh: Edinburgh University Press.

SHERIF, MUZAFER (1958). Superordinate Goals in the Reduction of Intergroup Conflict. *Journal of Sociology* 58(4): 349–56.

SHERIF, MUZAFER & SHERIF, CAROLYN W. (1953). *Groups in Harmony and Tension.* New York: Harper.

SILBERMAN, CHARLES E. (1964). *Crisis in Black and White.* New York: Random House; London: Jonathan Cape, 1965.

SILBERMAN, LEO & SPICE, BETTY (1950). Colour and Class in Six Liverpool Schools. Liverpool: Liverpool University Press.

SILCOCK, T. H. (1965). The Effects of Industrialisation on Race Relations in Malaya. In Guy Hunter (ed.), *Industrialisation and Race Relations: a symposium.* London: Oxford University Press, pp. 177–99.

SINGH, A. K. (1963). *Indian Students in Britain.* London: Asia Publishing House.

SIO, ARNOLD A. (1965). Interpretations of Slavery: the Slave States in the Americas. *Comparative Studies in Society and History* 7: 289–308.

SITHOLE, NDABANINGI (1959). *African Nationalism.* London: Oxford University Press.

SLADE, RUTH (1960). *The Belgian Congo: some recent changes.* London: Oxford University Press. 2nd edition, 1961.

SMITH, BERNARD (1960). *European Vision and the South Pacific 1768–1850: a study in the history of art and ideas.* Oxford: Clarendon Press.

SMITH, LILLIAN (1949). *Killers of the Dream.* New York: Norton; London: Cresset Press, 1950.

SMITH, M. G. (1965). *The Plural Society in the British West Indies.* Berkeley & Los Angeles: University of California Press.

SMITH, SAMUEL STANHOPE (1810). *An Essay on the Causes of the Variety of Complexion and Figure in the Human Species.* Revised edition, reprinted and edited by Winthrop D. Jordan. Cambridge, Mass: Belknap Press of Harvard University Press, 1965.

SOFER, CYRIL (1954). Working Groups in a Plural Society. *Industrial and Labor Relations Review* 8: 68–78.

SOFER, CYRIL & ROSS, RHONA (1951). Some Characteristics of an East African European Population. *British Journal of Sociology* 2(4): 315–27.

SOFER, CYRIL & SOFER, RHONA (1955). *Jinja Transformed* (East African Studies 4). Kampala: East African Institute of Social Research.

STAMPP, KENNETH M. (1956). *The Peculiar Institution: Negro slavery in the American South.* New York: Knopf; London: Eyre & Spottiswoode.

STANTON, WILLIAM (1960). *The Leopard's Spots: scientific attitudes towards race in America 1815–59.* Chicago: Chicago University Press.

STARK, W. (1961). Natural and Social Selection. In Michael Banton (ed.), *Darwinism and the Study of Society.* London: Tavistock Publications, pp. 49–61.

STOUFFER, SAMUEL A. *et al.* (1949). *The American Soldier: adjustment during army life.* Princeton, N.J.: Princeton University Press.

STROUD, GEORGE M. (1856). *A Sketch of the Laws relating to Slavery in the several States of the United States of America.* Philadelphia.

SUNDKLER, BENGT G. M. (1961). *Bantu Prophets in South Africa.* 2nd edition. London: Oxford University Press. (1st edition, London: Lutterworth, 1948.)

SYPHER, WYLIE (1942). *Guinea's Captive Kings.* Chapel Hill: University of North Carolina Press.

TAEUBER, KARL E. & TAEUBER, ALMA F. (1965). *Negroes in Cities: residential segregation and neighborhood change.* Chicago: Aldine.

TAJFEL, HENRI (1967). Social and Cultural Factors in Perception. In G. Lindzey and E. Aronson (eds.), *Handbook of Social Psychology.* 2nd edition. Reading, Mass.: Addison-Wesley.

TALMON, YONINA (1962). Pursuit of the Millennium: the relation between religious and social change. *Archives Européens de Sociologie* 3: 125–48.

TANNENBAUM, FRANK (1946). *Slave and Citizen: the Negro in the Americas.* New York: Knopf.

TANNER, R. E. S. (1966). European Leadership in Small Communities in Tanganyika prior to Independence: a study of conflicting social and political interracial roles. *Race* 7(3): 289–302.

TAYLOR, JOHN V. & LEHMANN, D. (1961). *Christians of the Copperbelt.* London: Student Christian Movement Press.

TEMPELS, P. PLACIDE (1945). *La Philosophie Bantoue.* Elisabethville: Lovania. (English trans., Paris: Présence Africaine, 1959.)

THOMPSON, EDGAR T. (1959). The Plantation as a Social System. In *Plantation Systems of the New World.* Washington, D.C.: Pan American Union, pp. 26–37.

THRUPP, SYLVIA (ed.) (1962). *Millennial Dreams in Action.* Supplement No. 2 to *Comparative Studies in Society and History.*

TOYNBEE, A. J. (1934). *A Study of History.* London: Oxford University Press. Vols. 1–3.

TRIANDIS, HARRY C., DAVIS, EARL E. & TAZEKAWA, SHIN-ICHI (1965). Some Determinants of Social Distance among American, German, and Japanese Students. *Journal of Personality and Social Psychology* 2(4): 540–51.

TRIANDIS, HARRY C. & TRIANDIS, LEIGH MINTURN (1960). Race, Social Class, Religion, and Nationality as Determinants of Social Distance. *Journal of Abnormal and Social Psychology* 61: 110–18.

TRIANDIS, HARRY C. & TRIANDIS, LEIGH MINTURN (1962). A Cross-cultural Study of Social Distance. *Psychological Monographs* 76, no. 21; whole no. 540.

TUMIN, MELVIN M. (1952). *Caste in a Peasant Society: a case study in the dynamics of caste.* Princeton: Princeton University Press.

TUMIN, MELVIN M. (1967). Ethnocentrism and Anti-Semitism in England, France and Germany. (Forthcoming.)

TURNBULL, COLIN M. (1963). *The Lonely African*. London: Chatto & Windus.

TURNBULL, COLIN M. (1965). *Wayward Servants: the two worlds of the African Pygmies*. London: Eyre & Spottiswoode; New York: Natural History Press; also New York: Doubleday.

TURNER, H. W. (1959). The Litany of an Independent West African Church. *Sierra Leone Bulletin of Religion* **1**: 48–55.

TURNER, H. W. (1960). The Catechism of an Independent West African Church. *Sierra Leone Bulletin of Religion* **2**: 45–57.

TURNER, H. W. (1962). The Church of the Lord: the expansion of a Nigerian Independent Church in Sierra Leone and Ghana. *Journal of African History* **3**(1): 91–110.

UNITED STATES (1965). Office of Policy Planning and Research, Department of Labor. *The Negro Family: the case for national action*. Washington, D.C.: Government Printing Office.

UNITED STATES (1967). *The Challenge of Crime in a Free Society: a report by the President's Commission on Law Enforcement and the Administration of Justice*. Washington, D.C.: Government Printing Office.

VAN DEN BERGHE, PIERRE L. (1960). Hypergamy, Hypergenation, and Miscegenation. *Human Relations* **13**: 83–91.

VAN DEN BERGHE, PIERRE L. (1965). *South Africa: a study in conflict*. Middletown, Conn.: Wesleyan University Press.

VAN DER HORST, SHEILA (1965). The Effects of Industrialisation on Race Relations in South Africa. In Guy Hunter (ed.), *Industrialisation and Race Relations: a symposium*. London: Oxford University Press, pp. 97–140.

VAN WING, J. (1958). Le Kibangisme vu par un témoin. *Zaire* **12**: 563–618.

VICKERY, WILLIAM & OPLER, MORRIS (1948). A Redefinition of Prejudice for Purposes of Social Science Research. *Human Relations* **1**: 419–28.

WADDINGTON, C. H. (1961). The Human Evolutionary System. In Michael Banton (ed.), *Darwinism and the Study of Society*. London: Tavistock Publications, pp. 63–81.

WADE, RICHARD C. (1964). *Slavery in the Cities: the South 1820–1860*. New York: Oxford University Press.

WAGLEY, CHARLES (ed.) (1952). *Race and Class in Rural Brazil*. Paris: UNESCO.

WAGLEY, CHARLES (1953). *Amazon Town*. New York: Macmillan.

WAGLEY, CHARLES & HARRIS, MARVIN (1958). *Minorities in the New World: six case studies*. New York: Columbia University Press.

WALLERSTEIN, IMMANUEL (1960). Ethnicity and National Integration in West Africa. *Cahiers d'Études Africaines* **3**: 129–39.

WALKER, H. J. (1957). Changes in the Status of the Negro in American Society. *International Social Science Bulletin* **9**(4): 438–74.

WARNER, W. LLOYD (1952). *The Structure of American Life*. Edinburgh: Edinburgh University Press. Revised edition, under the title of *American Life: dream and reality*, Chicago: University of Chicago Press, 1953.

WASHINGTON, BOOKER T. (1901). *Up from Slavery: an autobiography*. U.S.A.: Burt. Many editions (the page reference is to the Thomas Nelson edition). London: Longmans, 1951.

WEBER, MAX (1947). *From Max Weber: essays in sociology*. Edited by H. H. Gerth and C. Wright Mills. London: Routledge & Kegan Paul.

WEBER, MAX (1948). *The Protestant Ethic and the Spirit of Capitalism*. Trans. by Talcott Parsons. London: Allen & Unwin. (First published in Germany in 1920.)

WEBER, MAX (1965). *The Sociology of Religion*. Eng. trans. New York: Beacon Press, 1963; London: Methuen, 1965; also Social Science Paperback, 1966. (First published in Germany in 1922.)

WEBSTER, SHEILA (1954). Negroes in Bluebrick. Unpublished MS., Department of Social Anthropology, University of Edinburgh.

WELBOURN, F. B. (1961). *East African Rebels*. London: Student Christian Movement Press.

WERTHEIM, W. F. (1956). *Indonesian Society in Transition*. The Hague: von Hoeve. 2nd edition, 1959.

WHARTON, VERNON LANE (1947). *The Negro in Mississippi, 1865–1890*. Chapel Hill, N.C.: University of North Carolina Press; New York: Harper Torchbooks, 1965.

WHITAKER, IAN (1955). *Social Relations in a Nomadic Lappish Community*. Samiske Samlinger 2. Oslo: Norsk Folkemuseum.

WHITAKER, IAN (1956). Declining Transhumance as an Index of Culture-Change. *Arctica* (studies presented to Åke Campbell), Studia Ethnographica Upsaliensia 11. Uppsala: Almqvist & Wiksell.

WILLEY, BASIL (1961). Darwin's Place in the History of Thought. In Michael Banton (ed.), *Darwinism and the Study of Society*. London: Tavistock Publications, pp. 1–16.

WILLIAMS, E. E. (1944). *Capitalism and Slavery*. Chapel Hill, N.C.: University of North Carolina Press.

WILLIAMS, ERIC (1966). *British Historians and the West Indies*. London: Deutsch.

WILLIAMS, ROBIN, M., JR. (1964). *Strangers Next Door: ethnic relations in American communities*. Englewood Cliffs: Prentice Hall.

WILSON, JAMES Q. (1960). *Negro Politics: the search for leadership*. New York: The Free Press.

WILSON, MONICA (1959). The Early History of the Transkei and Ciskei, *African Studies* 18(4): 167–79.

WINDER, ALVIN E. (1956). White Attitudes towards Negro–White Interaction in a Number of Community Situations. *Journal of Social Psychology* 44: 15–32.

WISHLADE, R. L. (1965). *Sectarianism in Southern Nyasaland*. London: Oxford University Press.

WOODWARD, C. VANN (1938). *Tom Watson, agrarian rebel*. New York: Oxford University Press. New edition, 1963.

WOODWARD, C. VANN (1951). *Origins of the New South 1877–1913*.
Louisiana State University Press.

WOODWARD, C. VANN (1957). *The Strange Career of Jim Crow*. Revised
(Galaxy Book) edition. New York: Oxford University Press.

WOODWARD, C. VANN (1960). *The Burden of Southern History*. Baton
Rouge: Louisiana State University Press.

WORSLEY, PETER (1957). *The Trumpet Shall Sound: a study of 'Cargo'
Cults in Melanesia*. London: MacGibbon & Kee.

WRIGHT, RICHARD (1945). *Black Boy*. London: Gollancz.

ZINKIN, TAYA (1962). *Caste Today*. London: Oxford University Press.

Author Index

Subject Index

Soc
HT
✓ 1521
B34
1967

LUIS

3 1254 00148 4258

DATE DUE

~~DEC 2008~~			
HIGHSMITH 45230			